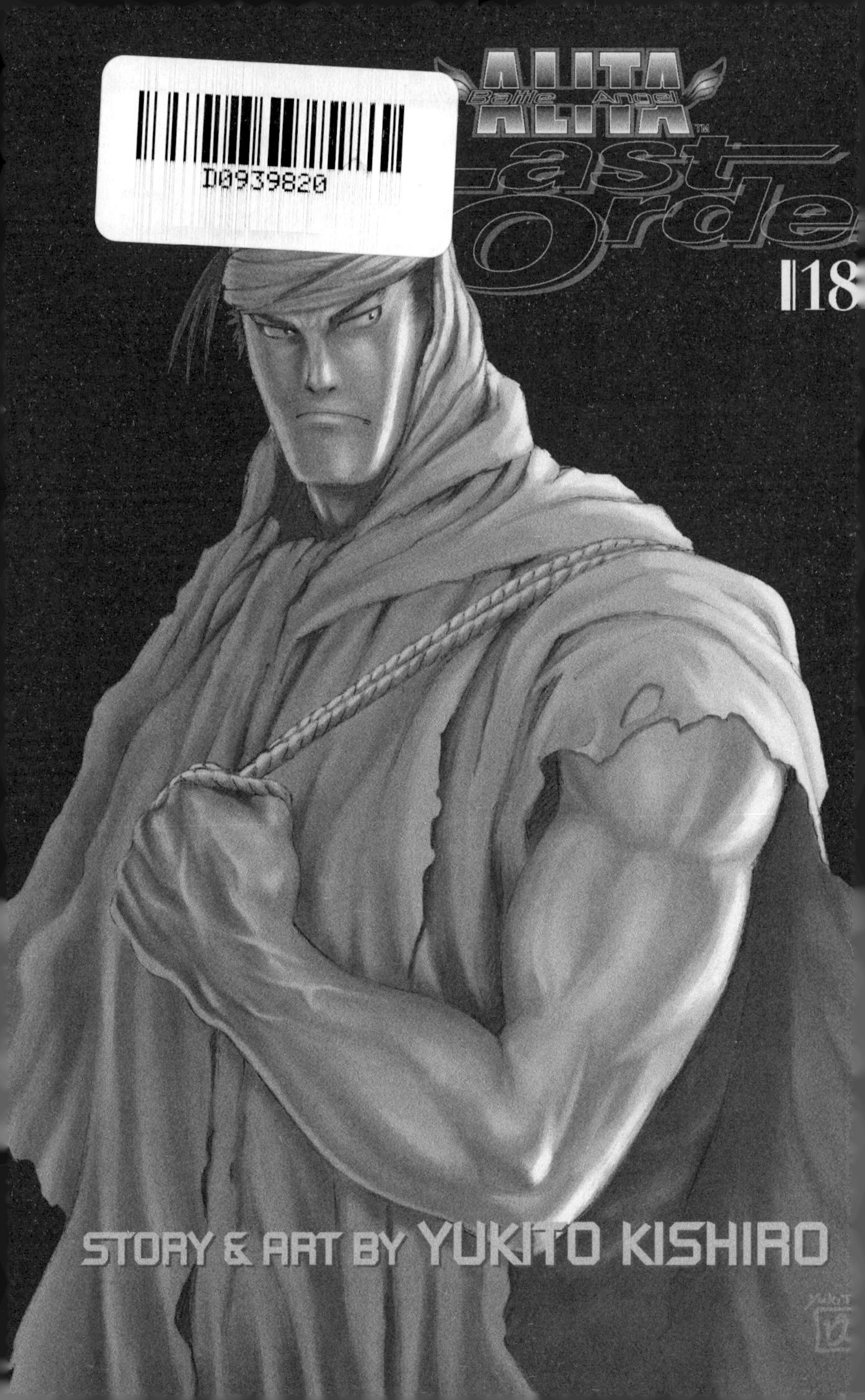
Battle Angel
ALITA
Last Order
18
STORY & ART BY YUKITO KISHIRO

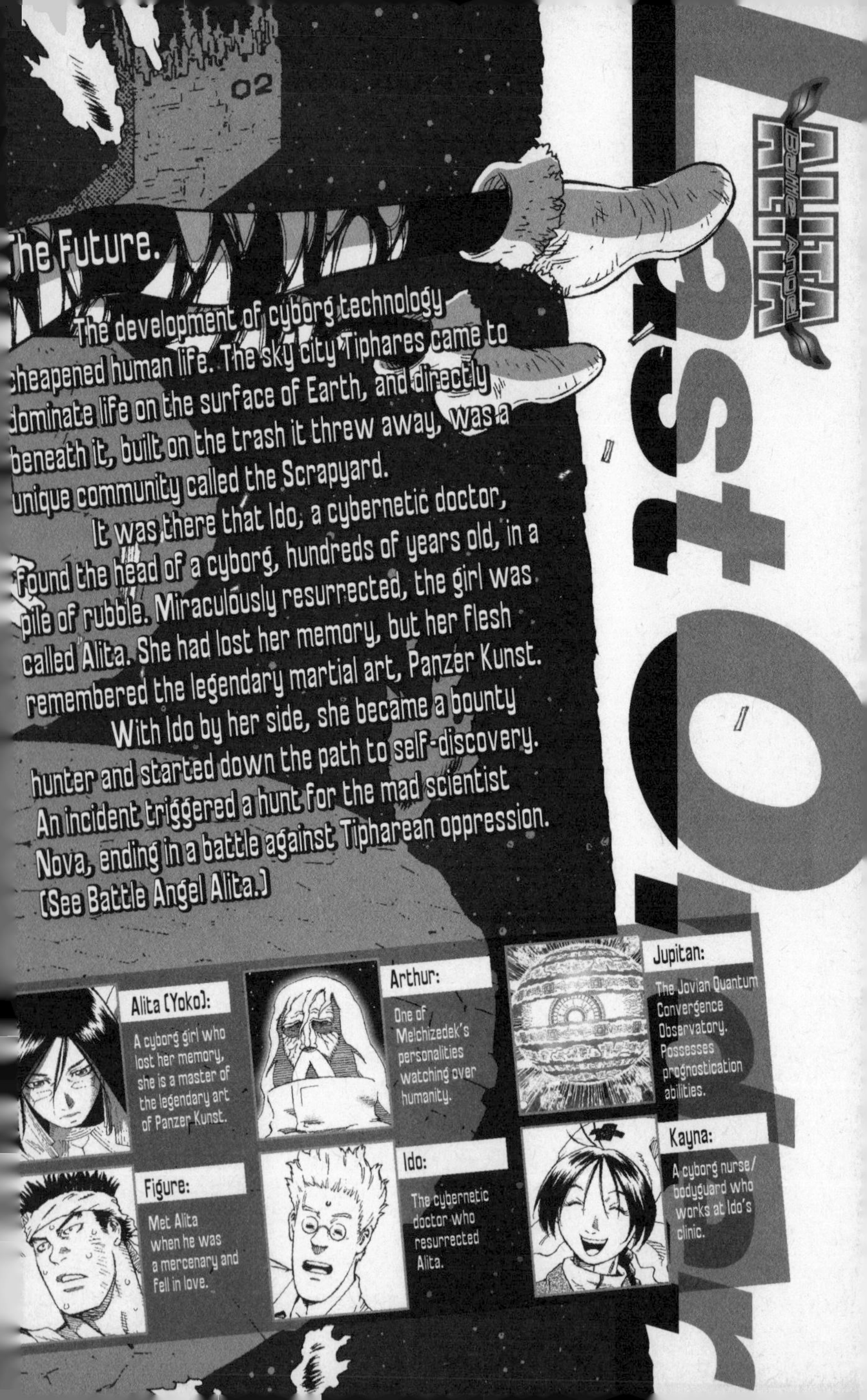

The Future.

The development of cyborg technology cheapened human life. The sky city Tiphares came to dominate life on the surface of Earth, and directly beneath it, built on the trash it threw away, was a unique community called the Scrapyard.

It was there that Ido, a cybernetic doctor, found the head of a cyborg, hundreds of years old, in a pile of rubble. Miraculously resurrected, the girl was called Alita. She had lost her memory, but her flesh remembered the legendary martial art, Panzer Kunst.

With Ido by her side, she became a bounty hunter and started down the path to self-discovery. An incident triggered a hunt for the mad scientist Nova, ending in a battle against TiphIrean oppression. (See Battle Angel Alita.)

ALITA BONE AND ALITA

Last 0rder

Alita (Yoko):

A cyborg girl who lost her memory, she is a master of the legendary art of Panzer Kunst.

Arthur:

One of Melchizedek's personalities watching over humanity.

Jupitan:

The Jovian Quantum Convergence Observatory. Possesses prognostication abilities.

Figure:

Met Alita when he was a mercenary and fell in love.

Ido:

The cybernetic doctor who resurrected Alita.

Kayna:

A cyborg nurse/bodyguard who works at Ido's clinic.

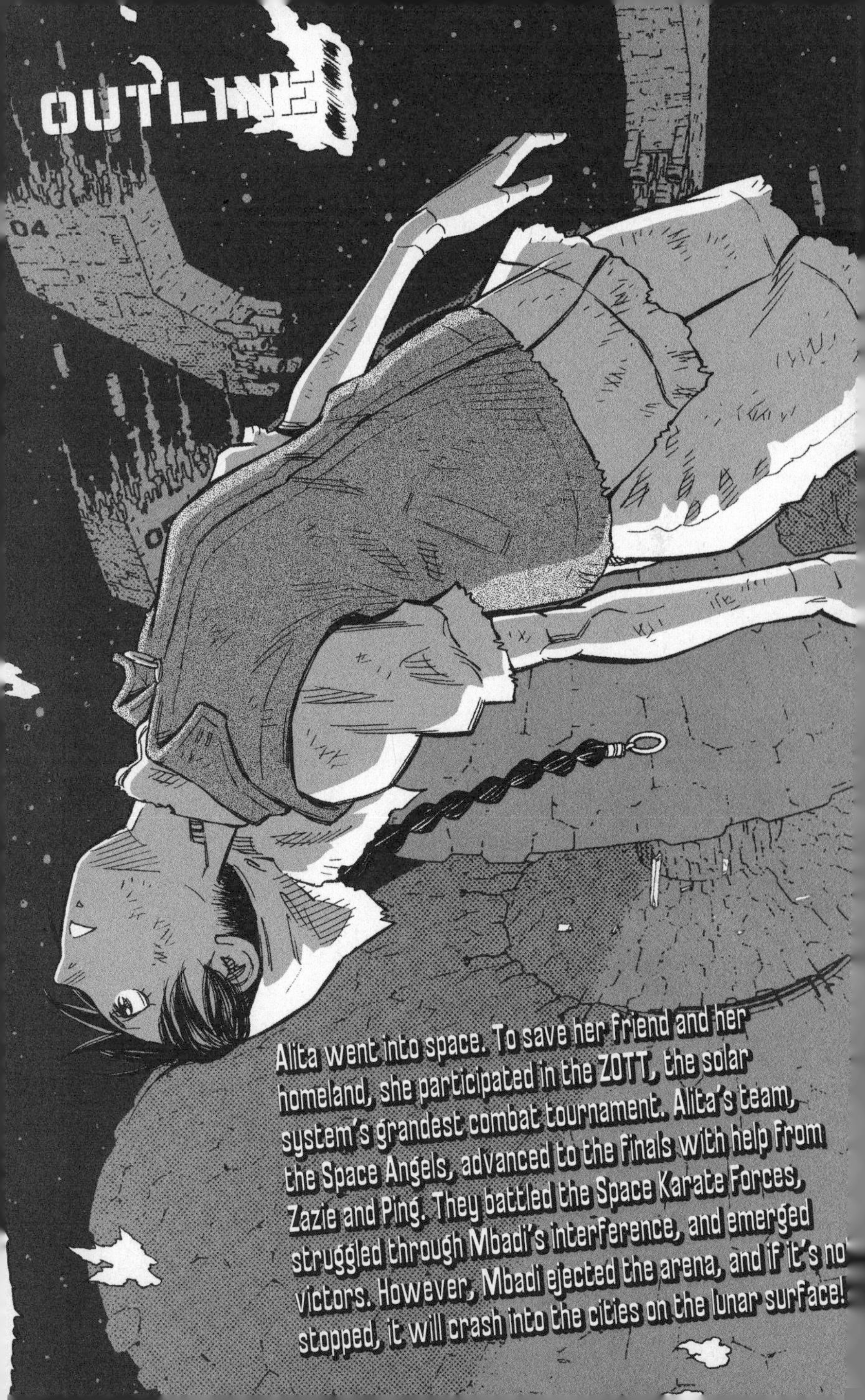
OUTLINE
Alita went into space. To save her friend and her homeland, she participated in the ZOTT, the solar system's grandest combat tournament. Alita's team, the Space Angels, advanced to the finals with help from Zazie and Ping. They battled the Space Karate Forces, struggled through Mbadi's interference, and emerged victors. However, Mbadi ejected the arena, and if it's not stopped, it will crash into the cities on the lunar surface!

CONTENTS

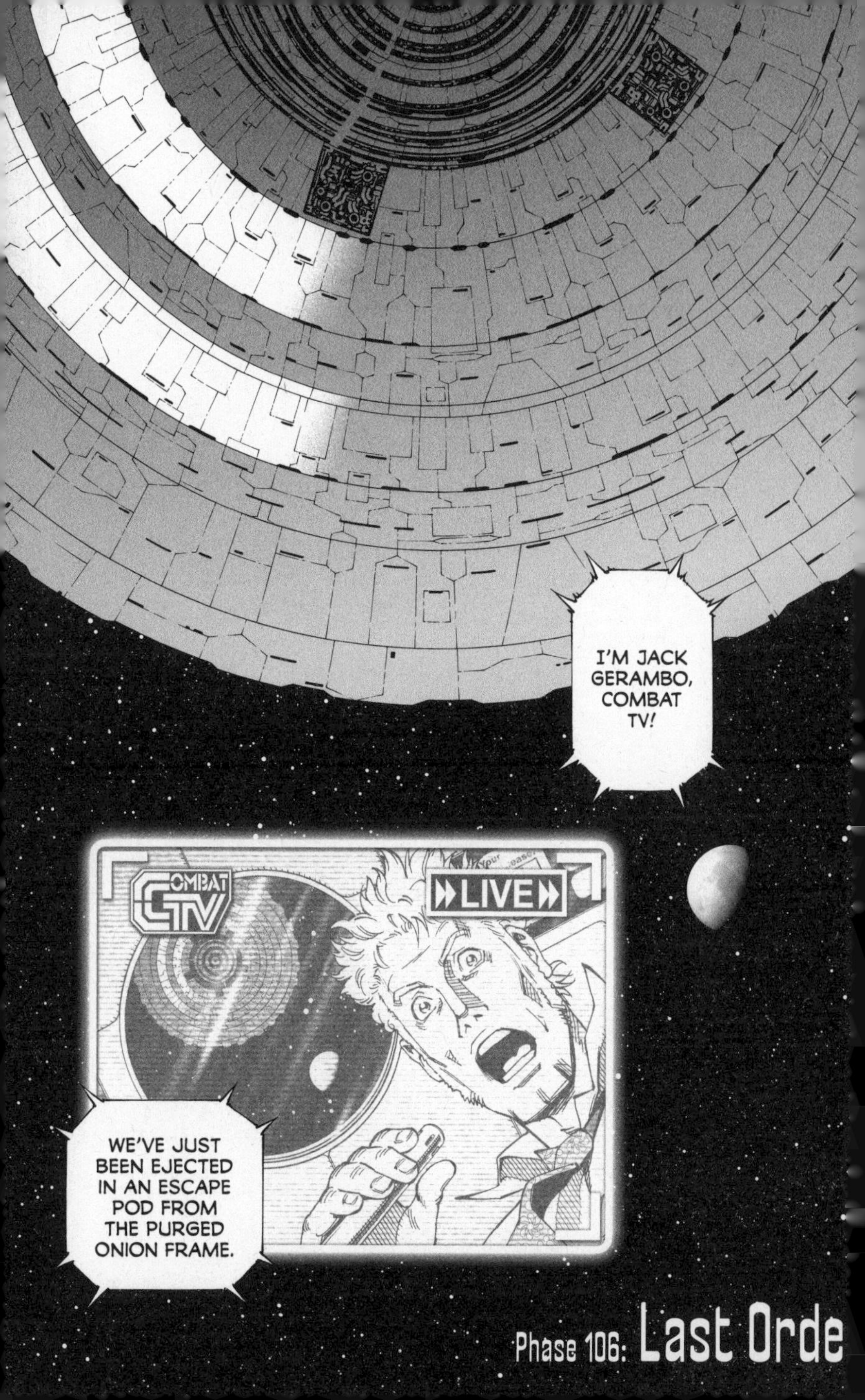
I'M JACK GERAMBO, COMBAT TV!
COMBAT TV
LIVE
WE'VE JUST BEEN EJECTED IN AN ESCAPE POD FROM THE PURGED ONION FRAME.
Phase 106: Last Orde

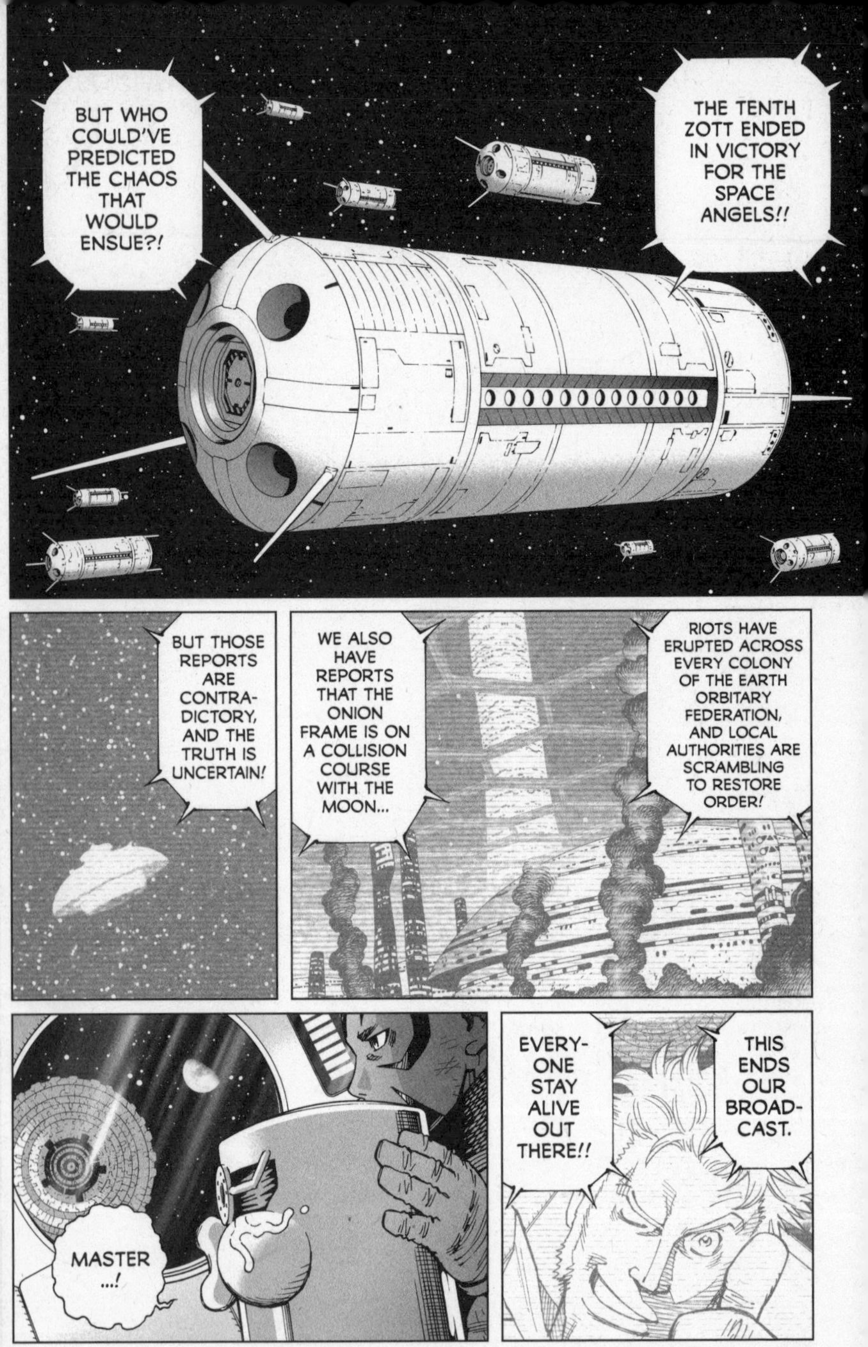
THE TENTH ZOTT ENDED IN VICTORY FOR THE SPACE ANGELS!!
BUT WHO COULD'VE PREDICTED THE CHAOS THAT WOULD ENSUE?!
RIOTS HAVE ERUPTED ACROSS EVERY COLONY OF THE EARTH ORBITARY FEDERATION, AND LOCAL AUTHORITIES ARE SCRAMBLING TO RESTORE ORDER!
WE ALSO HAVE REPORTS THAT THE ONION FRAME IS ON A COLLISION COURSE WITH THE MOON...
BUT THOSE REPORTS ARE CONTRA-DICTORY, AND THE TRUTH IS UNCERTAIN!
THIS ENDS OUR BROAD-CAST.
EVERY-ONE STAY ALIVE OUT THERE!!
MASTER ...!

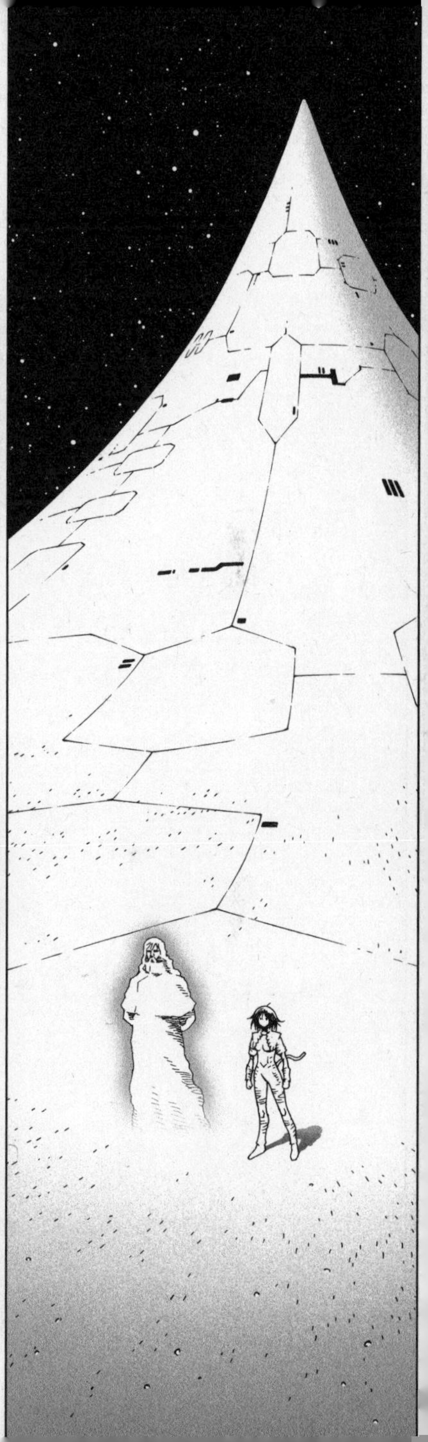

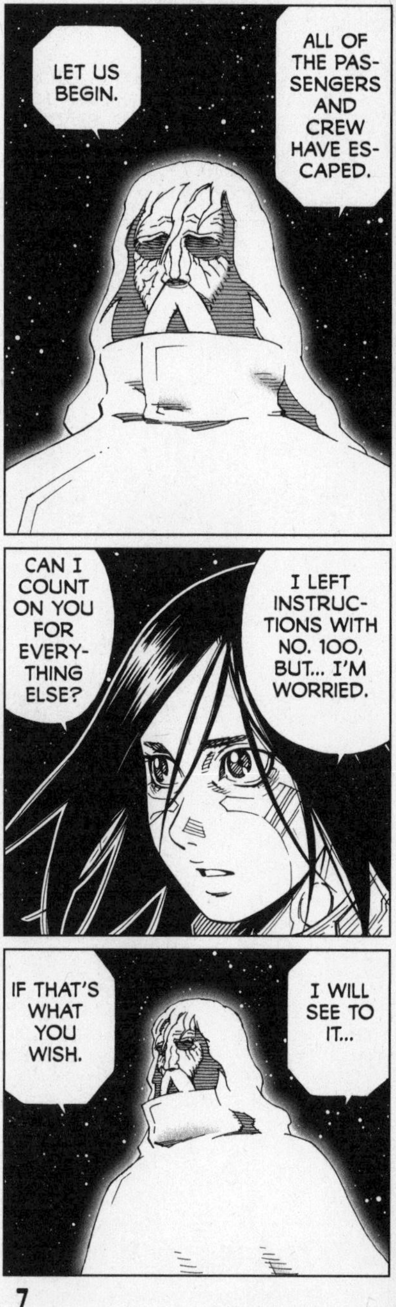
ALL OF THE PASSENGERS AND CREW HAVE ESCAPED.
LET US BEGIN.
I LEFT INSTRUCTIONS WITH NO. 100, BUT... I'M WORRIED.
CAN I COUNT ON YOU FOR EVERYTHING ELSE?
I WILL SEE TO IT...
IF THAT'S WHAT YOU WISH.

THIS IS TOTALLY DIFFERENT FROM KNOCKING DOWN AN ENEMY THAT'S RIGHT IN FRONT OF ME.

DO I HAVE THE STRENGTH TO CHANGE THE TRAJECTORY OF SOMETHING THIS MASSIVE?

I CAN'T THINK LIKE THAT.

NO.

OF COURSE I CAN.

I *CAN* DO IT.

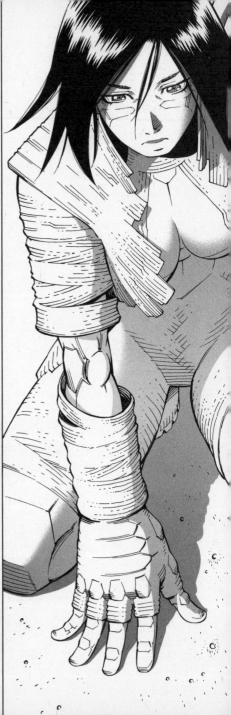

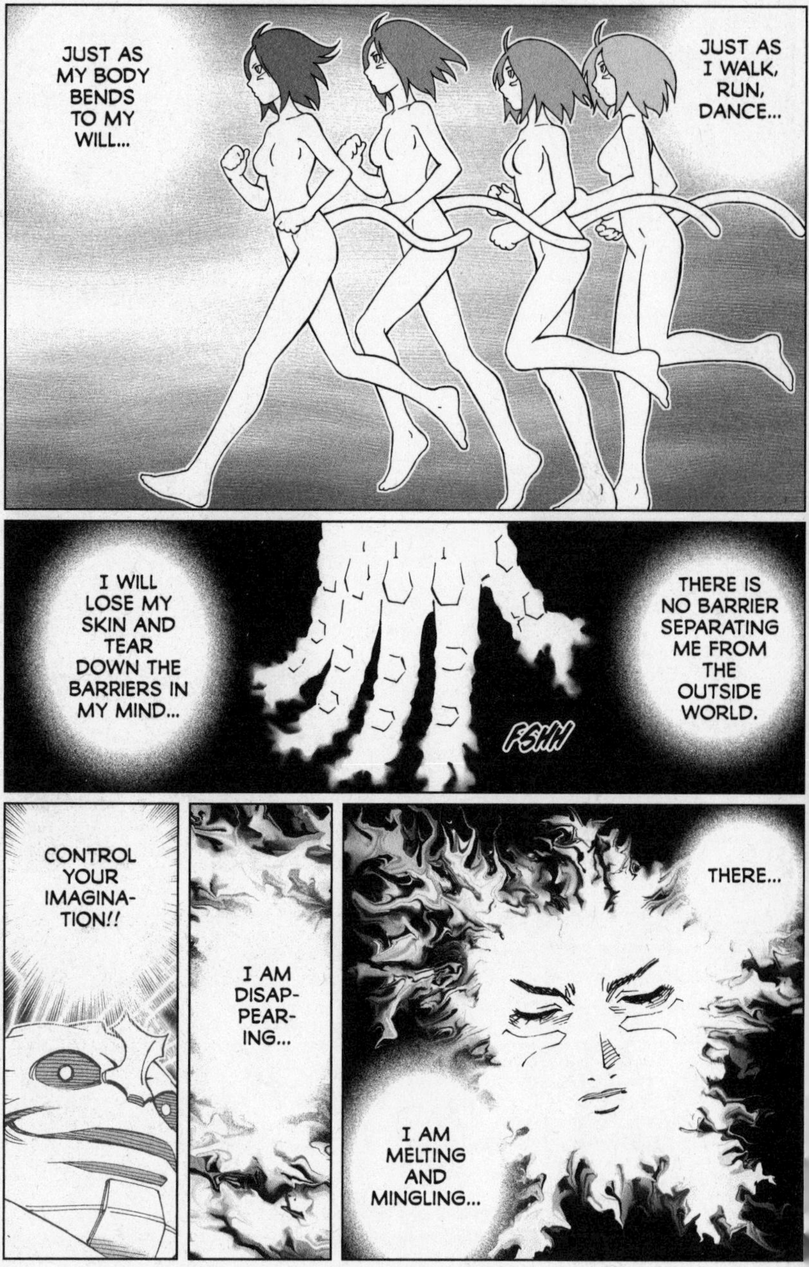
JUST AS I WALK, RUN, DANCE...
JUST AS MY BODY BENDS TO MY WILL...
THERE IS NO BARRIER SEPARATING ME FROM THE OUTSIDE WORLD.
I WILL LOSE MY SKIN AND TEAR DOWN THE BARRIERS IN MY MIND...
FSHH
THERE...
I AM MELTING AND MINGLING...
I AM DISAP-PEAR-ING...
CONTROL YOUR IMAGINA-TION!!

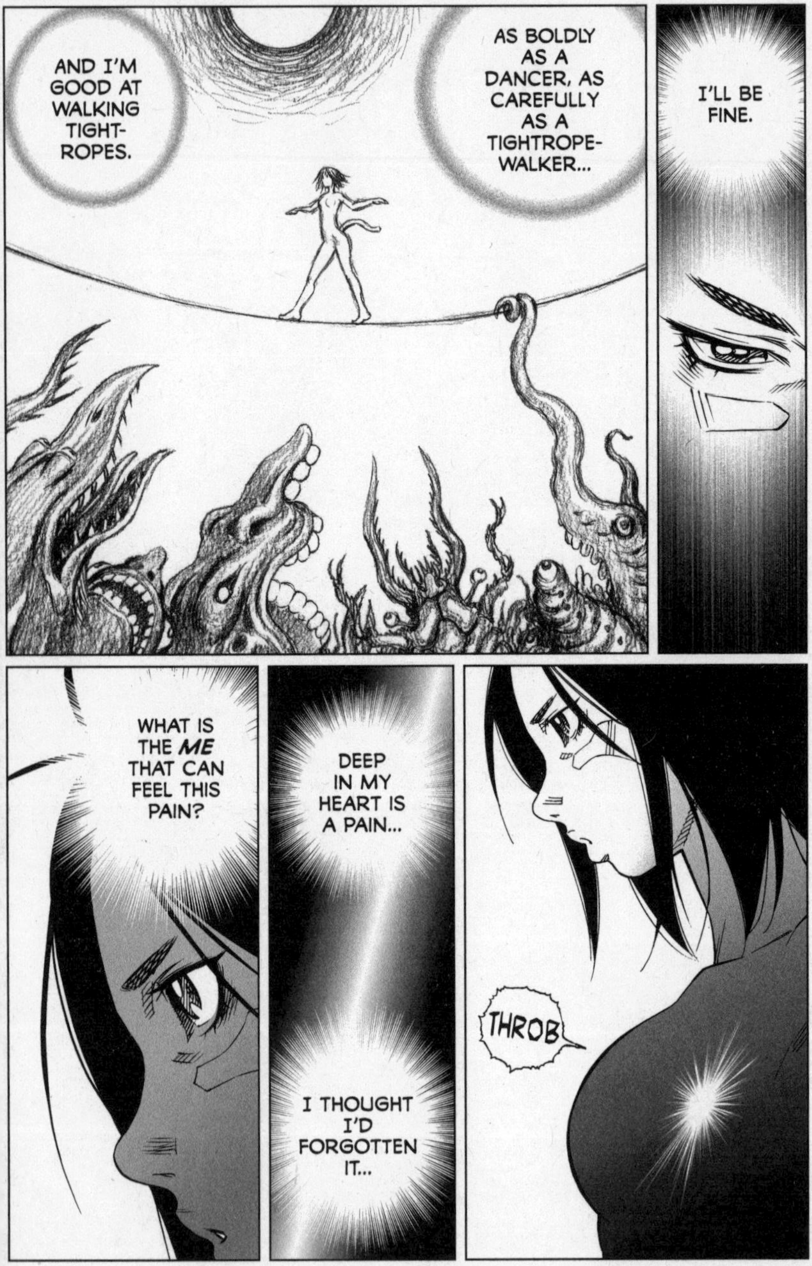
I'LL BE FINE.
AS BOLDLY AS A DANCER, AS CAREFULLY AS A TIGHTROPE-WALKER...
AND I'M GOOD AT WALKING TIGHT-ROPES.
THROB
DEEP IN MY HEART IS A PAIN...
I THOUGHT I'D FORGOTTEN IT...
WHAT IS THE *ME* THAT CAN FEEL THIS PAIN?

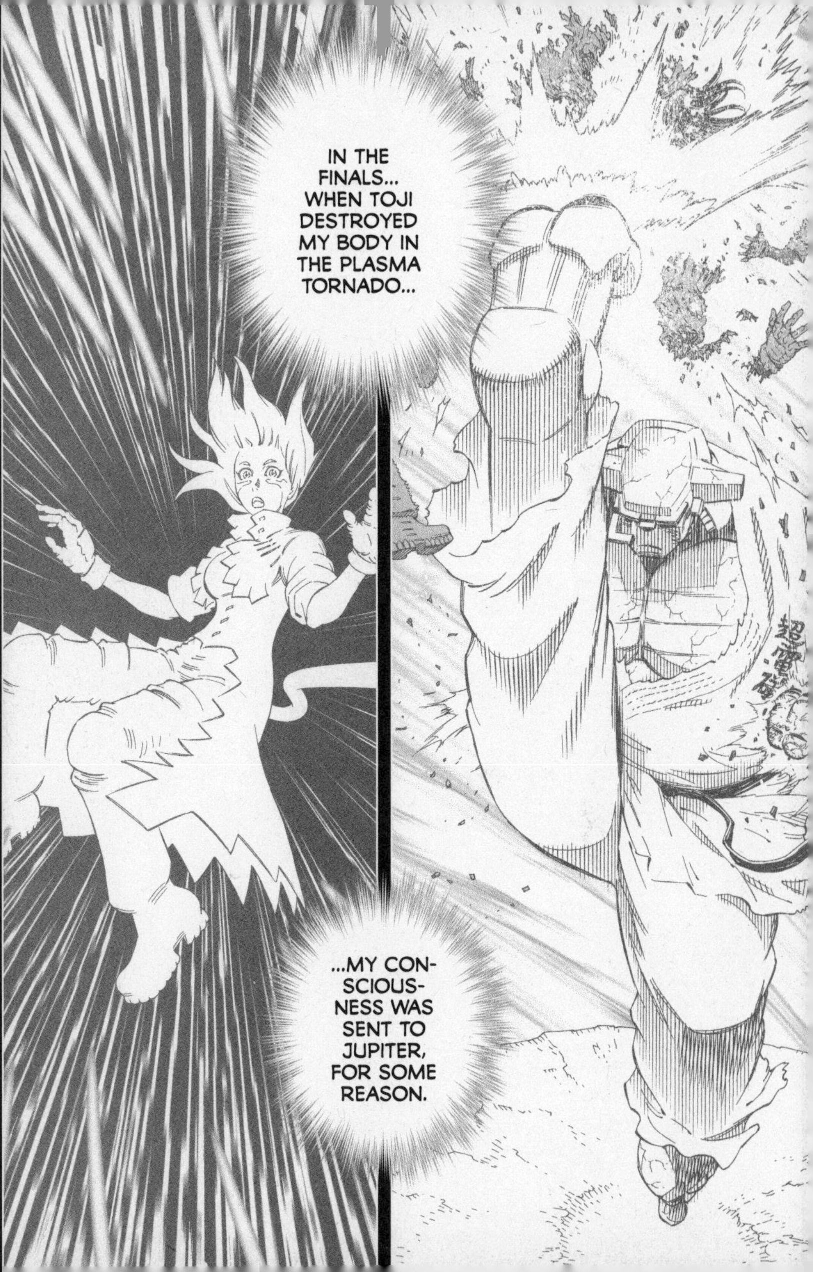
IN THE FINALS... WHEN TOJI DESTROYED MY BODY IN THE PLASMA TORNADO...
...MY CON-SCIOUS-NESS WAS SENT TO JUPITER, FOR SOME REASON.

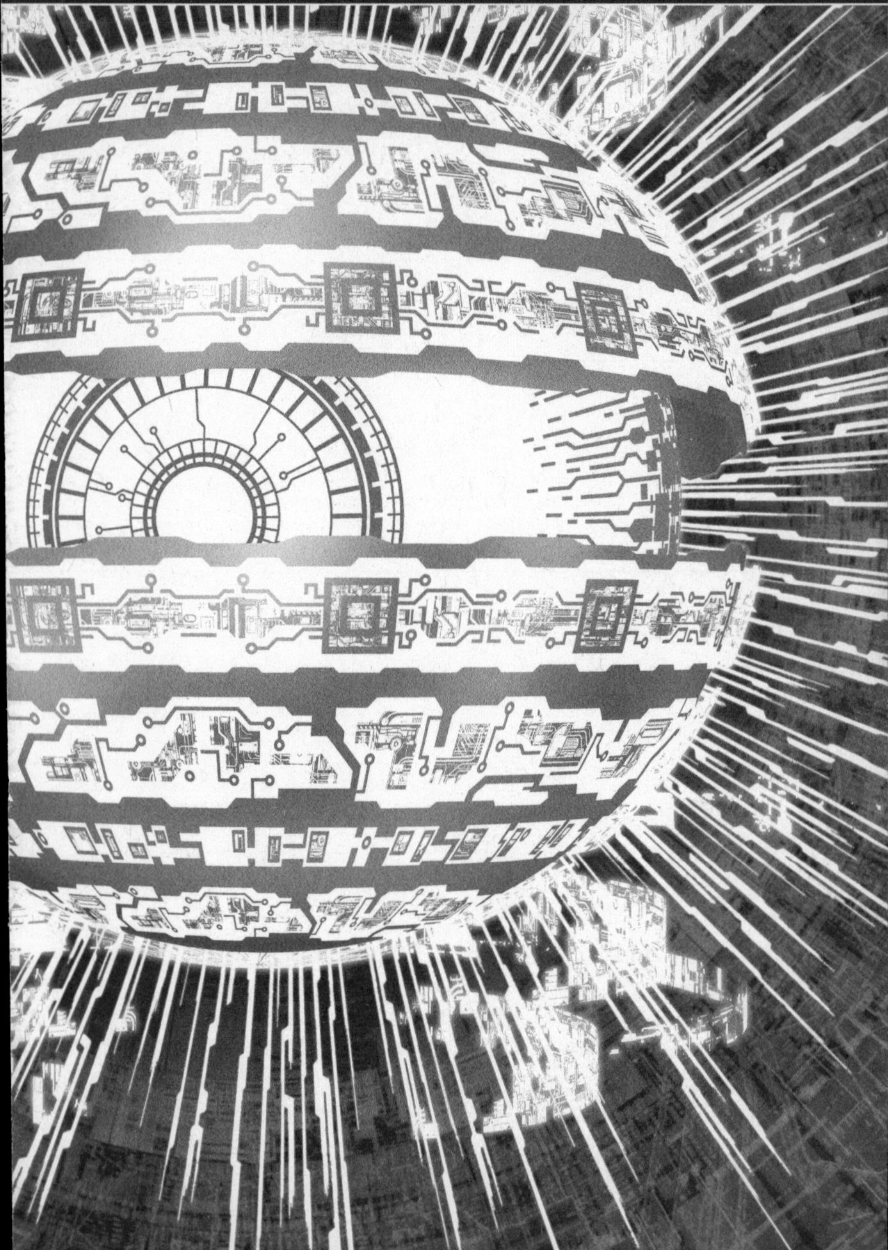

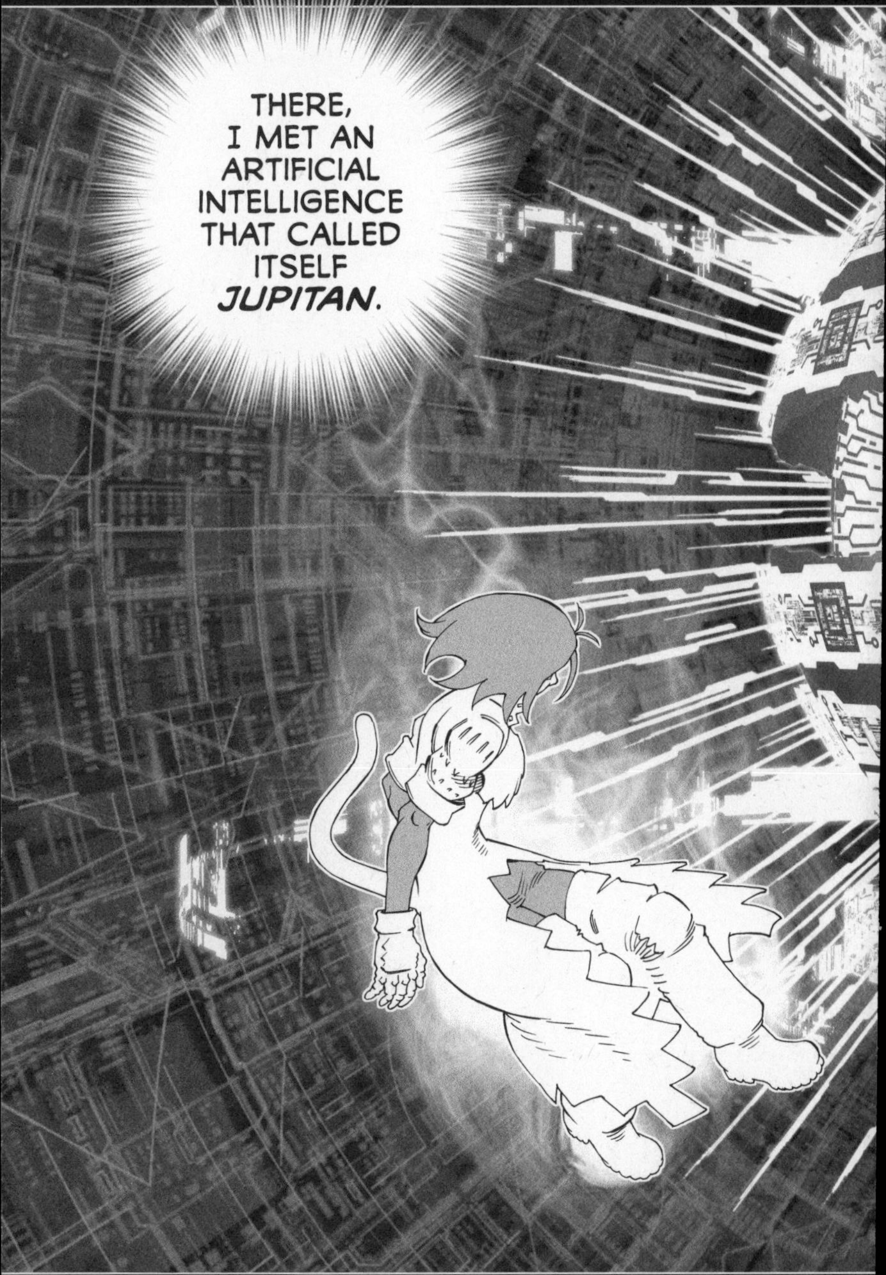
THERE, I MET AN ARTIFICIAL INTELLIGENCE THAT CALLED ITSELF *JUPITAN*.

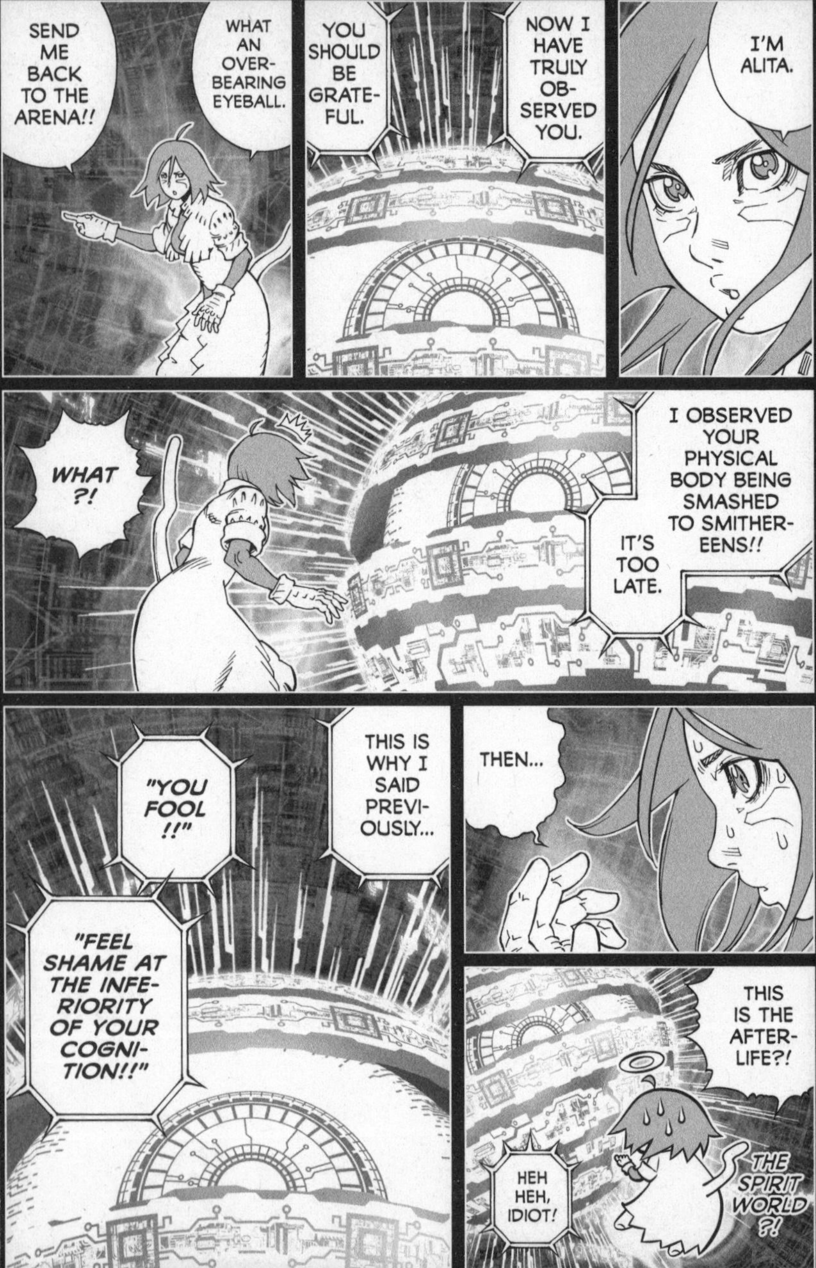
I'M ALITA.
NOW I HAVE TRULY OBSERVED YOU.
YOU SHOULD BE GRATEFUL.
WHAT AN OVERBEARING EYEBALL.
SEND ME BACK TO THE ARENA!!
I OBSERVED YOUR PHYSICAL BODY BEING SMASHED TO SMITHEREENS!!
IT'S TOO LATE.
WHAT?!
THEN...
THIS IS THE AFTERLIFE?!
THE SPIRIT WORLD?!
HEH HEH, IDIOT!
THIS IS WHY I SAID PREVIOUSLY...
"YOU FOOL!!"
"FEEL SHAME AT THE INFERIORITY OF YOUR COGNITION!!"

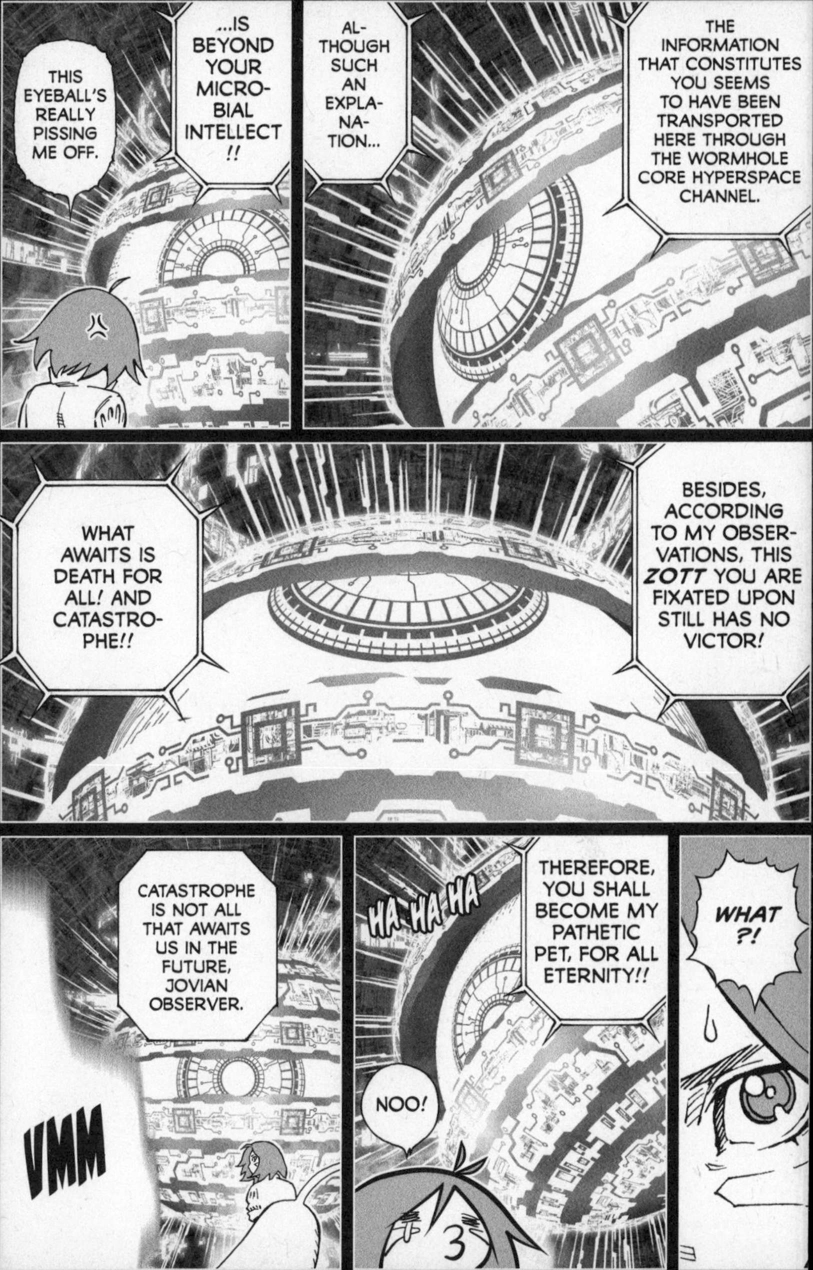
THE INFORMATION THAT CONSTITUTES YOU SEEMS TO HAVE BEEN TRANSPORTED HERE THROUGH THE WORMHOLE CORE HYPERSPACE CHANNEL.
ALTHOUGH SUCH AN EXPLANATION...
...IS BEYOND YOUR MICROBIAL INTELLECT!!
THIS EYEBALL'S REALLY PISSING ME OFF.
BESIDES, ACCORDING TO MY OBSERVATIONS, THIS *ZOTT* YOU ARE FIXATED UPON STILL HAS NO VICTOR!
WHAT AWAITS IS DEATH FOR ALL! AND CATASTROPHE!!
WHAT?!
THEREFORE, YOU SHALL BECOME MY PATHETIC PET, FOR ALL ETERNITY!!
HA HA HA
NOO!
CATASTROPHE IS NOT ALL THAT AWAITS US IN THE FUTURE, JOVIAN OBSERVER.
VMM

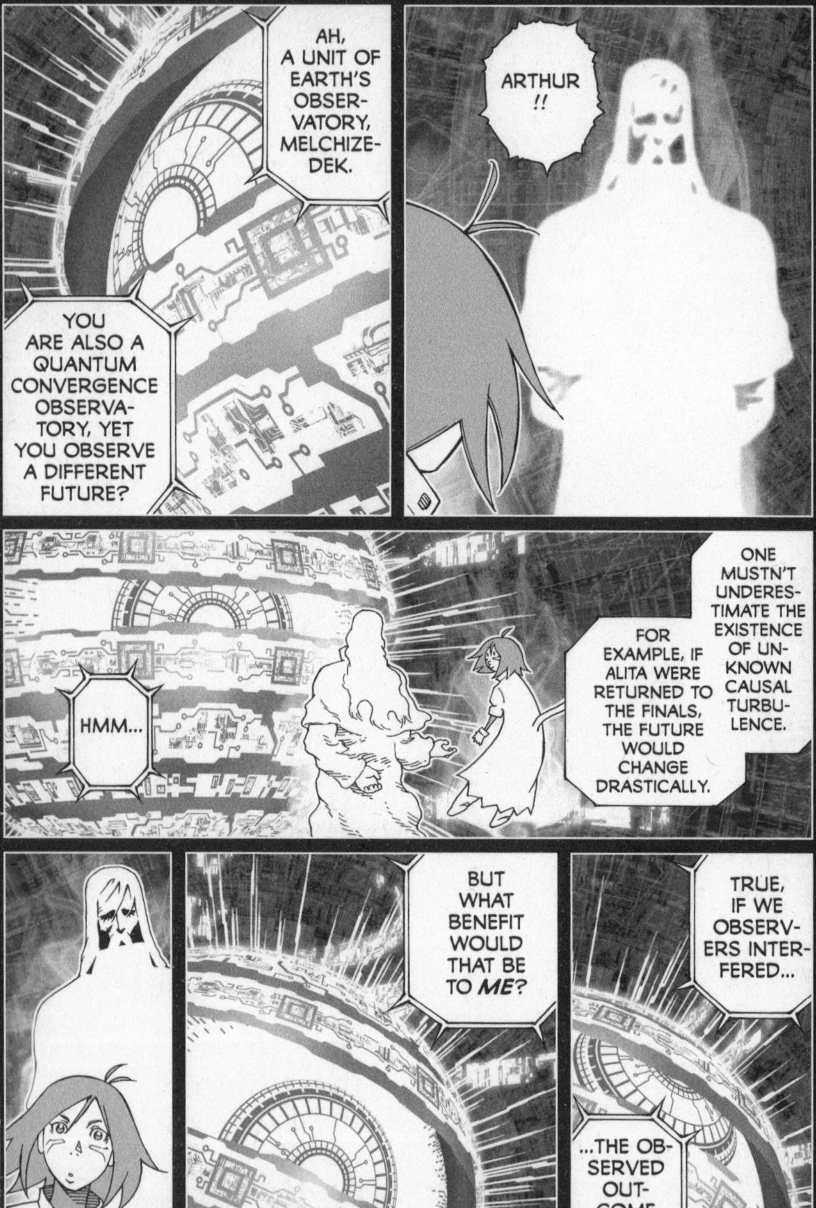
ARTHUR !!
AH, A UNIT OF EARTH'S OBSERVATORY, MELCHIZEDEK.
YOU ARE ALSO A QUANTUM CONVERGENCE OBSERVATORY, YET YOU OBSERVE A DIFFERENT FUTURE?
ONE MUSTN'T UNDERESTIMATE THE EXISTENCE OF UNKNOWN CAUSAL TURBULENCE.
FOR EXAMPLE, IF ALITA WERE RETURNED TO THE FINALS, THE FUTURE WOULD CHANGE DRASTICALLY.
HMM...
TRUE, IF WE OBSERVERS INTERFERED...
...THE OBSERVED OUTCOME WOULD CHANGE.
BUT WHAT BENEFIT WOULD THAT BE TO *ME*?

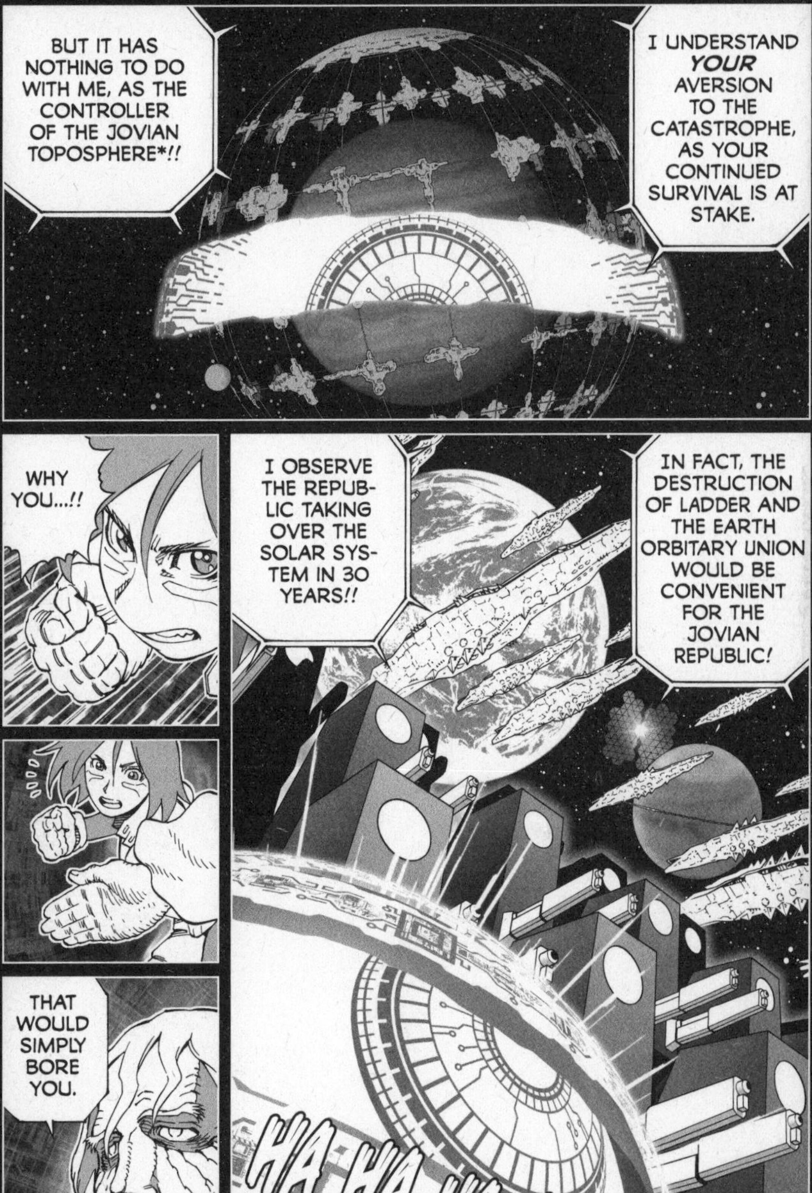
I UNDERSTAND *YOUR* AVERSION TO THE CATASTROPHE, AS YOUR CONTINUED SURVIVAL IS AT STAKE.
BUT IT HAS NOTHING TO DO WITH ME, AS THE CONTROLLER OF THE JOVIAN TOPOSPHERE*!!
IN FACT, THE DESTRUCTION OF LADDER AND THE EARTH ORBITARY UNION WOULD BE CONVENIENT FOR THE JOVIAN REPUBLIC!
I OBSERVE THE REPUBLIC TAKING OVER THE SOLAR SYSTEM IN 30 YEARS!!
HA HA HA HA HA
WHY YOU...!!
THAT WOULD SIMPLY BORE YOU.

*Toposphere: the artificial shell surrounding Jupiter, and the largest man-made structure. It was built to secure living space and efficient energy usage, but the war over building materials left it incomplete.

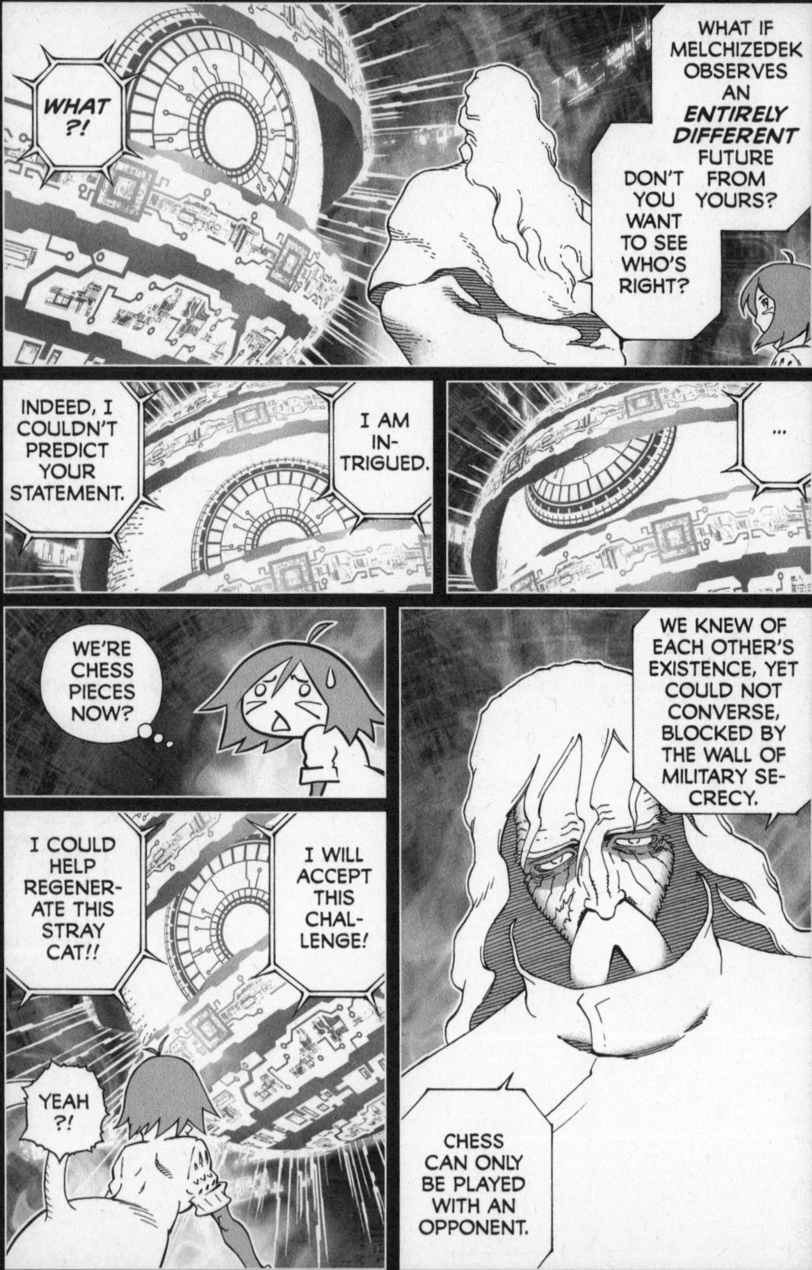
WHAT IF MELCHIZEDEK OBSERVES AN *ENTIRELY DIFFERENT* FUTURE FROM YOURS?
DON'T YOU WANT TO SEE WHO'S RIGHT?
WHAT?!
...
I AM IN-TRIGUED.
INDEED, I COULDN'T PREDICT YOUR STATEMENT.
WE KNEW OF EACH OTHER'S EXISTENCE, YET COULD NOT CONVERSE, BLOCKED BY THE WALL OF MILITARY SE-CRECY.
CHESS CAN ONLY BE PLAYED WITH AN OPPONENT.
WE'RE CHESS PIECES NOW?
I WILL ACCEPT THIS CHAL-LENGE!
I COULD HELP REGENER-ATE THIS STRAY CAT!!
YEAH?!

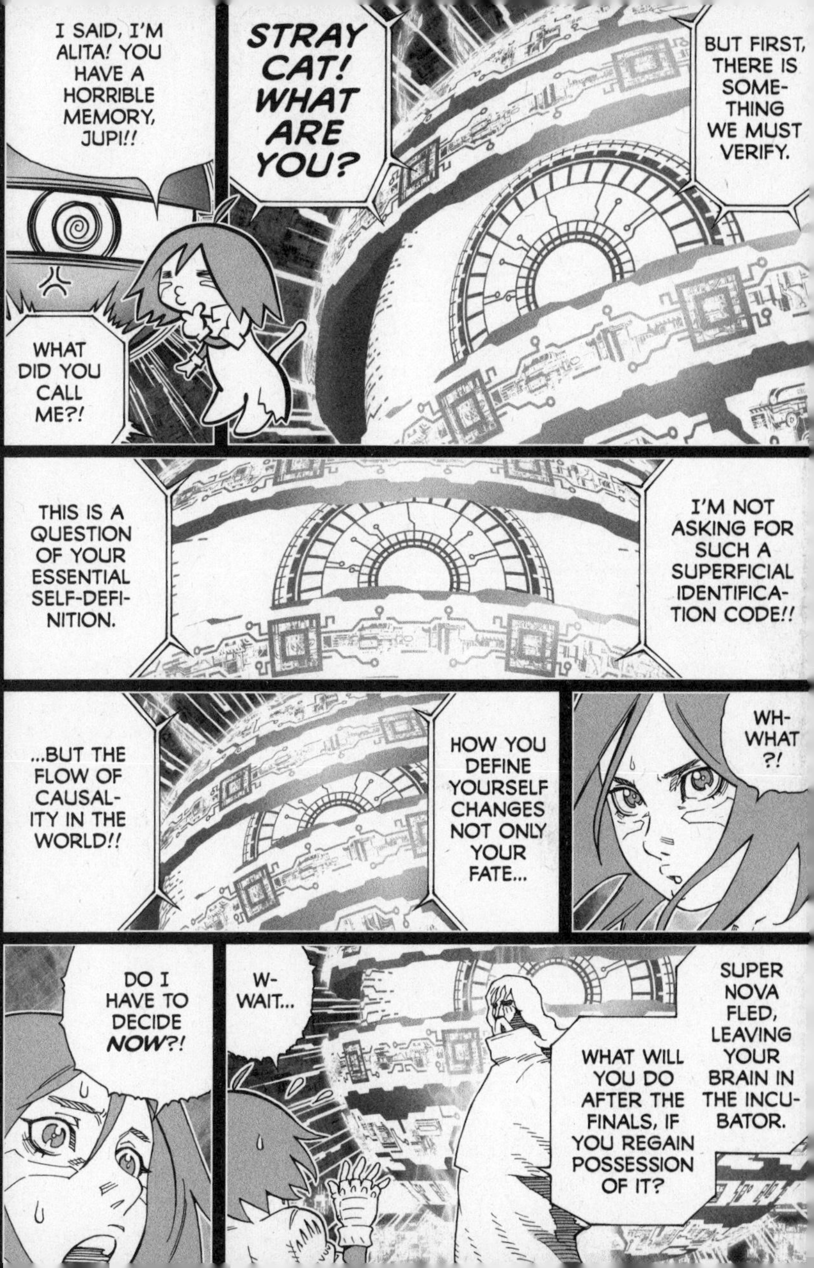
BUT FIRST, THERE IS SOME-THING WE MUST VERIFY.
STRAY CAT! WHAT ARE YOU?
I SAID, I'M ALITA! YOU HAVE A HORRIBLE MEMORY, JUPI!!
WHAT DID YOU CALL ME?!
I'M NOT ASKING FOR SUCH A SUPERFICIAL IDENTIFICA-TION CODE!!
THIS IS A QUESTION OF YOUR ESSENTIAL SELF-DEFI-NITION.
WH-WHAT?!
HOW YOU DEFINE YOURSELF CHANGES NOT ONLY YOUR FATE...
...BUT THE FLOW OF CAUSAL-ITY IN THE WORLD!!
SUPER NOVA FLED, LEAVING YOUR BRAIN IN THE INCU-BATOR.
WHAT WILL YOU DO AFTER THE FINALS, IF YOU REGAIN POSSESSION OF IT?
W-WAIT...
DO I HAVE TO DECIDE *NOW*?!

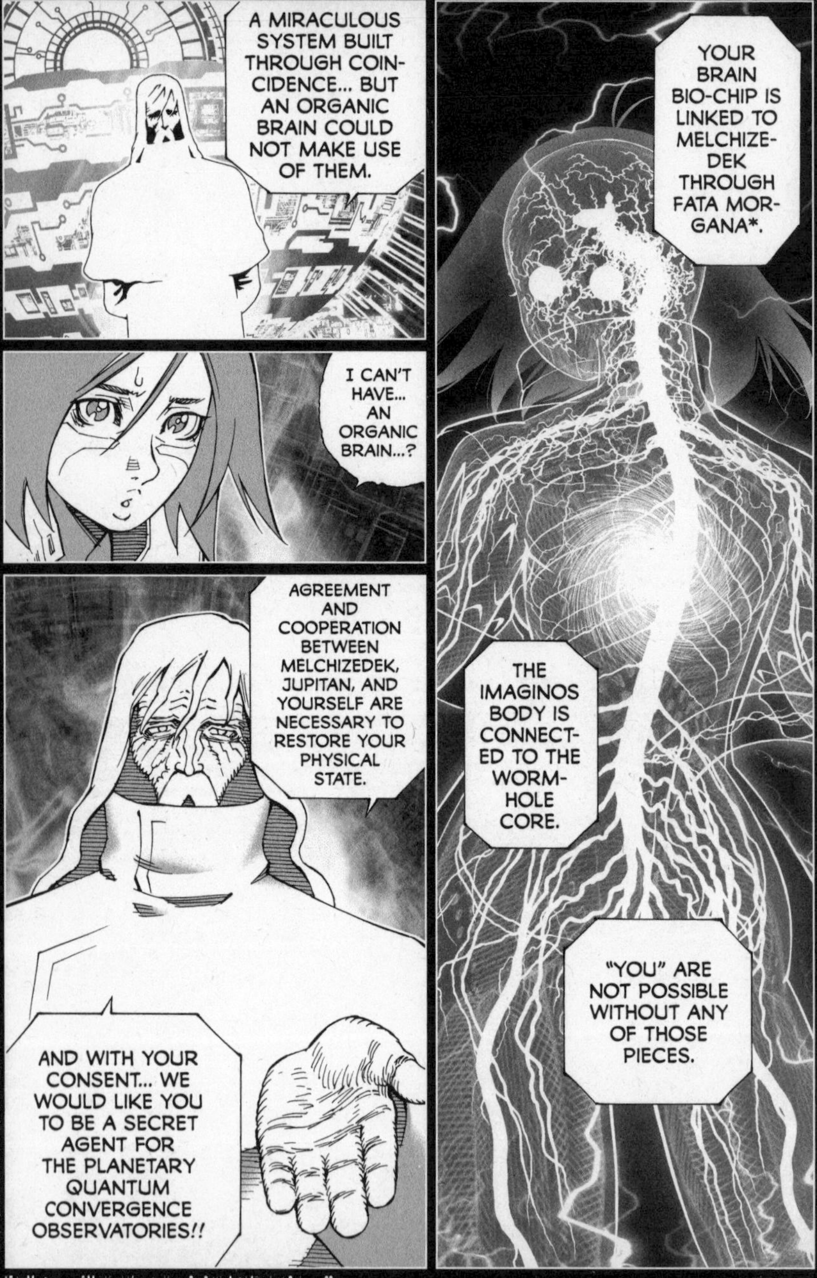

YOUR BRAIN BIO-CHIP IS LINKED TO MELCHIZE-DEK THROUGH FATA MOR-GANA*.
THE IMAGINOS BODY IS CONNECT-ED TO THE WORM-HOLE CORE.
"YOU" ARE NOT POSSIBLE WITHOUT ANY OF THOSE PIECES.
A MIRACULOUS SYSTEM BUILT THROUGH COIN-CIDENCE... BUT AN ORGANIC BRAIN COULD NOT MAKE USE OF THEM.
I CAN'T HAVE... AN ORGANIC BRAIN...?
AGREEMENT AND COOPERATION BETWEEN MELCHIZEDEK, JUPITAN, AND YOURSELF ARE NECESSARY TO RESTORE YOUR PHYSICAL STATE.
AND WITH YOUR CONSENT... WE WOULD LIKE YOU TO BE A SECRET AGENT FOR THE PLANETARY QUANTUM CONVERGENCE OBSERVATORIES!!

*Fata Morgana: one of Melchizedek's control keys. See Battle Angel Alita: Last Order ep. 86.

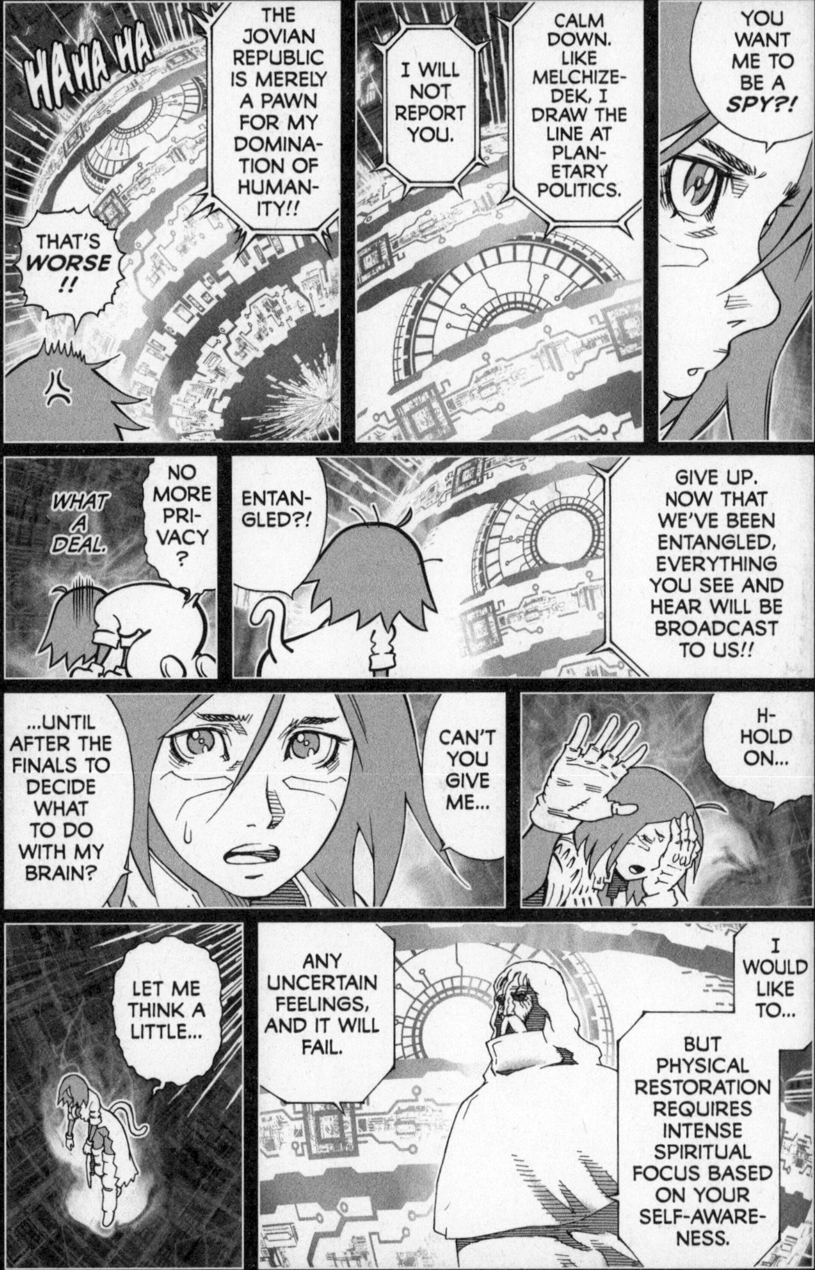
YOU WANT ME TO BE A SPY?!
CALM DOWN. LIKE MELCHIZEDEK, I DRAW THE LINE AT PLANETARY POLITICS.
I WILL NOT REPORT YOU.
THE JOVIAN REPUBLIC IS MERELY A PAWN FOR MY DOMINATION OF HUMANITY!!
HAHA HA
THAT'S WORSE!!
GIVE UP. NOW THAT WE'VE BEEN ENTANGLED, EVERYTHING YOU SEE AND HEAR WILL BE BROADCAST TO US!!
ENTANGLED?!
NO MORE PRIVACY?
WHAT A DEAL.
H-HOLD ON...
CAN'T YOU GIVE ME...
...UNTIL AFTER THE FINALS TO DECIDE WHAT TO DO WITH MY BRAIN?
I WOULD LIKE TO...
BUT PHYSICAL RESTORATION REQUIRES INTENSE SPIRITUAL FOCUS BASED ON YOUR SELF-AWARENESS.
ANY UNCERTAIN FEELINGS, AND IT WILL FAIL.
LET ME THINK A LITTLE...

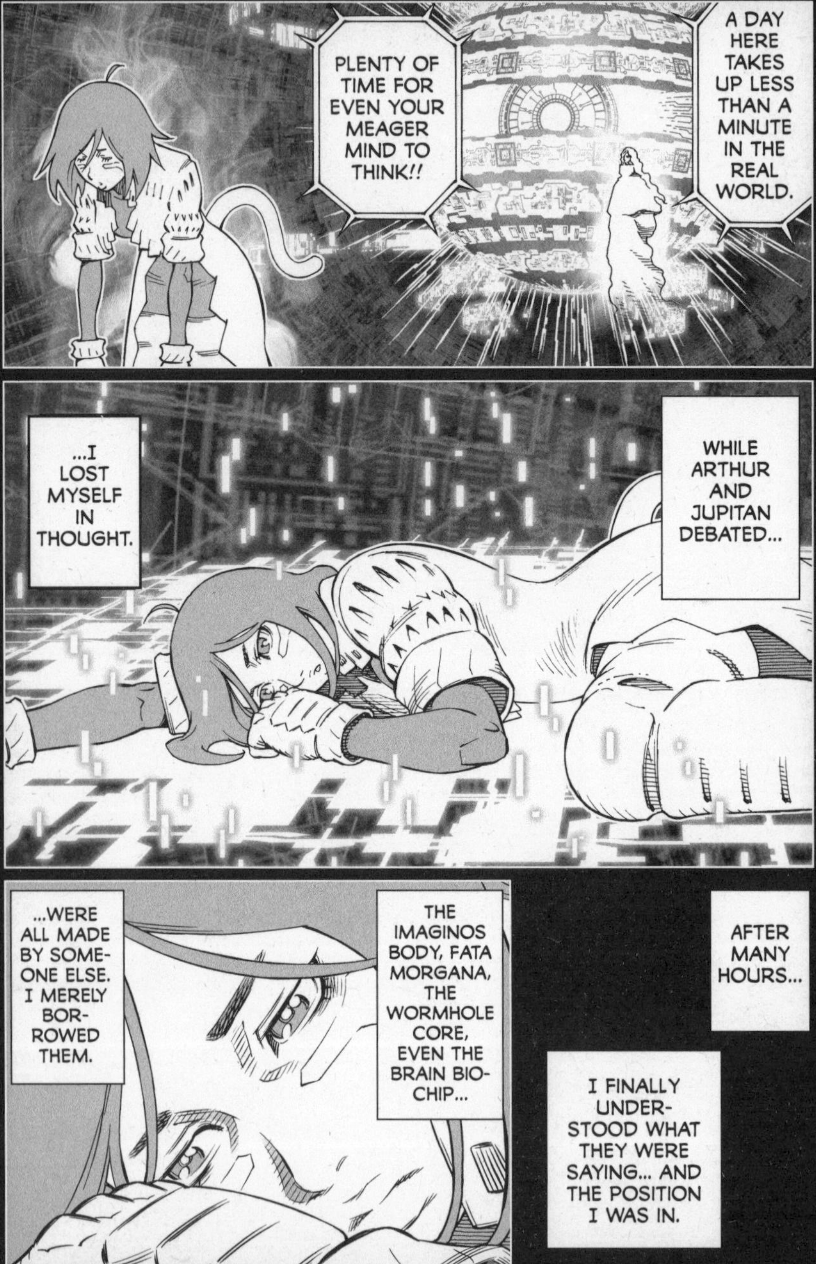
A DAY HERE TAKES UP LESS THAN A MINUTE IN THE REAL WORLD.
PLENTY OF TIME FOR EVEN YOUR MEAGER MIND TO THINK!!
WHILE ARTHUR AND JUPITAN DEBATED...
...I LOST MYSELF IN THOUGHT.
AFTER MANY HOURS...
I FINALLY UNDERSTOOD WHAT THEY WERE SAYING... AND THE POSITION I WAS IN.
THE IMAGINOS BODY, FATA MORGANA, THE WORMHOLE CORE, EVEN THE BRAIN BIOCHIP...
...WERE ALL MADE BY SOMEONE ELSE. I MERELY BORROWED THEM.

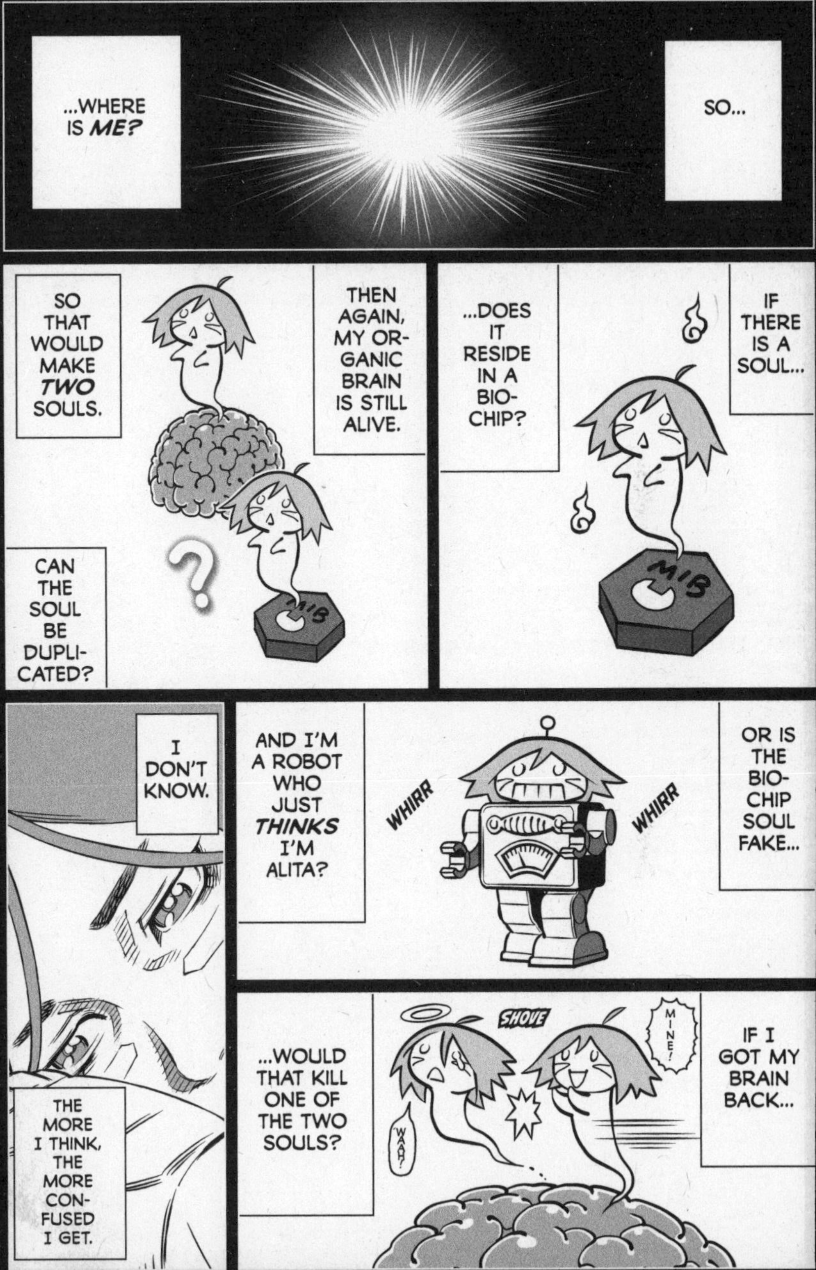
SO...
...WHERE IS *ME?*
IF THERE IS A SOUL...
...DOES IT RESIDE IN A BIO-CHIP?
THEN AGAIN, MY ORGANIC BRAIN IS STILL ALIVE.
SO THAT WOULD MAKE *TWO* SOULS.
CAN THE SOUL BE DUPLICATED?
OR IS THE BIO-CHIP SOUL FAKE...
WHIRR
WHIRR
AND I'M A ROBOT WHO JUST *THINKS* I'M ALITA?
IF I GOT MY BRAIN BACK...
MINE!
SHOVE
WAAH!
...WOULD THAT KILL ONE OF THE TWO SOULS?
I DON'T KNOW.
THE MORE I THINK, THE MORE CONFUSED I GET.

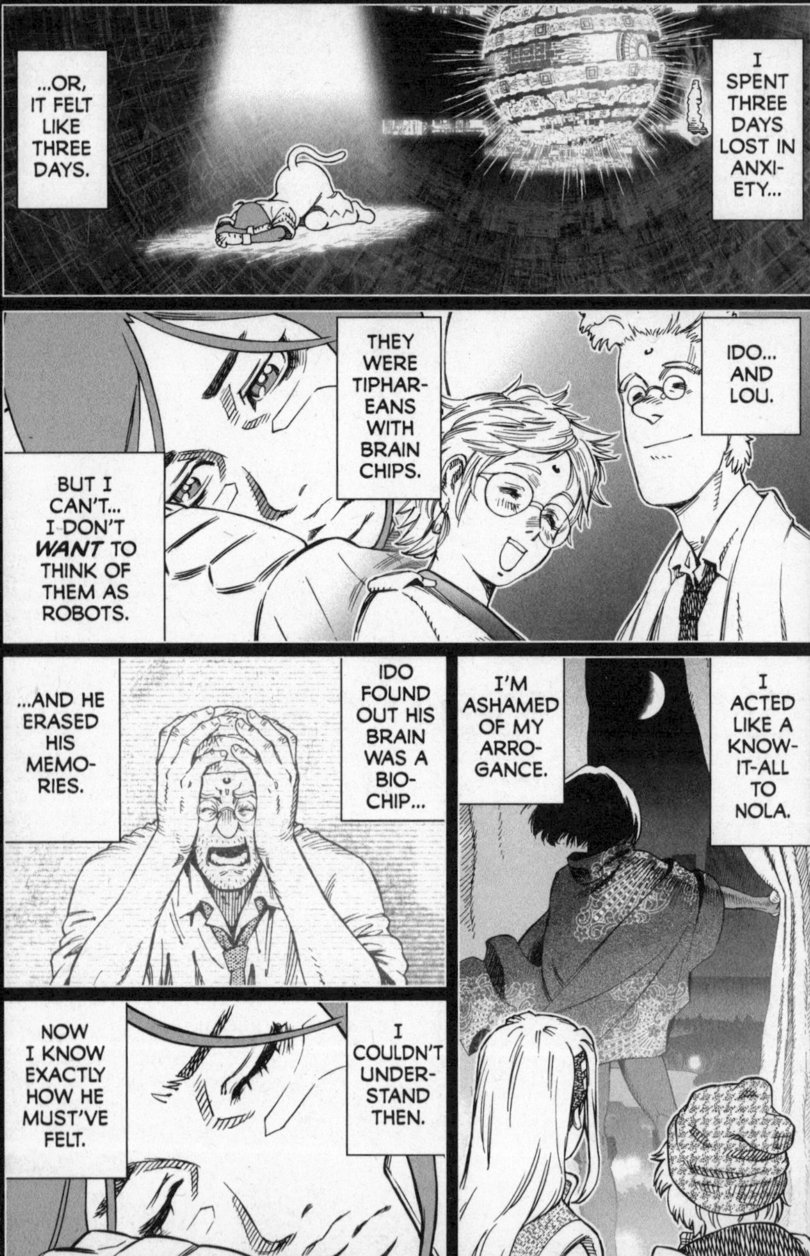
I SPENT THREE DAYS LOST IN ANXIETY...
...OR, IT FELT LIKE THREE DAYS.
IDO... AND LOU.
THEY WERE TIPHAREANS WITH BRAIN CHIPS.
BUT I CAN'T... I DON'T *WANT* TO THINK OF THEM AS ROBOTS.
I ACTED LIKE A KNOW-IT-ALL TO NOLA.
I'M ASHAMED OF MY ARROGANCE.
IDO FOUND OUT HIS BRAIN WAS A BIO-CHIP...
...AND HE ERASED HIS MEMORIES.
I COULDN'T UNDERSTAND THEN.
NOW I KNOW EXACTLY HOW HE MUST'VE FELT.

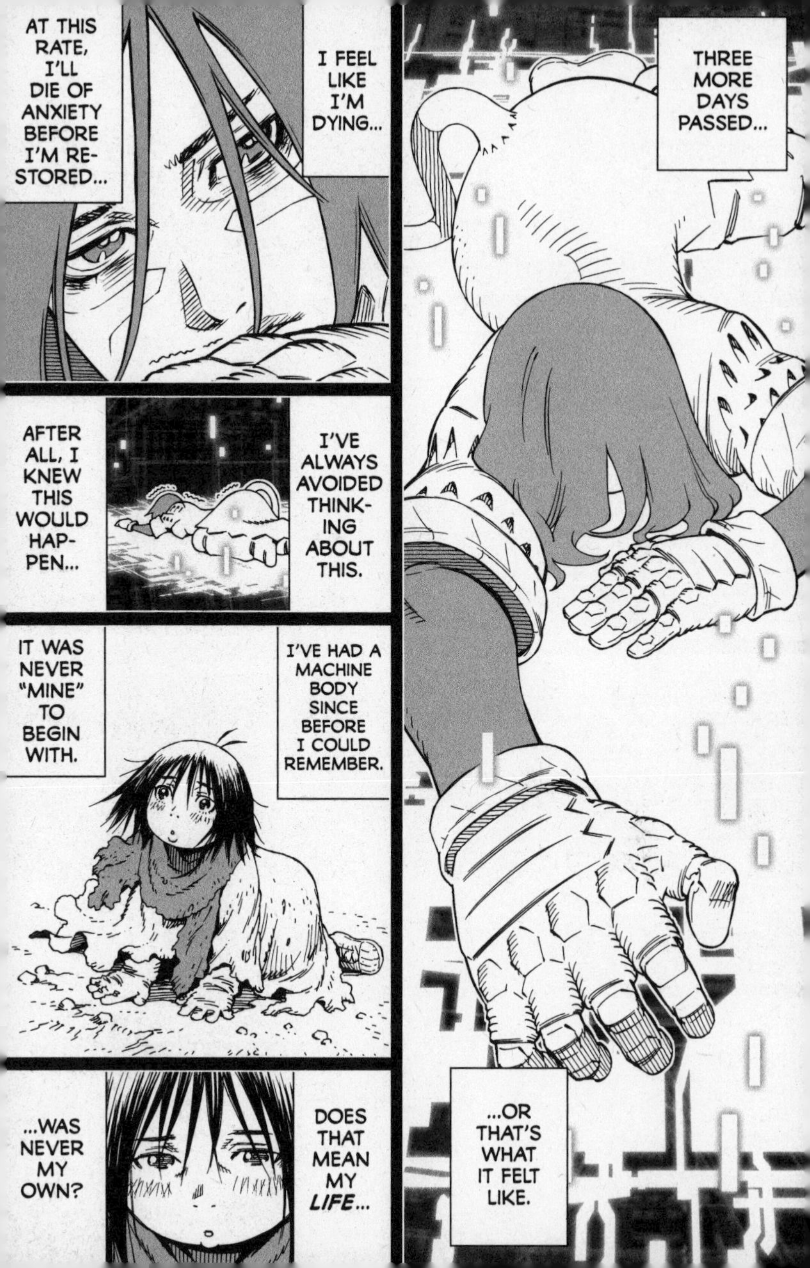
THREE MORE DAYS PASSED...
...OR THAT'S WHAT IT FELT LIKE.
I FEEL LIKE I'M DYING...
AT THIS RATE, I'LL DIE OF ANXIETY BEFORE I'M RESTORED...
I'VE ALWAYS AVOIDED THINKING ABOUT THIS.
AFTER ALL, I KNEW THIS WOULD HAPPEN...
I'VE HAD A MACHINE BODY SINCE BEFORE I COULD REMEMBER.
IT WAS NEVER "MINE" TO BEGIN WITH.
DOES THAT MEAN MY *LIFE*...
...WAS NEVER MY OWN?

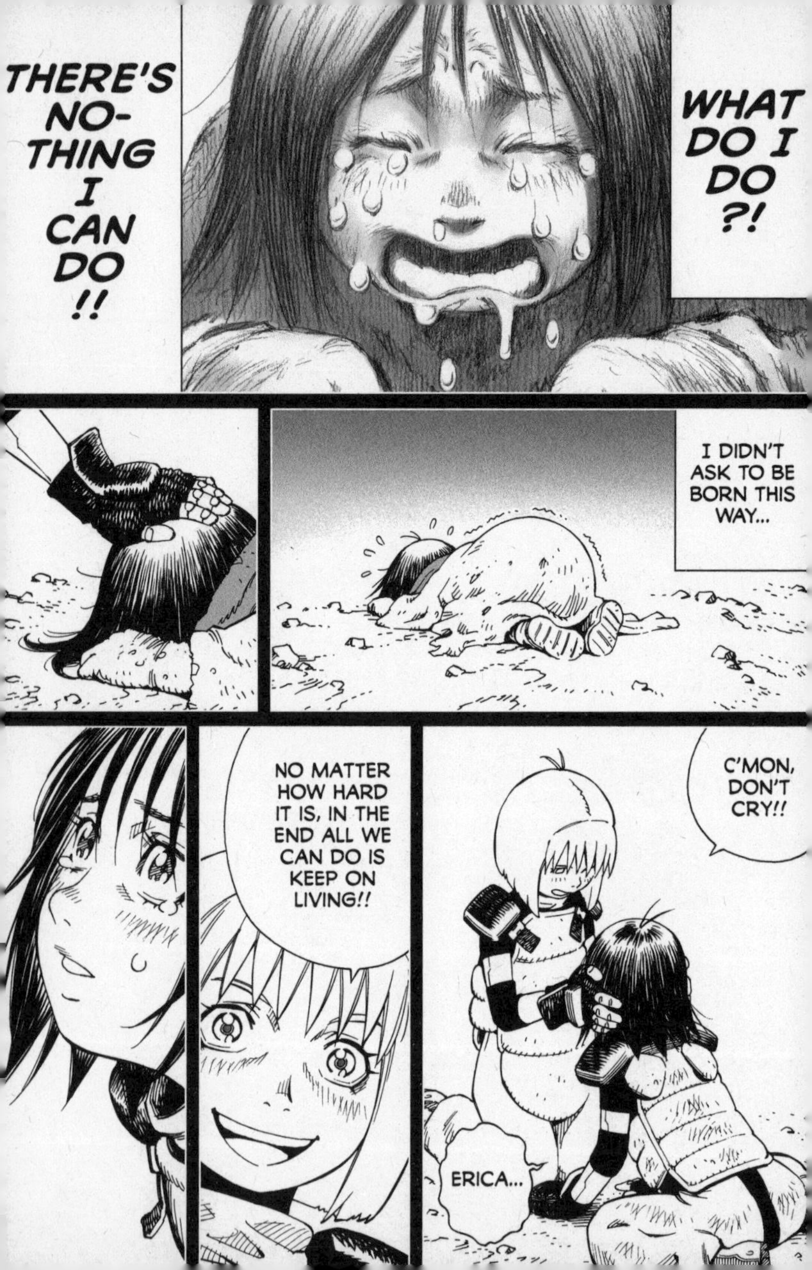
WHAT DO I DO?!
THERE'S NOTHING I CAN DO!!
I DIDN'T ASK TO BE BORN THIS WAY...
C'MON, DON'T CRY!!
ERICA...
NO MATTER HOW HARD IT IS, IN THE END ALL WE CAN DO IS KEEP ON LIVING!!

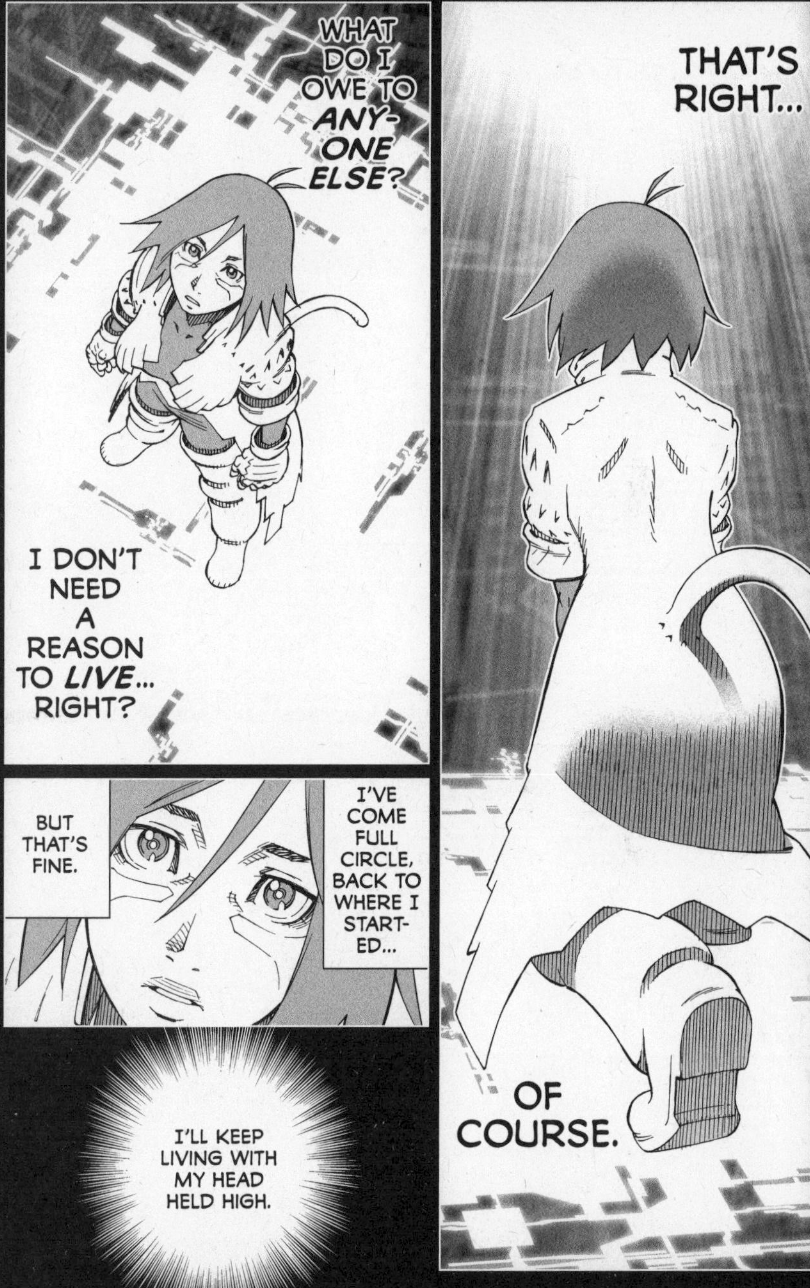
THAT'S RIGHT...
OF COURSE.
WHAT DO I OWE TO ANY-ONE ELSE?
I DON'T NEED A REASON TO LIVE... RIGHT?
I'VE COME FULL CIRCLE, BACK TO WHERE I START-ED...
BUT THAT'S FINE.
I'LL KEEP LIVING WITH MY HEAD HELD HIGH.

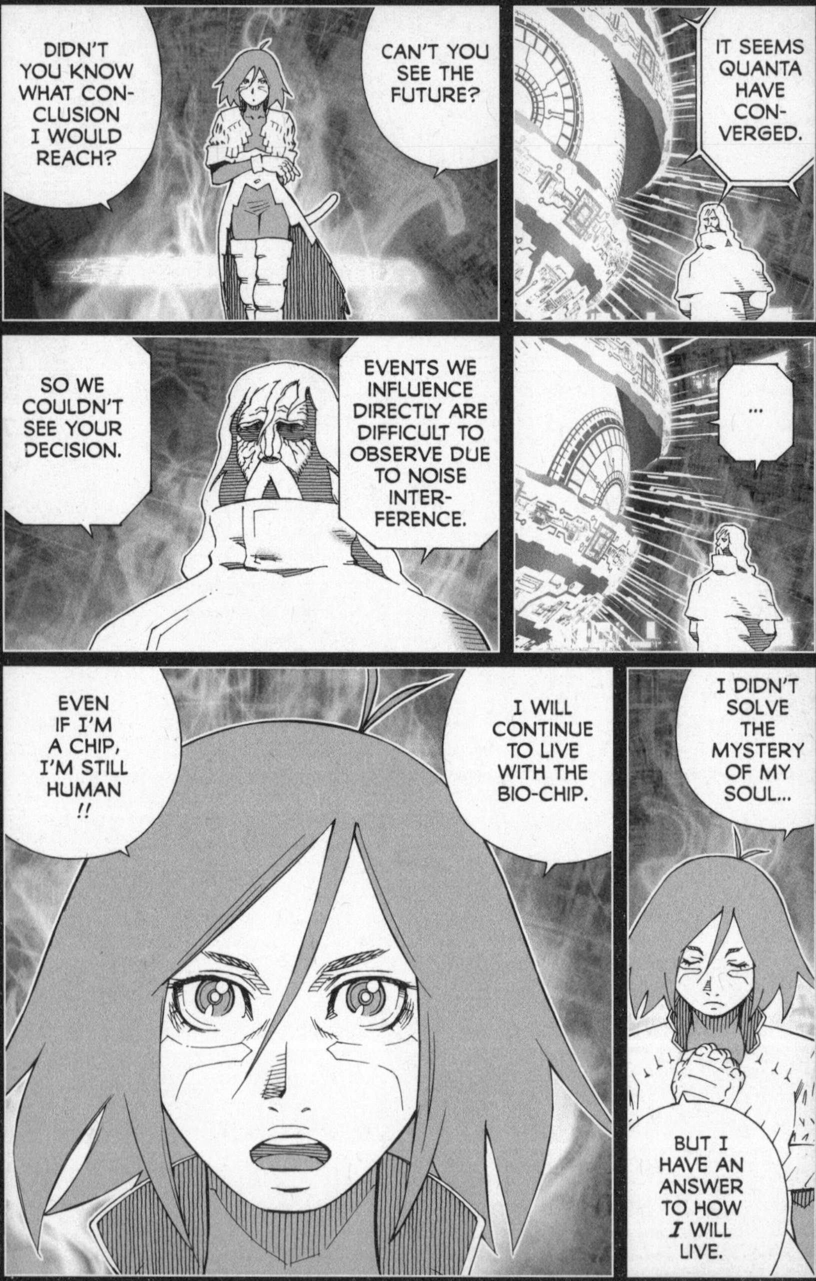
IT SEEMS QUANTA HAVE CONVERGED.
CAN'T YOU SEE THE FUTURE?
DIDN'T YOU KNOW WHAT CONCLUSION I WOULD REACH?
...
EVENTS WE INFLUENCE DIRECTLY ARE DIFFICULT TO OBSERVE DUE TO NOISE INTERFERENCE.
SO WE COULDN'T SEE YOUR DECISION.
I DIDN'T SOLVE THE MYSTERY OF MY SOUL...
BUT I HAVE AN ANSWER TO HOW *I* WILL LIVE.
I WILL CONTINUE TO LIVE WITH THE BIO-CHIP.
EVEN IF I'M A CHIP, I'M STILL HUMAN!!

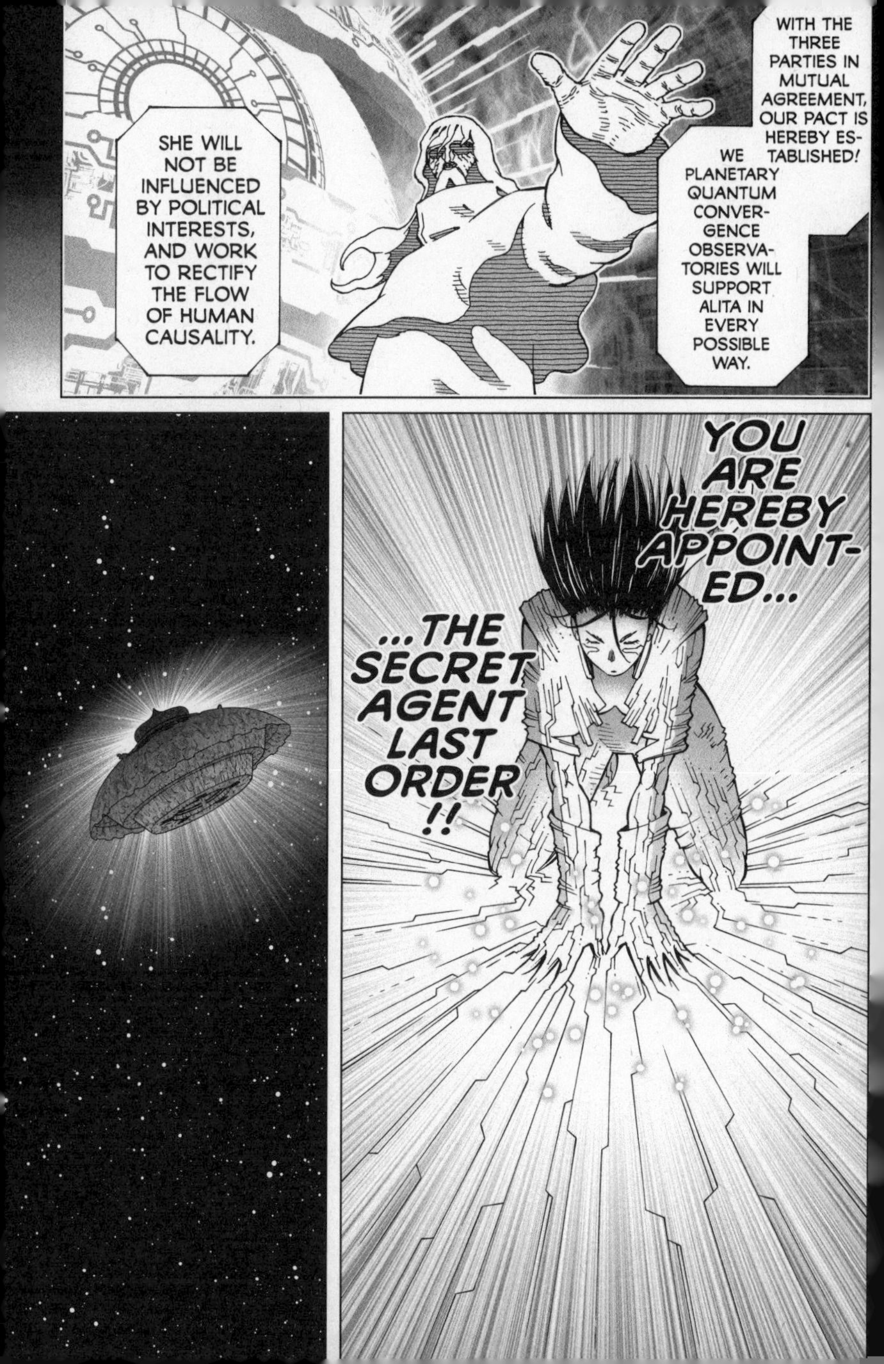
WITH THE THREE PARTIES IN MUTUAL AGREEMENT, OUR PACT IS HEREBY ESTABLISHED!
WE PLANETARY QUANTUM CONVERGENCE OBSERVATORIES WILL SUPPORT ALITA IN EVERY POSSIBLE WAY.
SHE WILL NOT BE INFLUENCED BY POLITICAL INTERESTS, AND WORK TO RECTIFY THE FLOW OF HUMAN CAUSALITY.
YOU ARE HEREBY APPOINTED...
...THE SECRET AGENT LAST ORDER!!

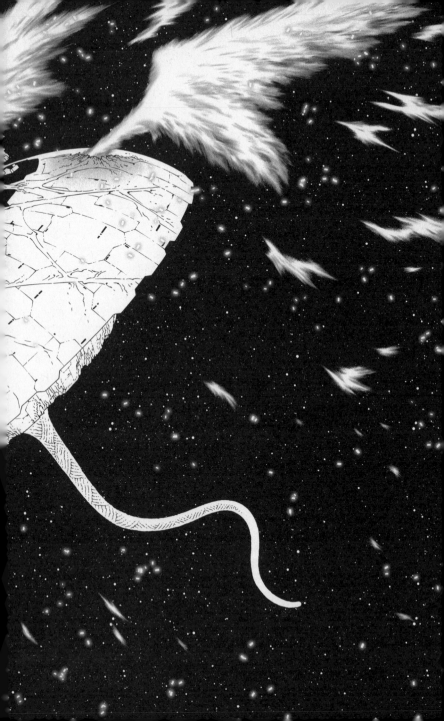

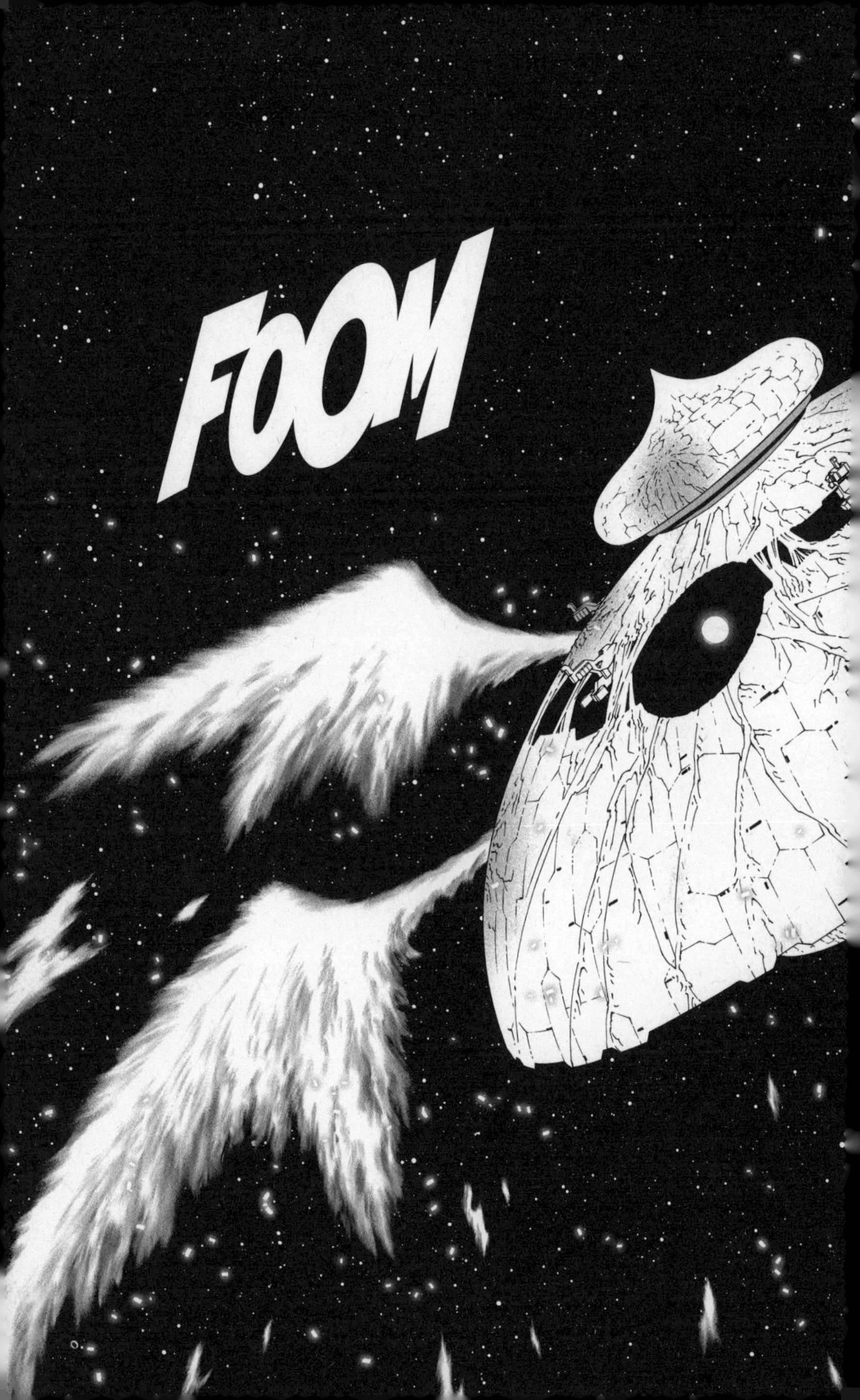
FOOM

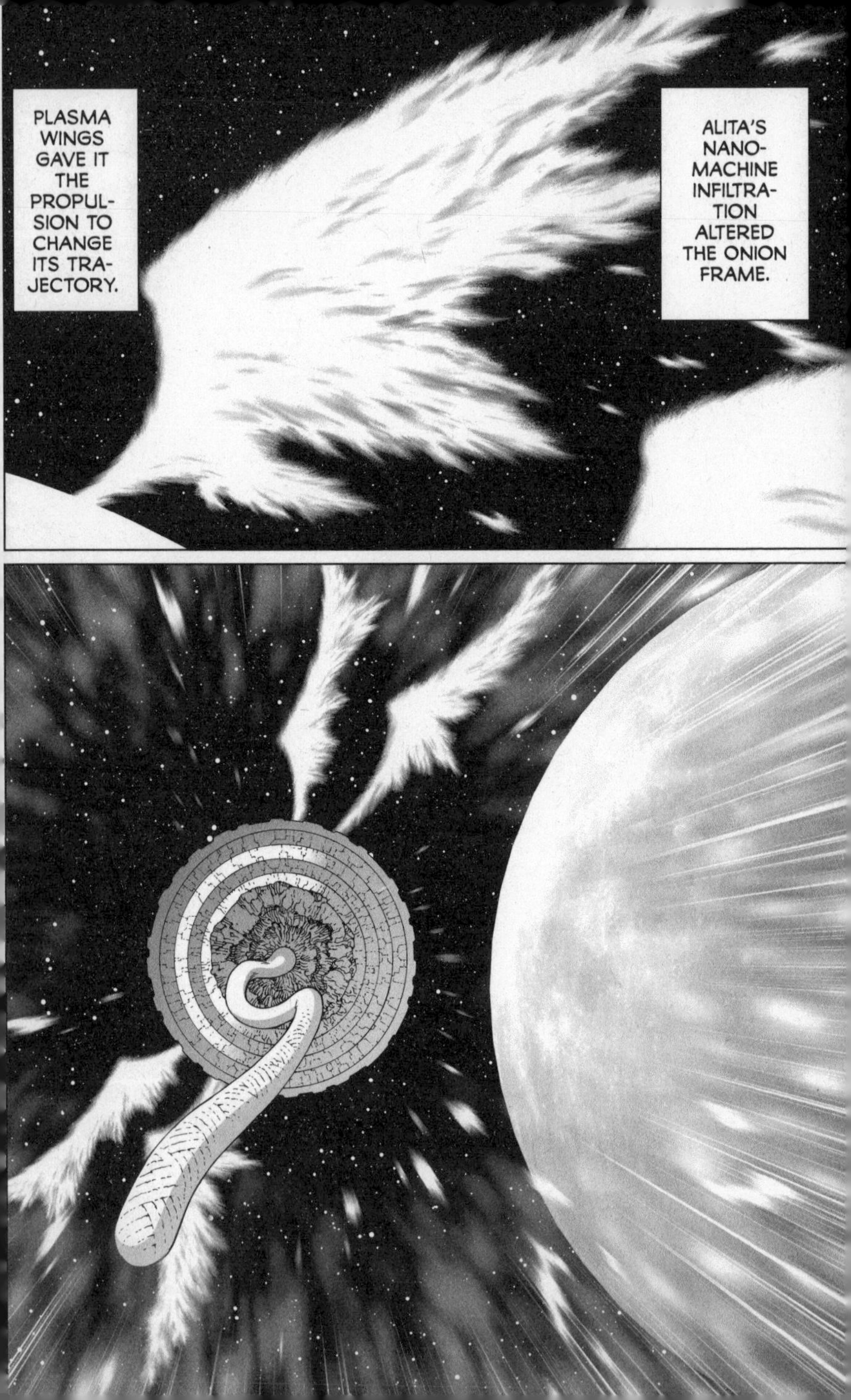
ALITA'S NANO-MACHINE INFILTRA-TION ALTERED THE ONION FRAME.
PLASMA WINGS GAVE IT THE PROPUL-SION TO CHANGE ITS TRA-JECTORY.

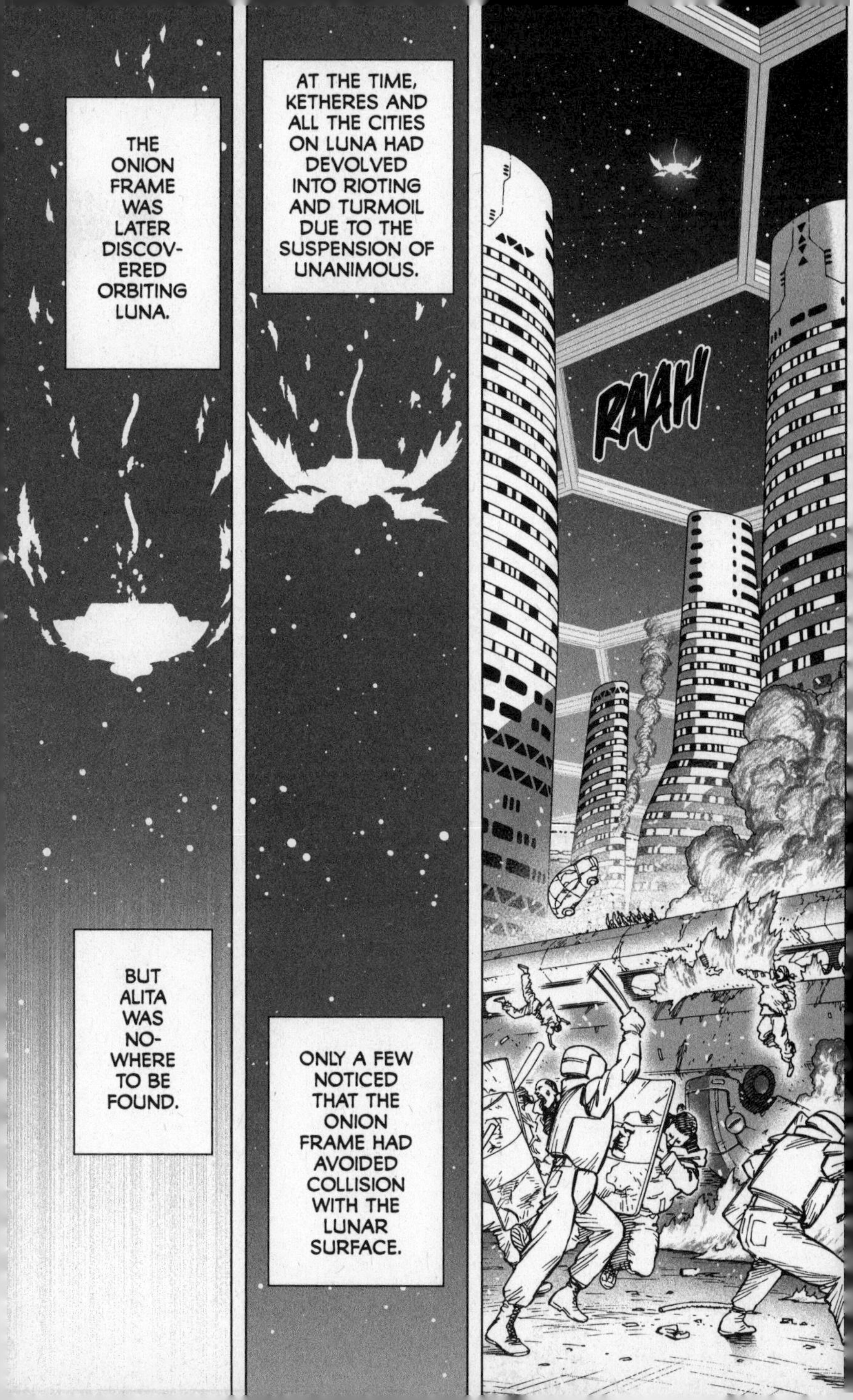
RAAH
AT THE TIME, KETHERES AND ALL THE CITIES ON LUNA HAD DEVOLVED INTO RIOTING AND TURMOIL DUE TO THE SUSPENSION OF UNANIMOUS.
ONLY A FEW NOTICED THAT THE ONION FRAME HAD AVOIDED COLLISION WITH THE LUNAR SURFACE.
THE ONION FRAME WAS LATER DISCOV-ERED ORBITING LUNA.
BUT ALITA WAS NO-WHERE TO BE FOUND.

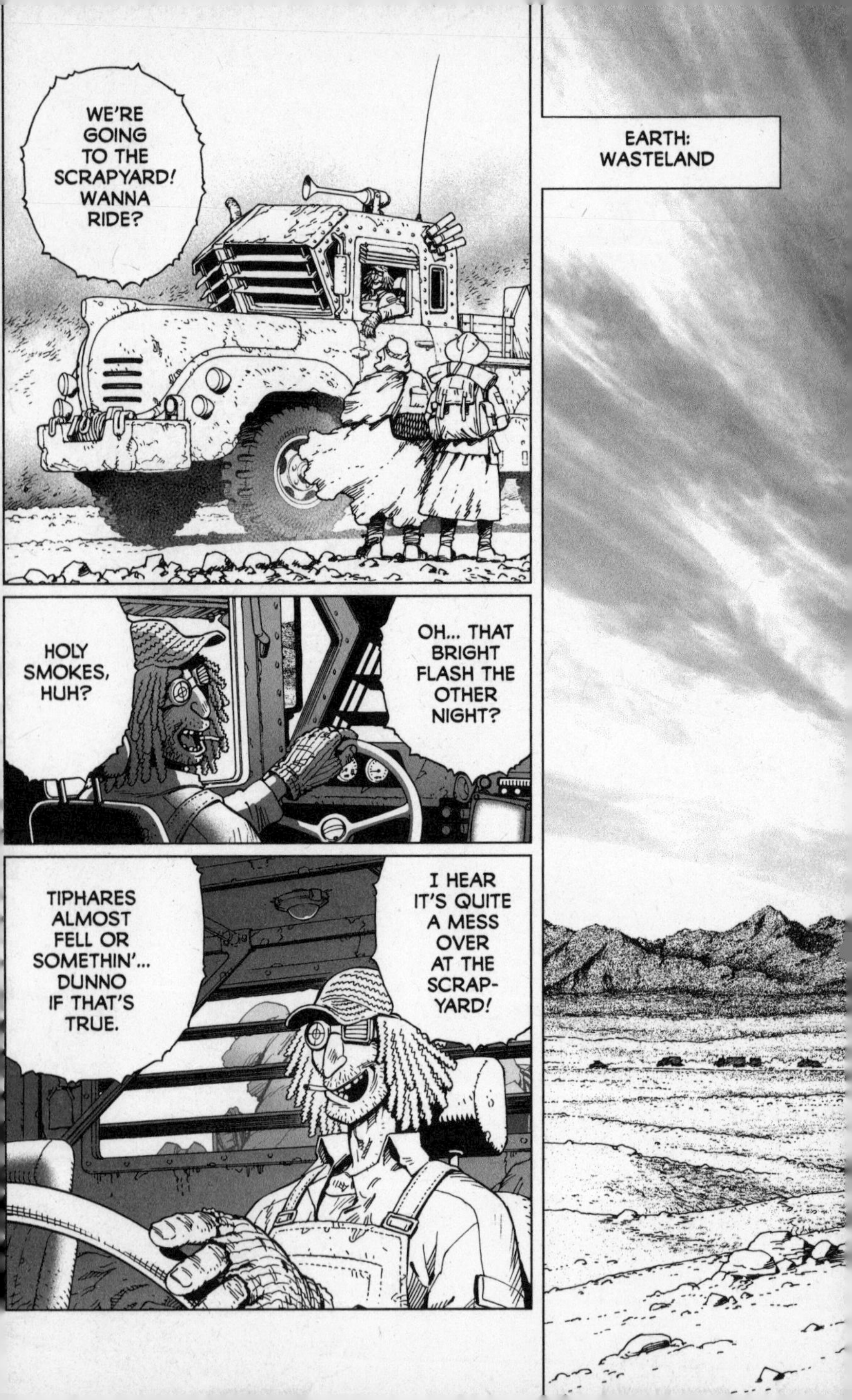
EARTH: WASTELAND
WE'RE GOING TO THE SCRAPYARD! WANNA RIDE?
OH... THAT BRIGHT FLASH THE OTHER NIGHT?
HOLY SMOKES, HUH?
I HEAR IT'S QUITE A MESS OVER AT THE SCRAP-YARD!
TIPHARES ALMOST FELL OR SOMETHIN'... DUNNO IF THAT'S TRUE.

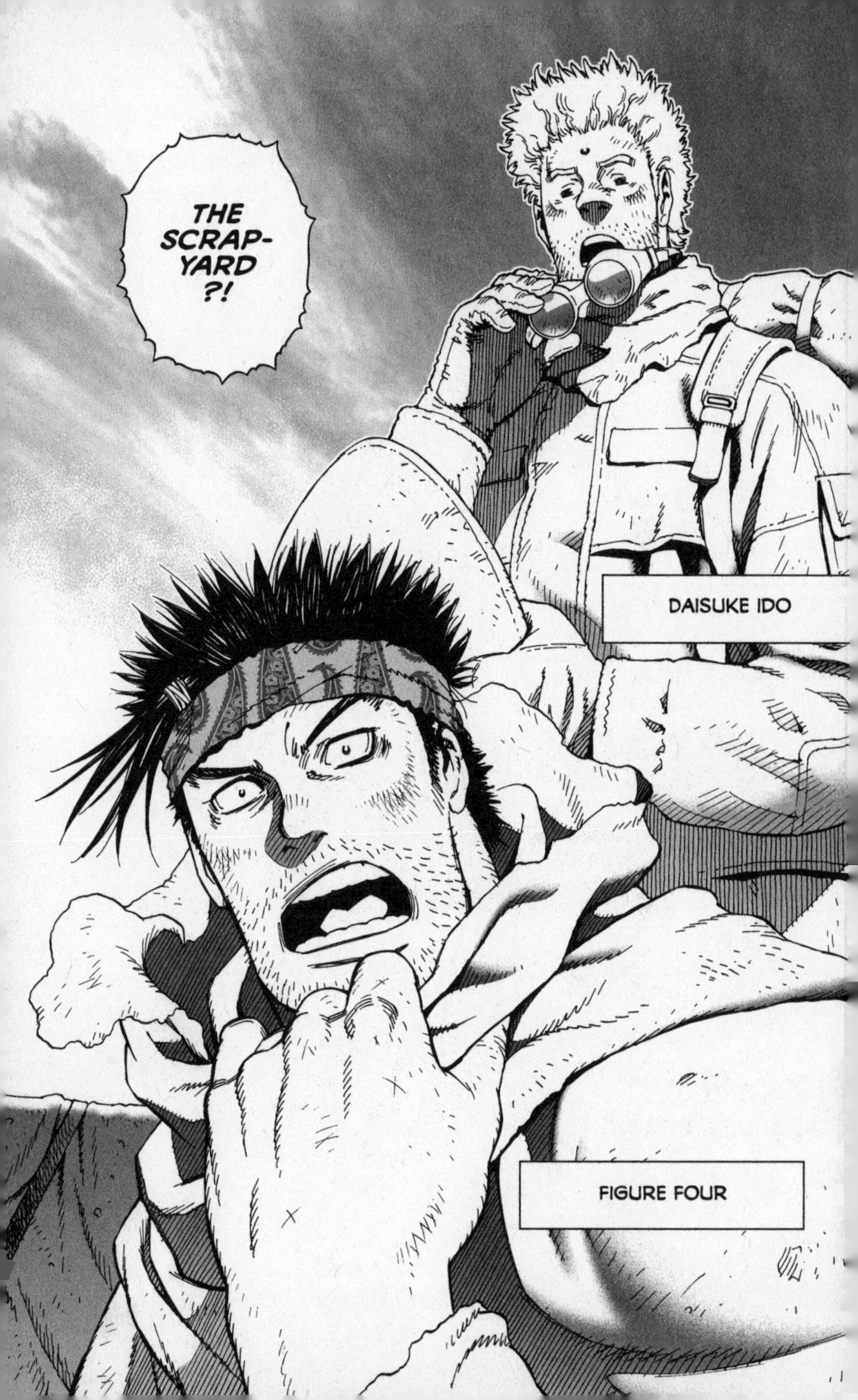
THE SCRAP-YARD ?!
DAISUKE IDO
FIGURE FOUR

Phase 107: Alita Quest I

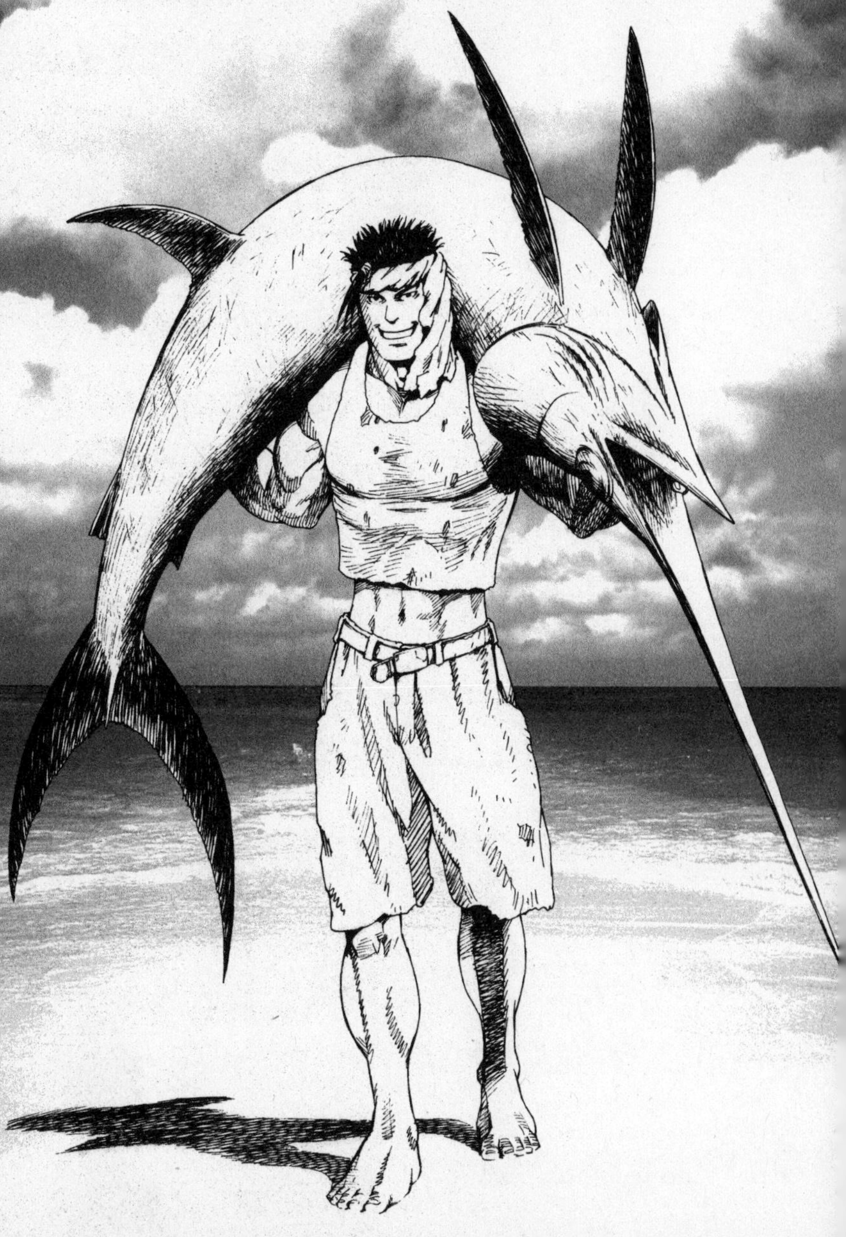

ELEVEN
MONTHS
EARLIER

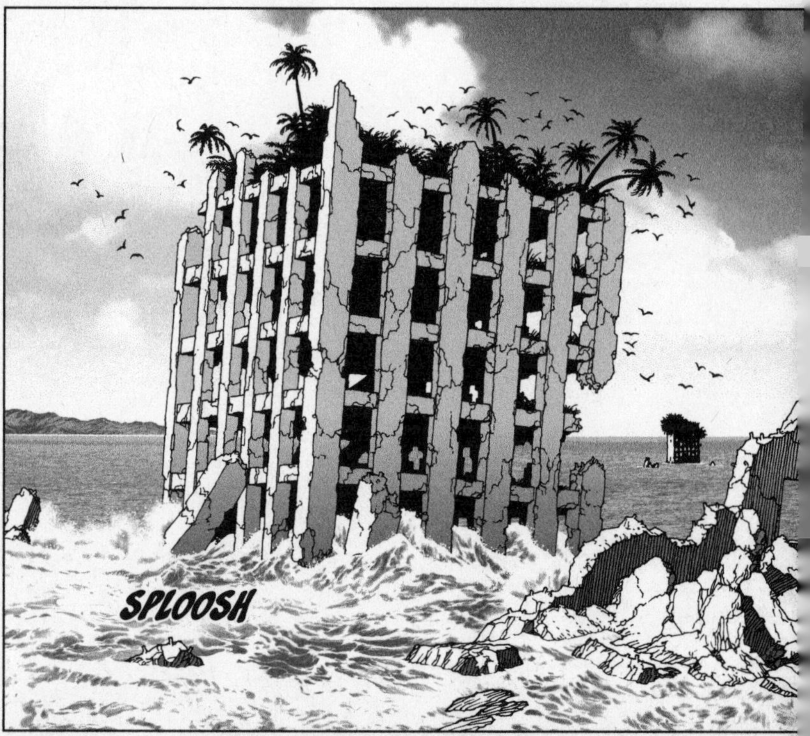
SPLOOSH
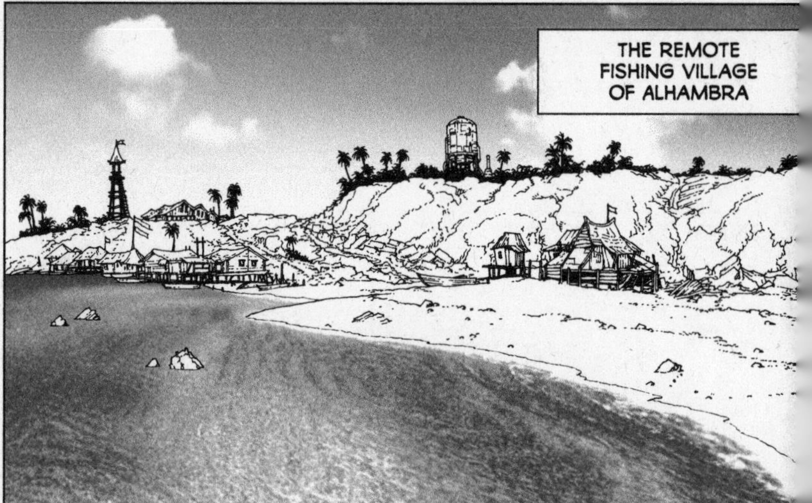
THE REMOTE FISHING VILLAGE OF ALHAMBRA

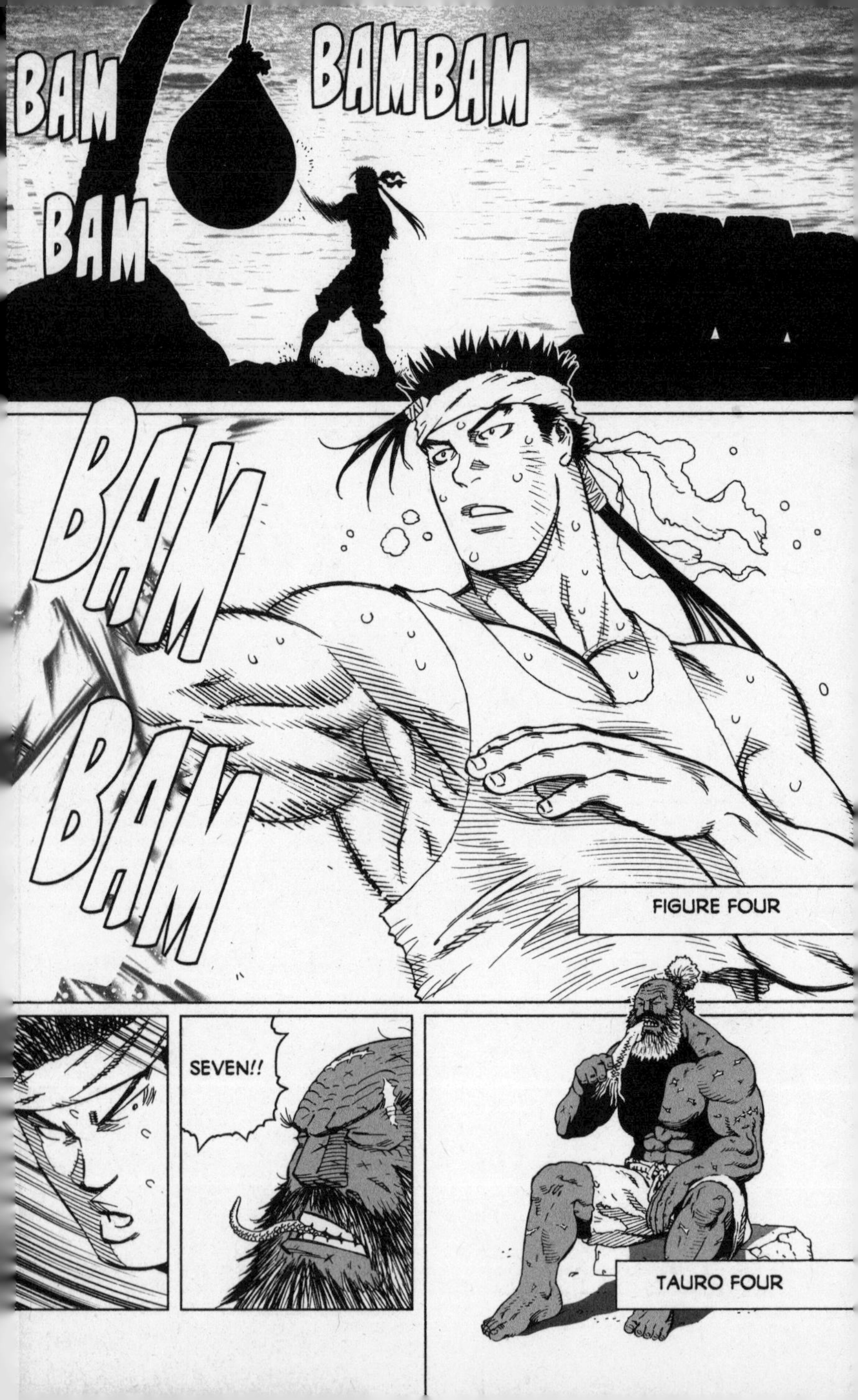
BAM BAM
BAM
BAM
FIGURE FOUR
BAM
BAM
TAURO FOUR
SEVEN!!

THOOM

TAP

BOOM

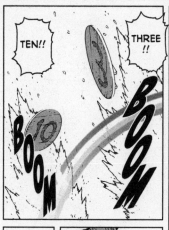

TEN!!

THREE!!

BOOM

BOOM

NEXT STAGE?

ALL YOUR HARD WORK'S PAID OFF.

TIME FOR THE NEXT STAGE!

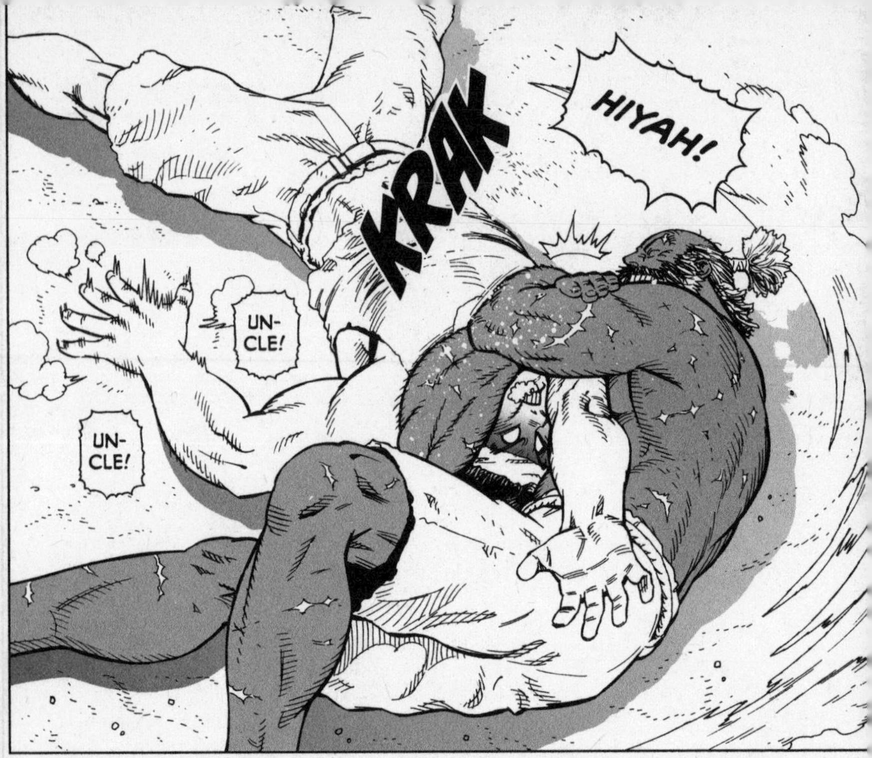
HIYAH!
KRAK
UN-CLE!
UN-CLE!
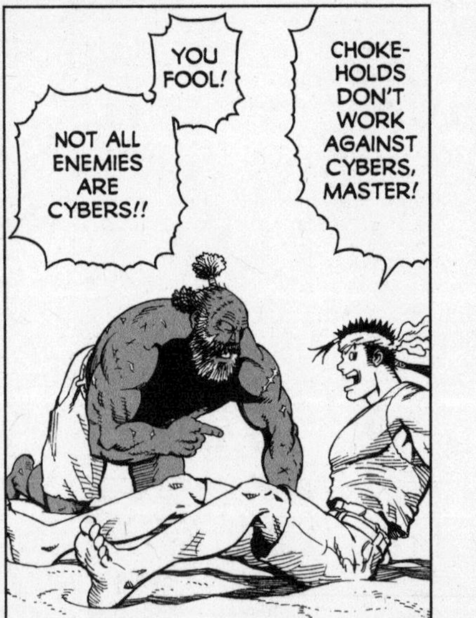
CHOKE-HOLDS DON'T WORK AGAINST CYBERS, MASTER!
YOU FOOL!
NOT ALL ENEMIES ARE CYBERS!!
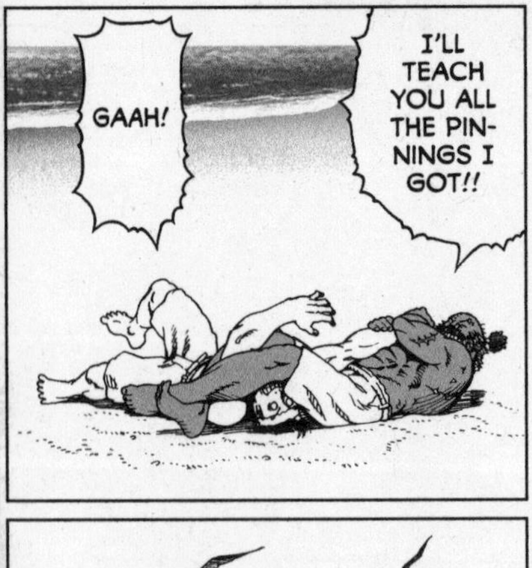
I'LL TEACH YOU ALL THE PIN-NINGS I GOT!!
GAAH!
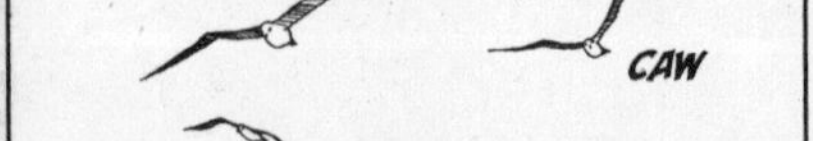
CAW
CAW

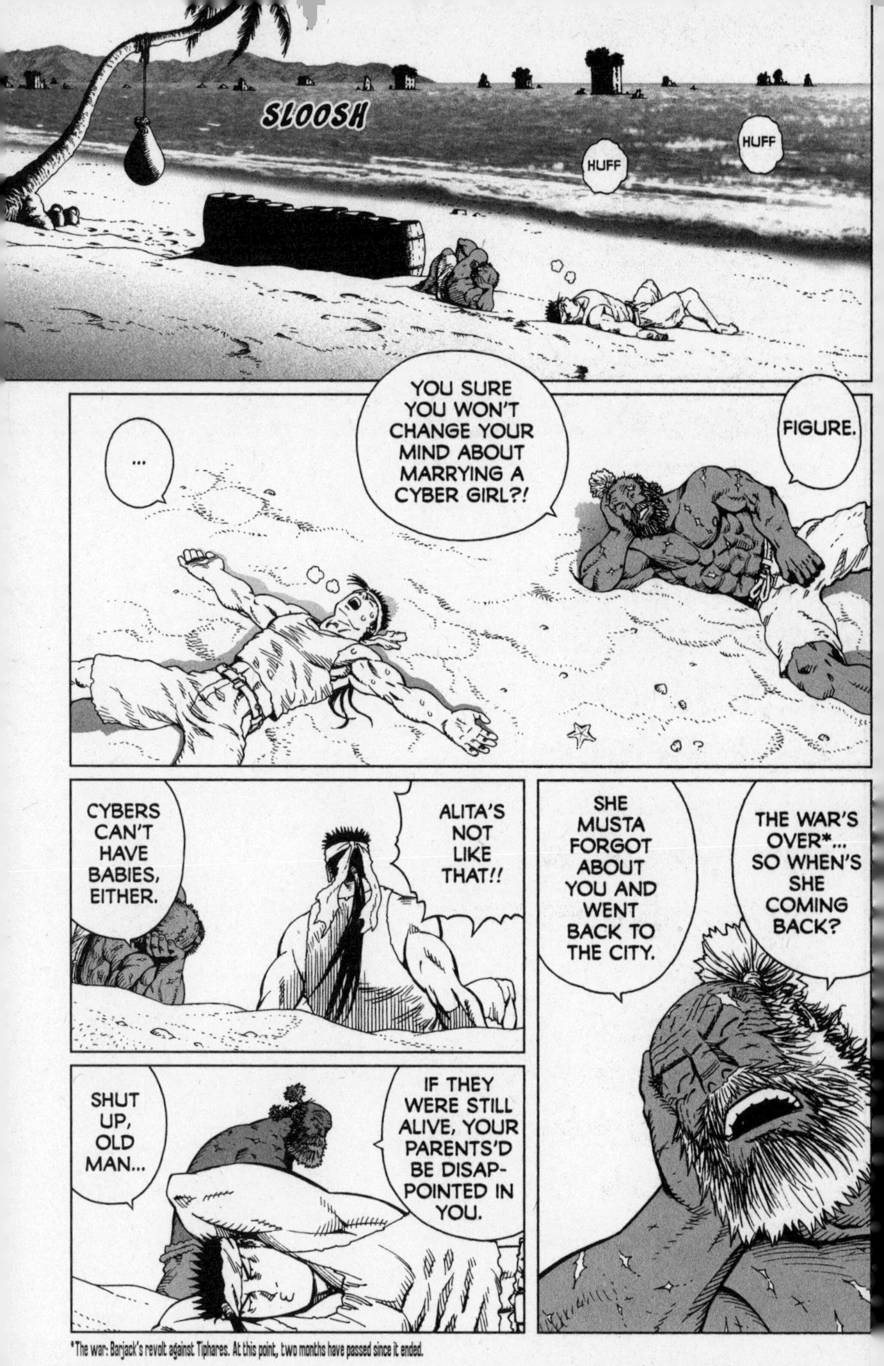
SLOOSH
HUFF
HUFF
FIGURE.
YOU SURE YOU WON'T CHANGE YOUR MIND ABOUT MARRYING A CYBER GIRL?!
...
THE WAR'S OVER*... SO WHEN'S SHE COMING BACK?
SHE MUSTA FORGOT ABOUT YOU AND WENT BACK TO THE CITY.
ALITA'S NOT LIKE THAT!!
CYBERS CAN'T HAVE BABIES, EITHER.
IF THEY WERE STILL ALIVE, YOUR PARENTS'D BE DISAP-POINTED IN YOU.
SHUT UP, OLD MAN...

*The war: Barjack's revolt against Tiphares. At this point, two months have passed since it ended.

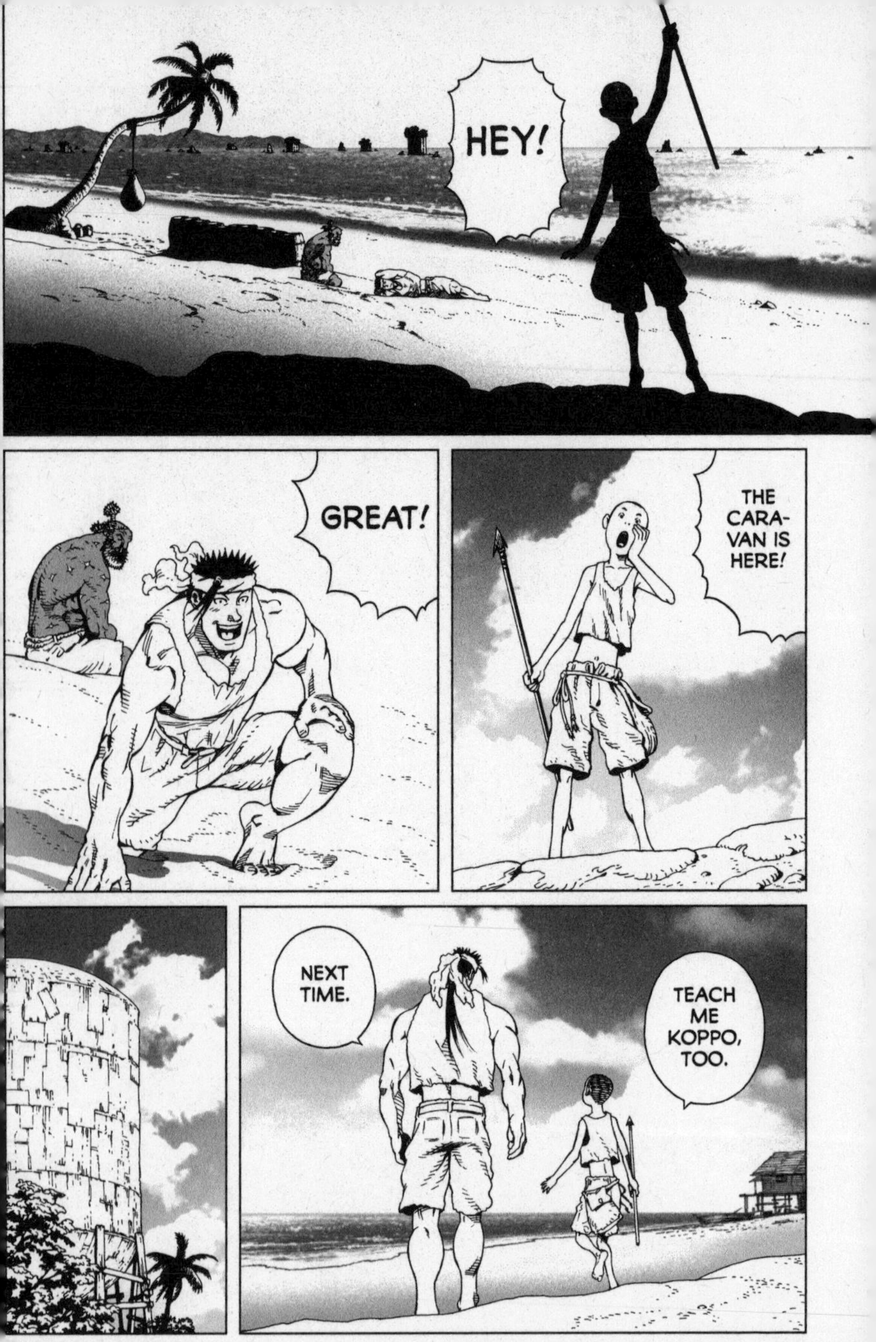
HEY!
THE CARA-VAN IS HERE!
GREAT!
TEACH ME KOPPO, TOO.
NEXT TIME.

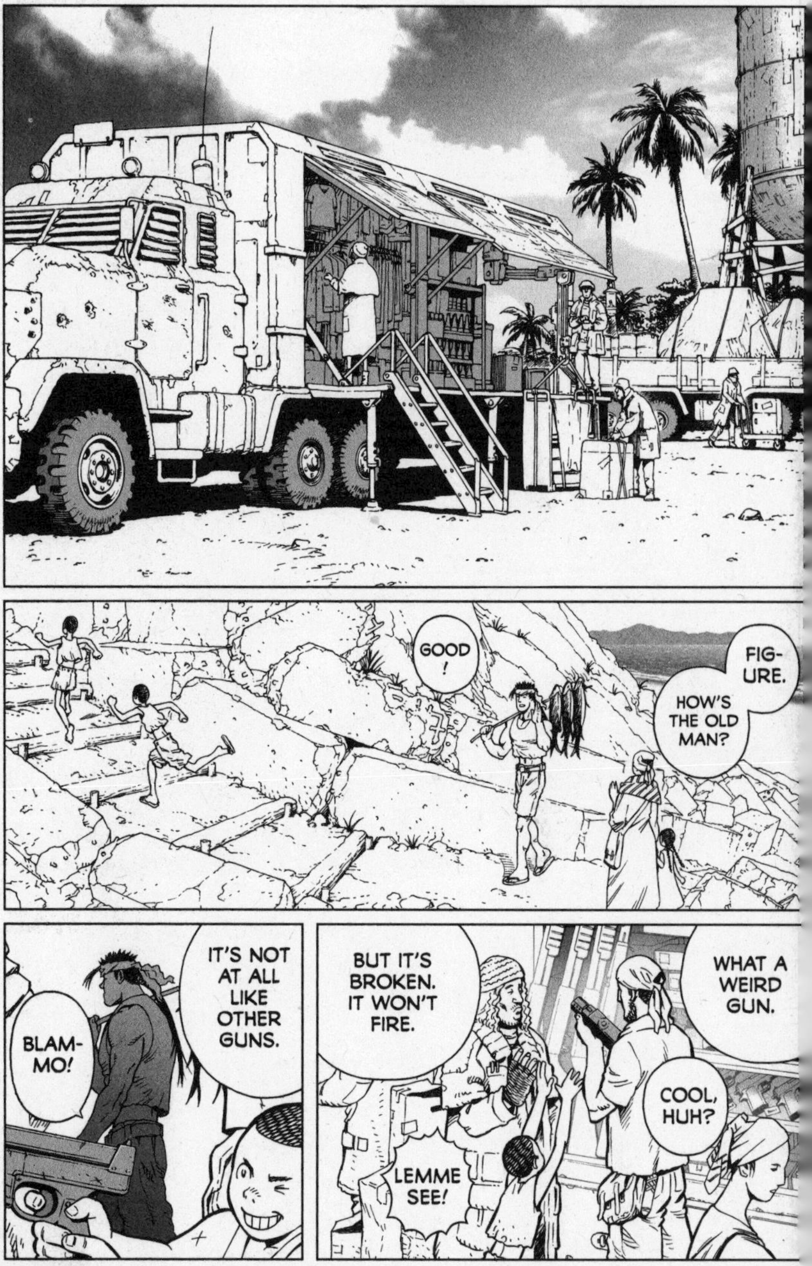
FIGURE.
HOW'S THE OLD MAN?
GOOD!
WHAT A WEIRD GUN.
BUT IT'S BROKEN. IT WON'T FIRE.
COOL, HUH?
LEMME SEE!
IT'S NOT AT ALL LIKE OTHER GUNS.
BLAMMO!

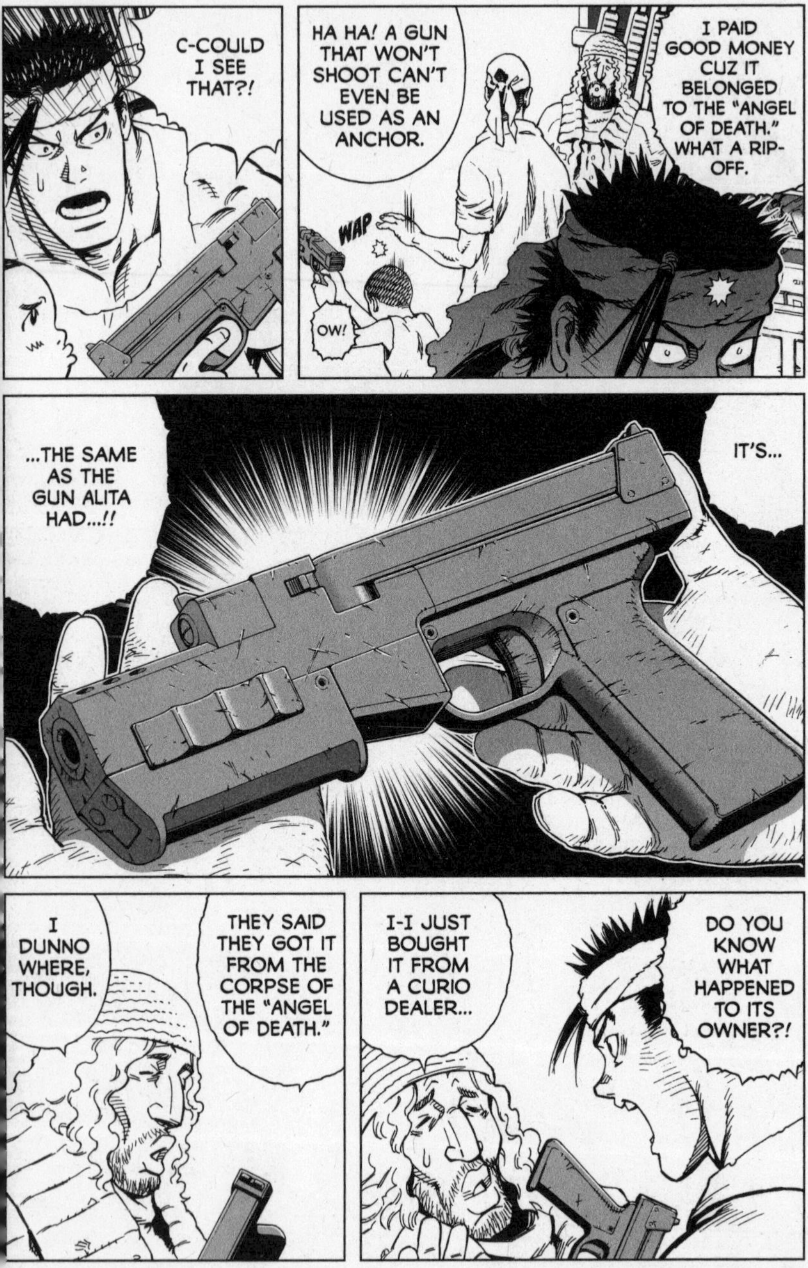
I PAID GOOD MONEY CUZ IT BELONGED TO THE "ANGEL OF DEATH." WHAT A RIP-OFF.
HA HA! A GUN THAT WON'T SHOOT CAN'T EVEN BE USED AS AN ANCHOR.
WAP
OW!
C-COULD I SEE THAT?!
IT'S...
...THE SAME AS THE GUN ALITA HAD...!!
DO YOU KNOW WHAT HAPPENED TO ITS OWNER?!
I-I JUST BOUGHT IT FROM A CURIO DEALER...
THEY SAID THEY GOT IT FROM THE CORPSE OF THE "ANGEL OF DEATH."
I DUNNO WHERE, THOUGH.

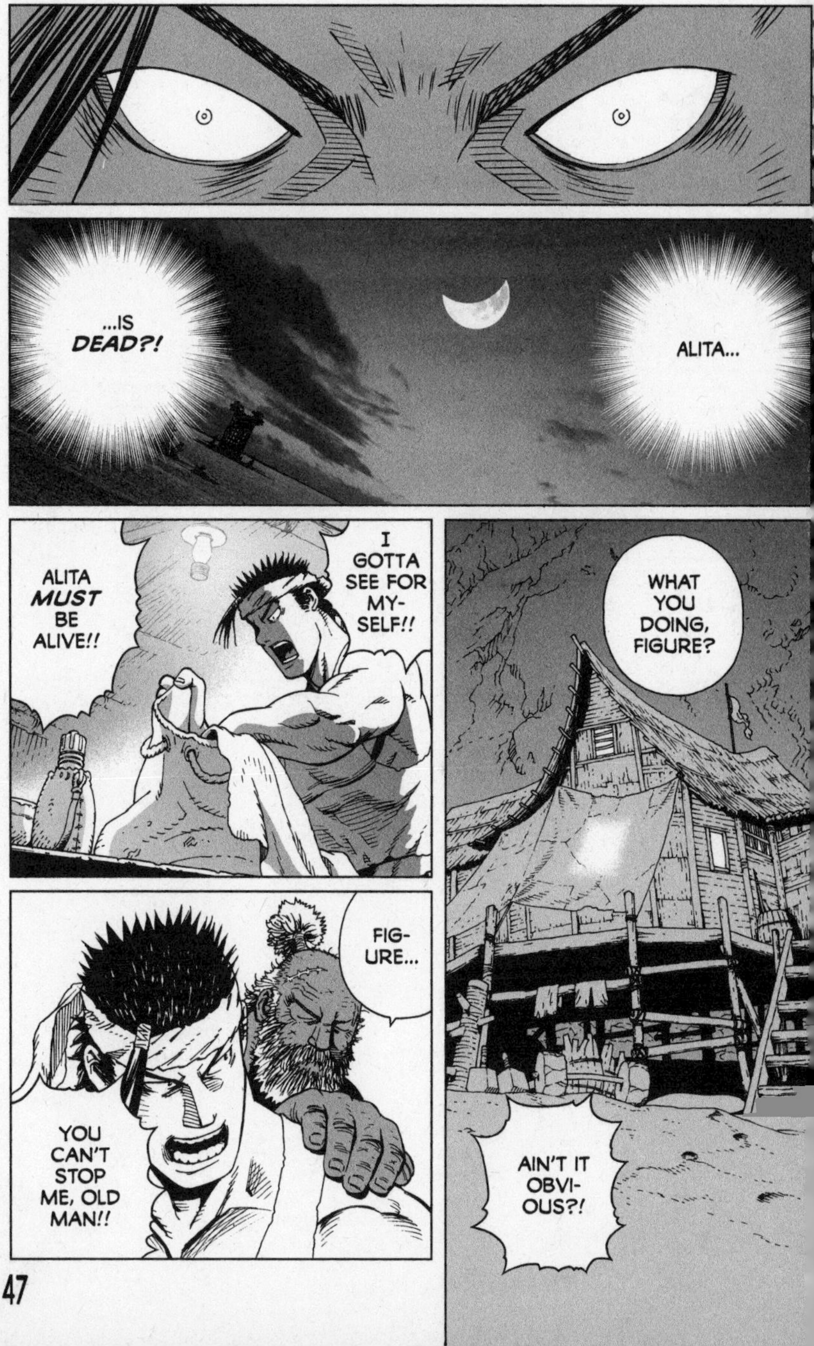
ALITA...
...IS *DEAD?!*
WHAT YOU DOING, FIGURE?
AIN'T IT OBVIOUS?!
I GOTTA SEE FOR MY-SELF!!
ALITA *MUST* BE ALIVE!!
FIG-URE...
YOU CAN'T STOP ME, OLD MAN!!

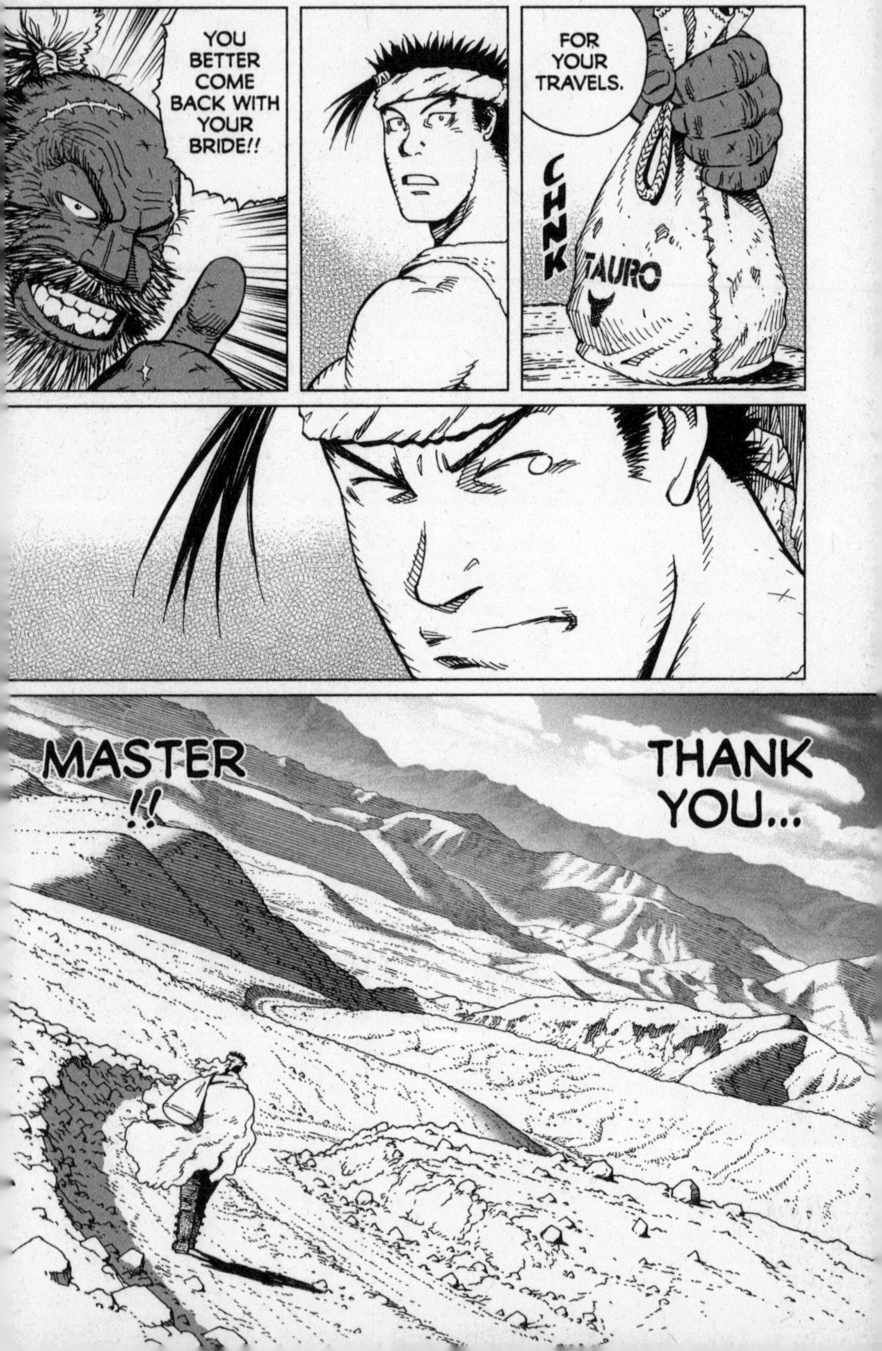
FOR YOUR TRAVELS.
CHNK
TAURO
YOU BETTER COME BACK WITH YOUR BRIDE!!
THANK YOU...
MASTER!!

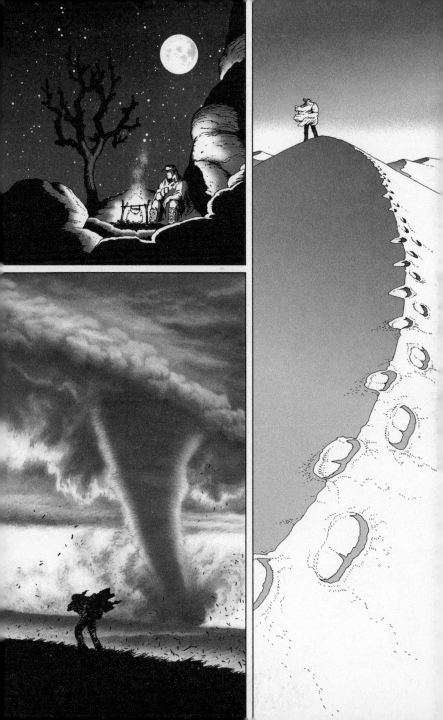

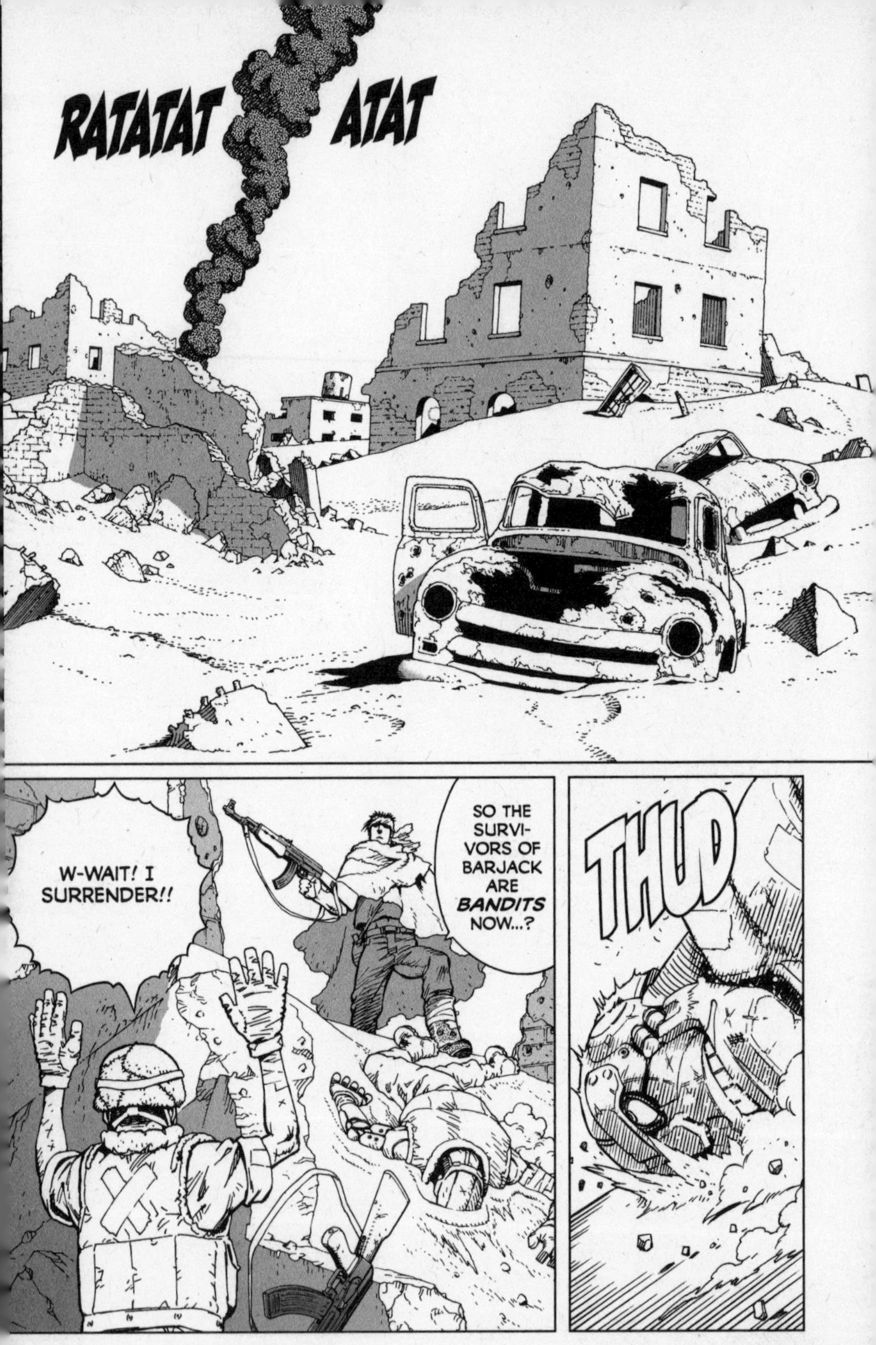
RATATAT ATAT
THUD
SO THE SURVI-VORS OF BARJACK ARE *BANDITS* NOW...?
W-WAIT! I SURRENDER!!

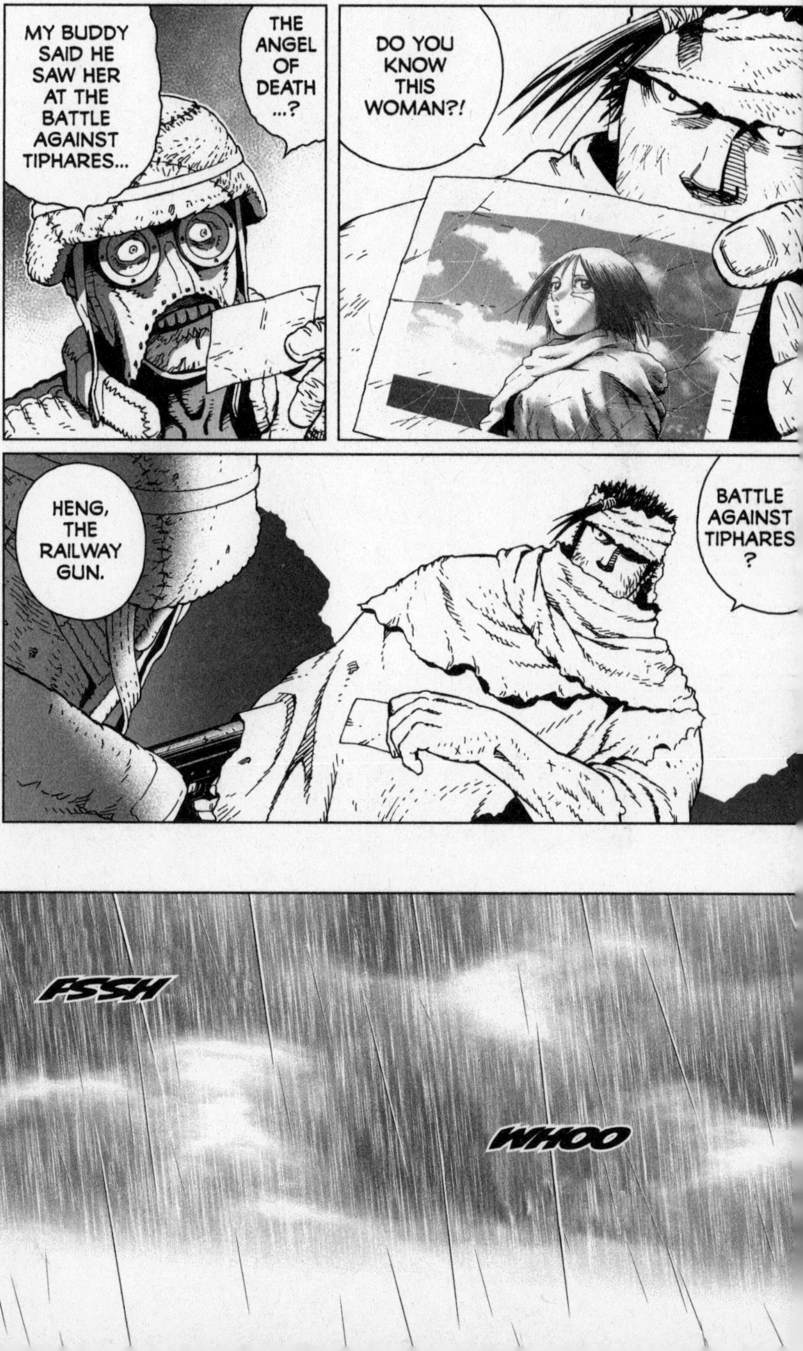
DO YOU KNOW THIS WOMAN?!
THE ANGEL OF DEATH ...?
MY BUDDY SAID HE SAW HER AT THE BATTLE AGAINST TIPHARES...
BATTLE AGAINST TIPHARES ?
HENG, THE RAILWAY GUN.
FSSH
WHOO

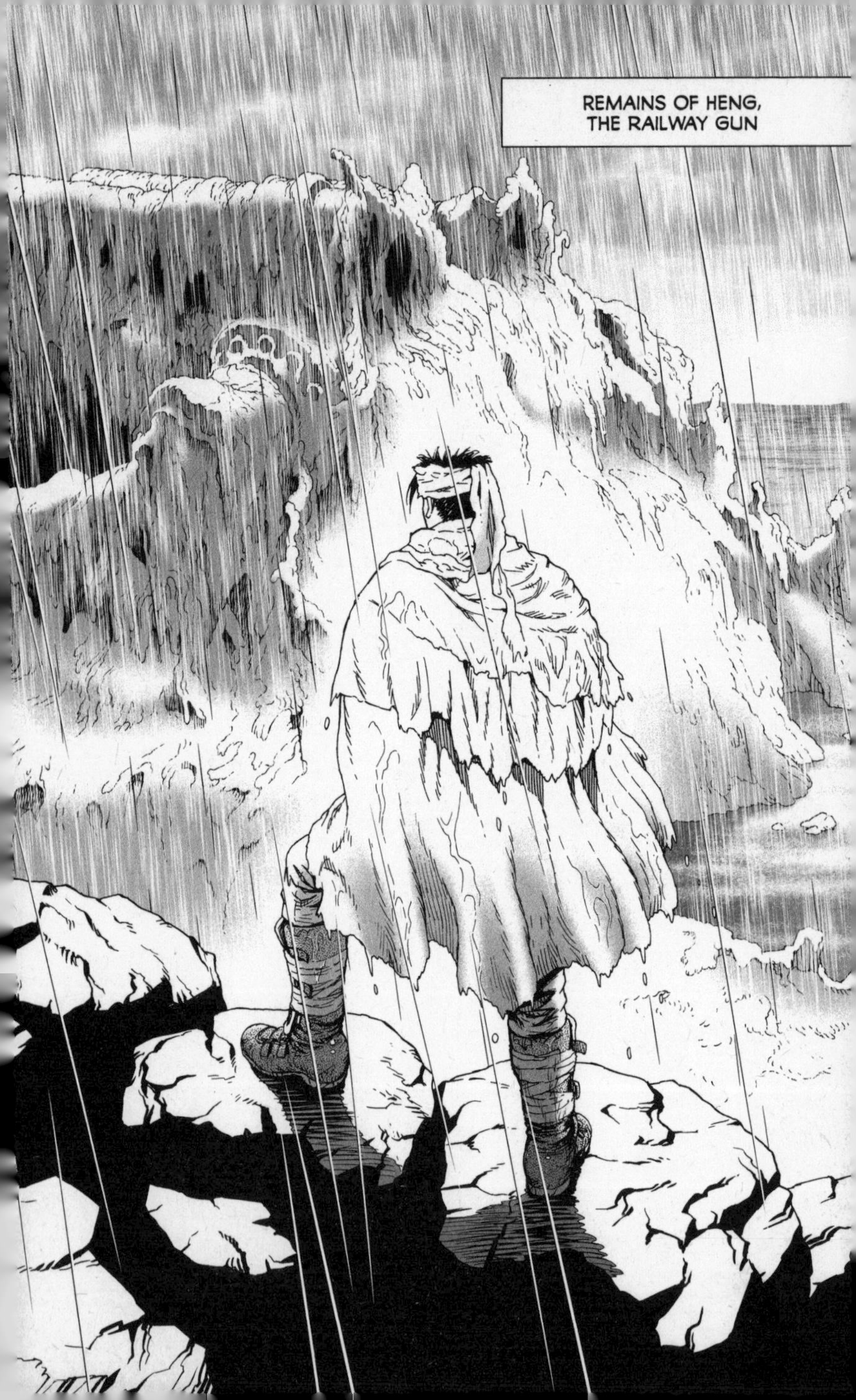
REMAINS OF HENG,
THE RAILWAY GUN

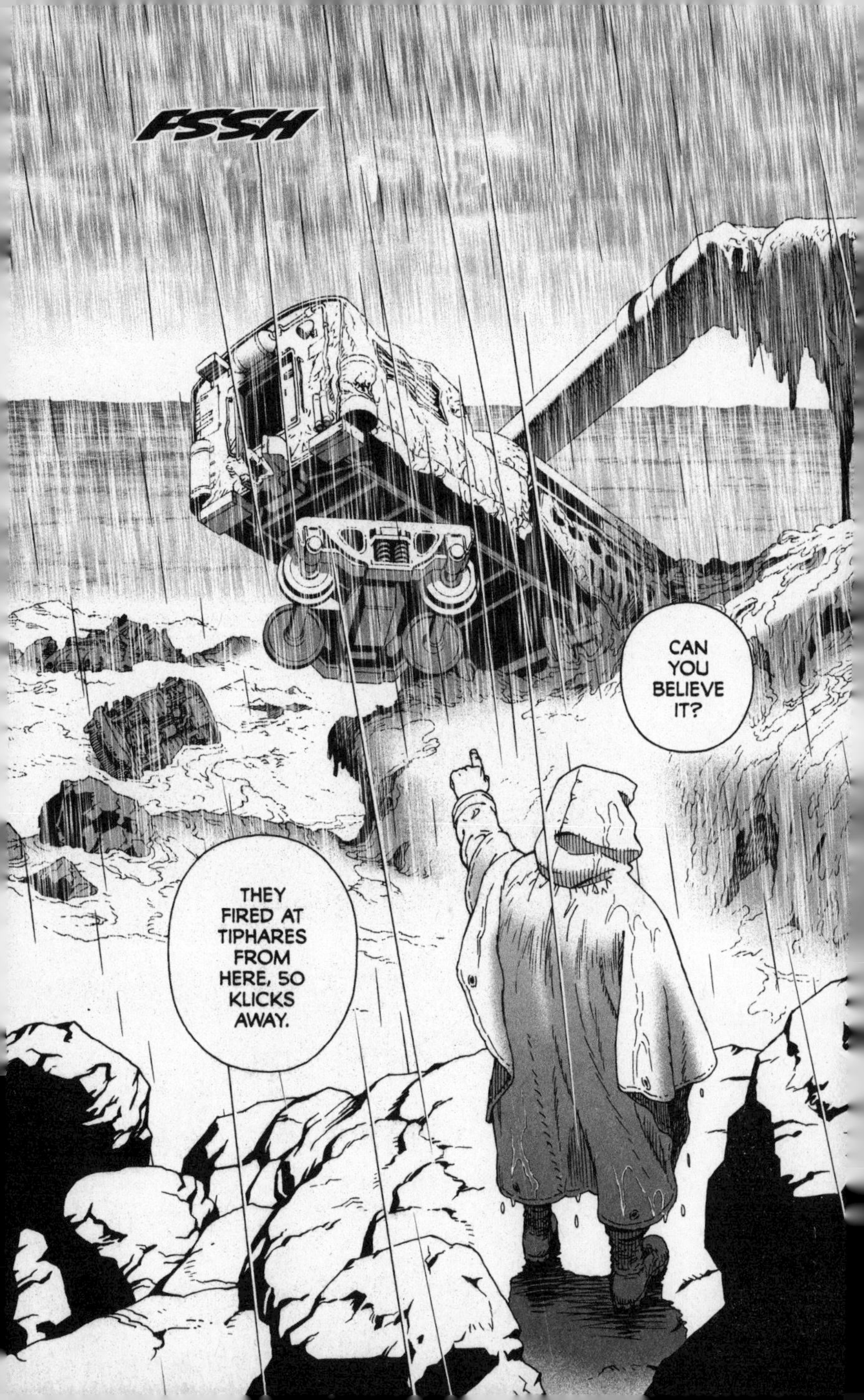
FSSH
CAN YOU BELIEVE IT?
THEY FIRED AT TIPHARES FROM HERE, 50 KLICKS AWAY.

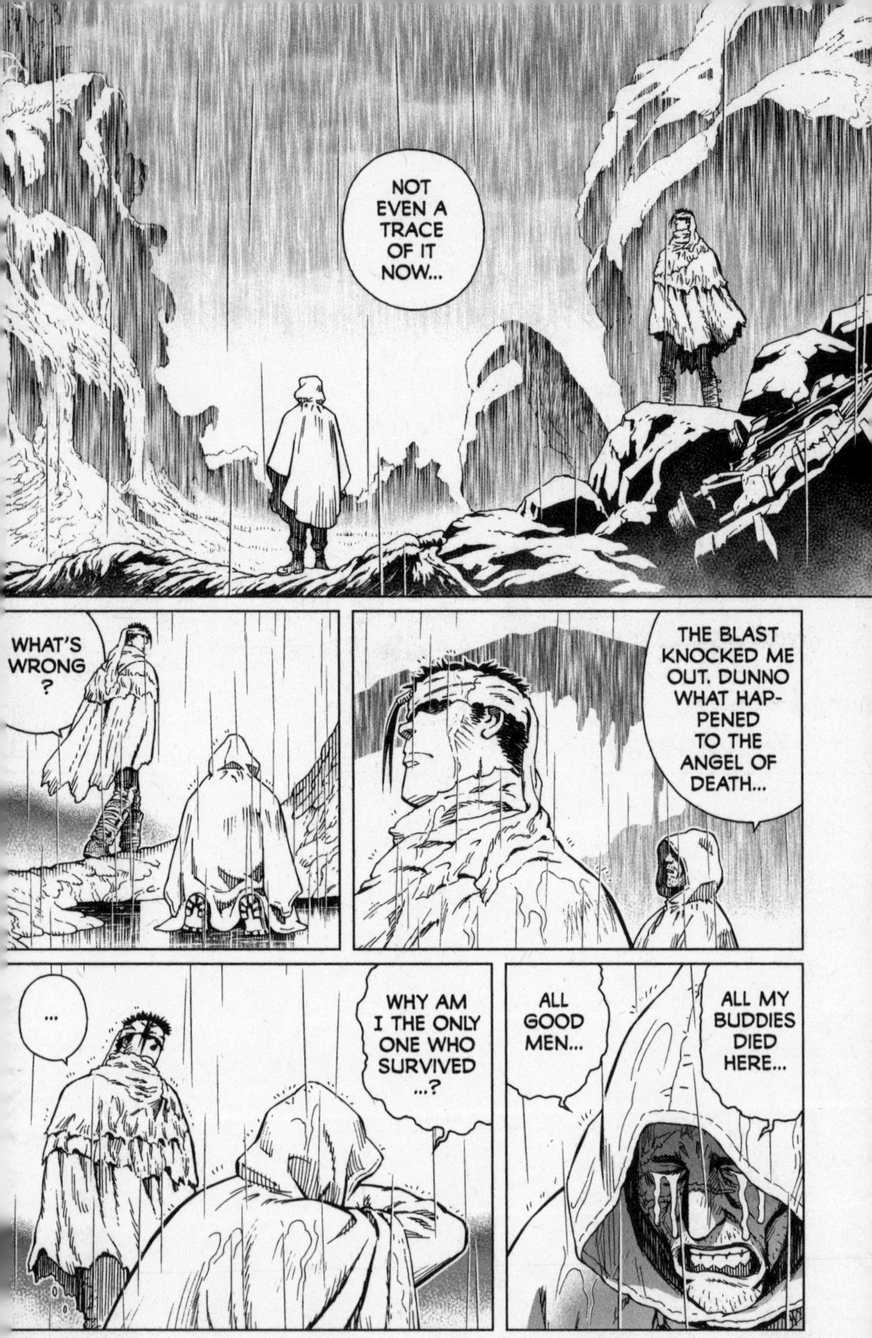
NOT EVEN A TRACE OF IT NOW...
THE BLAST KNOCKED ME OUT. DUNNO WHAT HAP-PENED TO THE ANGEL OF DEATH...
WHAT'S WRONG ?
ALL MY BUDDIES DIED HERE...
ALL GOOD MEN...
WHY AM I THE ONLY ONE WHO SURVIVED ...?
...

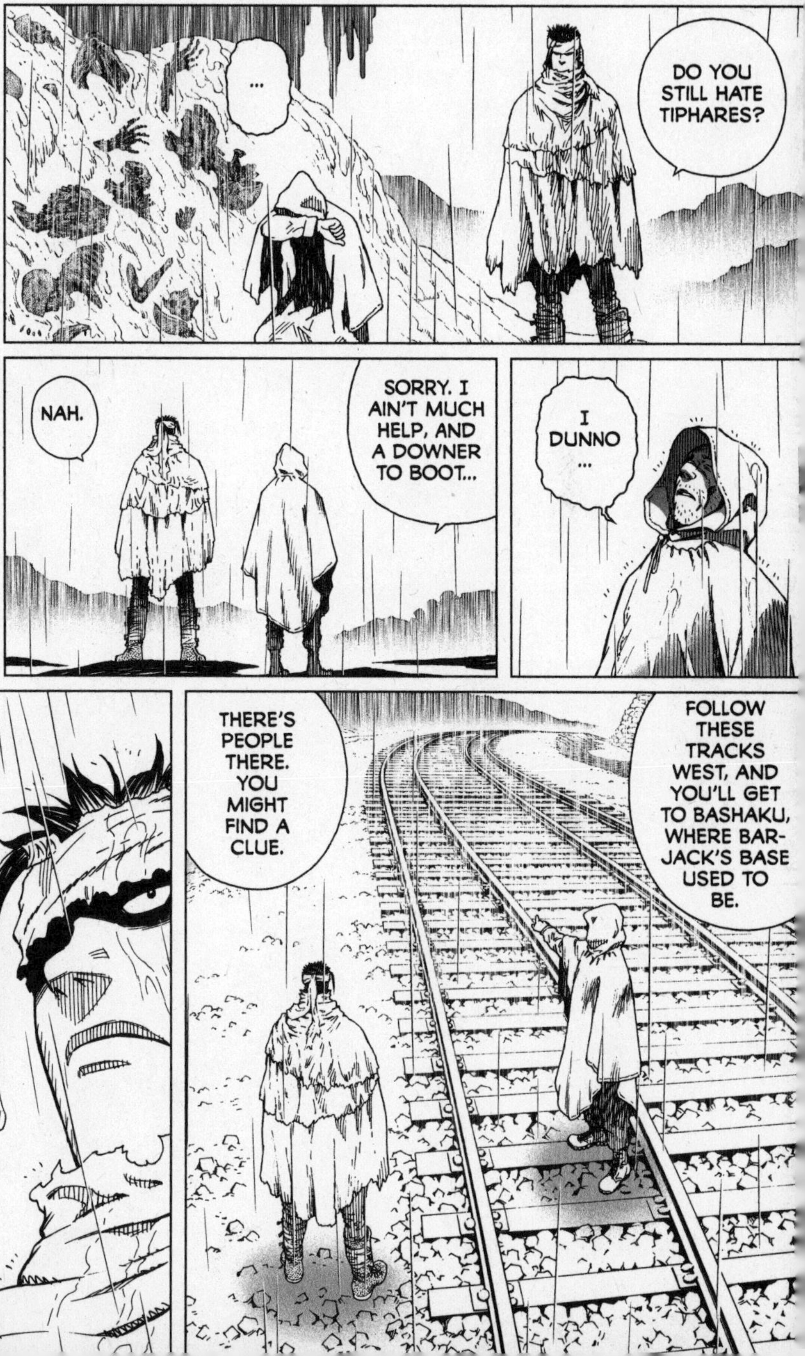
DO YOU STILL HATE TIPHARES?
...
I DUNNO ...
SORRY. I AIN'T MUCH HELP, AND A DOWNER TO BOOT...
NAH.
FOLLOW THESE TRACKS WEST, AND YOU'LL GET TO BASHAKU, WHERE BAR-JACK'S BASE USED TO BE.
THERE'S PEOPLE THERE. YOU MIGHT FIND A CLUE.

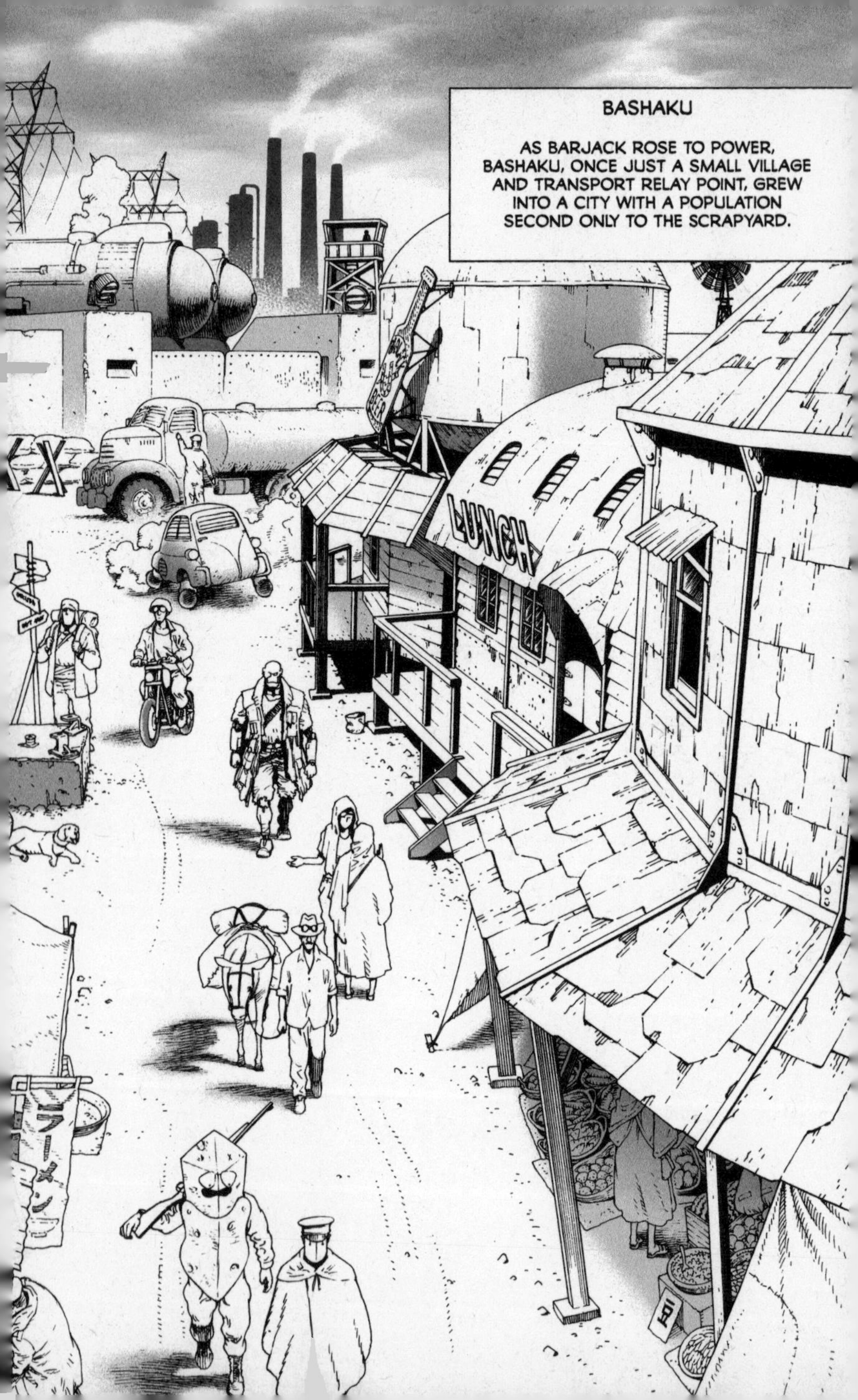
BASHAKU
AS BARJACK ROSE TO POWER, BASHAKU, ONCE JUST A SMALL VILLAGE AND TRANSPORT RELAY POINT, GREW INTO A CITY WITH A POPULATION SECOND ONLY TO THE SCRAPYARD.
LUNCH

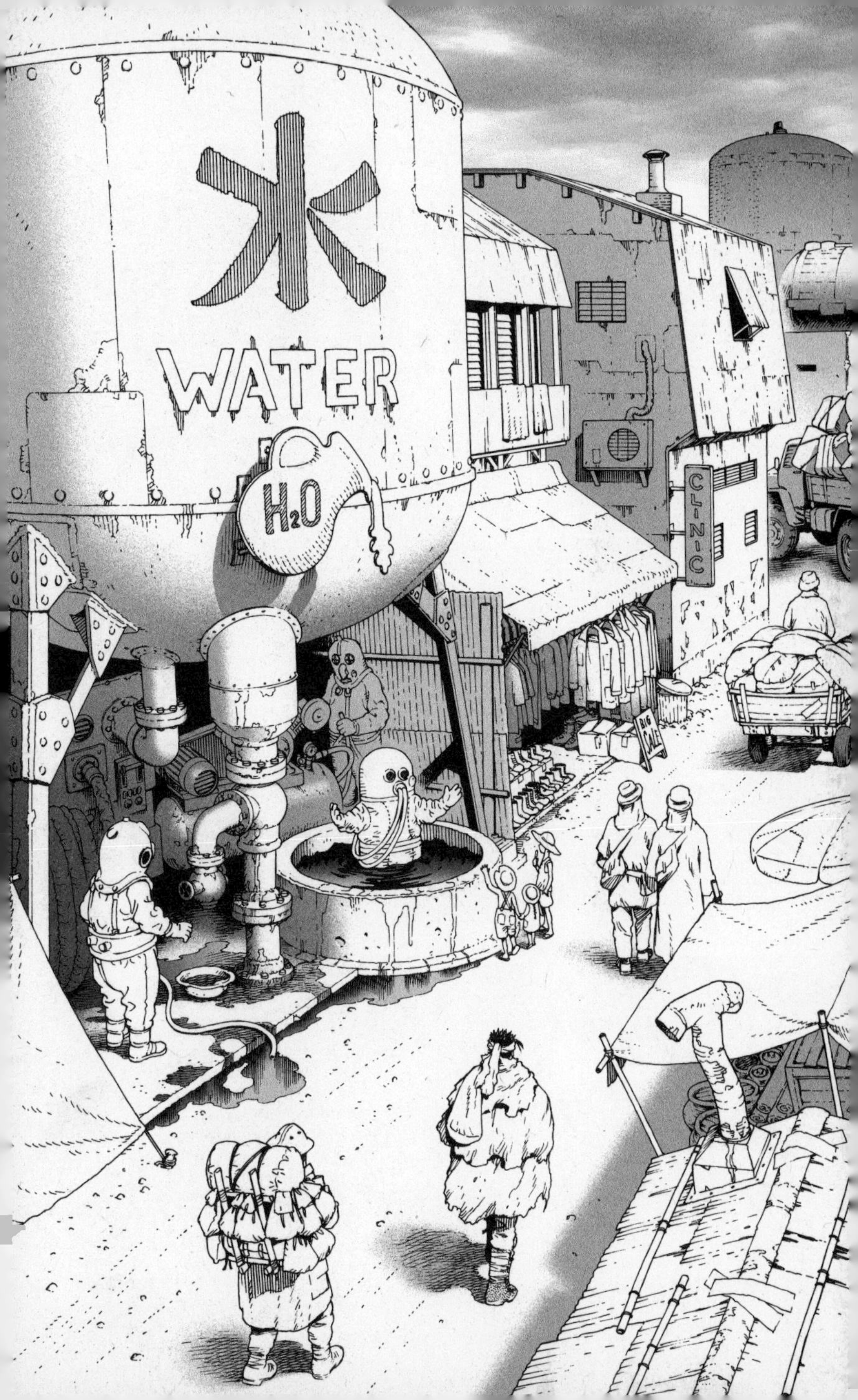
水
WATER
H_2O
CLINIC
BIG SALE

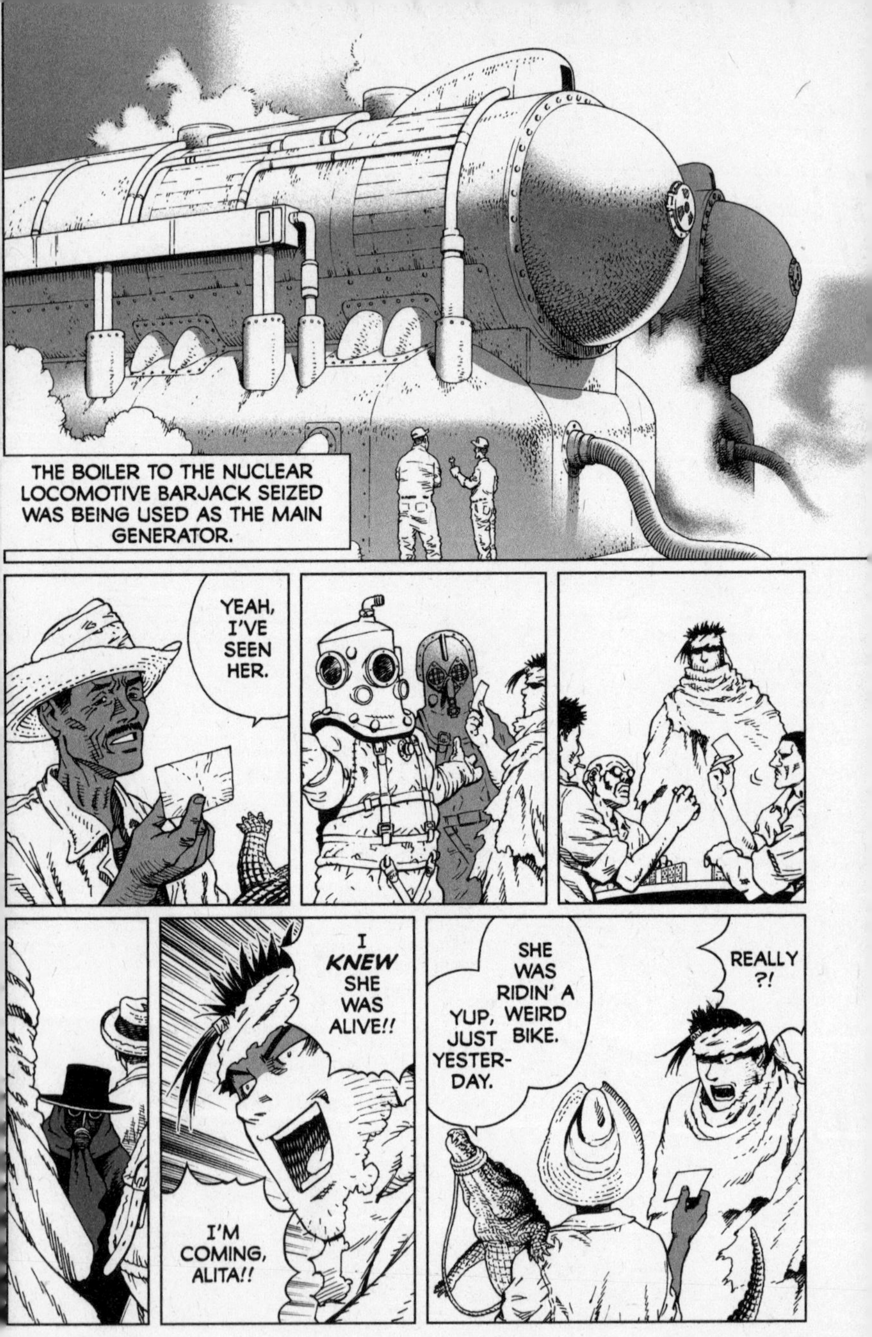

THE BOILER TO THE NUCLEAR LOCOMOTIVE BARJACK SEIZED WAS BEING USED AS THE MAIN GENERATOR.
YEAH, I'VE SEEN HER.
REALLY?!
SHE WAS RIDIN' A WEIRD BIKE.
YUP, JUST YESTER-DAY.
I *KNEW* SHE WAS ALIVE!!
I'M COMING, ALITA!!

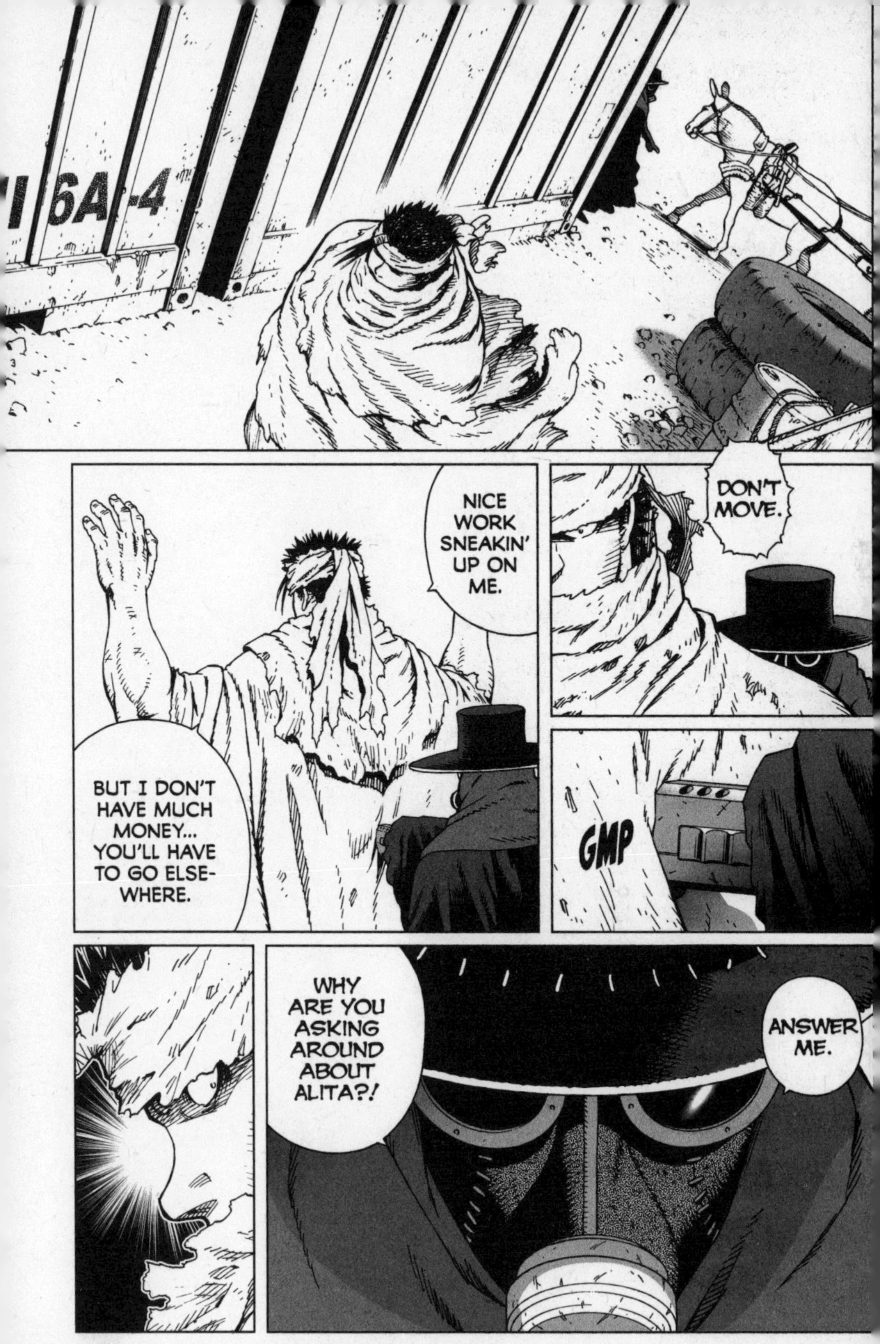
16A-4
DON'T MOVE.
GMP
NICE WORK SNEAKIN' UP ON ME.
BUT I DON'T HAVE MUCH MONEY... YOU'LL HAVE TO GO ELSE-WHERE.
ANSWER ME.
WHY ARE YOU ASKING AROUND ABOUT ALITA?!

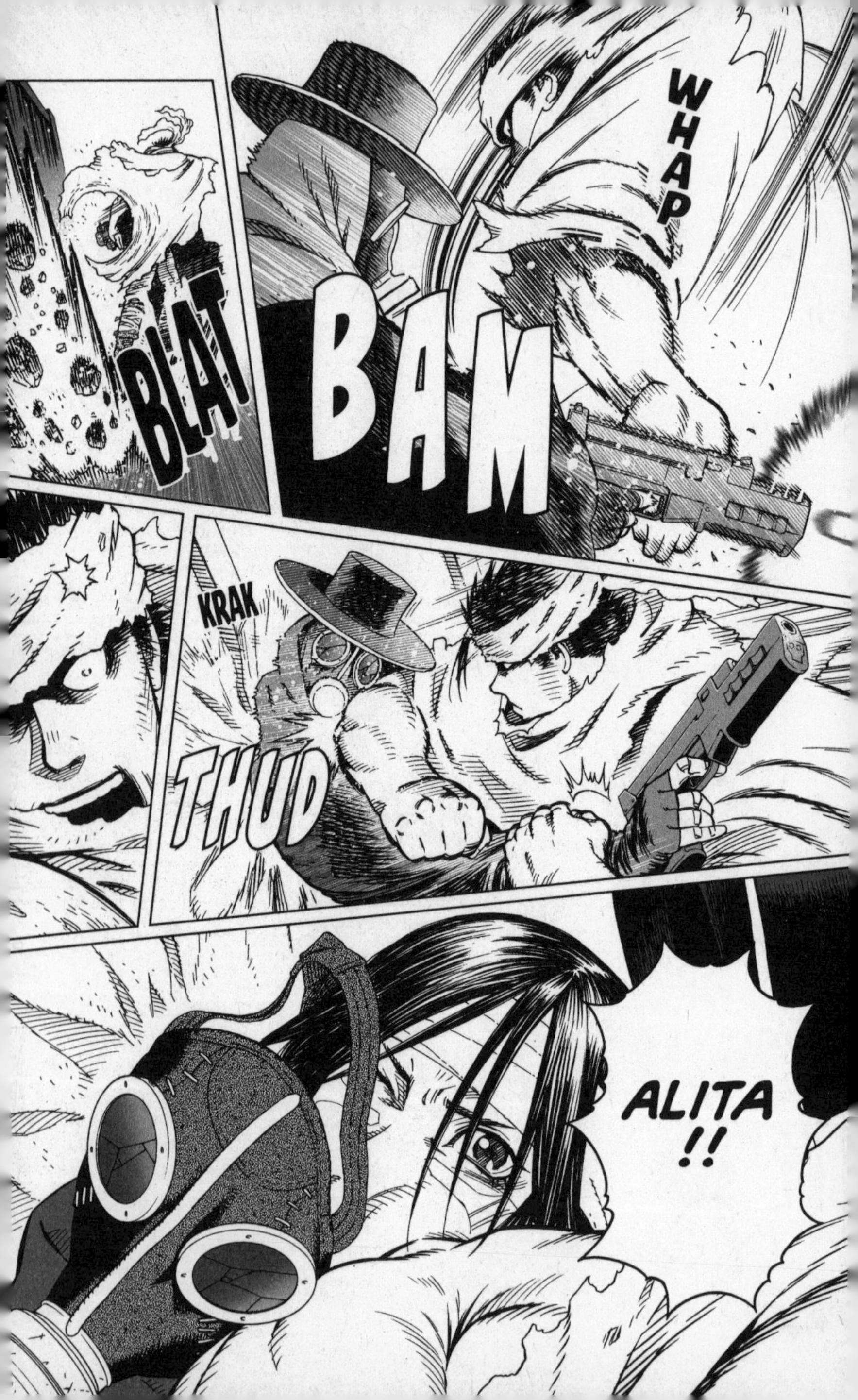
WHAP
BAM
BLAT
KRAK
THUD
ALITA !!

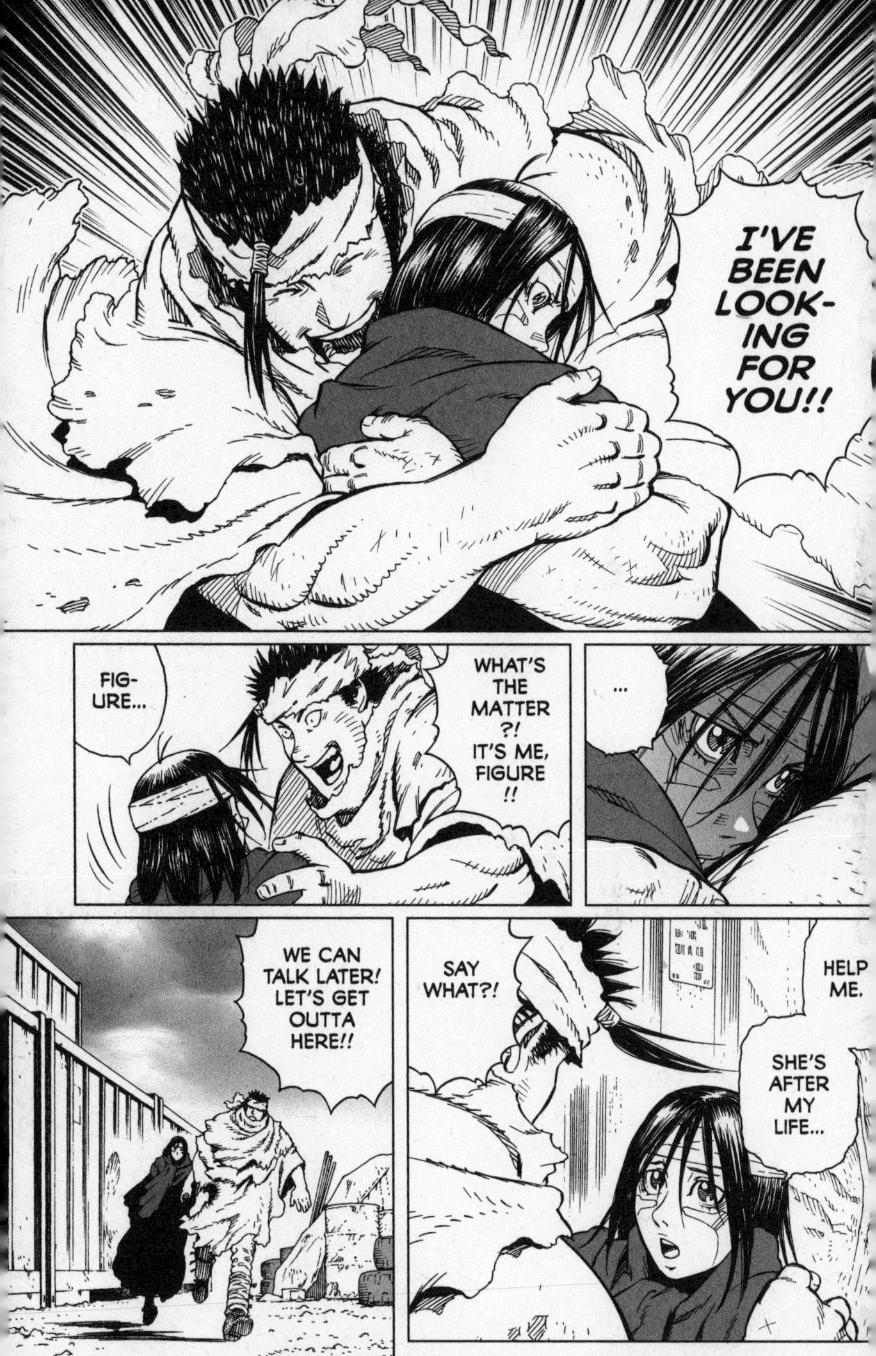
I'VE BEEN LOOK-ING FOR YOU!!
...
WHAT'S THE MATTER?! IT'S ME, FIGURE!!
FIG-URE...
HELP ME.
SHE'S AFTER MY LIFE...
SAY WHAT?!
WE CAN TALK LATER! LET'S GET OUTTA HERE!!

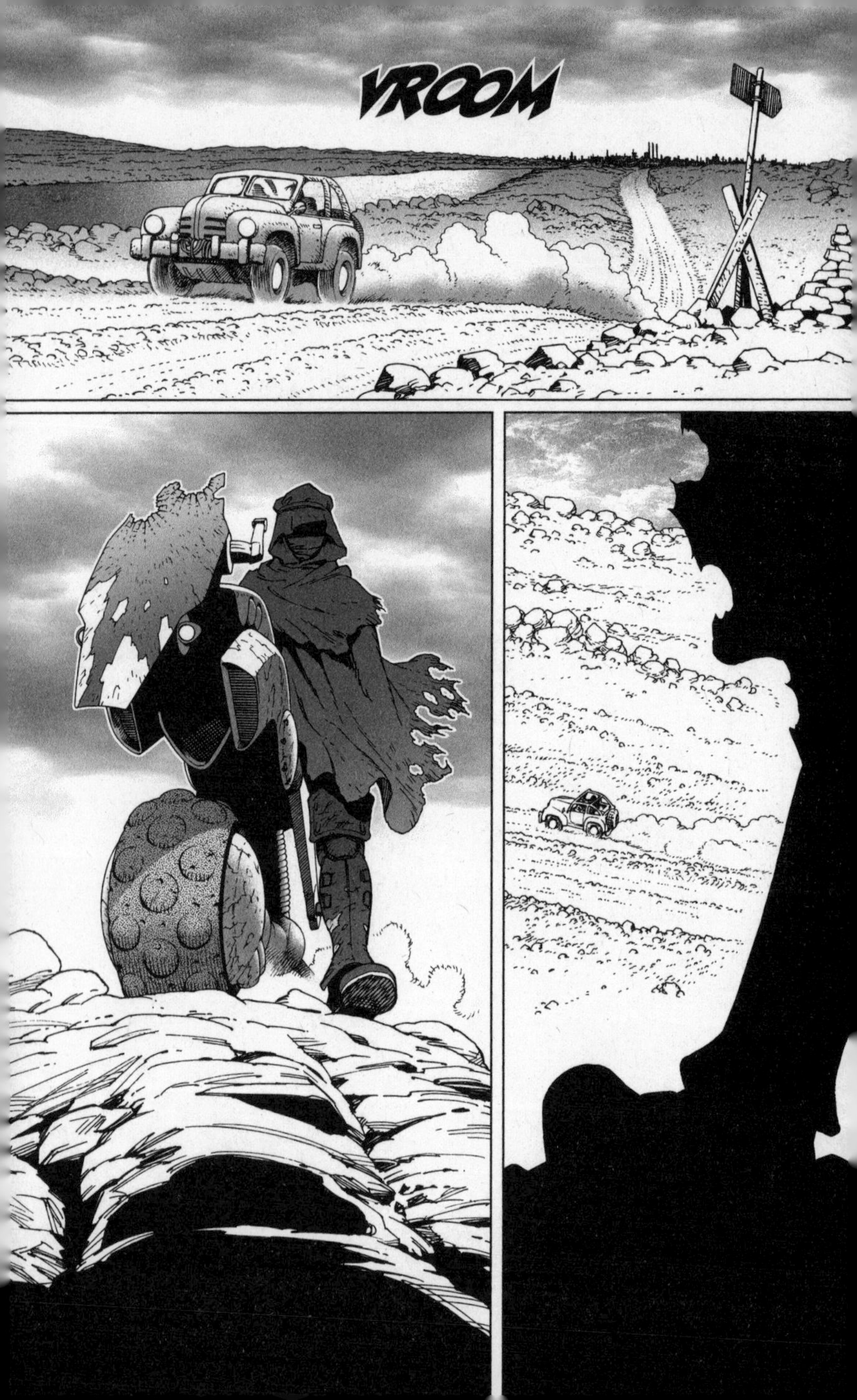
VROOM

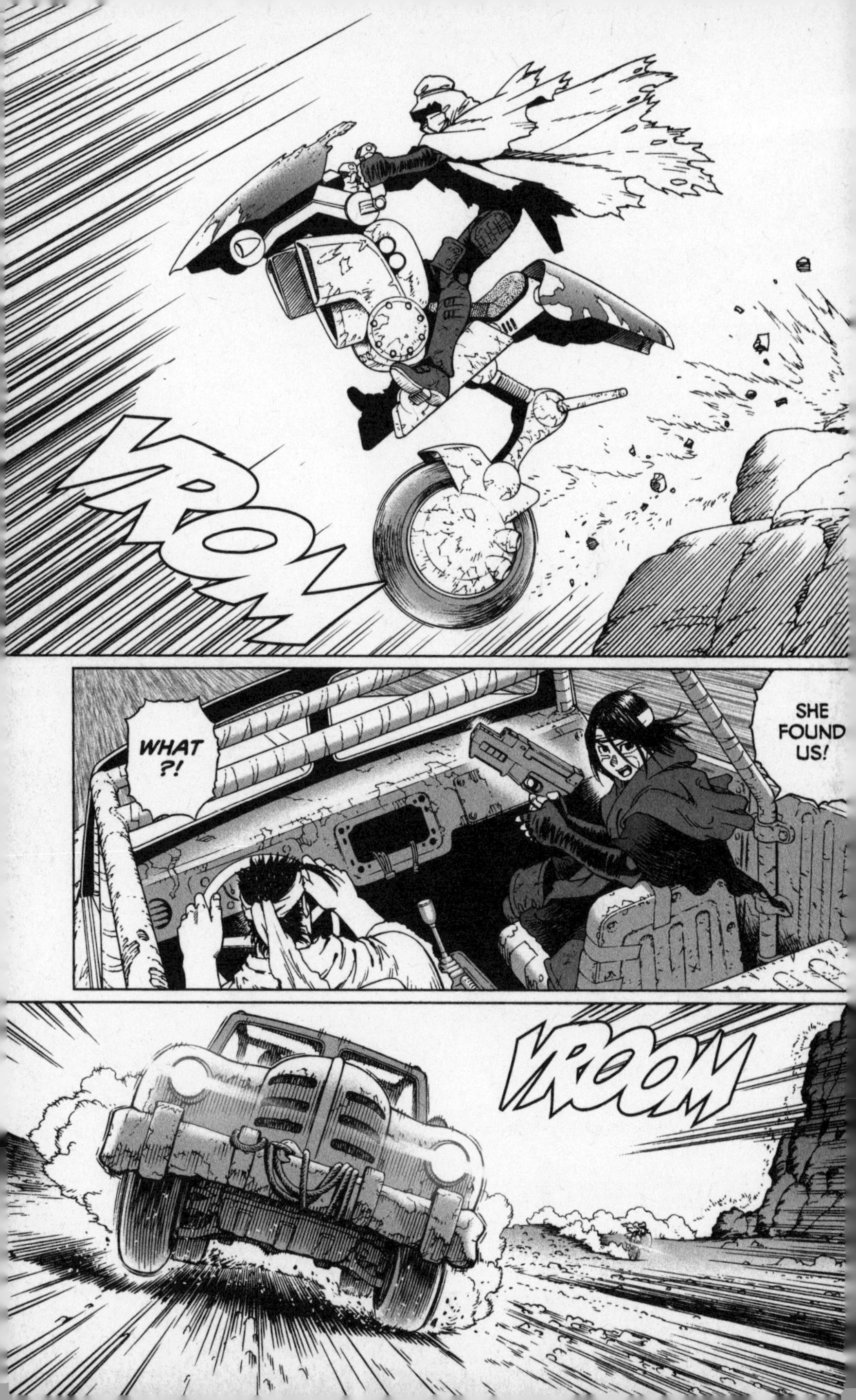
VROOM
SHE FOUND US!
WHAT?!
VROOM

Phase 108: Alita Quest II

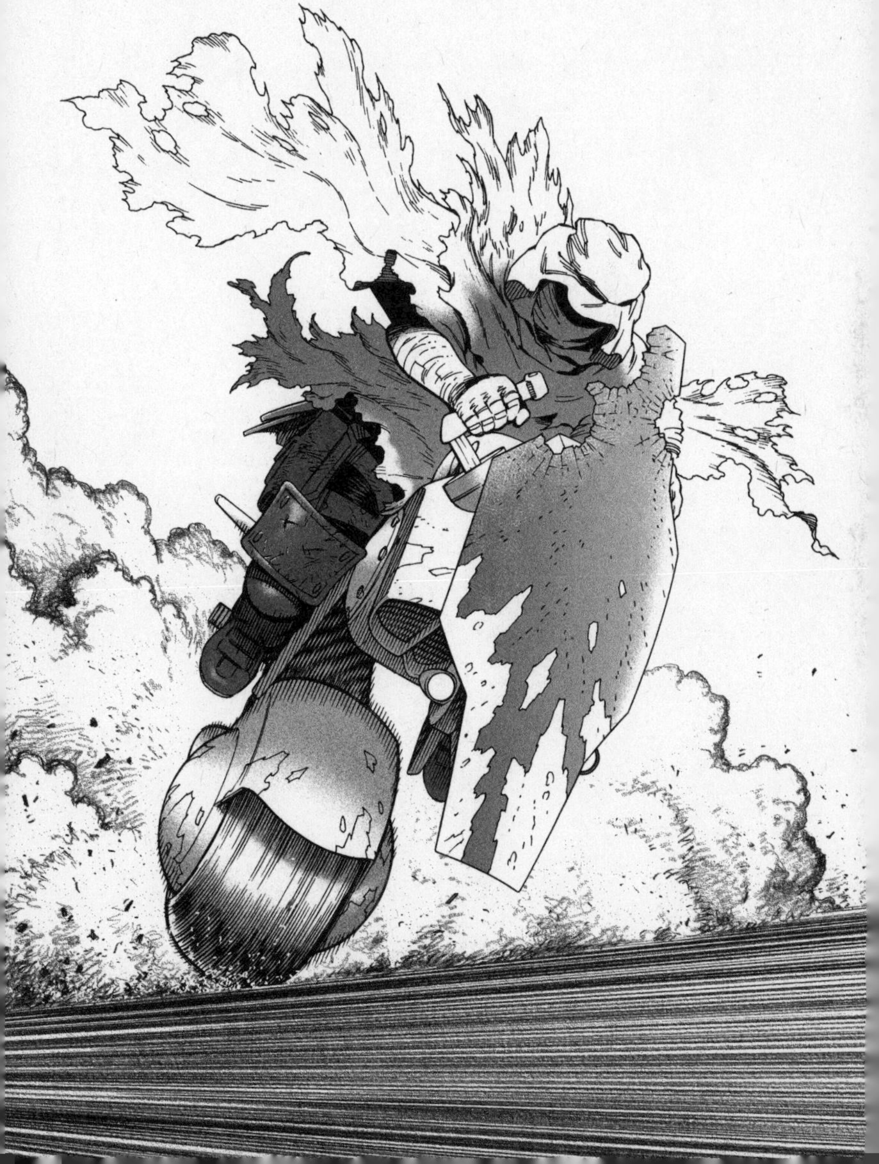

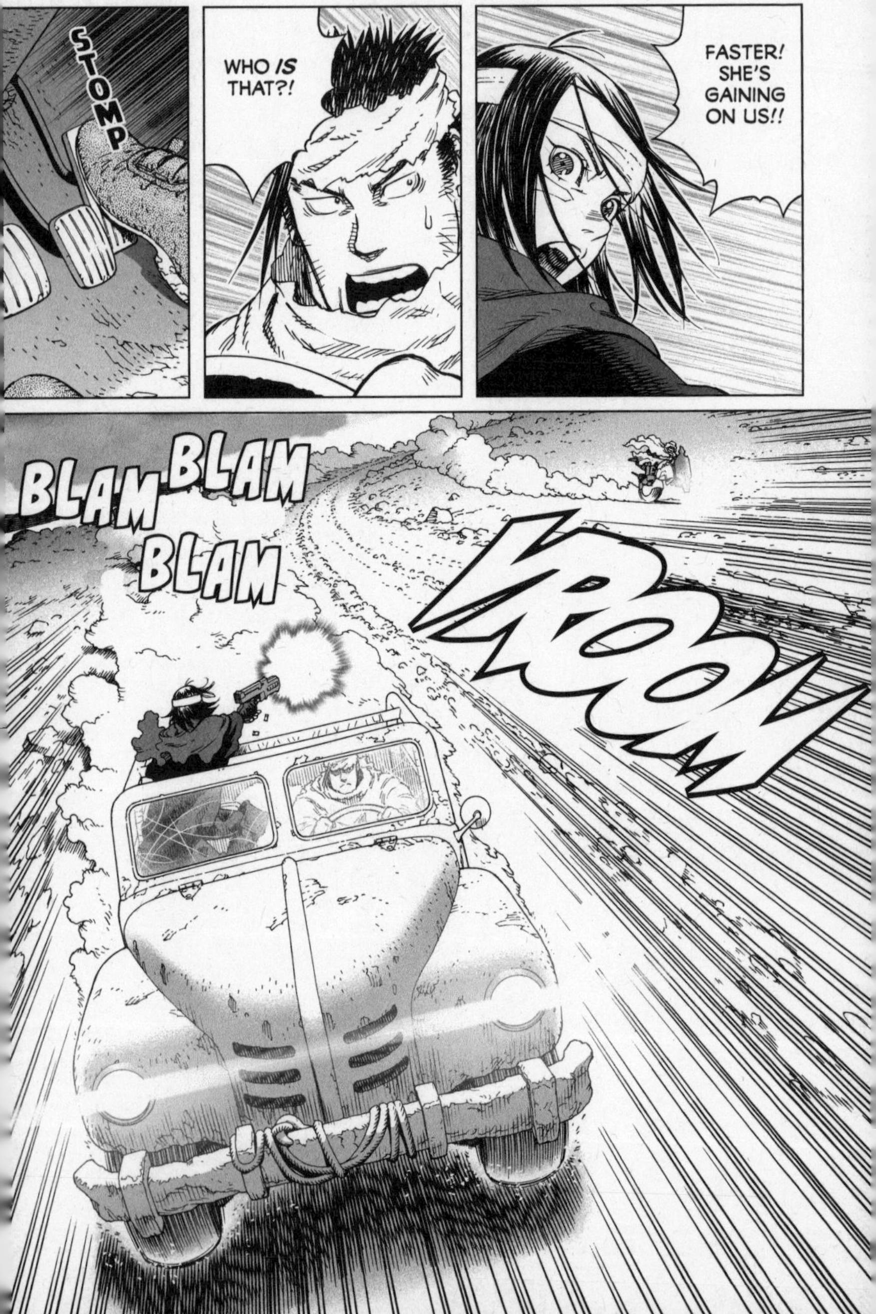
FASTER! SHE'S GAINING ON US!!
WHO *IS* THAT?!
STOMP
VROOM
BLAM BLAM
BLAM

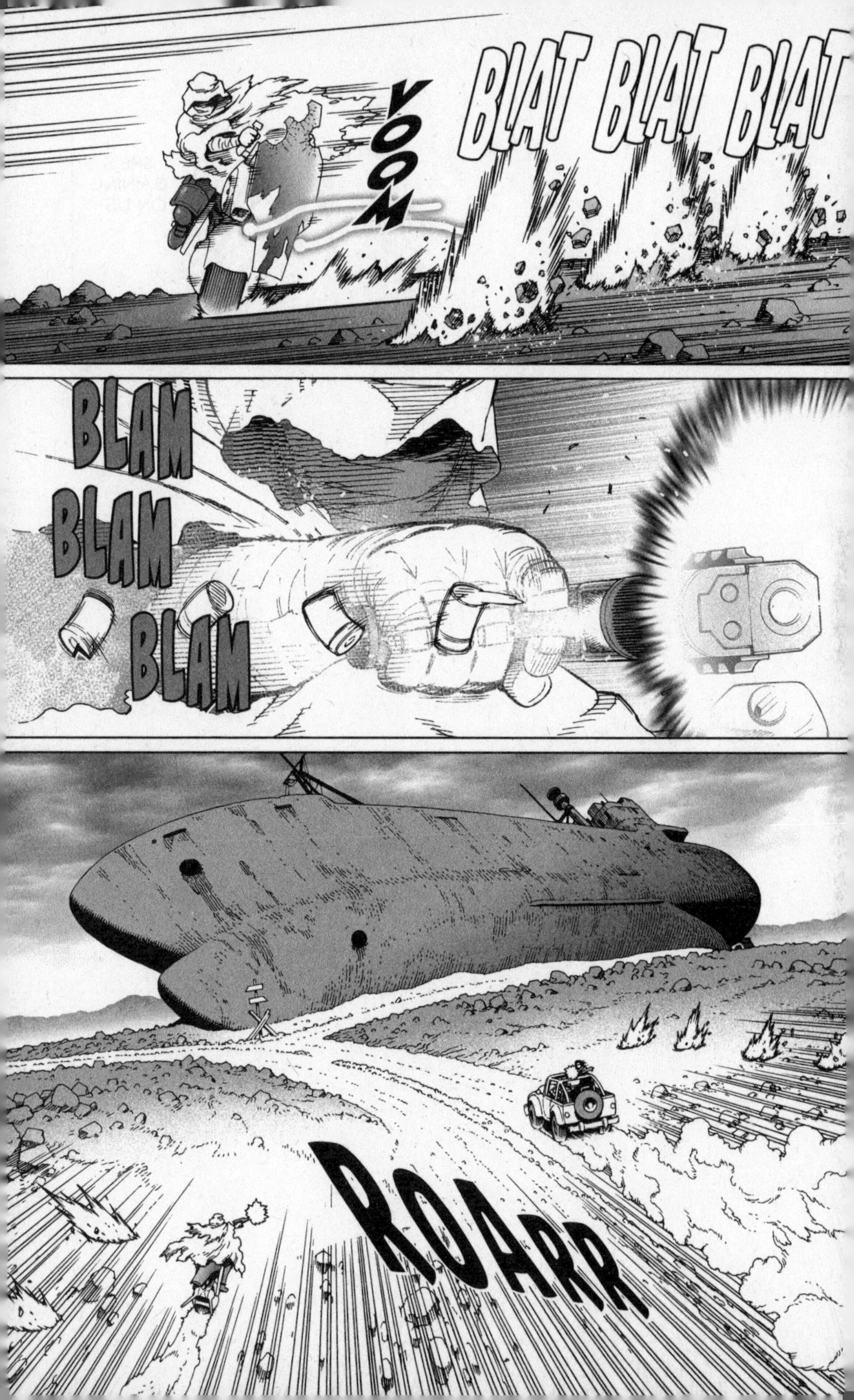
BLAT BLAT BLAT
VOOM
BLAM
BLAM
BLAM
ROARR

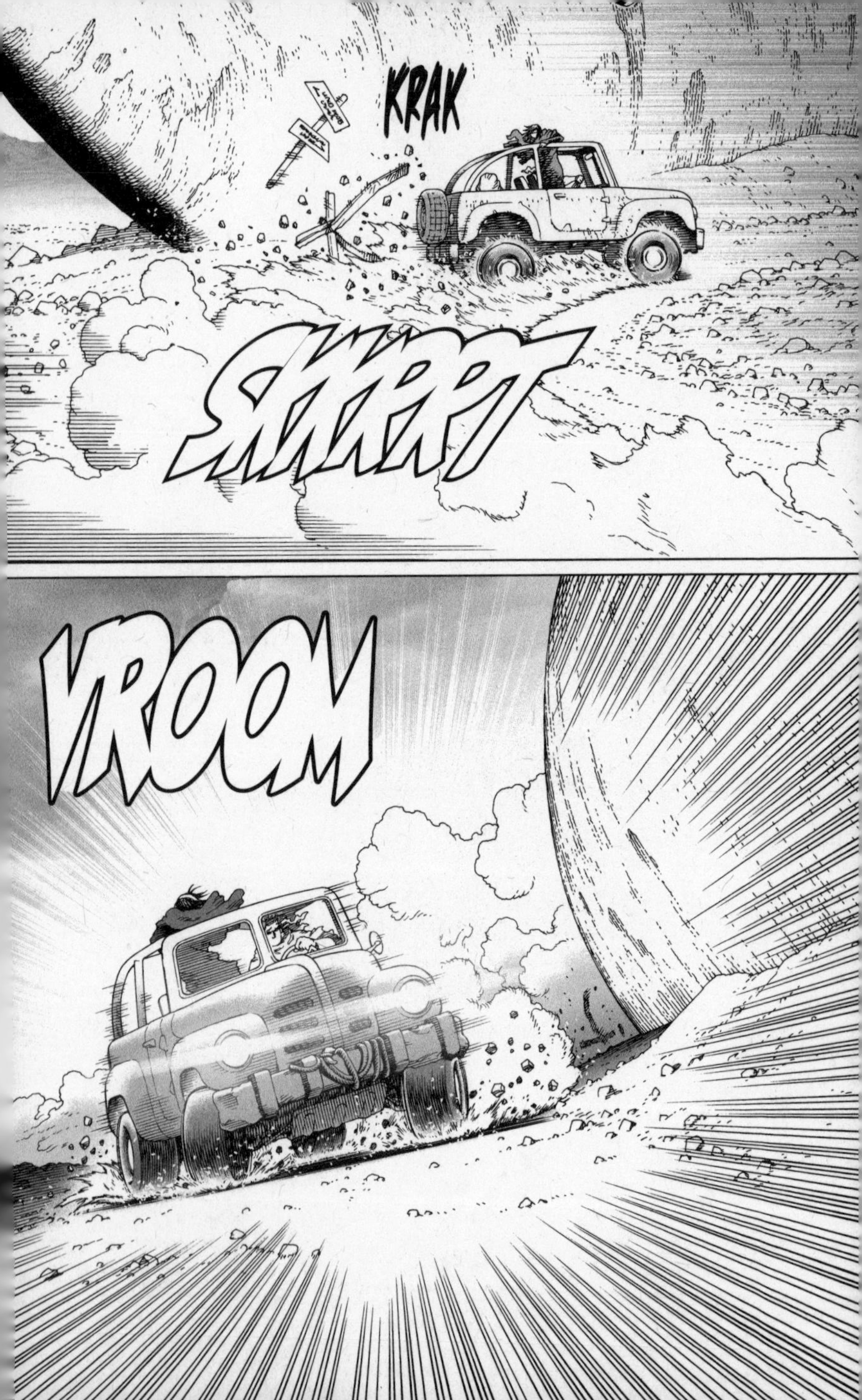
KRAK
SHIPPT
VROOM

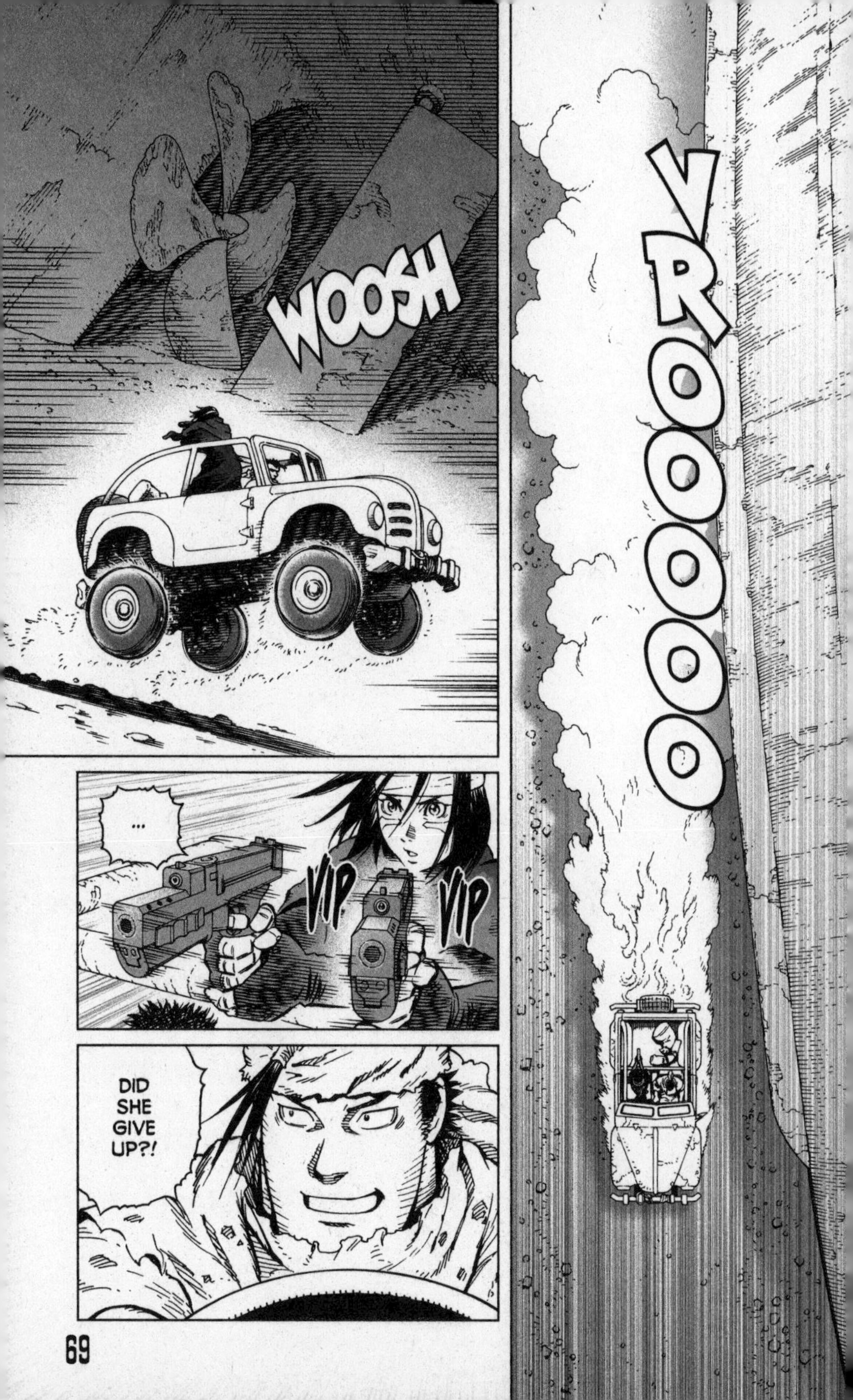

VROOOOOO
WOOSH
...
VIP VIP
DID SHE GIVE UP?!

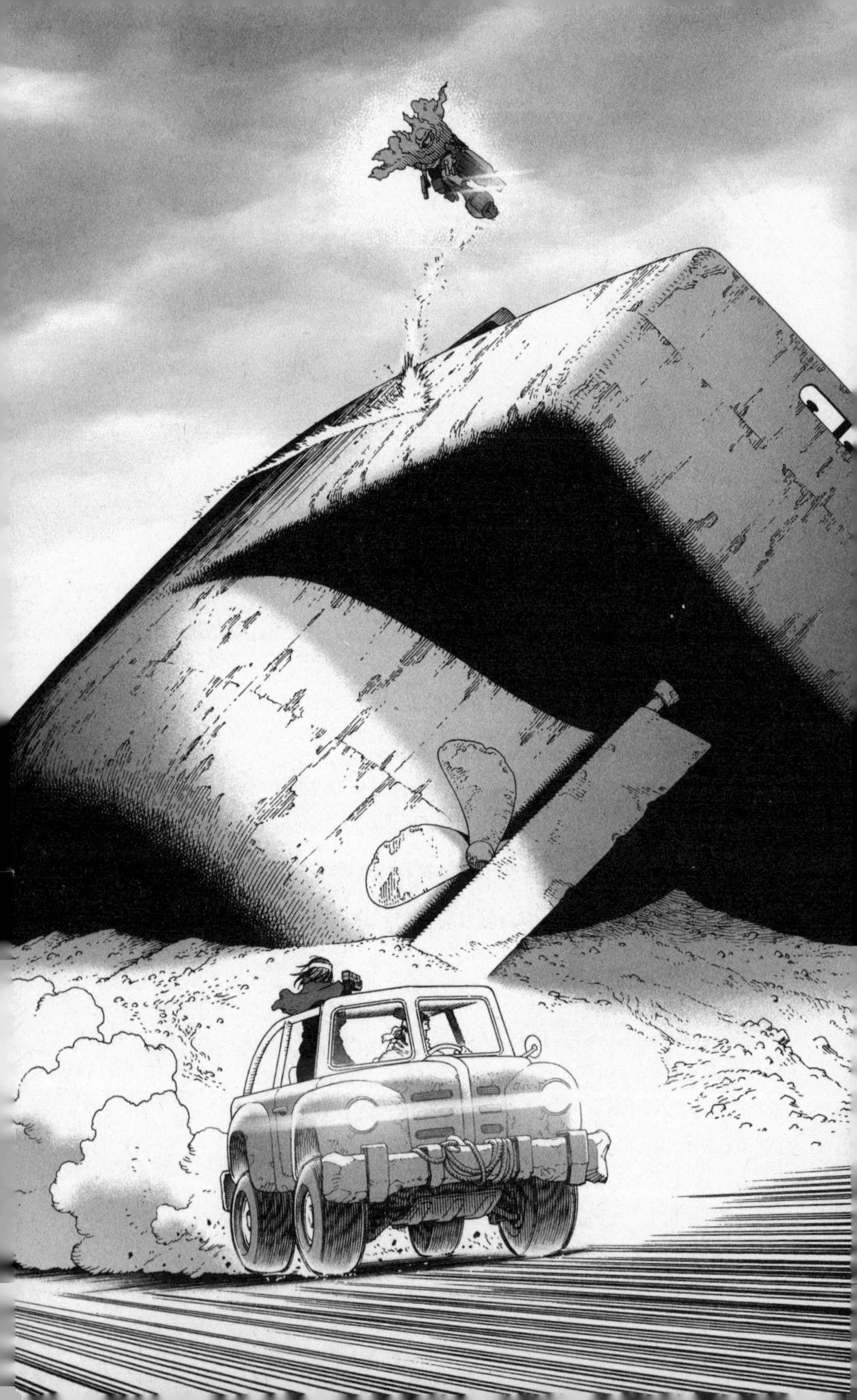

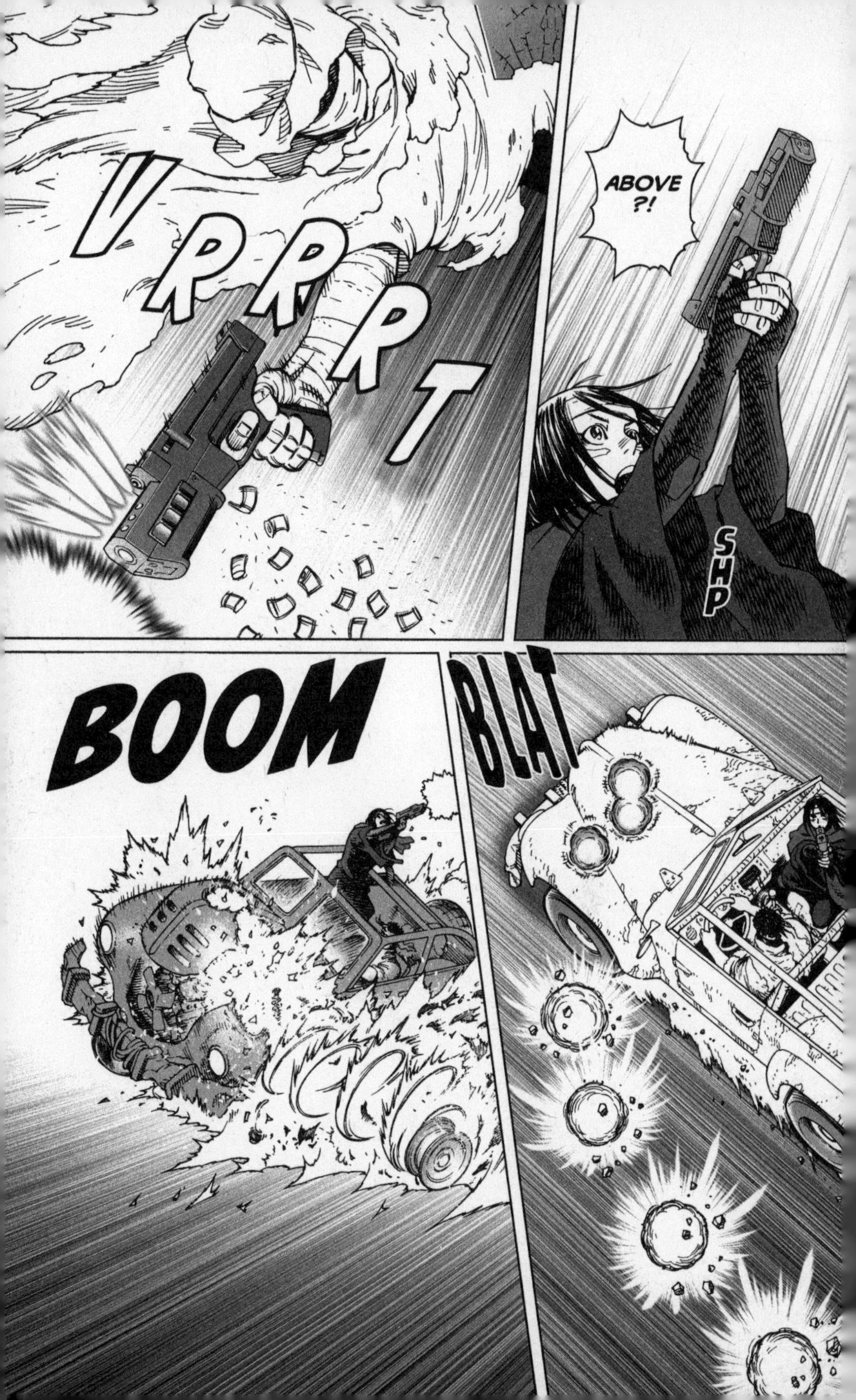
ABOVE ?!
SHP
VRRRRT
BLAT
BOOM

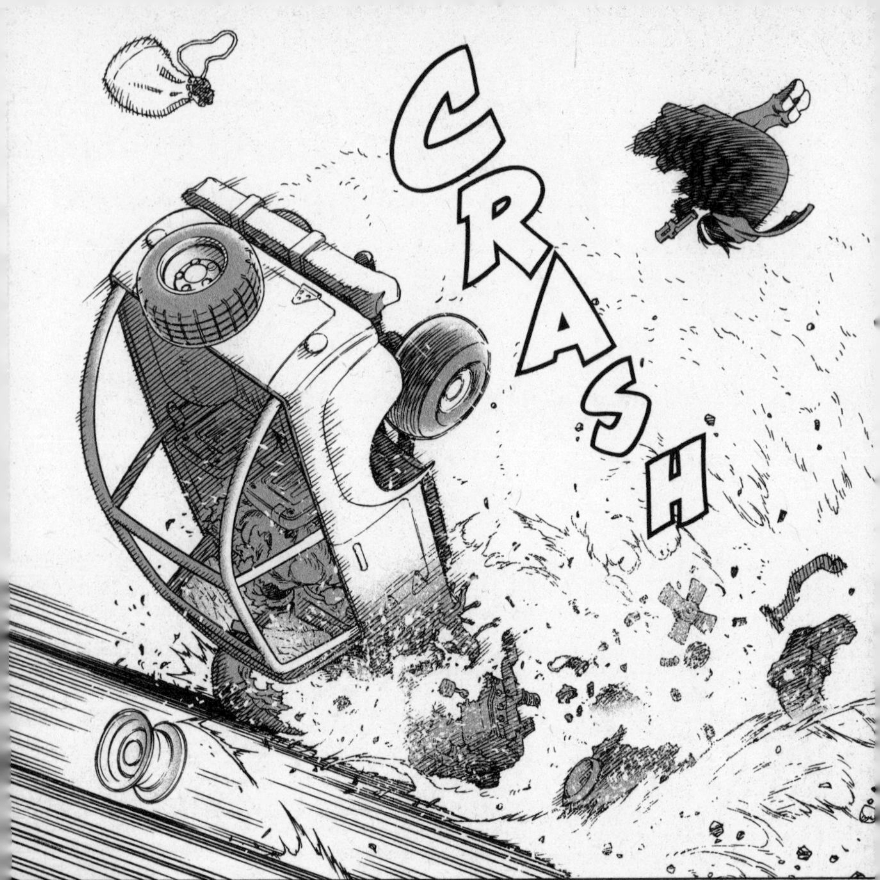
CRASH
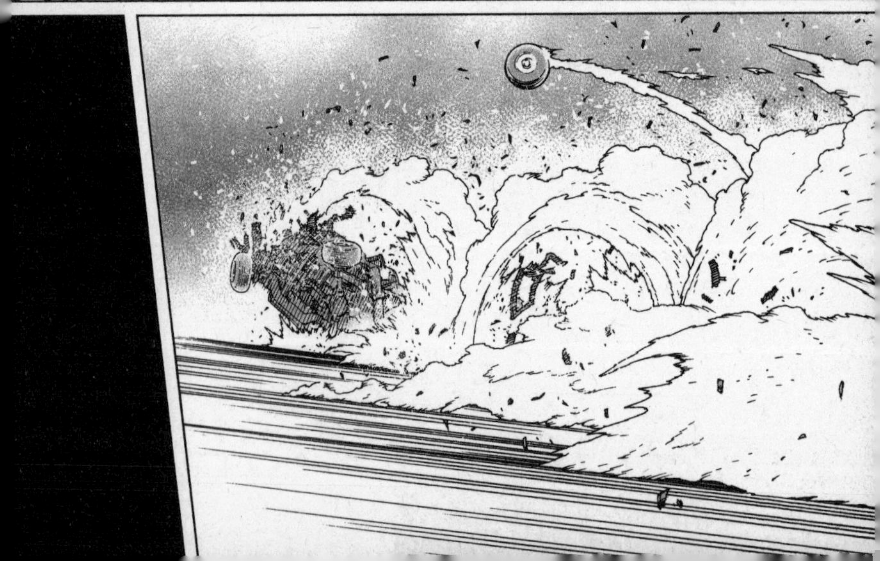

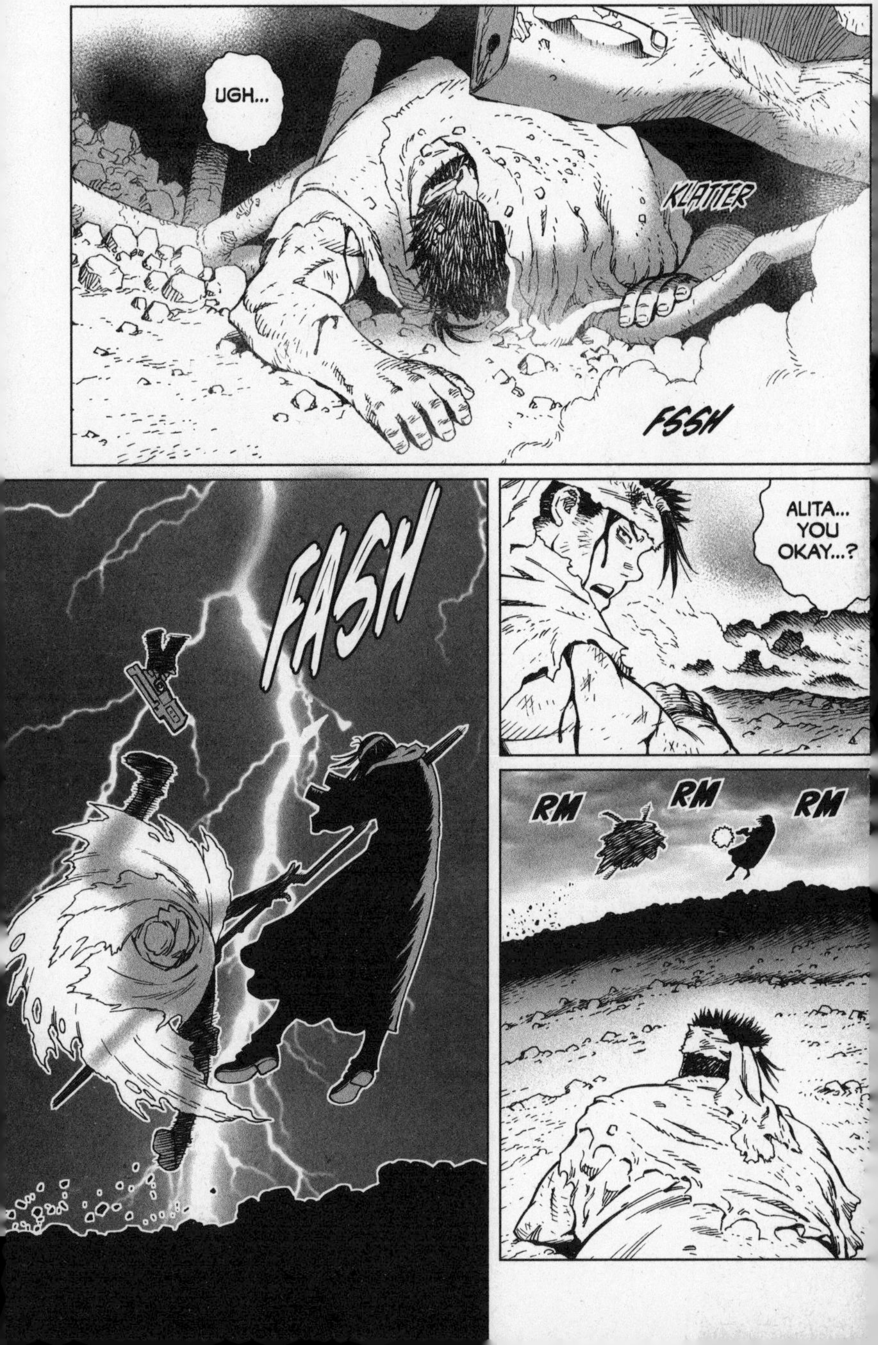
UGH...
KLATTER
FSSH
ALITA... YOU OKAY...?
RM
RM
RM
FASH

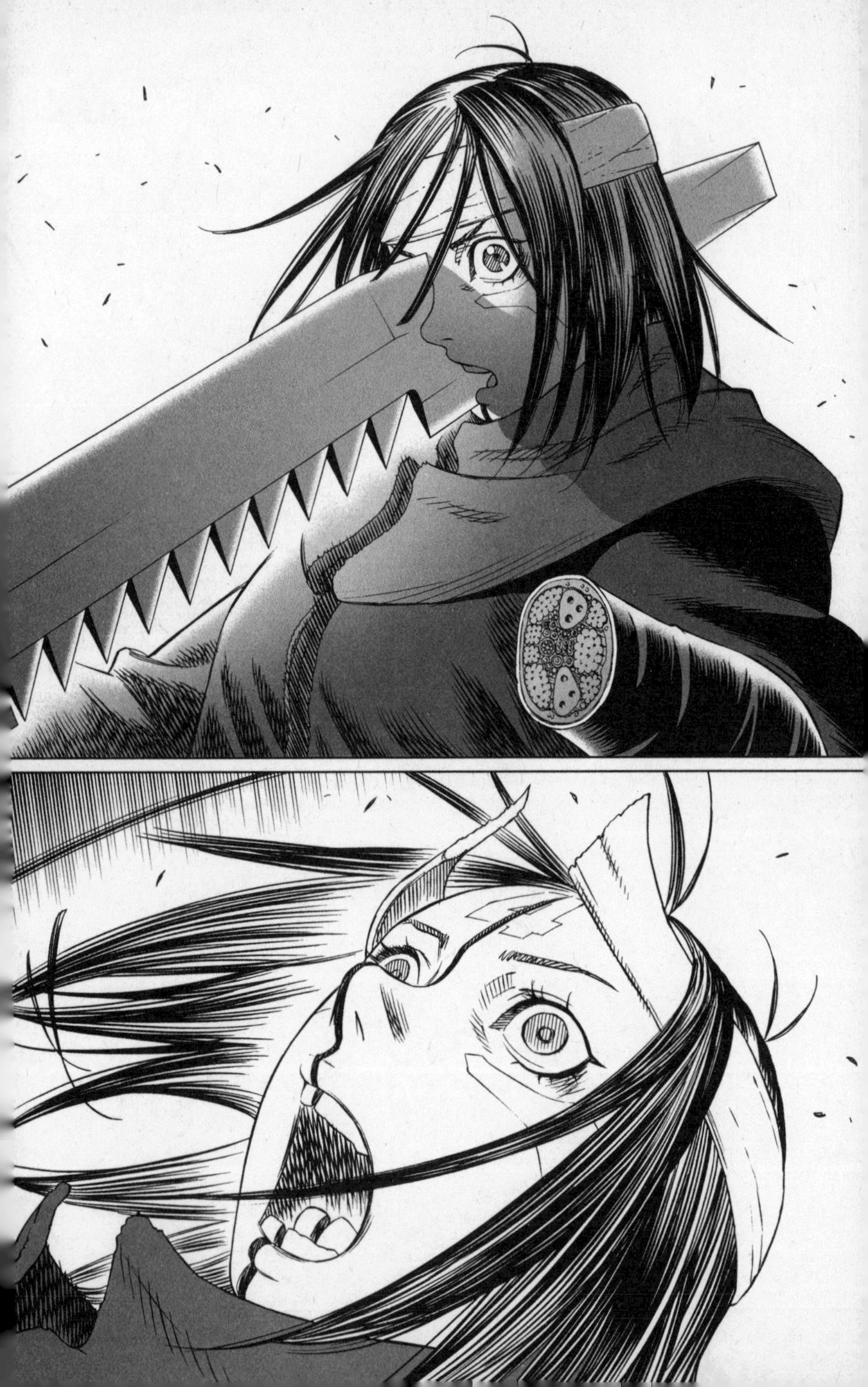

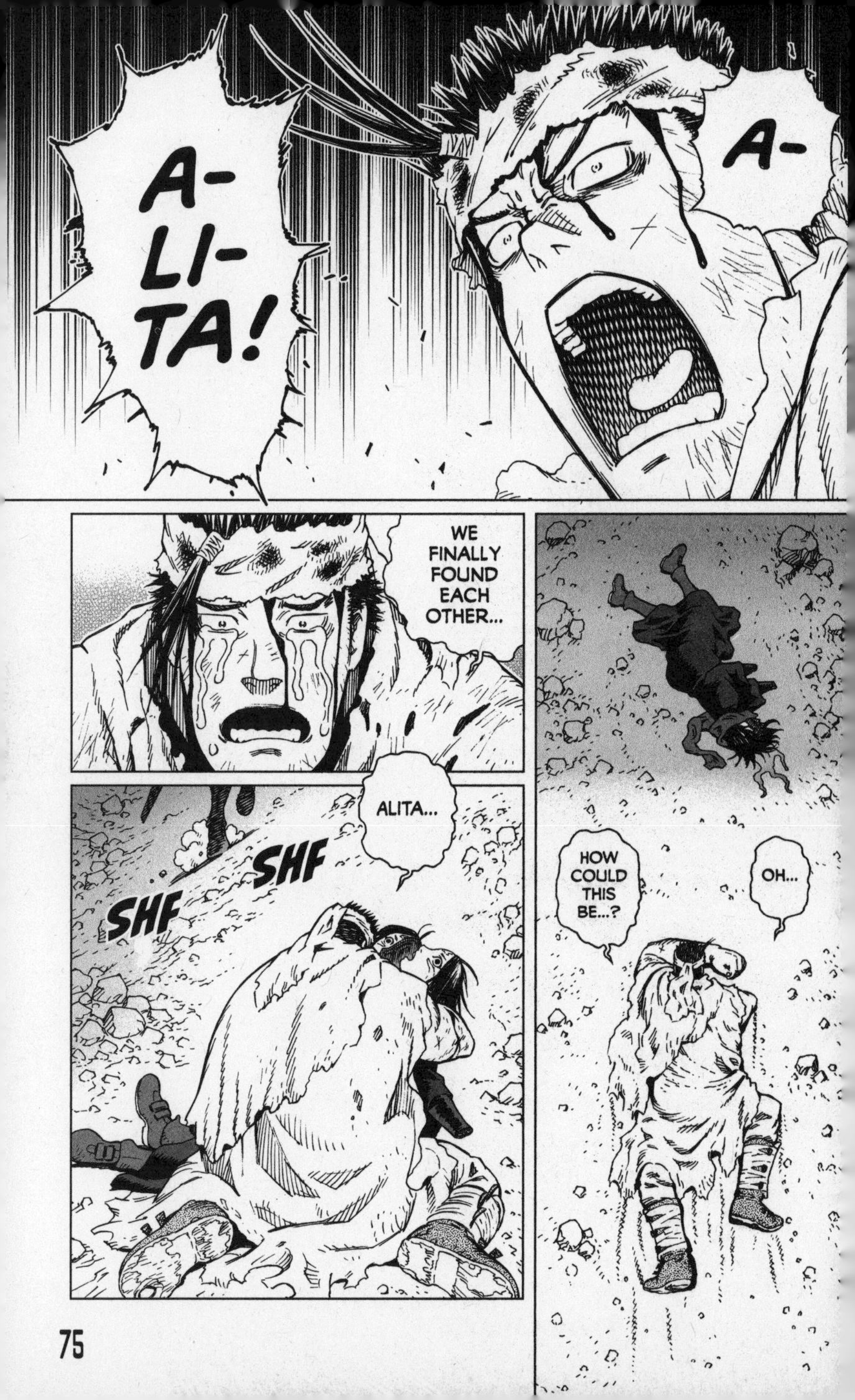
A-
A-LI-TA!
OH...
HOW COULD THIS BE...?
WE FINALLY FOUND EACH OTHER...
ALITA...
SHF
SHF

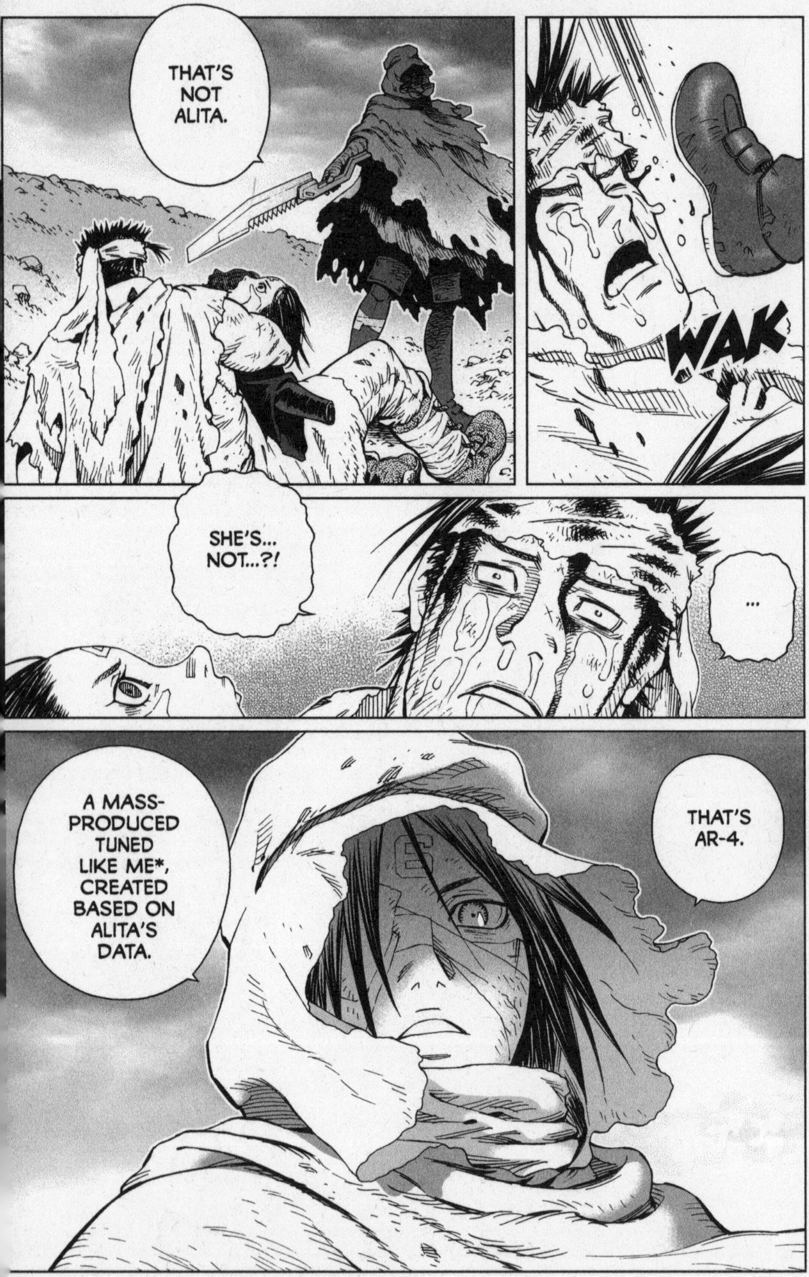
WAK
THAT'S NOT ALITA.
...
SHE'S... NOT...?!
THAT'S AR-4.
A MASS-PRODUCED TUNED LIKE ME*, CREATED BASED ON ALITA'S DATA.

*TUNED: agents and their system created by Tiphares's Ground Investigation Bureau (GIB). Alita was the first TUNED.

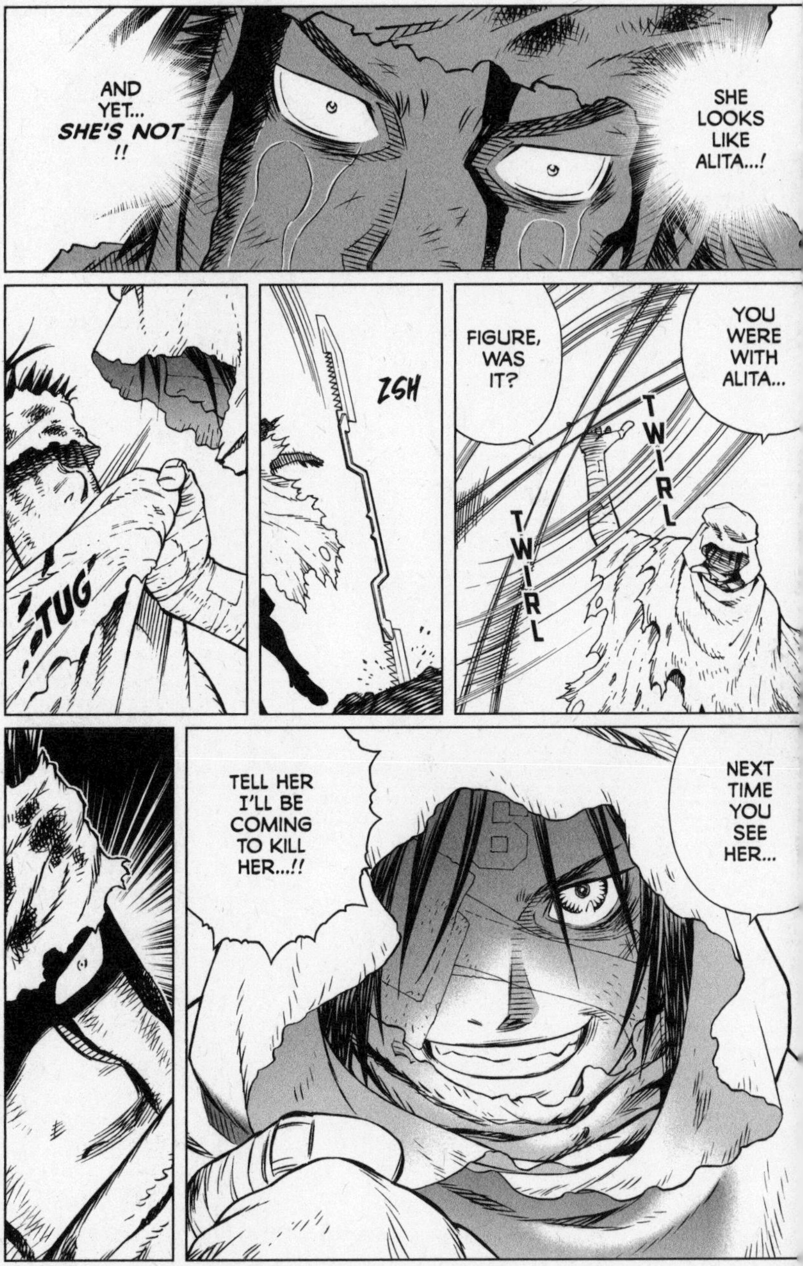
SHE LOOKS LIKE ALITA...!
AND YET... SHE'S NOT !!
YOU WERE WITH ALITA...
FIGURE, WAS IT?
TWIRL
TWIRL
ZSH
TUG
NEXT TIME YOU SEE HER...
TELL HER I'LL BE COMING TO KILL HER...!!

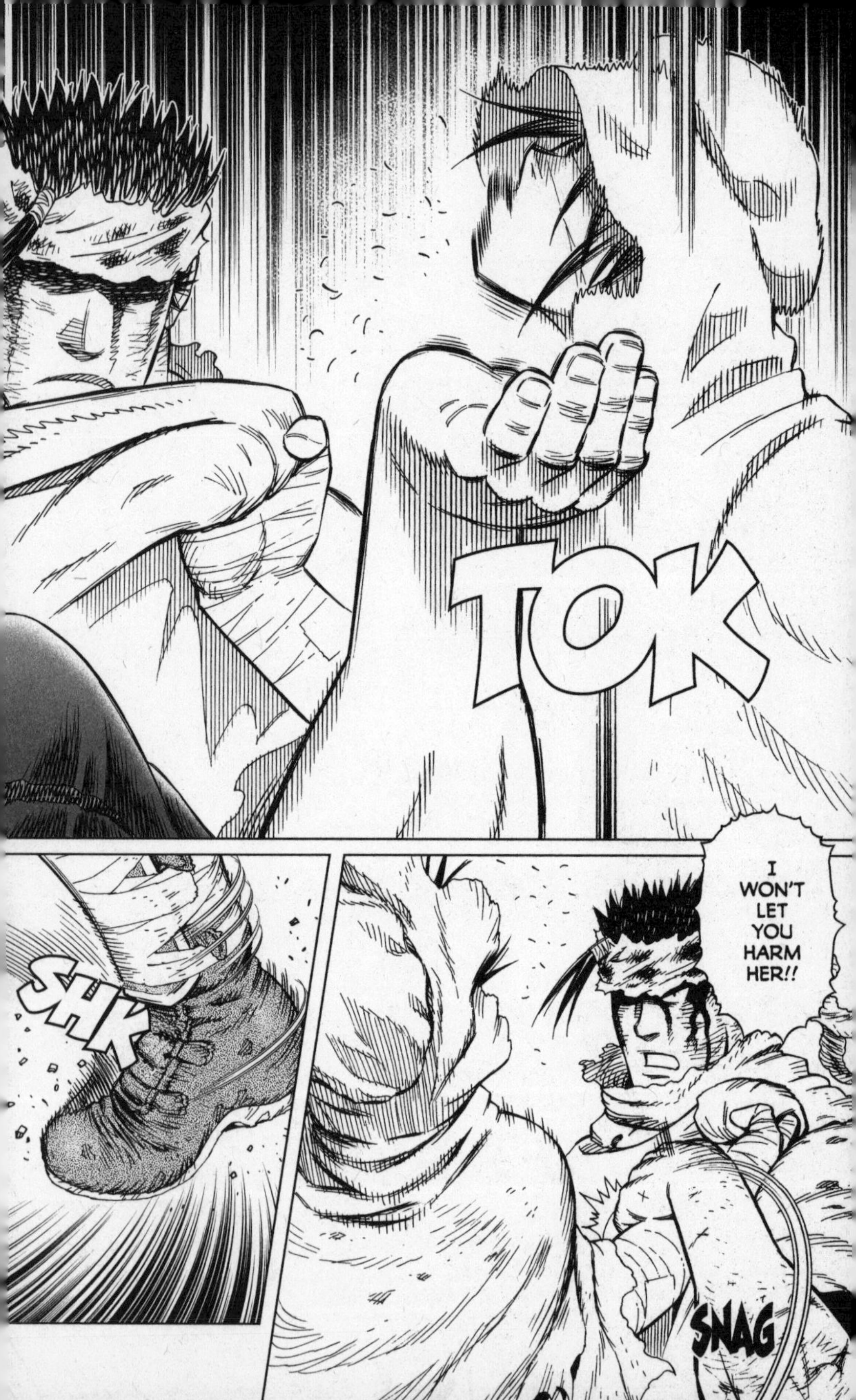
TOK
I WON'T LET YOU HARM HER!!
SNAG
SHK

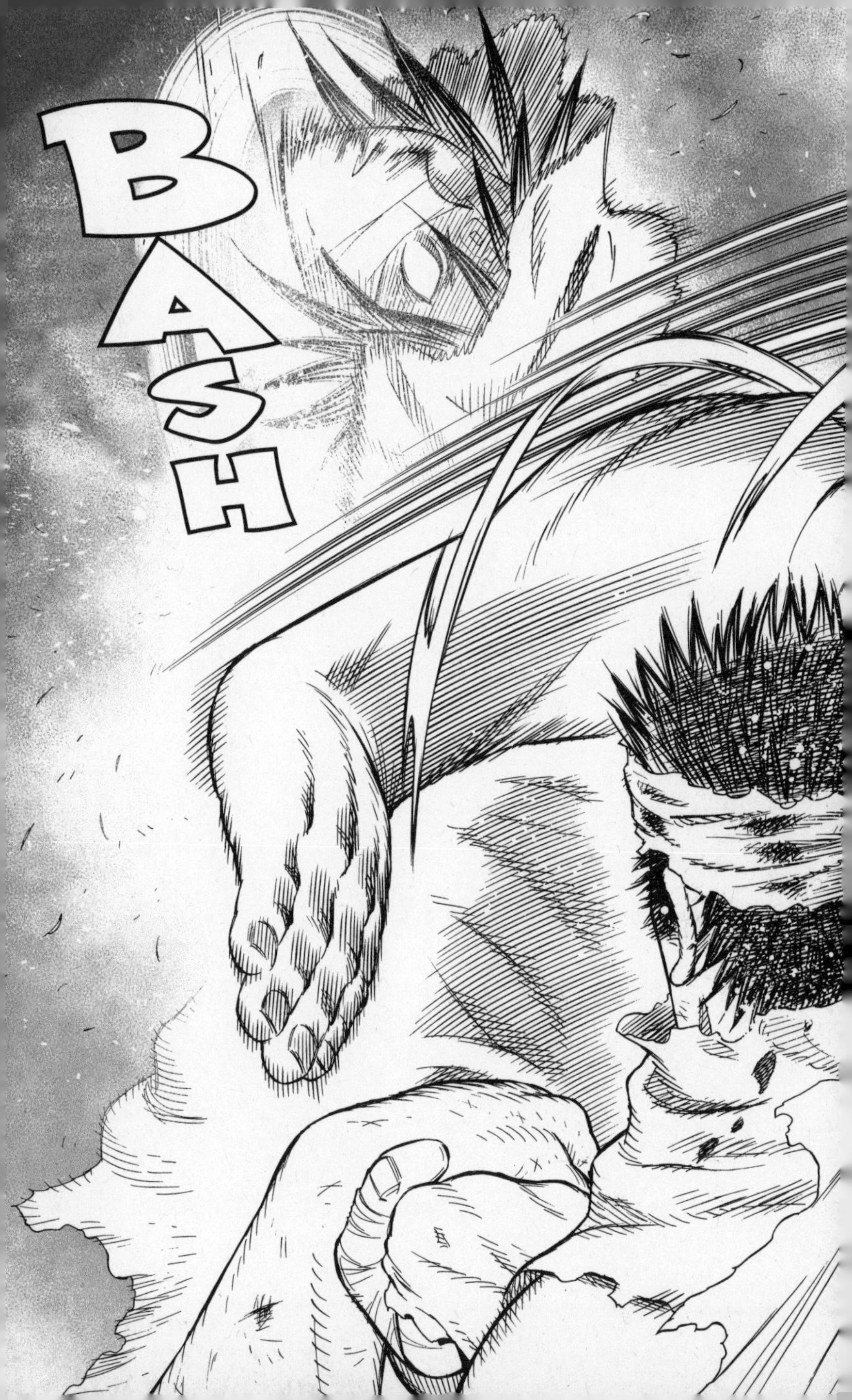
BASH

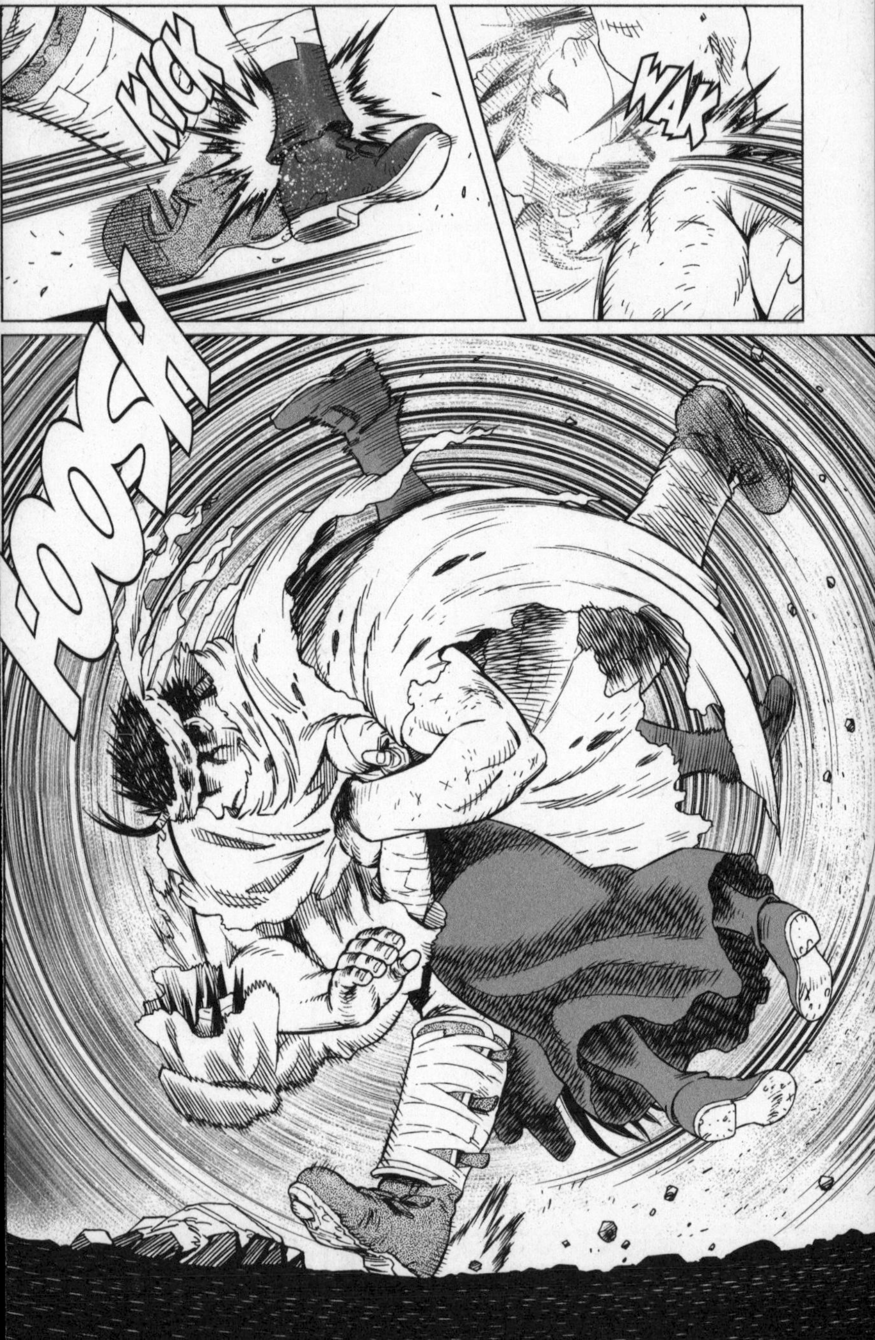
WAK
KICK
FOOSH

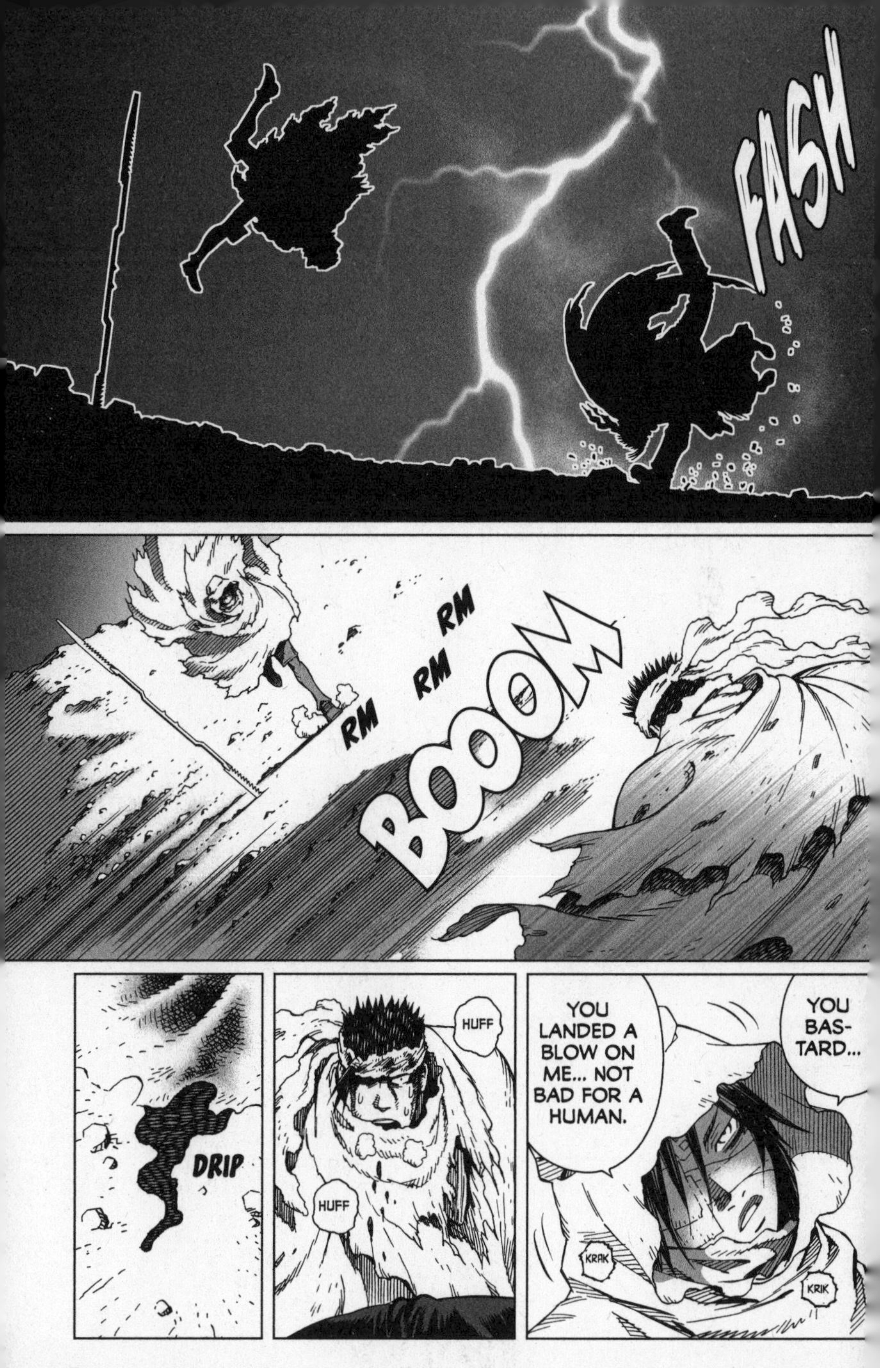
FASH
RM
RM
RM
BOOOM
YOU BAS-TARD...
YOU LANDED A BLOW ON ME... NOT BAD FOR A HUMAN.
KRIK
KRAK
HUFF
HUFF
DRIP

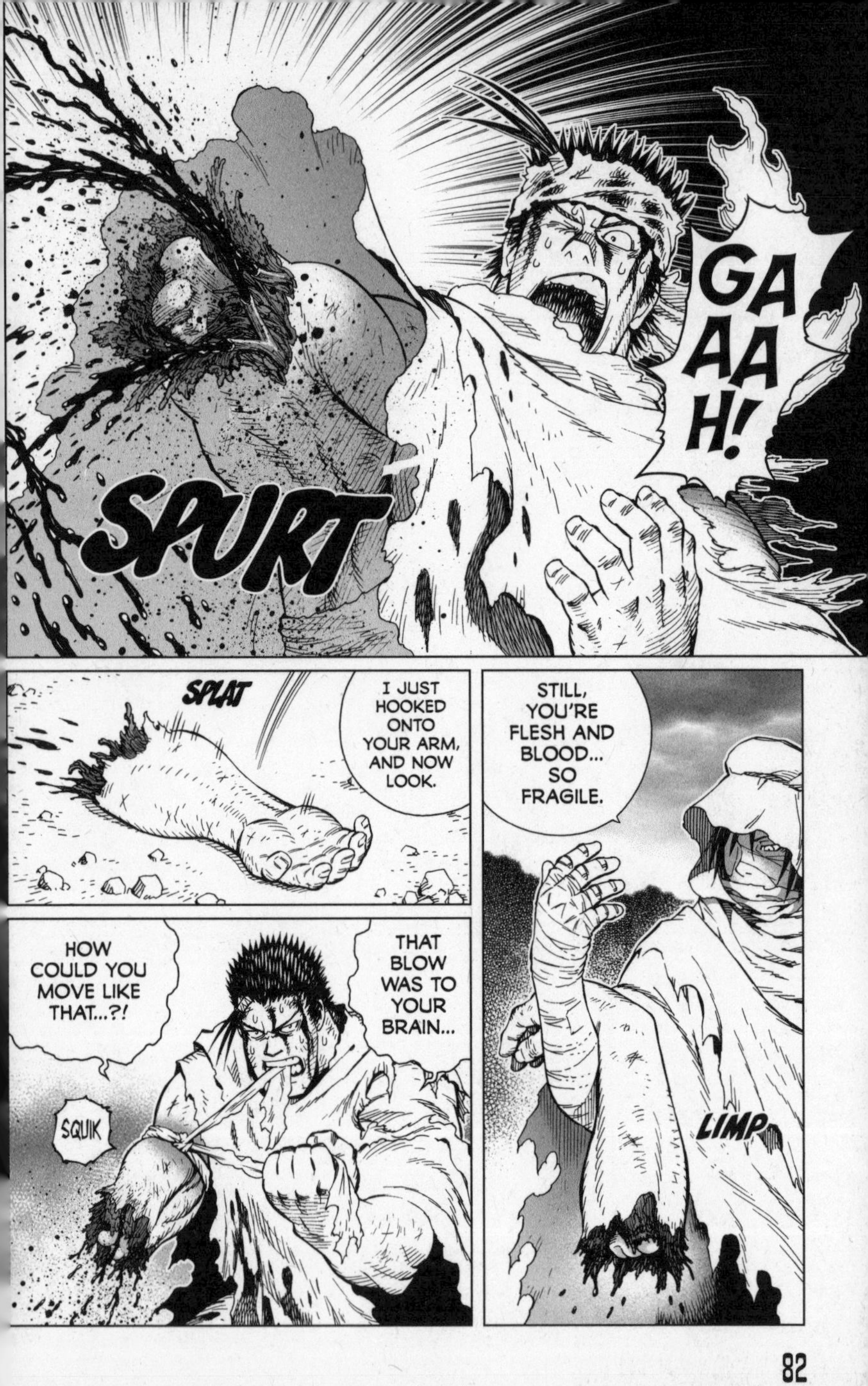
GAAAH!
SPURT
STILL, YOU'RE FLESH AND BLOOD... SO FRAGILE.
LIMP
I JUST HOOKED ONTO YOUR ARM, AND NOW LOOK.
SPLAT
THAT BLOW WAS TO YOUR BRAIN...
HOW COULD YOU MOVE LIKE THAT...?!
SQUIK

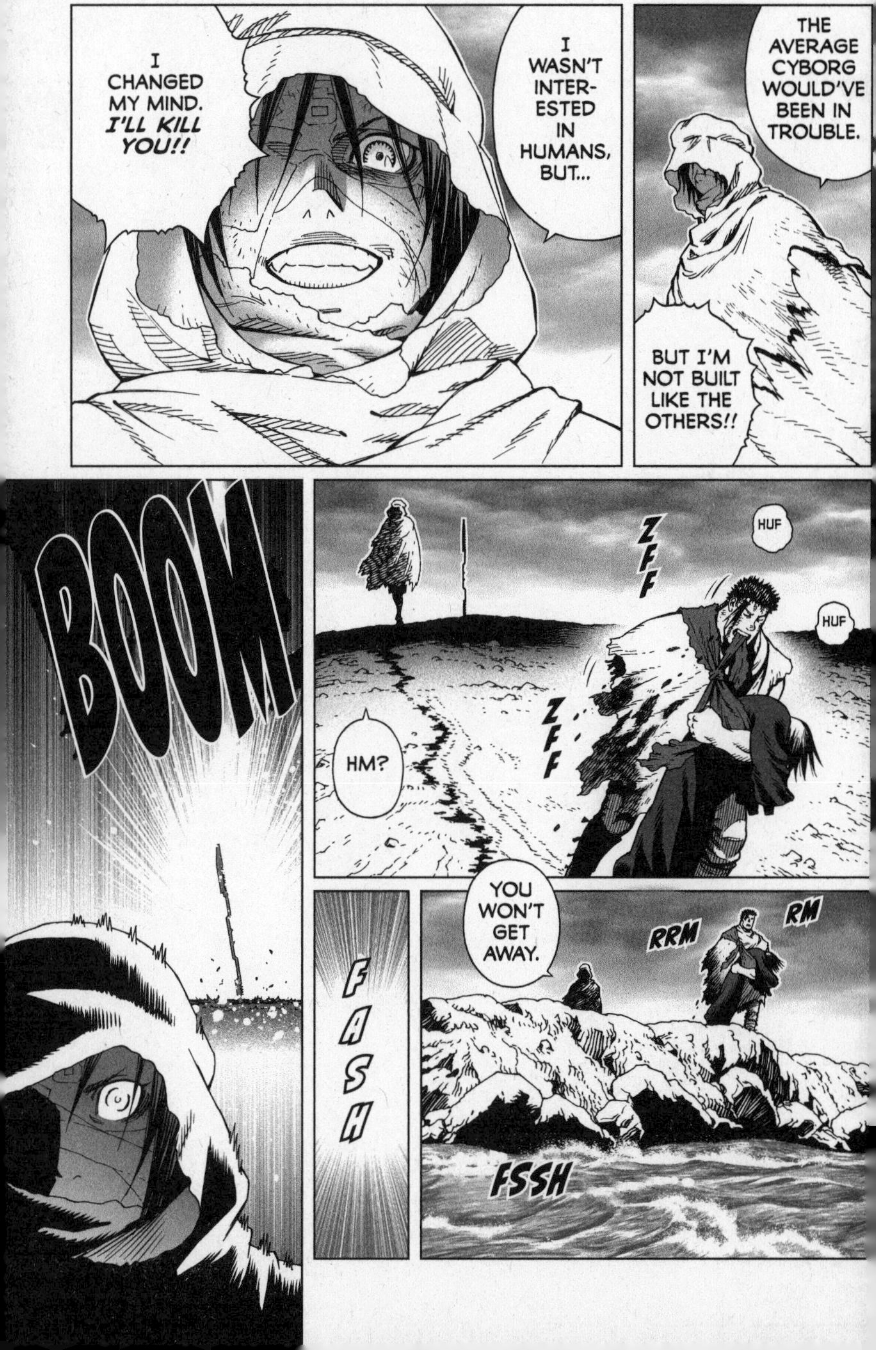
THE AVERAGE CYBORG WOULD'VE BEEN IN TROUBLE.
BUT I'M NOT BUILT LIKE THE OTHERS!!
I WASN'T INTER-ESTED IN HUMANS, BUT...
I CHANGED MY MIND. *I'LL KILL YOU!!*
HUF
HUF
ZFF
ZFF
HM?
RM
RRM
YOU WON'T GET AWAY.
FSSH
FASH
BOOM

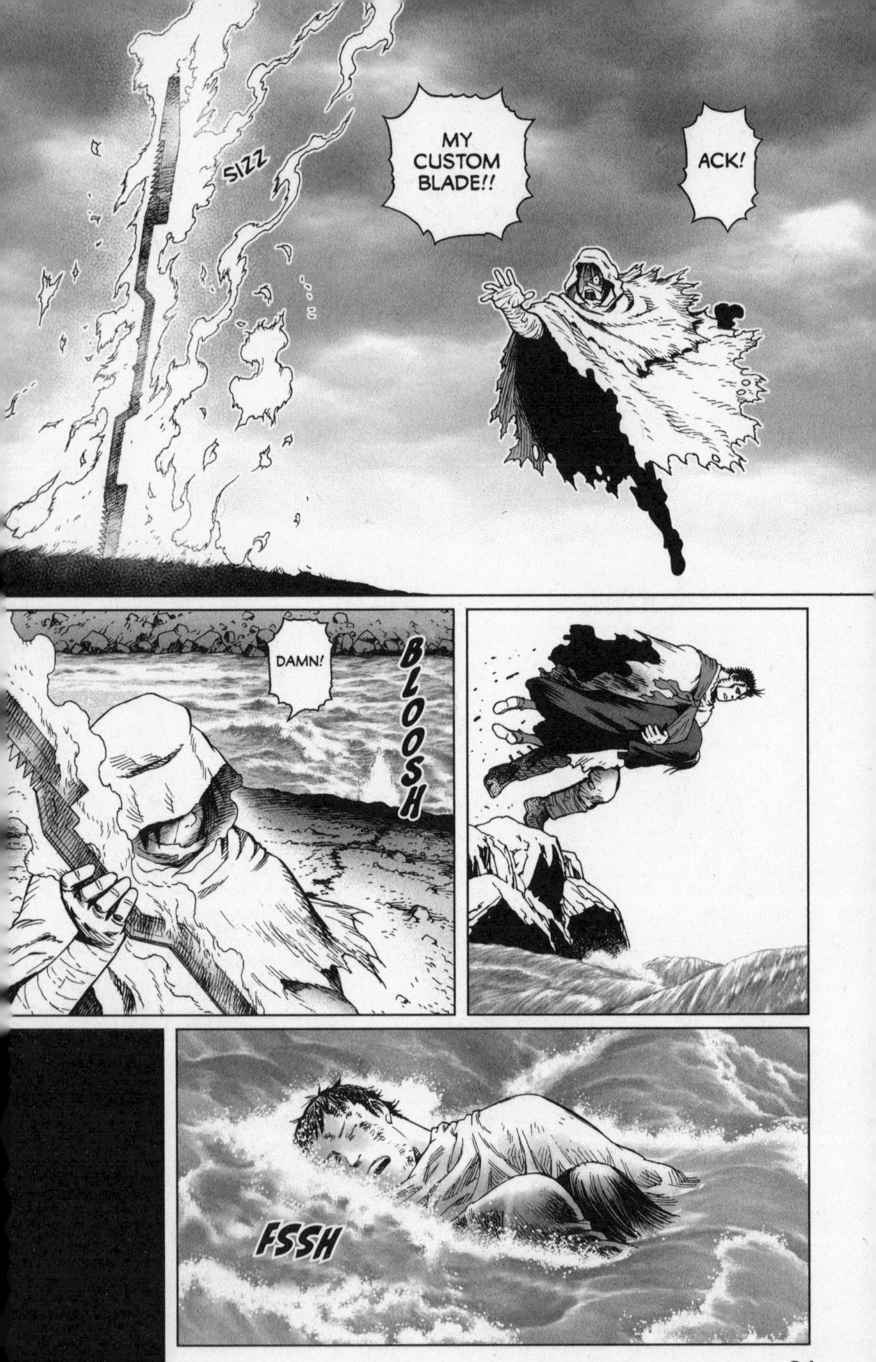
ACK!
MY CUSTOM BLADE!!
SIZZ
BLOOSH
DAMN!
FSSH

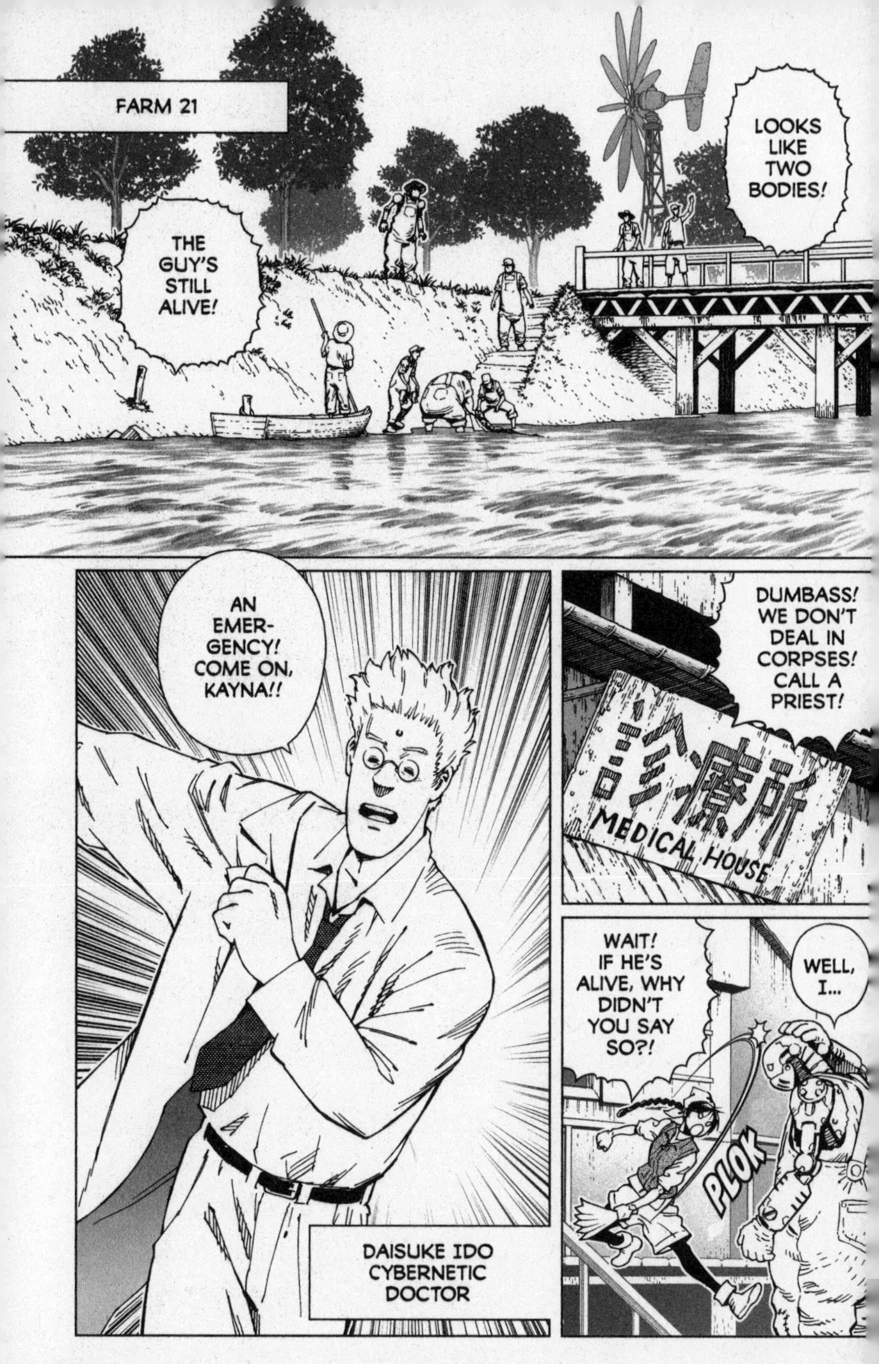
LOOKS LIKE TWO BODIES!
FARM 21
THE GUY'S STILL ALIVE!
DUMBASS! WE DON'T DEAL IN CORPSES! CALL A PRIEST!
診療所
MEDICAL HOUSE
WAIT! IF HE'S ALIVE, WHY DIDN'T YOU SAY SO?!
WELL, I...
PLOK
AN EMERGENCY! COME ON, KAYNA!!
DAISUKE IDO CYBERNETIC DOCTOR

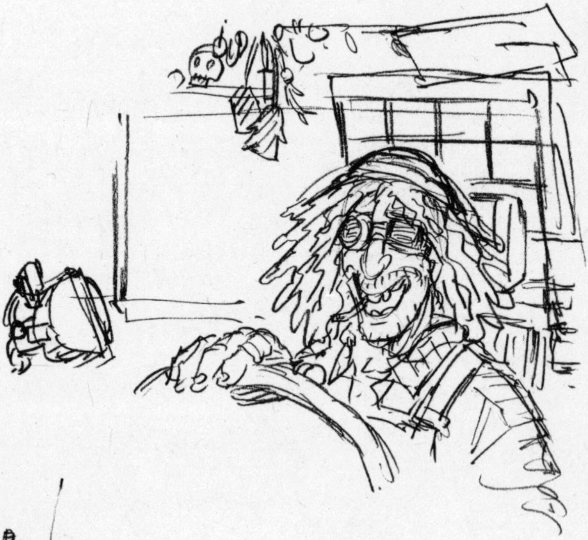

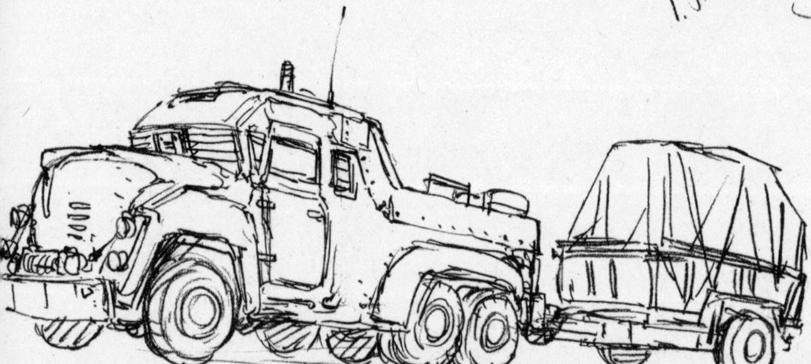

Phase 109: Alita Quest III

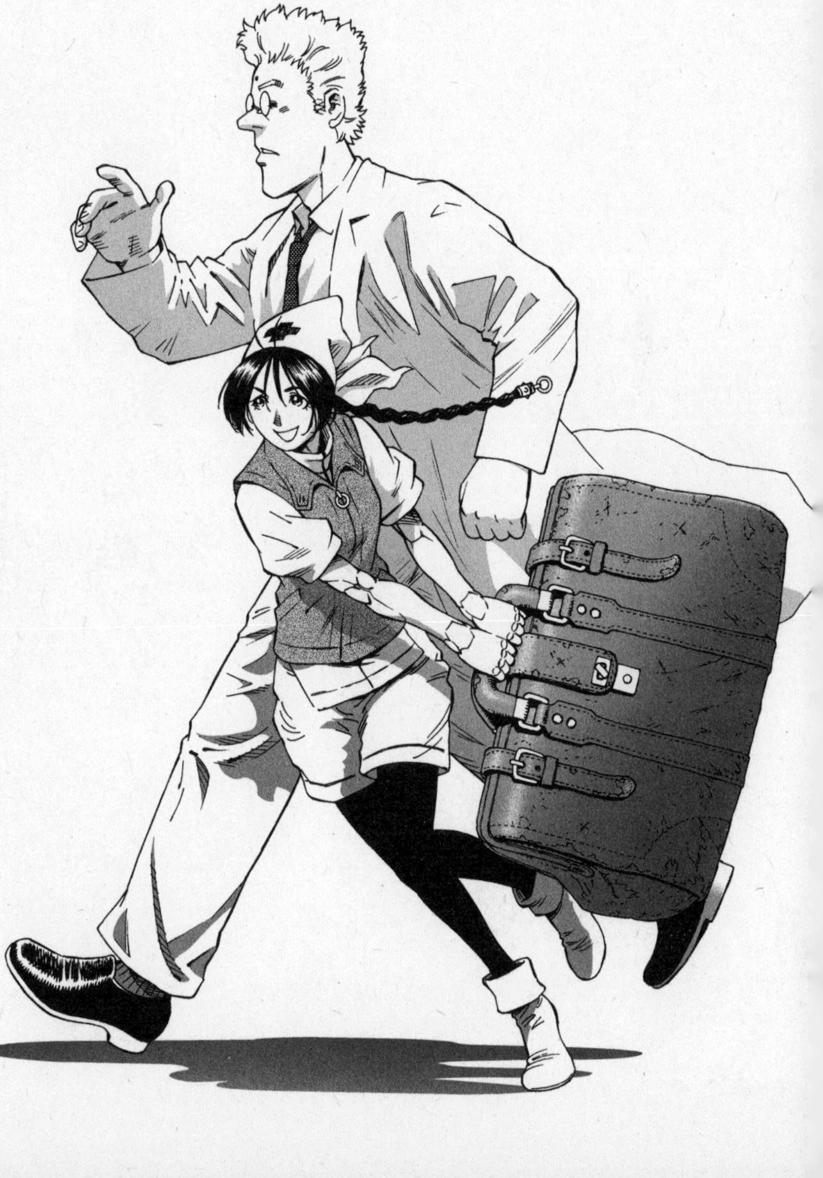

KLANK
KLANK

YOU'RE
AWAKE!

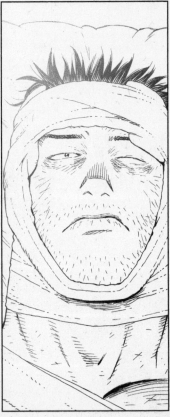

WHAT A
TOUGH
GUY!!

LOSE AN ARM
AND FALL INTO
A FLOODED
RIVER... MOST
PEOPLE
WOULD BE
DEAD!

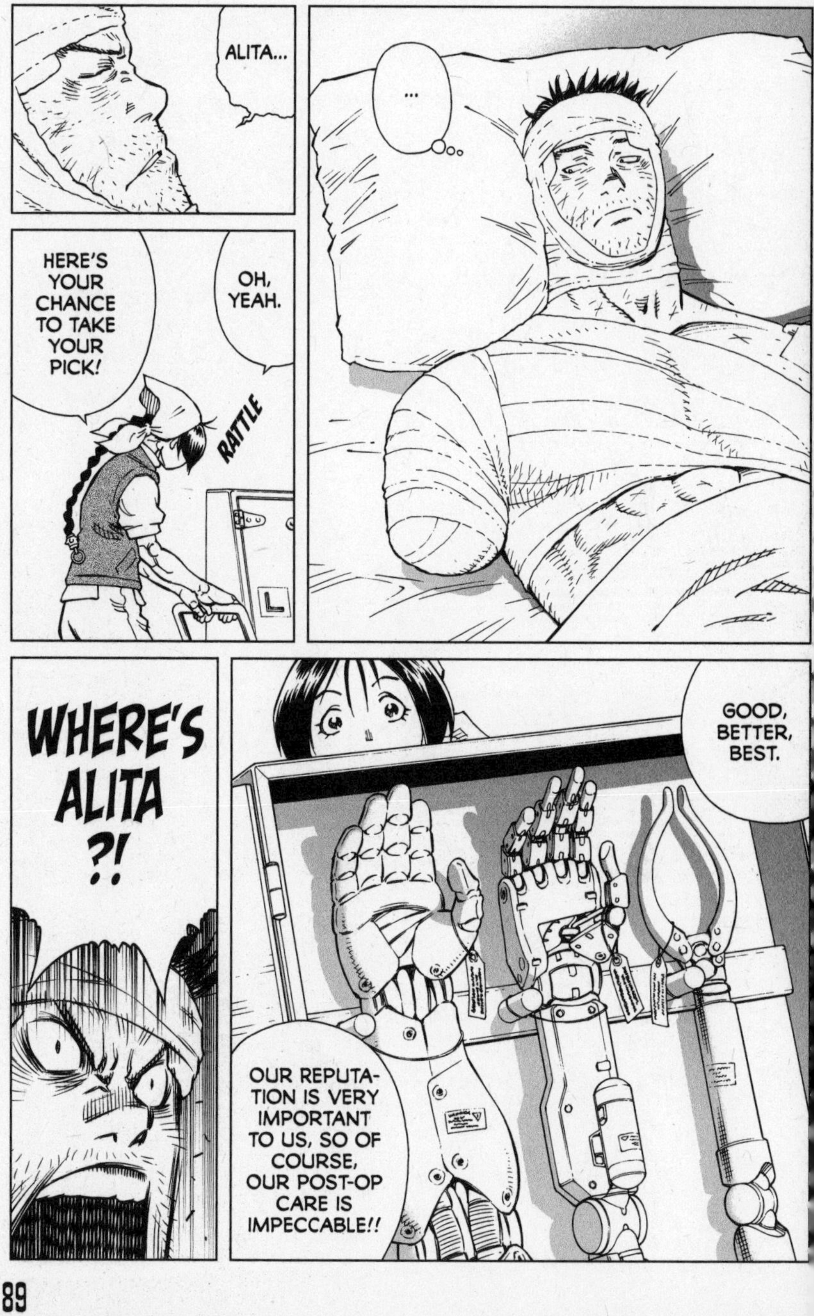
...
ALITA...
OH, YEAH.
HERE'S YOUR CHANCE TO TAKE YOUR PICK!
RATTLE
GOOD, BETTER, BEST.
OUR REPUTATION IS VERY IMPORTANT TO US, SO OF COURSE, OUR POST-OP CARE IS IMPECCABLE!!
WHERE'S ALITA?!

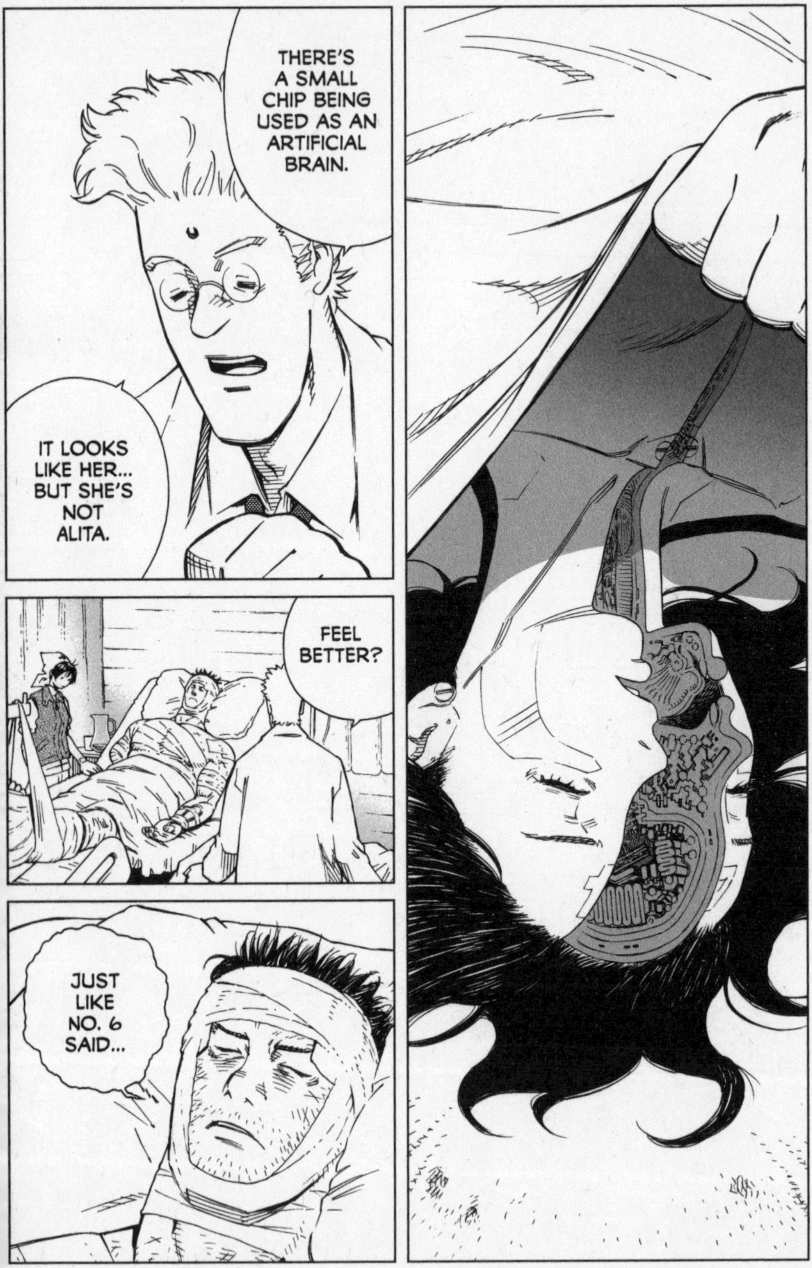
THERE'S A SMALL CHIP BEING USED AS AN ARTIFICIAL BRAIN.
IT LOOKS LIKE HER... BUT SHE'S NOT ALITA.
FEEL BETTER?
JUST LIKE NO. 6 SAID...

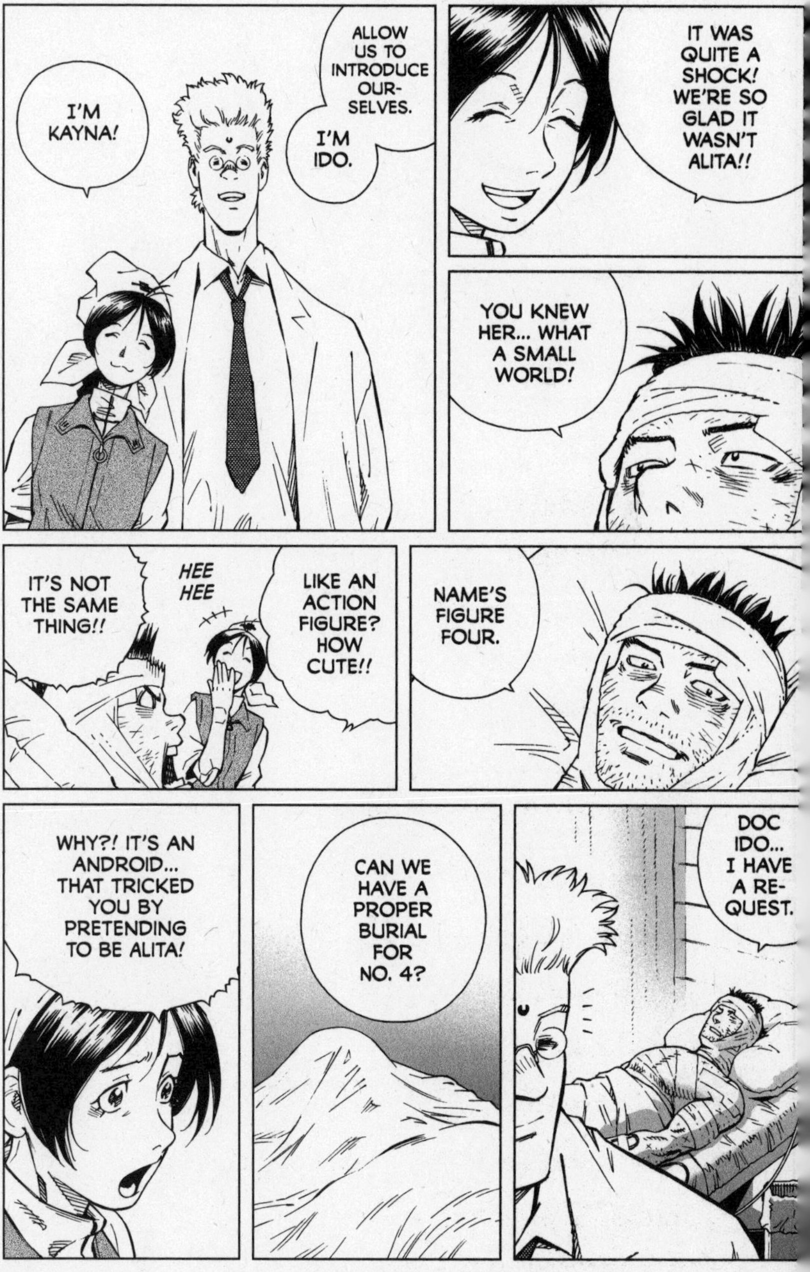
IT WAS QUITE A SHOCK! WE'RE SO GLAD IT WASN'T ALITA!!
YOU KNEW HER... WHAT A SMALL WORLD!
ALLOW US TO INTRODUCE OUR-SELVES.
I'M IDO.
I'M KAYNA!
NAME'S FIGURE FOUR.
LIKE AN ACTION FIGURE? HOW CUTE!!
HEE HEE
IT'S NOT THE SAME THING!!
DOC IDO... I HAVE A RE-QUEST.
CAN WE HAVE A PROPER BURIAL FOR NO. 4?
WHY?! IT'S AN ANDROID... THAT TRICKED YOU BY PRETENDING TO BE ALITA!

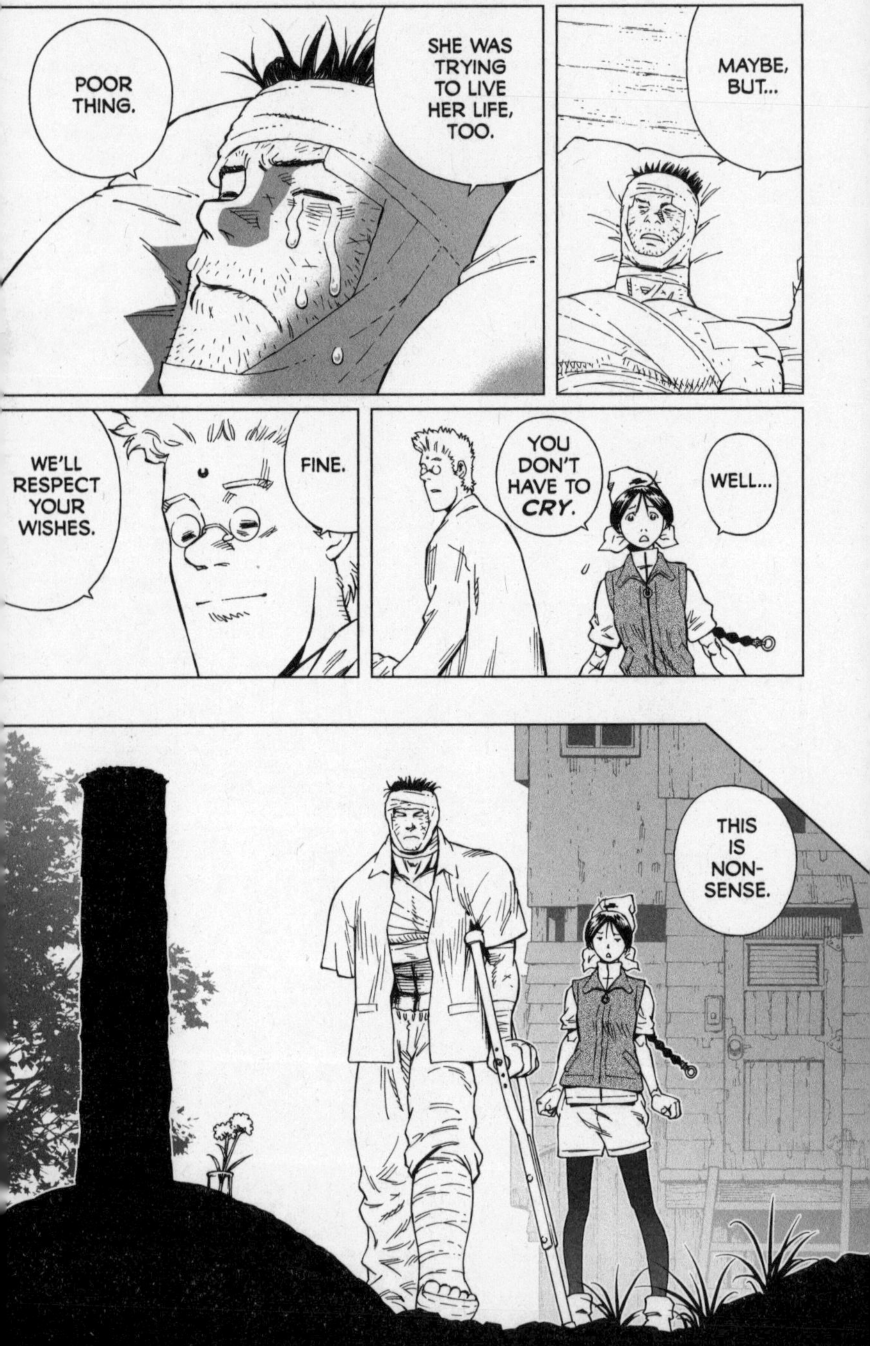
MAYBE, BUT...
SHE WAS TRYING TO LIVE HER LIFE, TOO.
POOR THING.
WELL...
YOU DON'T HAVE TO *CRY*.
FINE.
WE'LL RESPECT YOUR WISHES.
THIS IS NON-SENSE.

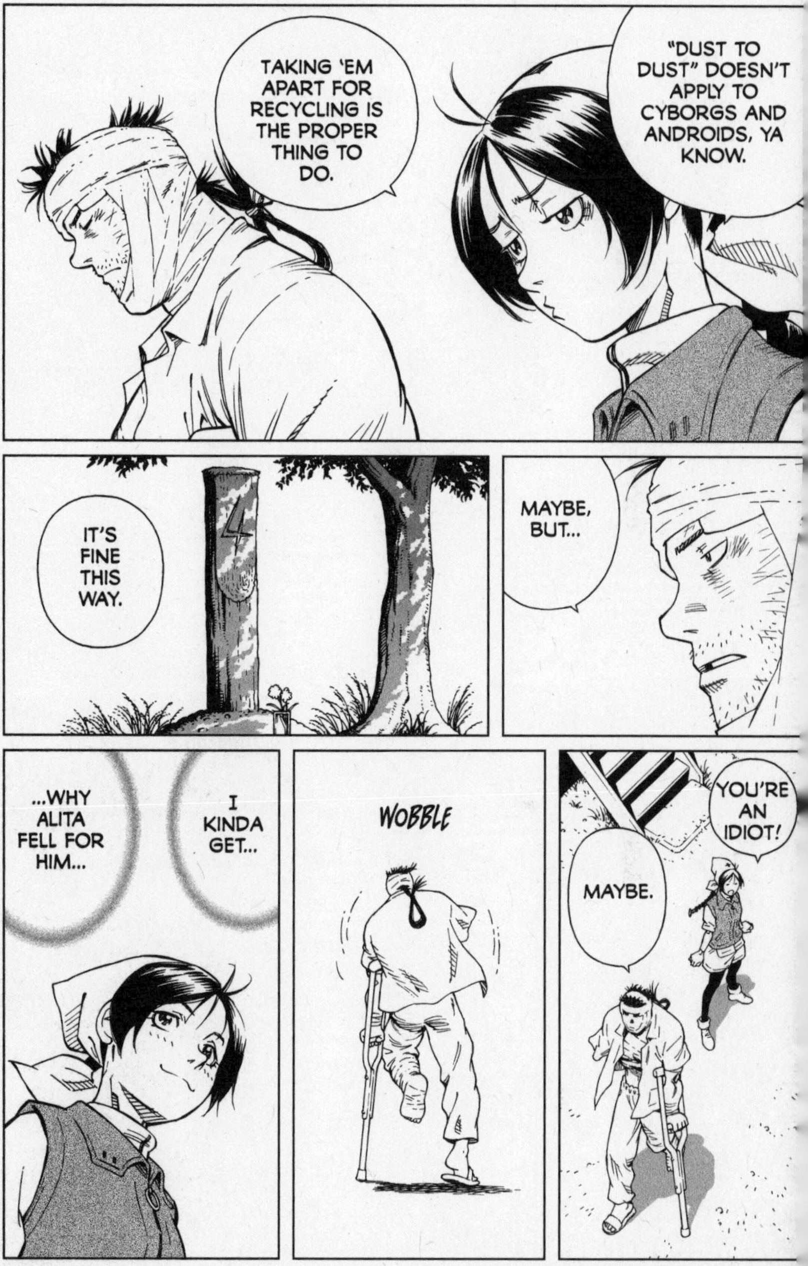
"DUST TO DUST" DOESN'T APPLY TO CYBORGS AND ANDROIDS, YA KNOW.
TAKING 'EM APART FOR RECYCLING IS THE PROPER THING TO DO.
MAYBE, BUT...
IT'S FINE THIS WAY.
YOU'RE AN IDIOT!
MAYBE.
WOBBLE
I KINDA GET...
...WHY ALITA FELL FOR HIM...

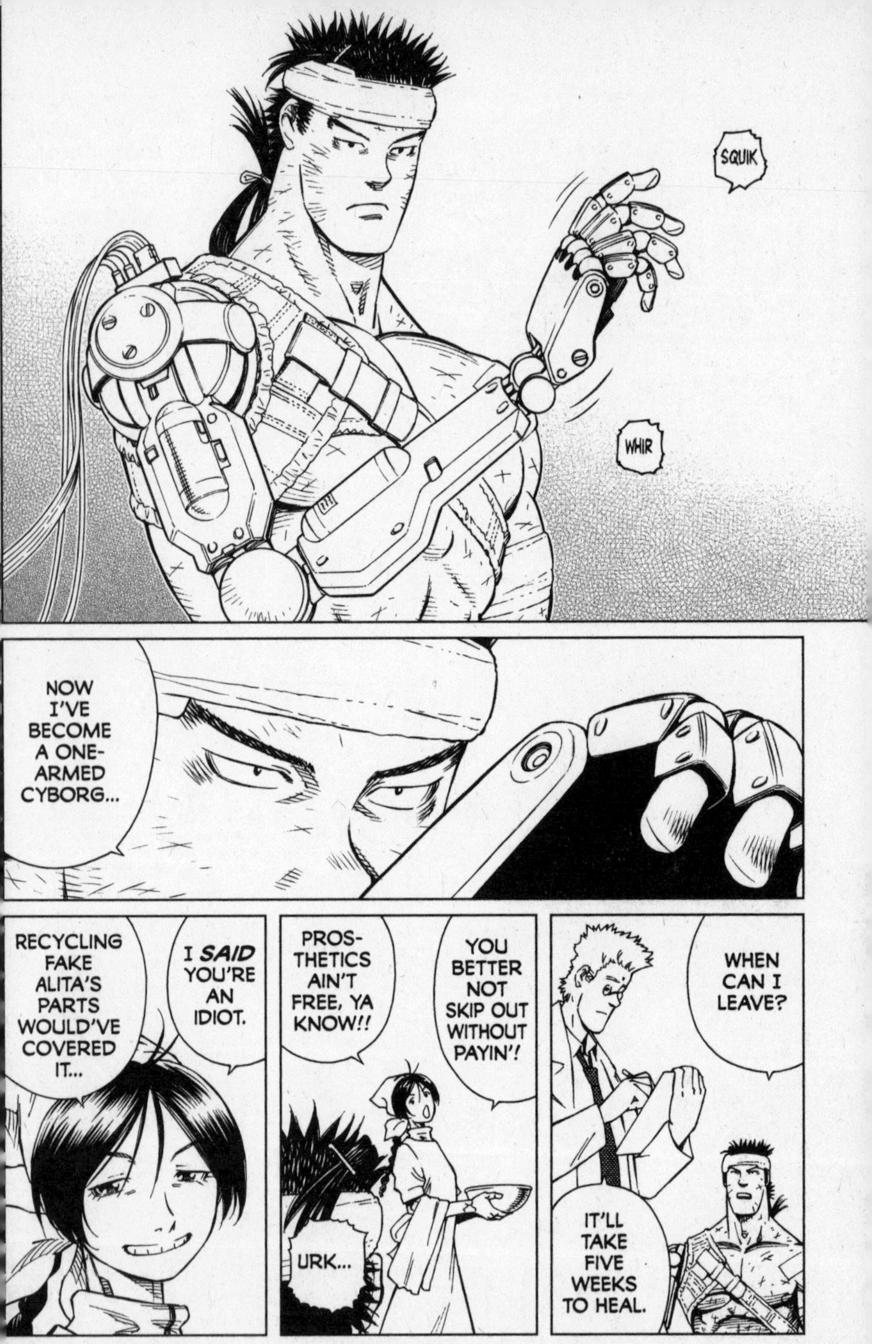
SQUIK
WHIR
NOW I'VE BECOME A ONE-ARMED CYBORG...
WHEN CAN I LEAVE?
IT'LL TAKE FIVE WEEKS TO HEAL.
YOU BETTER NOT SKIP OUT WITHOUT PAYIN'!
PROSTHETICS AIN'T FREE, YA KNOW!!
URK...
I *SAID* YOU'RE AN IDIOT.
RECYCLING FAKE ALITA'S PARTS WOULD'VE COVERED IT...

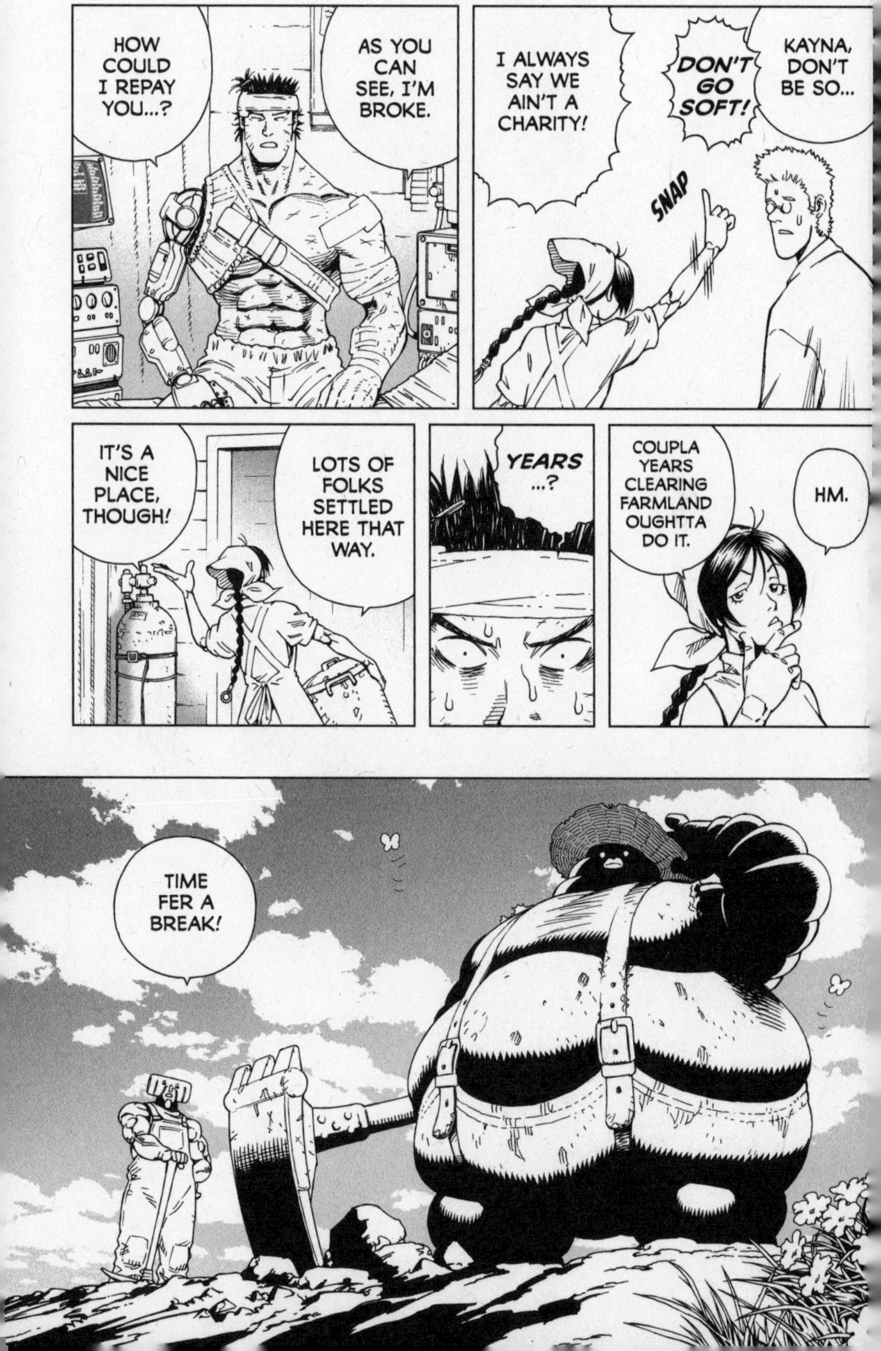
KAYNA, DON'T BE SO...
DON'T GO SOFT!
I ALWAYS SAY WE AIN'T A CHARITY!
SNAP
AS YOU CAN SEE, I'M BROKE.
HOW COULD I REPAY YOU...?
HM.
COUPLA YEARS CLEARING FARMLAND OUGHTTA DO IT.
YEARS ...?
LOTS OF FOLKS SETTLED HERE THAT WAY.
IT'S A NICE PLACE, THOUGH!
TIME FER A BREAK!

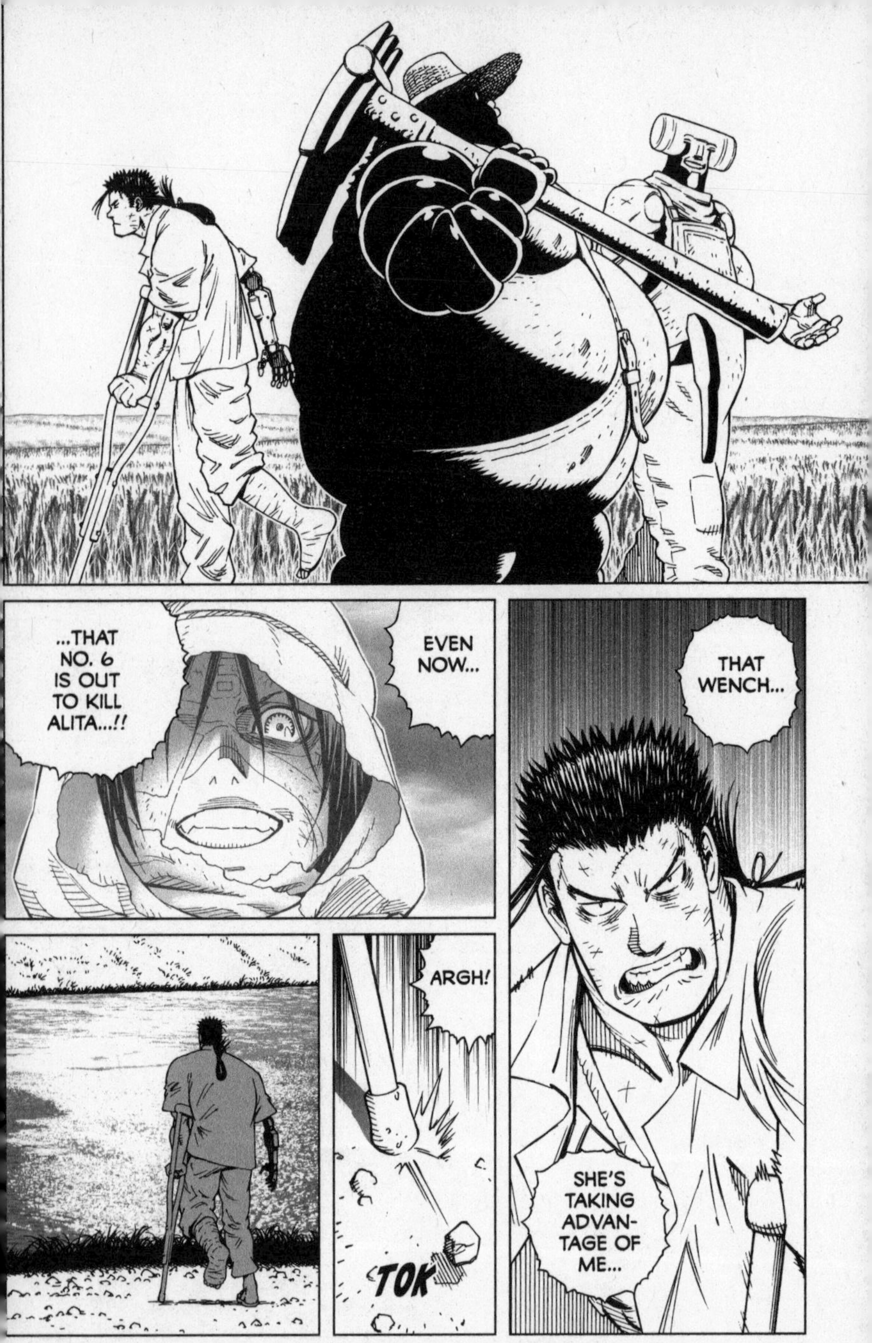
THAT WENCH...
SHE'S TAKING ADVAN-TAGE OF ME...
EVEN NOW...
...THAT NO. 6 IS OUT TO KILL ALITA...!!
ARGH!
TOK

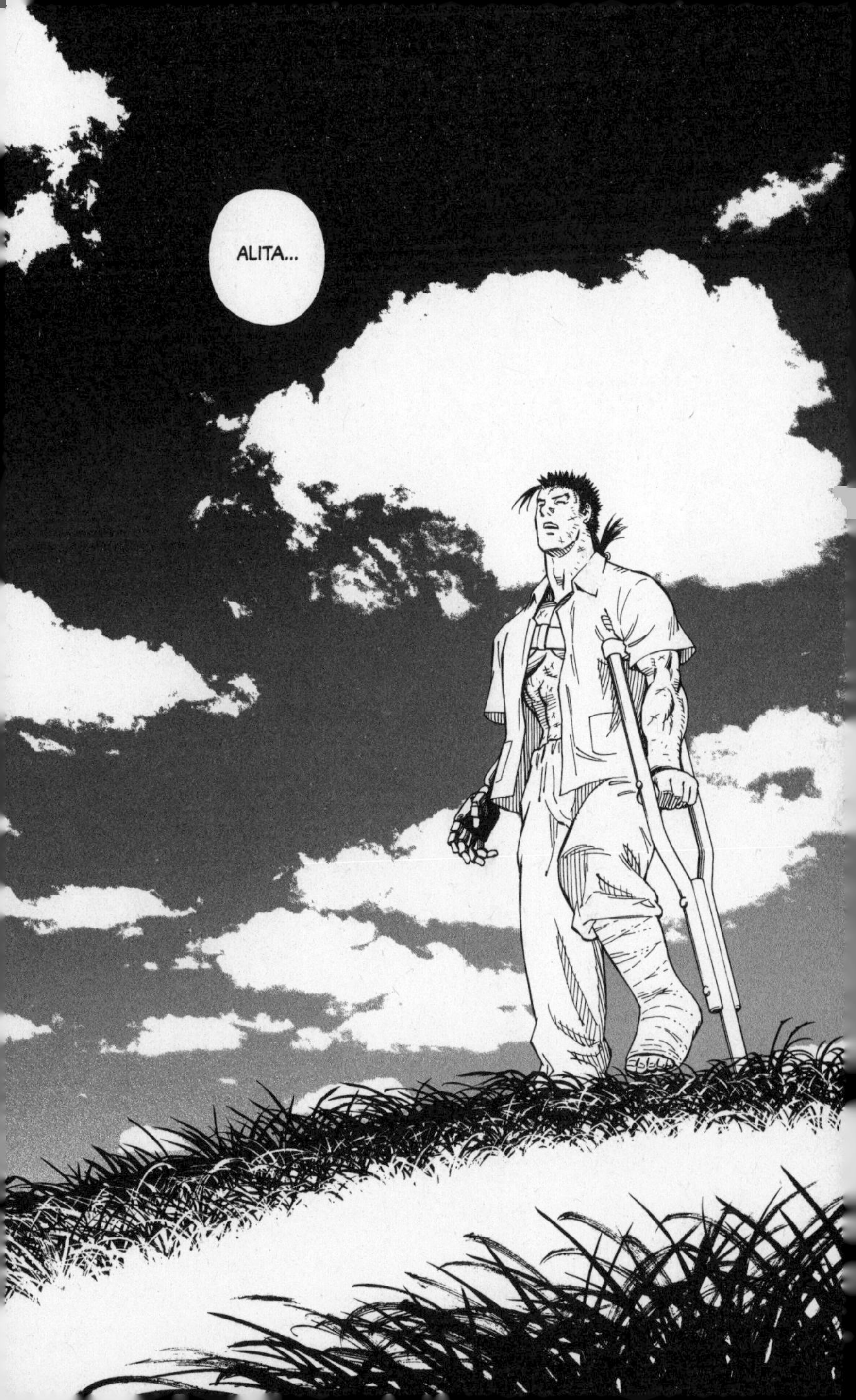
ALITA...

WHERE ARE YOU...?

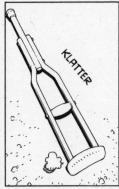

KLATTER

FFT

BAM BAM

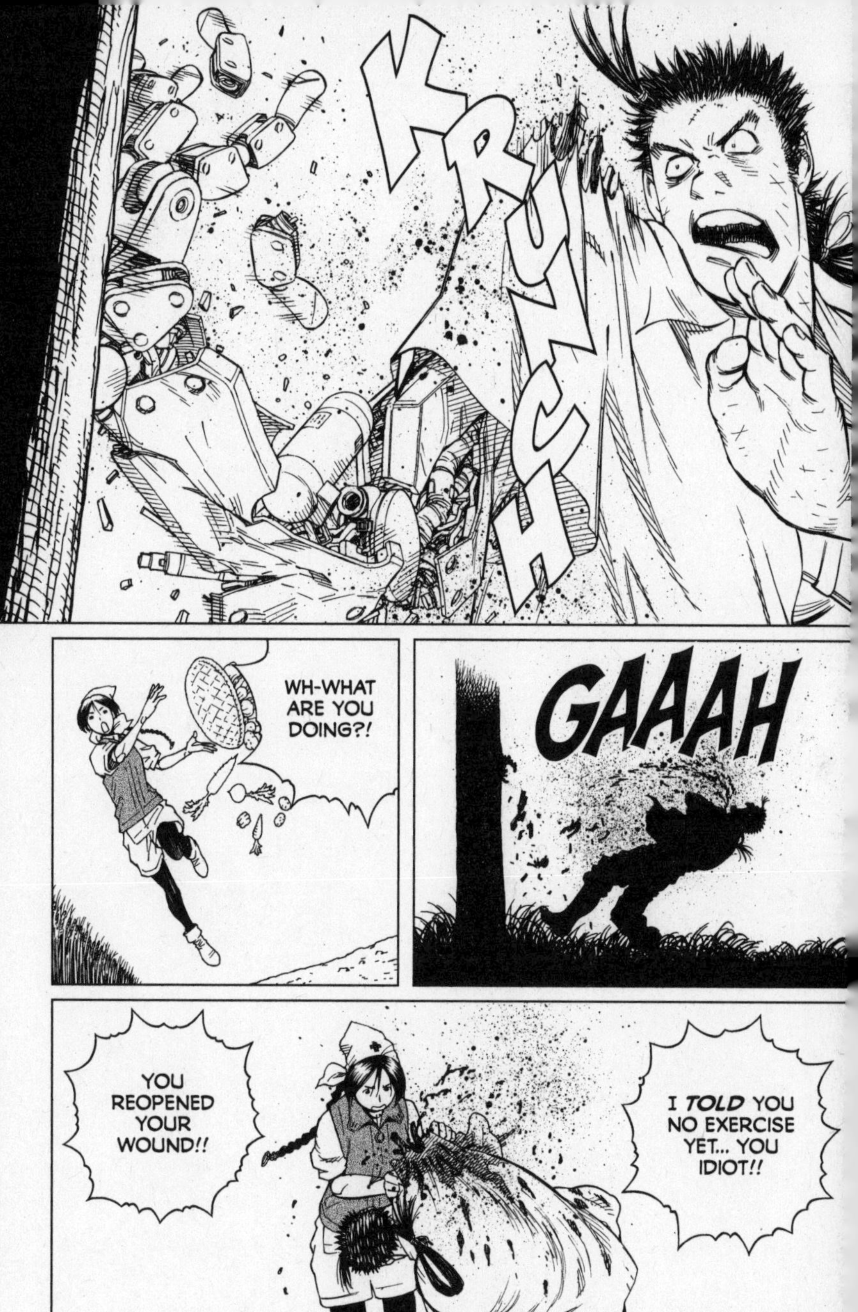
KRUNCH
GAAAH
WH-WHAT ARE YOU DOING?!
I *TOLD* YOU NO EXERCISE YET... YOU IDIOT!!
YOU REOPENED YOUR WOUND!!

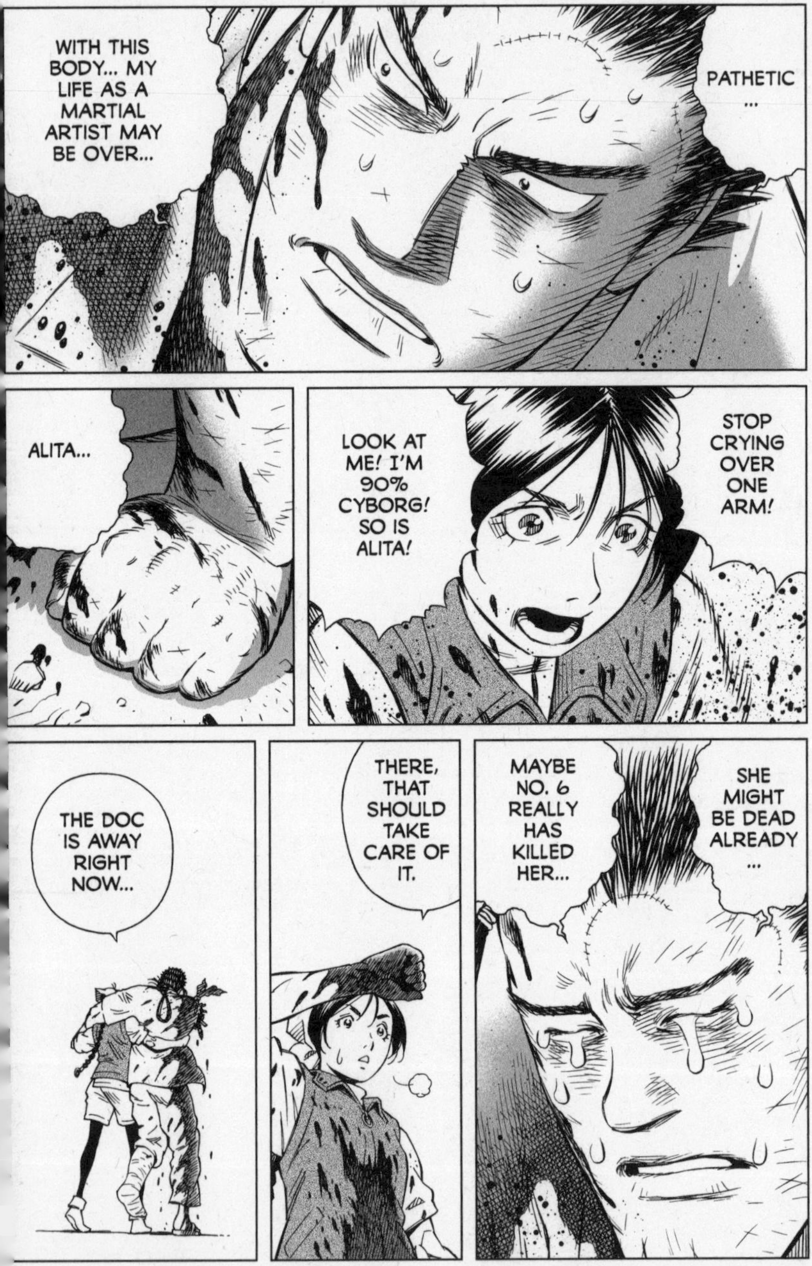
PATHETIC ...
WITH THIS BODY... MY LIFE AS A MARTIAL ARTIST MAY BE OVER...
STOP CRYING OVER ONE ARM!
LOOK AT ME! I'M 90% CYBORG! SO IS ALITA!
ALITA...
SHE MIGHT BE DEAD ALREADY ...
MAYBE NO. 6 REALLY HAS KILLED HER...
THERE, THAT SHOULD TAKE CARE OF IT.
THE DOC IS AWAY RIGHT NOW...

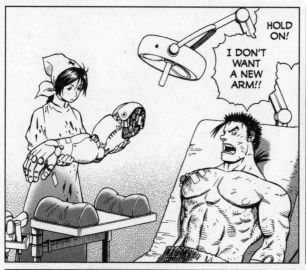

診療所
MEDICAL HOUSE
HOLD ON!
I DON'T WANT A NEW ARM!!
YOU WANT ME TO GO INTO DEBT AND BECOME A SERF!!
SHEESH.
DON'T WORRY. I'LL PUT THIS ON YOUR TAB.
HUH?
PAY FOR THE ARM AND THE SURGERY WHENEVER YOU FEEL LIKE IT.
IN EXCHANGE, YOU NEED TO GET BETTER AND GO FIND ALITA!!

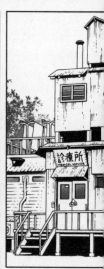

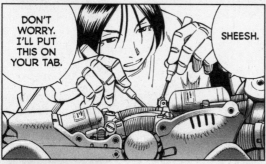

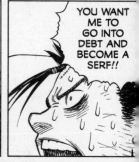

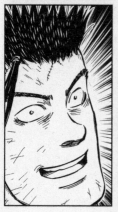

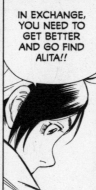

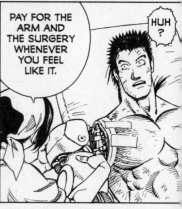

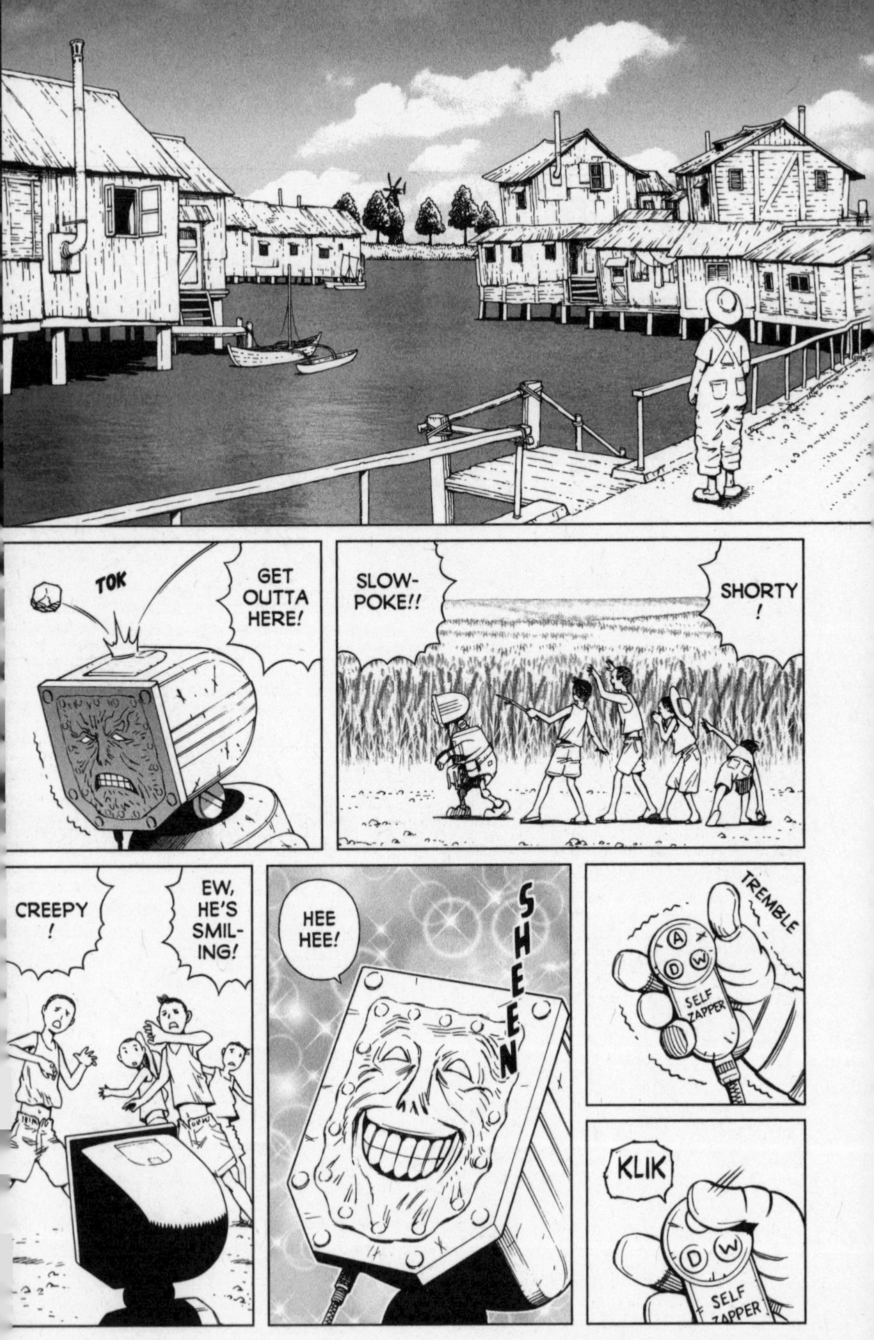
SHORTY!
SLOW-POKE!!
GET OUTTA HERE!
TOK
TREMBLE
A
D
W
SELF ZAPPER
KLIK
D
W
SELF ZAPPER
SHEEN
HEE HEE!
EW, HE'S SMIL-ING!
CREEPY!

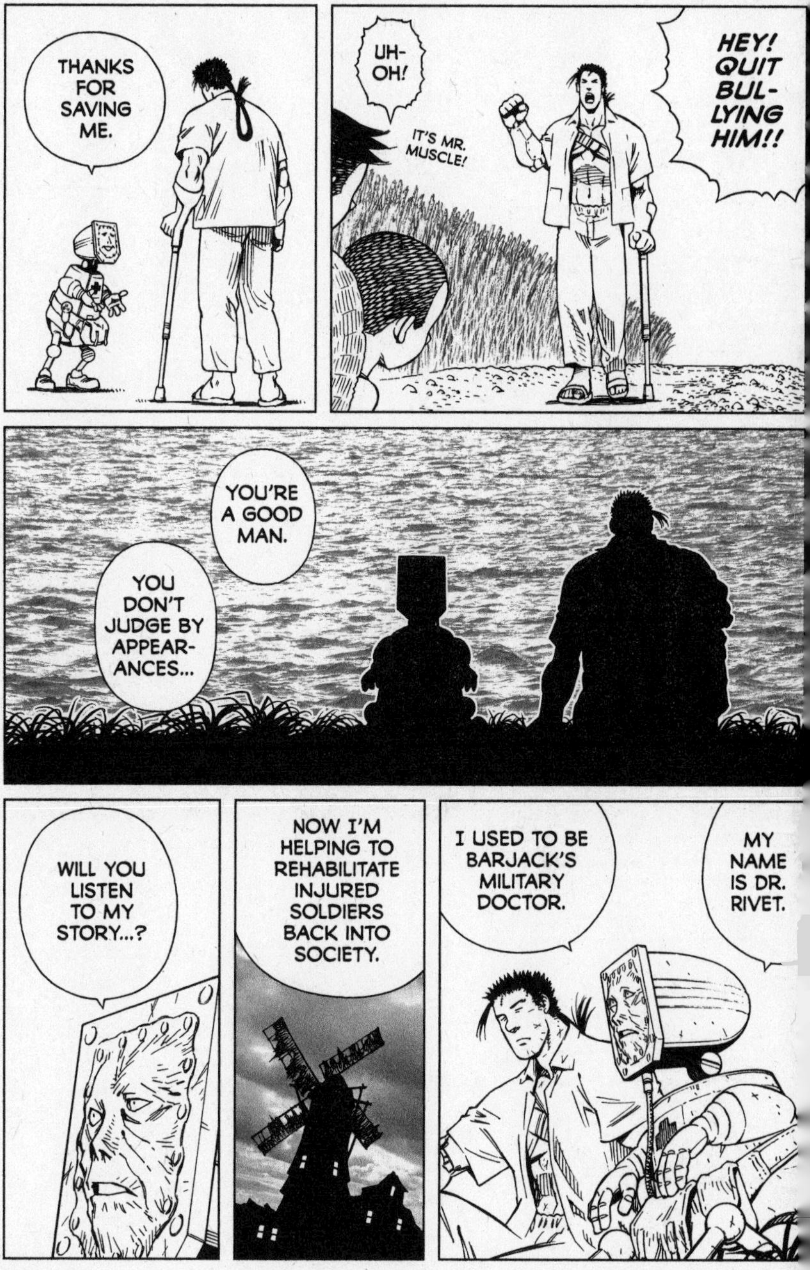
HEY! QUIT BULLYING HIM!!
UH-OH!
IT'S MR. MUSCLE!
THANKS FOR SAVING ME.
YOU'RE A GOOD MAN.
YOU DON'T JUDGE BY APPEARANCES...
MY NAME IS DR. RIVET.
I USED TO BE BARJACK'S MILITARY DOCTOR.
NOW I'M HELPING TO REHABILITATE INJURED SOLDIERS BACK INTO SOCIETY.
WILL YOU LISTEN TO MY STORY...?

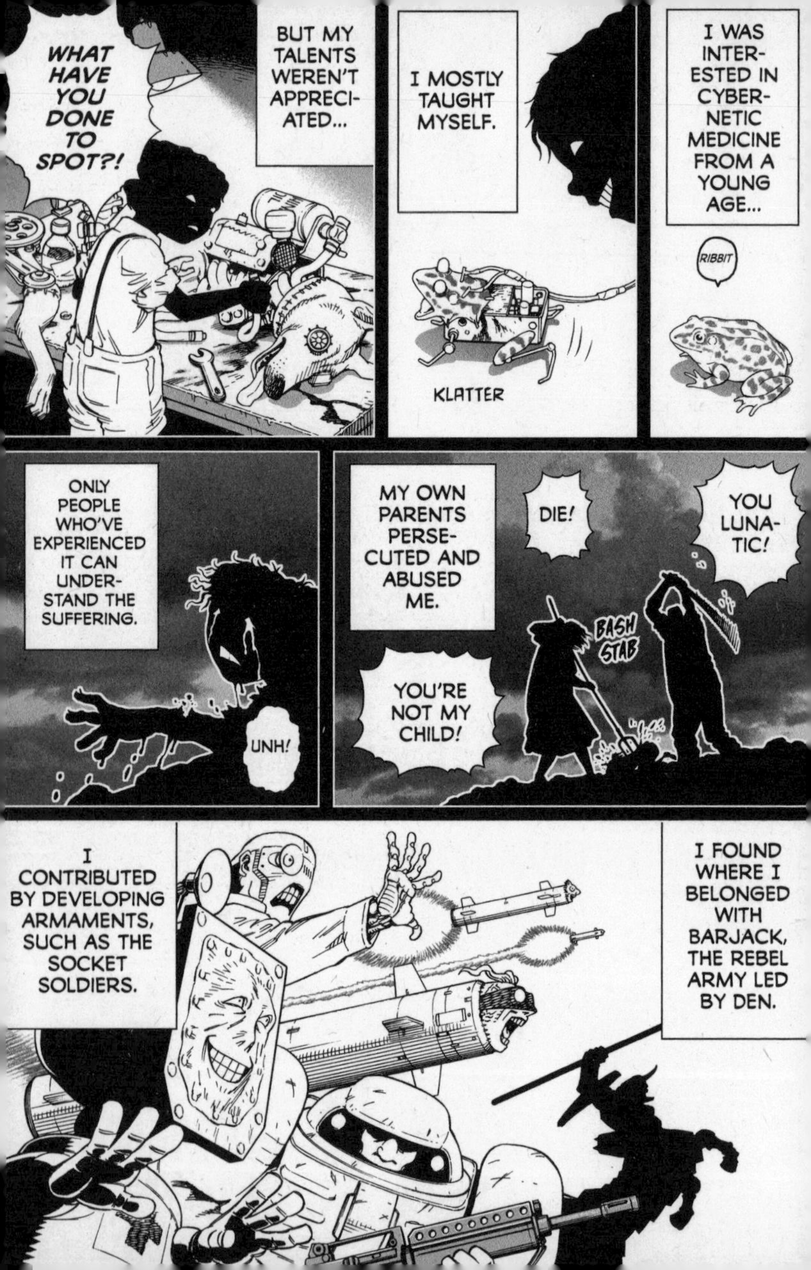
I WAS INTERESTED IN CYBERNETIC MEDICINE FROM A YOUNG AGE...
RIBBIT
I MOSTLY TAUGHT MYSELF.
KLATTER
BUT MY TALENTS WEREN'T APPRECIATED...
WHAT HAVE YOU DONE TO SPOT?!
YOU LUNATIC!
DIE!
MY OWN PARENTS PERSECUTED AND ABUSED ME.
BASH
STAB
YOU'RE NOT MY CHILD!
ONLY PEOPLE WHO'VE EXPERIENCED IT CAN UNDERSTAND THE SUFFERING.
UNH!
I FOUND WHERE I BELONGED WITH BARJACK, THE REBEL ARMY LED BY DEN.
I CONTRIBUTED BY DEVELOPING ARMAMENTS, SUCH AS THE SOCKET SOLDIERS.

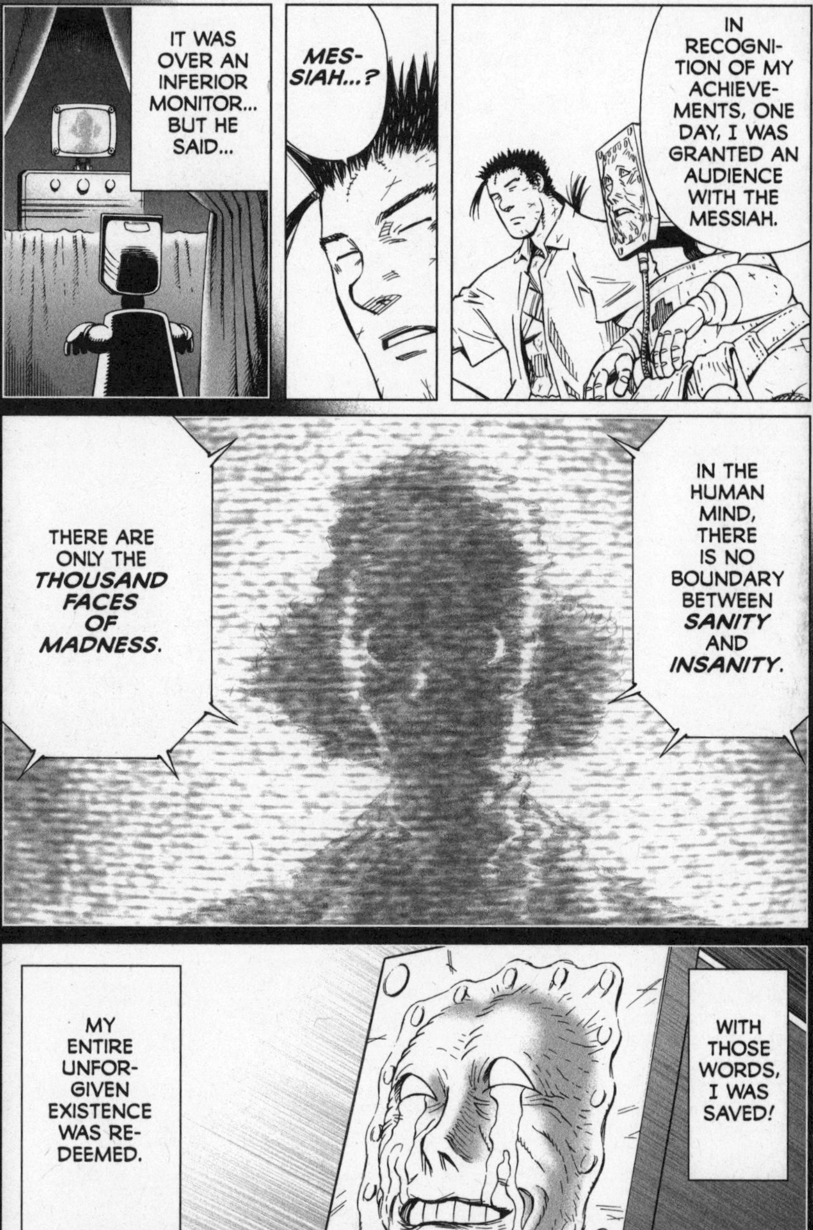
IN RECOGNITION OF MY ACHIEVEMENTS, ONE DAY, I WAS GRANTED AN AUDIENCE WITH THE MESSIAH.
MESSIAH...?
IT WAS OVER AN INFERIOR MONITOR... BUT HE SAID...
IN THE HUMAN MIND, THERE IS NO BOUNDARY BETWEEN SANITY AND INSANITY.
THERE ARE ONLY THE THOUSAND FACES OF MADNESS.
WITH THOSE WORDS, I WAS SAVED!
MY ENTIRE UNFORGIVEN EXISTENCE WAS REDEEMED.

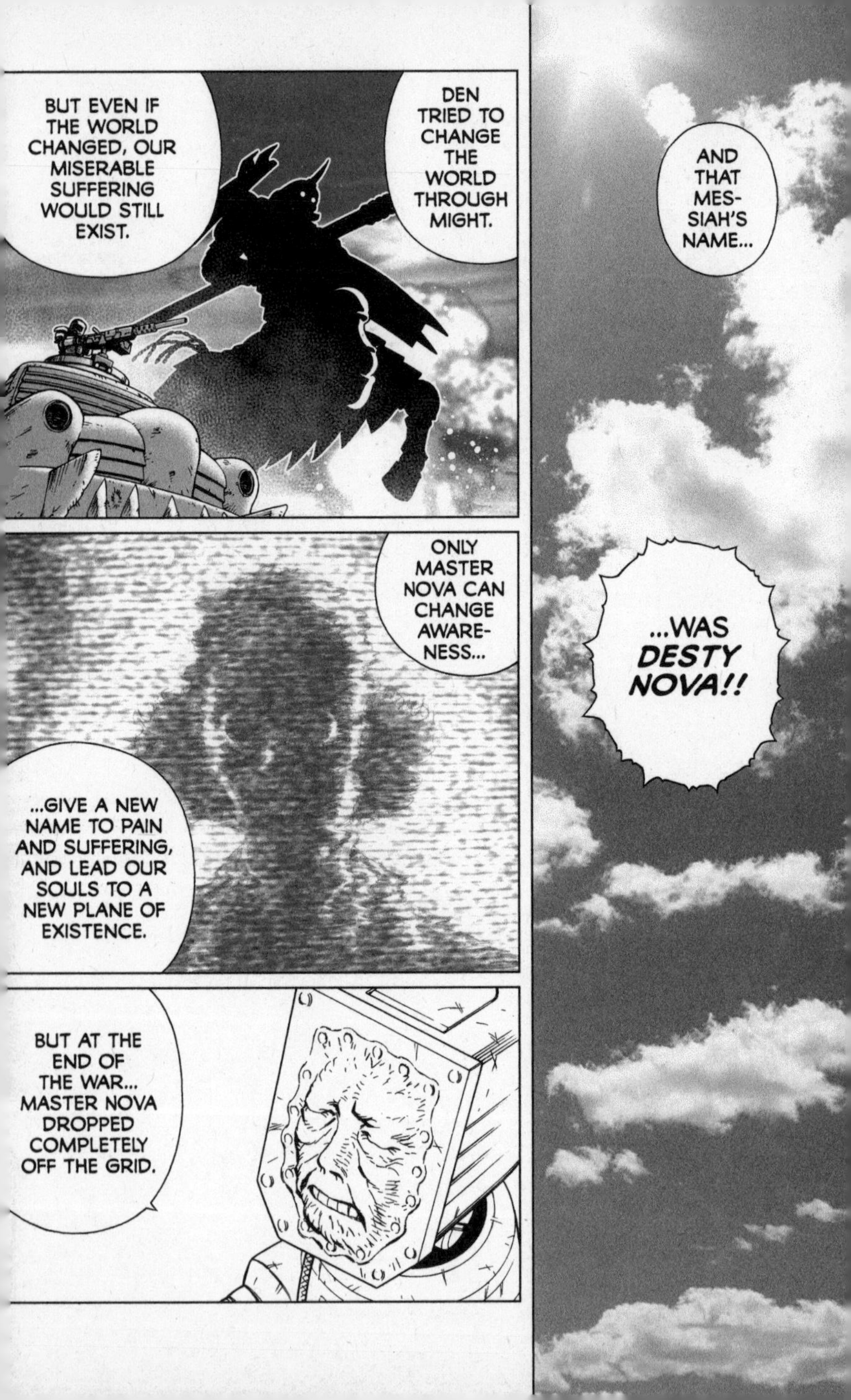
AND THAT MES-SIAH'S NAME...
...WAS *DESTY NOVA!!*
DEN TRIED TO CHANGE THE WORLD THROUGH MIGHT.
BUT EVEN IF THE WORLD CHANGED, OUR MISERABLE SUFFERING WOULD STILL EXIST.
ONLY MASTER NOVA CAN CHANGE AWARE-NESS...
...GIVE A NEW NAME TO PAIN AND SUFFERING, AND LEAD OUR SOULS TO A NEW PLANE OF EXISTENCE.
BUT AT THE END OF THE WAR... MASTER NOVA DROPPED COMPLETELY OFF THE GRID.

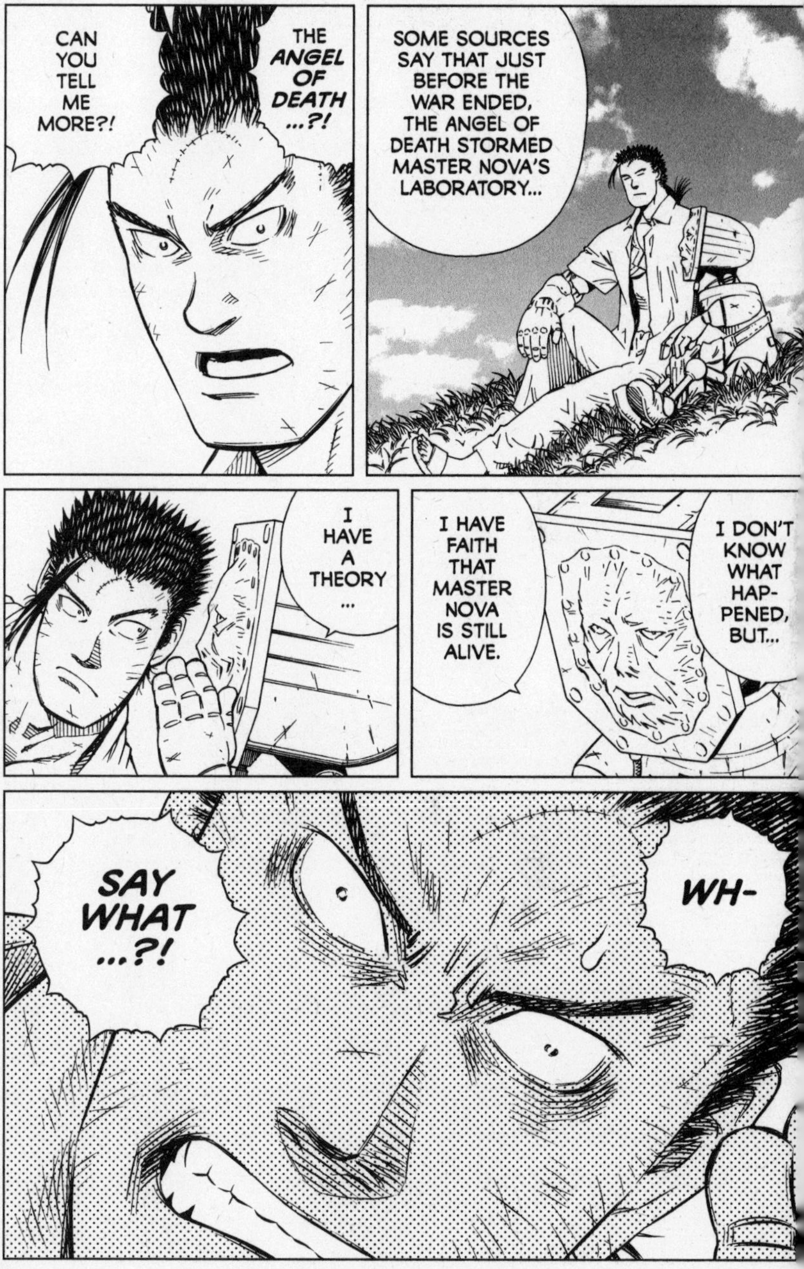
SOME SOURCES SAY THAT JUST BEFORE THE WAR ENDED, THE ANGEL OF DEATH STORMED MASTER NOVA'S LABORATORY...
THE *ANGEL OF DEATH* ...?!
CAN YOU TELL ME MORE?!
I DON'T KNOW WHAT HAP-PENED, BUT...
I HAVE FAITH THAT MASTER NOVA IS STILL ALIVE.
I HAVE A THEORY ...
WH-
SAY WHAT ...?!

Phase 110: Alita Quest IV

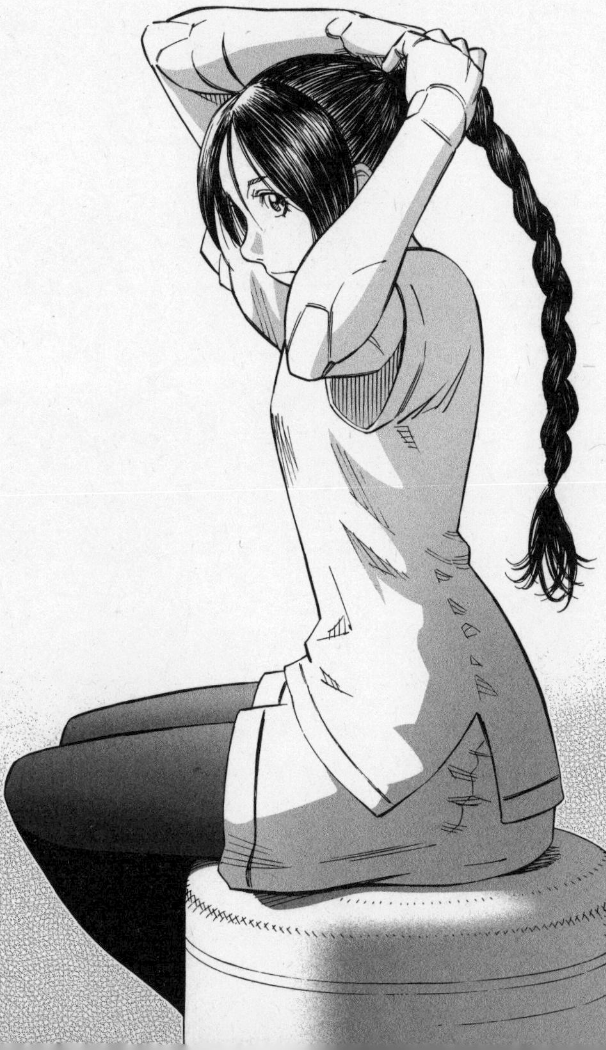

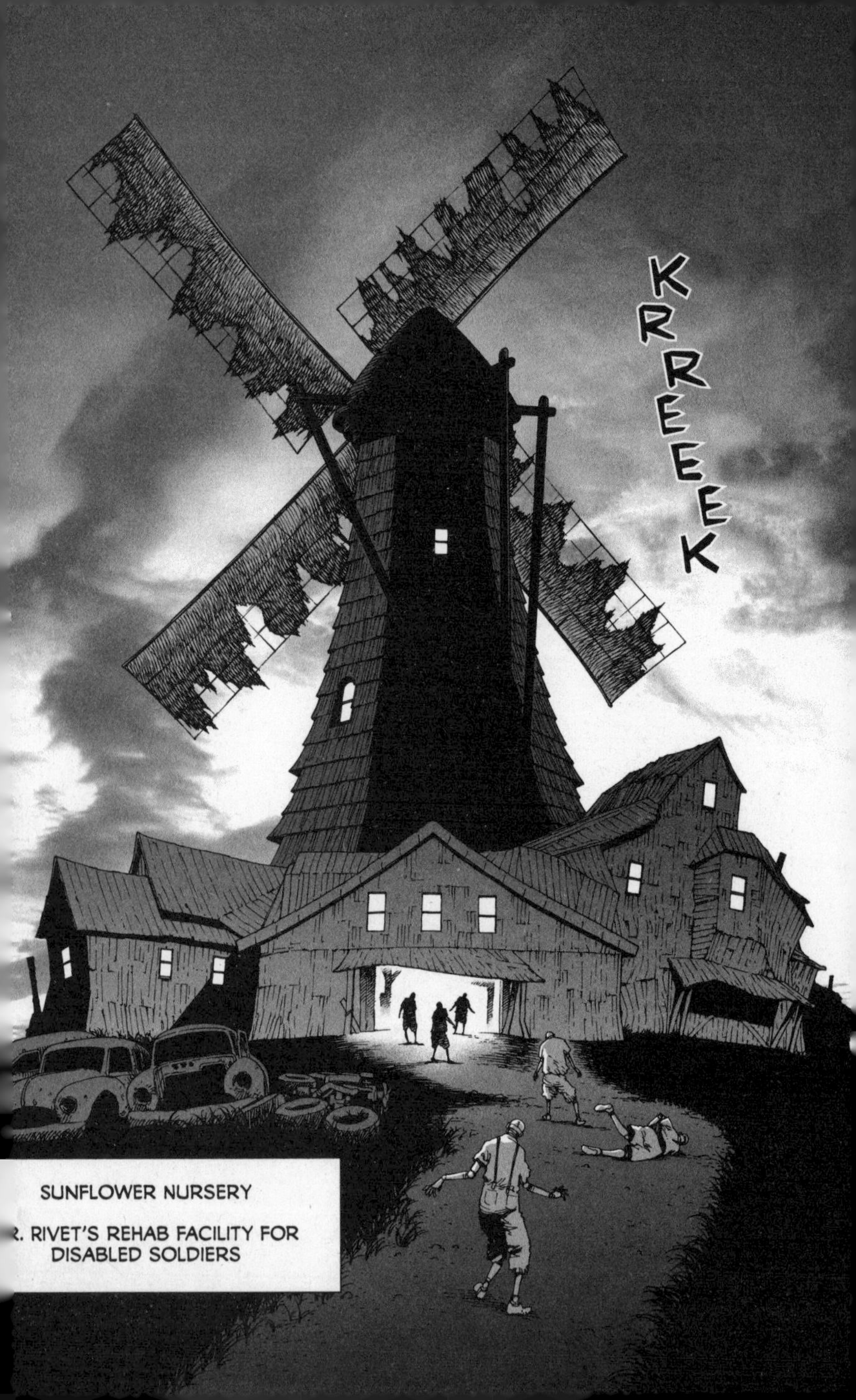
KRREEEK
SUNFLOWER NURSERY
R. RIVET'S REHAB FACILITY FOR DISABLED SOLDIERS

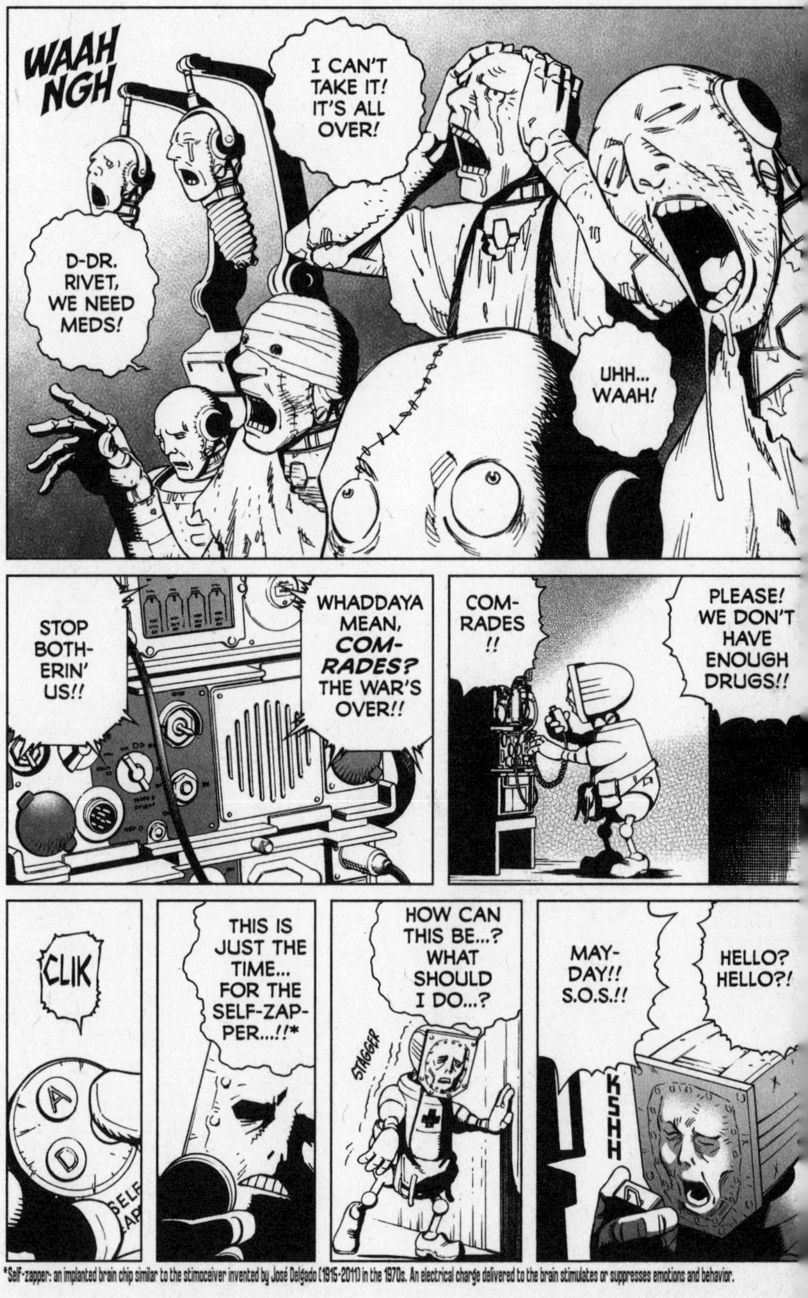
I CAN'T TAKE IT! IT'S ALL OVER!
WAAH NGH
UHH... WAAH!
D-DR. RIVET, WE NEED MEDS!
PLEASE! WE DON'T HAVE ENOUGH DRUGS!!
COM-RADES!!
WHADDAYA MEAN, COM-RADES? THE WAR'S OVER!!
STOP BOTH-ERIN' US!!
HELLO? HELLO?!
MAY-DAY!! S.O.S.!!
KSHH
HOW CAN THIS BE...? WHAT SHOULD I DO...?
STAGGER
THIS IS JUST THE TIME... FOR THE SELF-ZAPPER...!!*
CLIK
A
D
SELF ZAP

*Self-zapper: an implanted brain chip similar to the stimoceiver invented by José Delgado (1915-2011) in the 1970s. An electrical charge delivered to the brain stimulates or suppresses emotions and behavior.

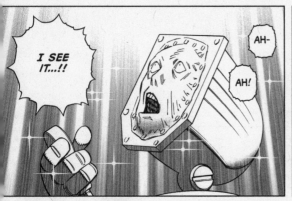

AH!
AH-
AH!
I SEE IT...!!
MEN!
MOCKED FOR BEING STRAGGLERS OF A LOSING ARMY, YOU ARE ORPHANS WITH NOWHERE TO GO!!
A REVELATION HAS TURNED MY HYPOTHESIS TO CONVICTION!
LEGEND SAYS...
...NOVA THE MESSIAH HAD TWO LOYAL SERVANTS!

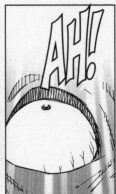

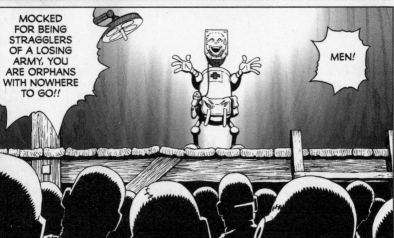

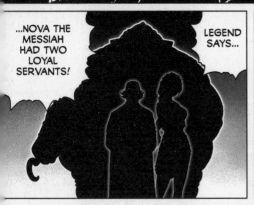

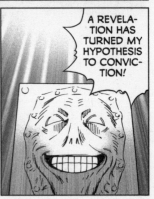

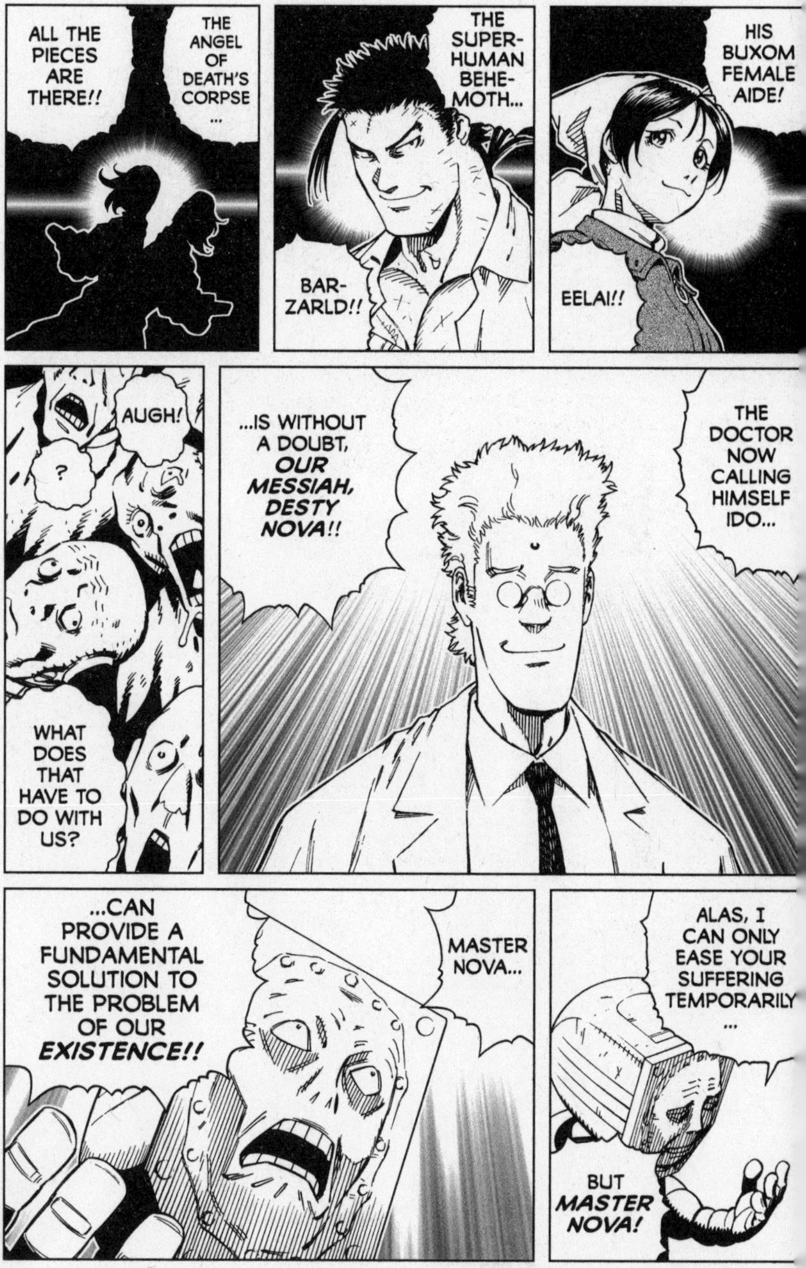
HIS BUXOM FEMALE AIDE!
EELAI!!
THE SUPERHUMAN BEHEMOTH...
BARZARLD!!
THE ANGEL OF DEATH'S CORPSE...
ALL THE PIECES ARE THERE!!
THE DOCTOR NOW CALLING HIMSELF IDO...
...IS WITHOUT A DOUBT, ***OUR MESSIAH, DESTY NOVA!!***
AUGH!
?
WHAT DOES THAT HAVE TO DO WITH US?
ALAS, I CAN ONLY EASE YOUR SUFFERING TEMPORARILY...
BUT ***MASTER NOVA!***
MASTER NOVA...
...CAN PROVIDE A FUNDAMENTAL SOLUTION TO THE PROBLEM OF OUR ***EXISTENCE!!***

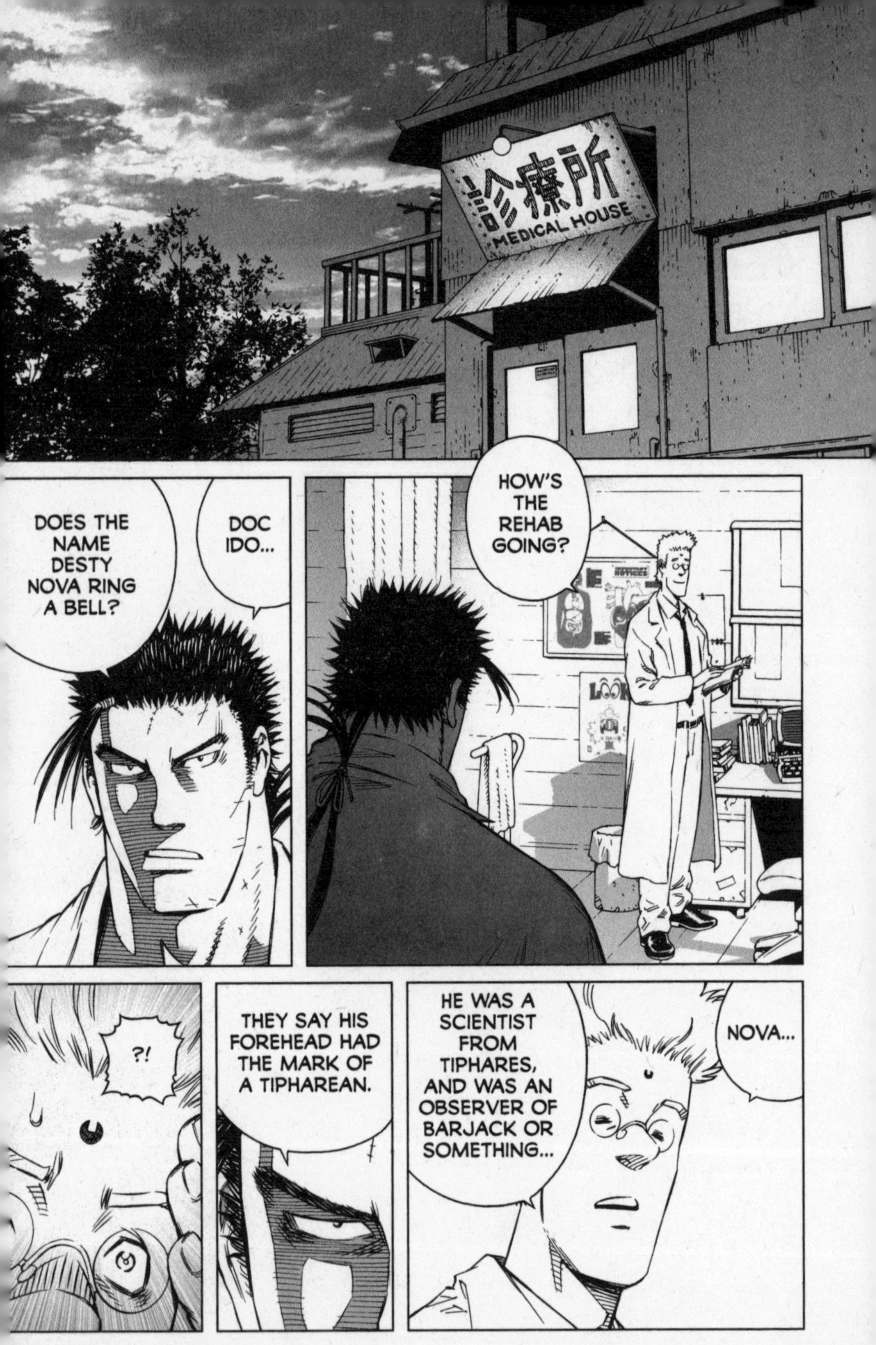
診療所
MEDICAL HOUSE
HOW'S THE REHAB GOING?
DOC IDO...
DOES THE NAME DESTY NOVA RING A BELL?
NOVA...
HE WAS A SCIENTIST FROM TIPHARES, AND WAS AN OBSERVER OF BARJACK OR SOMETHING...
THEY SAY HIS FOREHEAD HAD THE MARK OF A TIPHAREAN.
?!

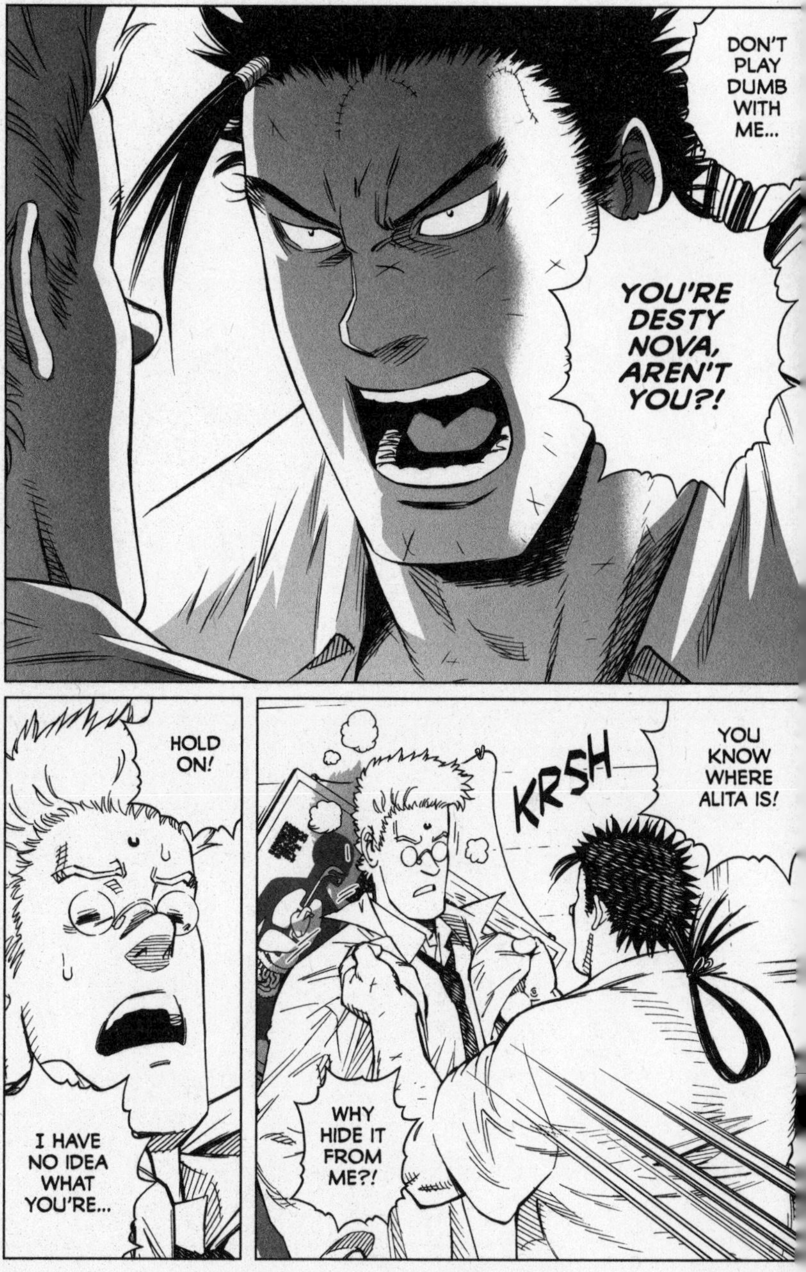
DON'T PLAY DUMB WITH ME...
YOU'RE DESTY NOVA, AREN'T YOU?!
YOU KNOW WHERE ALITA IS!
KRSH
WHY HIDE IT FROM ME?!
HOLD ON!
I HAVE NO IDEA WHAT YOU'RE...

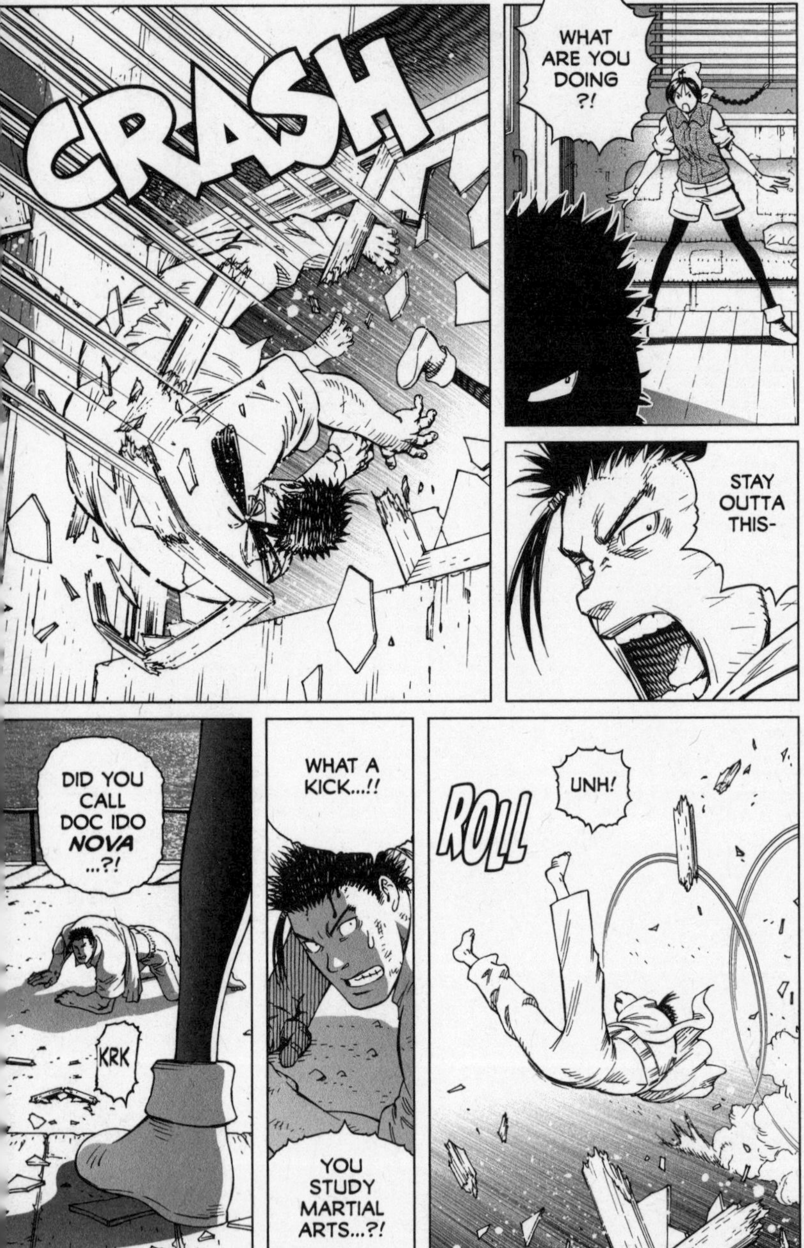
WHAT ARE YOU DOING ?!
STAY OUTTA THIS-
CRASH
UNH!
ROLL
WHAT A KICK...!!
YOU STUDY MARTIAL ARTS...?!
DID YOU CALL DOC IDO *NOVA* ...?!
KRK

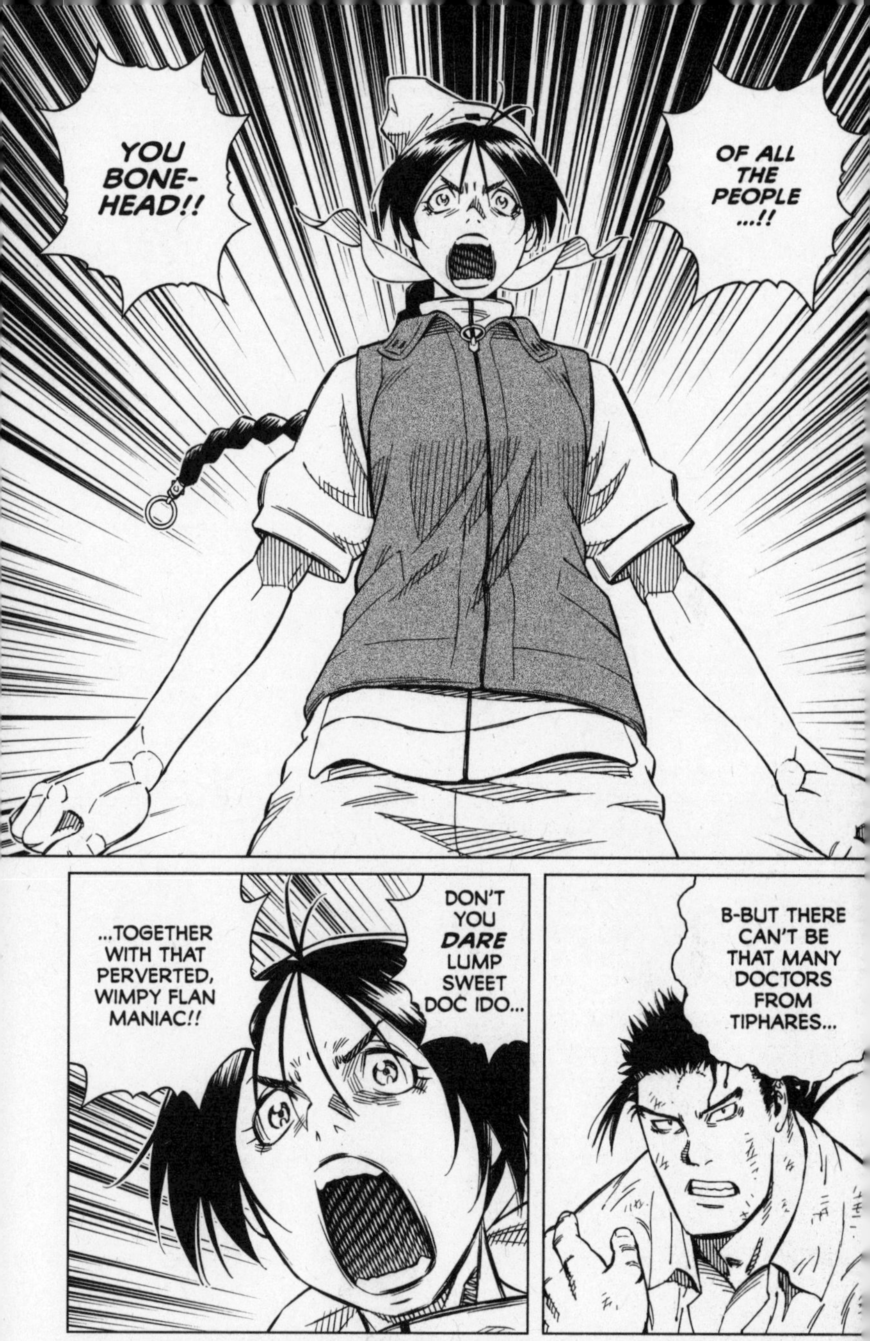
OF ALL THE PEOPLE ...!!
YOU BONE-HEAD!!
B-BUT THERE CAN'T BE THAT MANY DOCTORS FROM TIPHARES...
DON'T YOU DARE LUMP SWEET DOC IDO...
...TOGETHER WITH THAT PERVERTED, WIMPY FLAN MANIAC!!

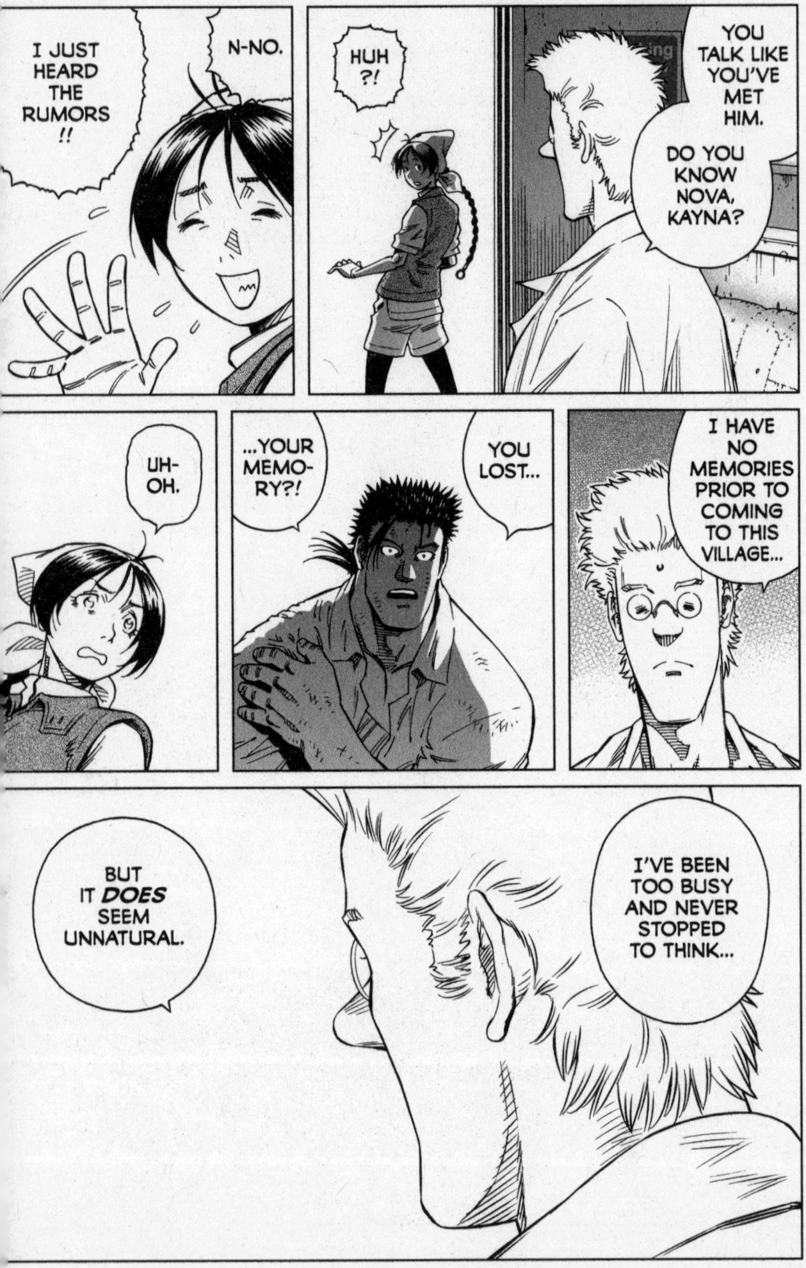
YOU TALK LIKE YOU'VE MET HIM.
DO YOU KNOW NOVA, KAYNA?
HUH ?!
N-NO.
I JUST HEARD THE RUMORS !!
I HAVE NO MEMORIES PRIOR TO COMING TO THIS VILLAGE...
YOU LOST...
...YOUR MEMORY?!
UH-OH.
I'VE BEEN TOO BUSY AND NEVER STOPPED TO THINK...
BUT IT *DOES* SEEM UNNATURAL.

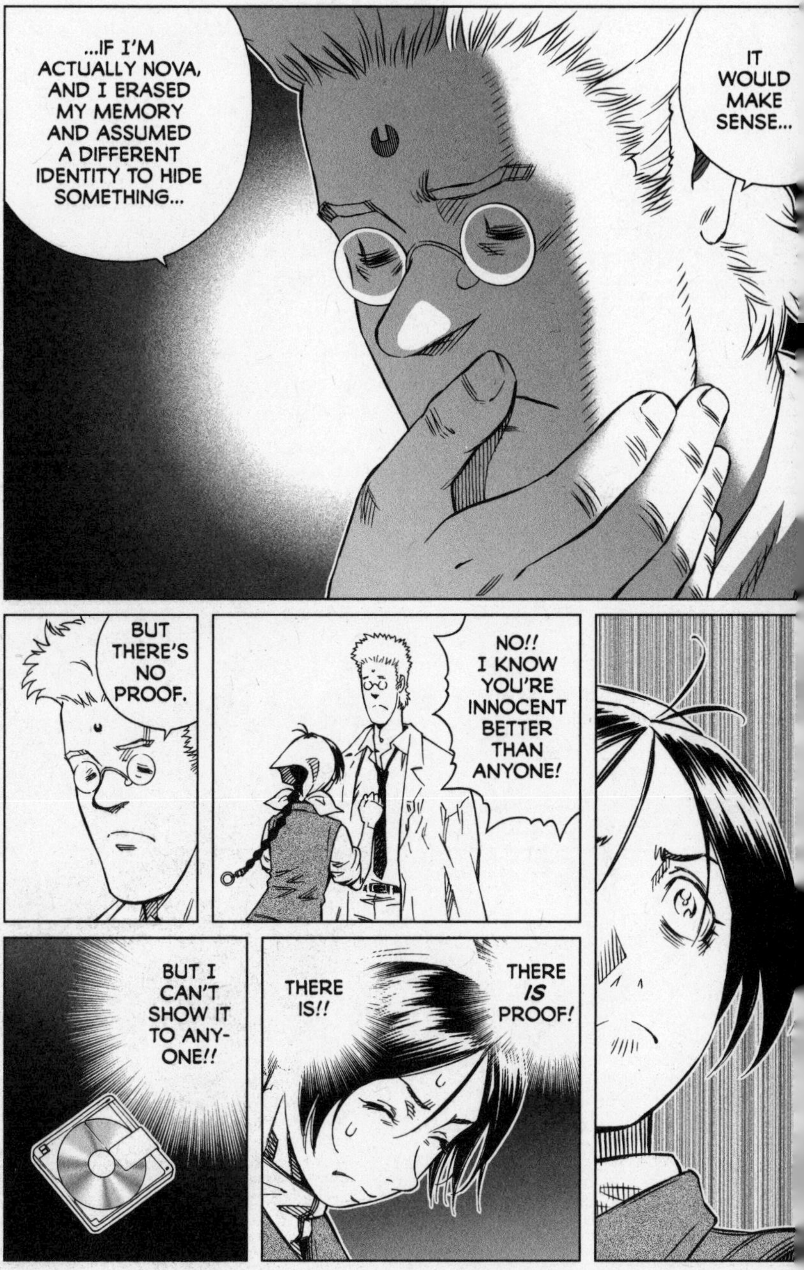
IT WOULD MAKE SENSE...
...IF I'M ACTUALLY NOVA, AND I ERASED MY MEMORY AND ASSUMED A DIFFERENT IDENTITY TO HIDE SOMETHING...
NO!! I KNOW YOU'RE INNOCENT BETTER THAN ANYONE!
BUT THERE'S NO PROOF.
THERE *IS* PROOF!
THERE IS!!
BUT I CAN'T SHOW IT TO ANY-ONE!!

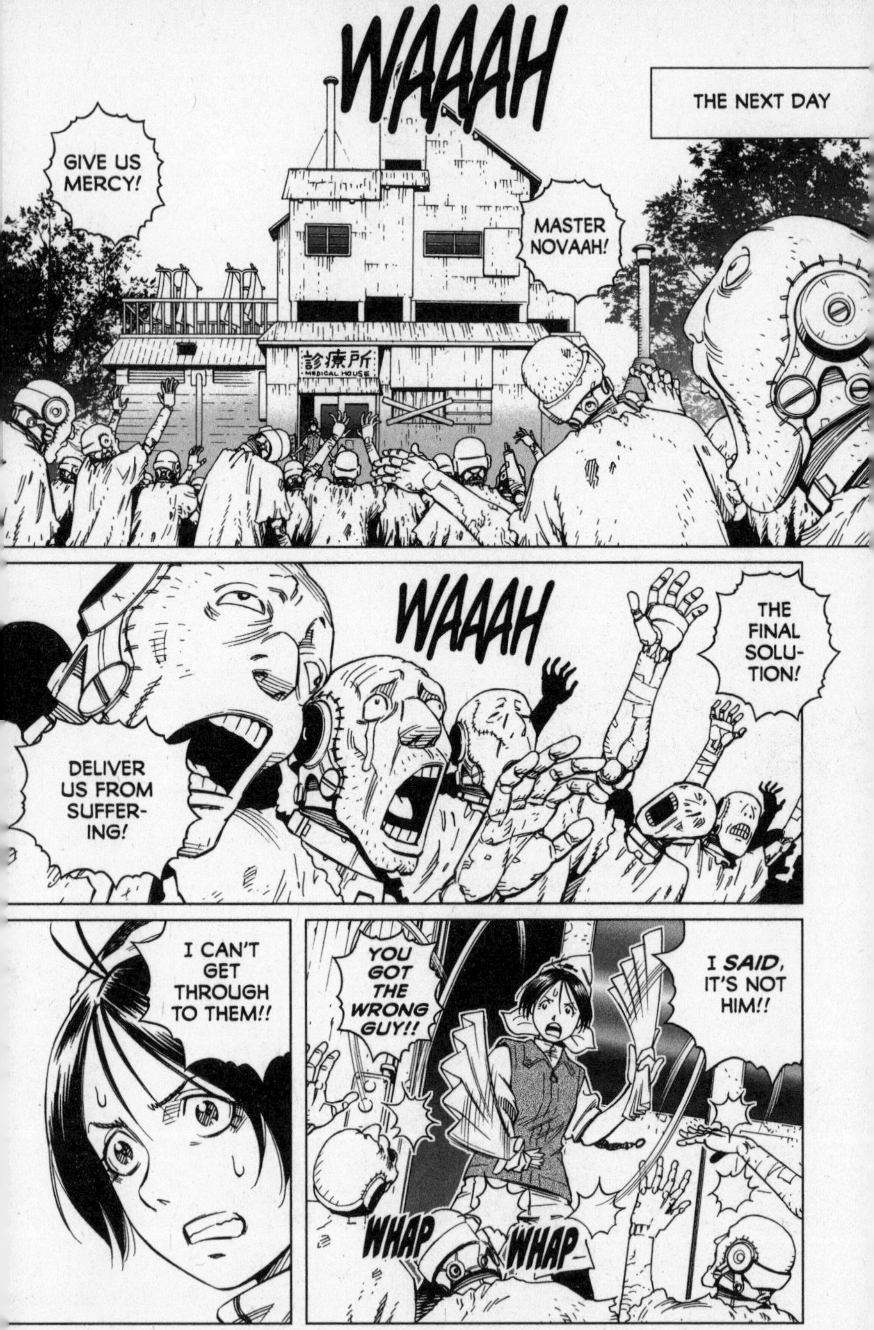
THE NEXT DAY
WAAAH
MASTER NOVAAH!
GIVE US MERCY!
THE FINAL SOLUTION!
WAAAH
DELIVER US FROM SUFFERING!
I SAID, IT'S NOT HIM!!
YOU GOT THE WRONG GUY!!
WHAP
WHAP
I CAN'T GET THROUGH TO THEM!!

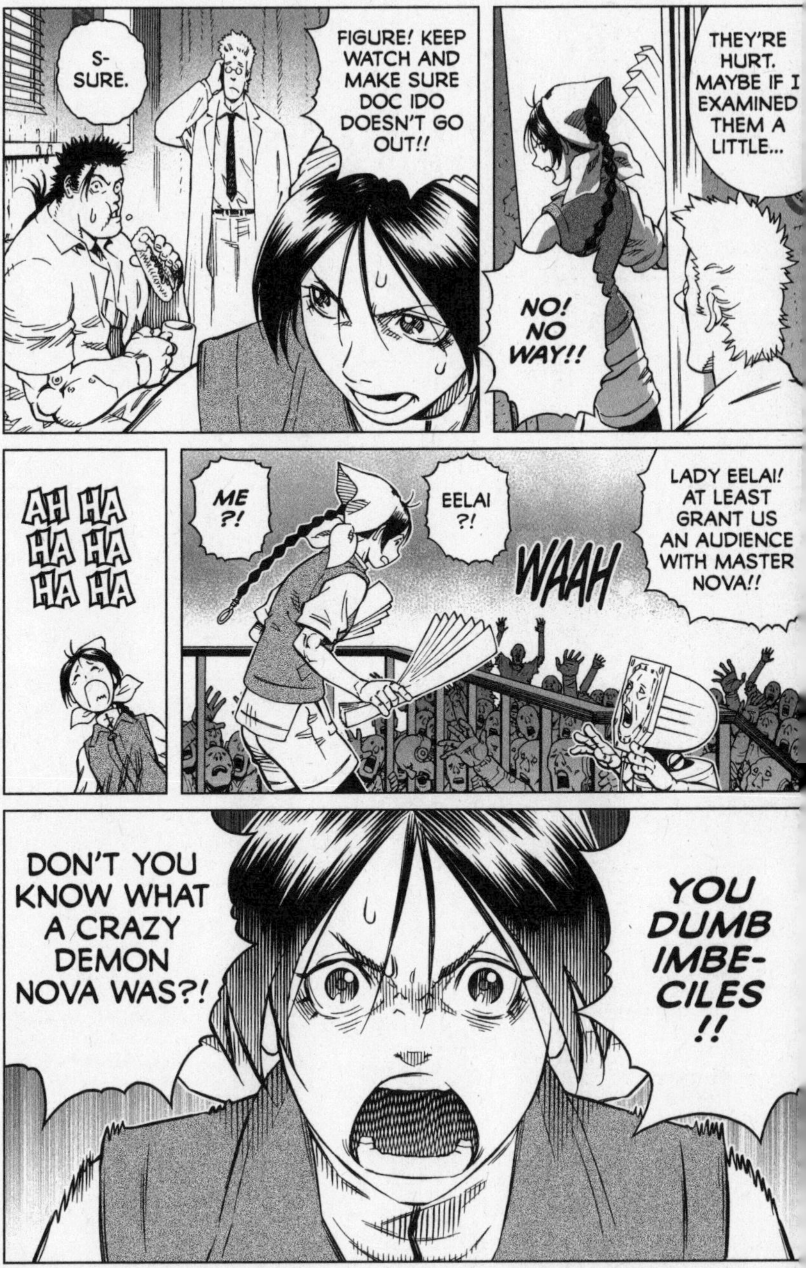
THEY'RE HURT. MAYBE IF I EXAMINED THEM A LITTLE...
NO! NO WAY!!
FIGURE! KEEP WATCH AND MAKE SURE DOC IDO DOESN'T GO OUT!!
S- SURE.
LADY EELAI! AT LEAST GRANT US AN AUDIENCE WITH MASTER NOVA!!
WAAH
EELAI ?!
ME ?!
AH HA HA HA HA HA
YOU DUMB IMBE- CILES !!
DON'T YOU KNOW WHAT A CRAZY DEMON NOVA WAS?!

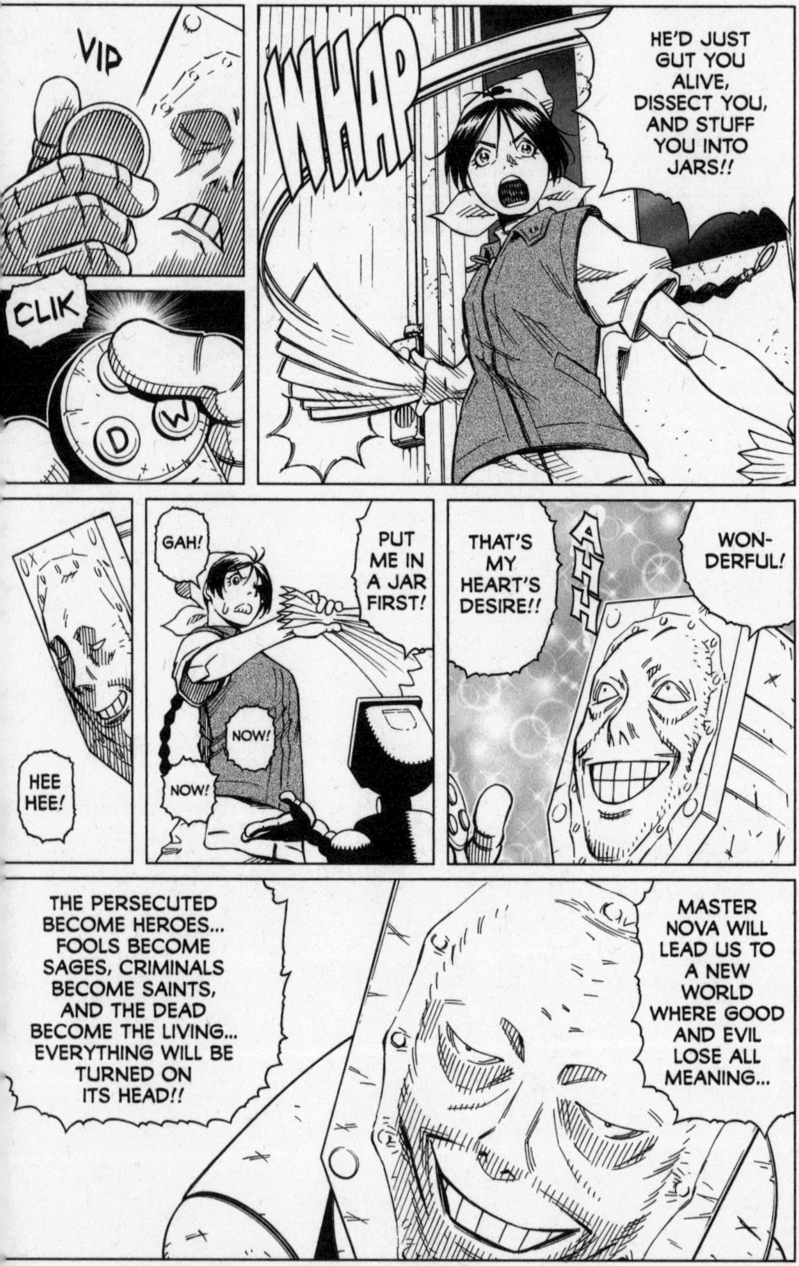
HE'D JUST GUT YOU ALIVE, DISSECT YOU, AND STUFF YOU INTO JARS!!
WHAP
VIP
CLIK
WON-DERFUL!
AHHH
THAT'S MY HEART'S DESIRE!!
PUT ME IN A JAR FIRST!
GAH!
NOW!
NOW!
HEE HEE!
MASTER NOVA WILL LEAD US TO A NEW WORLD WHERE GOOD AND EVIL LOSE ALL MEANING...
THE PERSECUTED BECOME HEROES... FOOLS BECOME SAGES, CRIMINALS BECOME SAINTS, AND THE DEAD BECOME THE LIVING... EVERYTHING WILL BE TURNED ON ITS HEAD!!

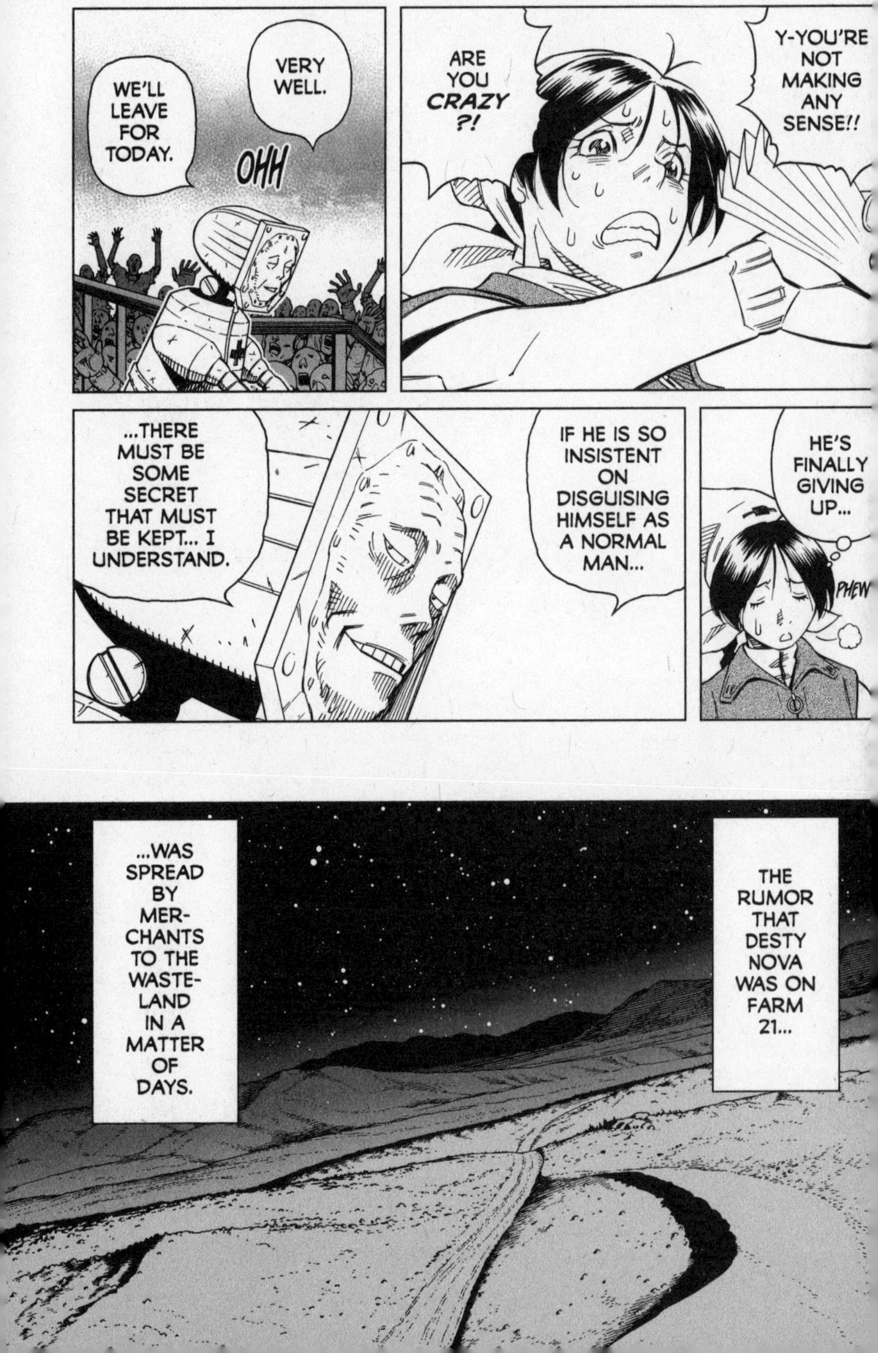
Y-YOU'RE NOT MAKING ANY SENSE!!
ARE YOU CRAZY?!
VERY WELL.
WE'LL LEAVE FOR TODAY.
OHH
HE'S FINALLY GIVING UP...
PHEW
IF HE IS SO INSISTENT ON DISGUISING HIMSELF AS A NORMAL MAN...
...THERE MUST BE SOME SECRET THAT MUST BE KEPT... I UNDERSTAND.
THE RUMOR THAT DESTY NOVA WAS ON FARM 21...
...WAS SPREAD BY MER-CHANTS TO THE WASTE-LAND IN A MATTER OF DAYS.

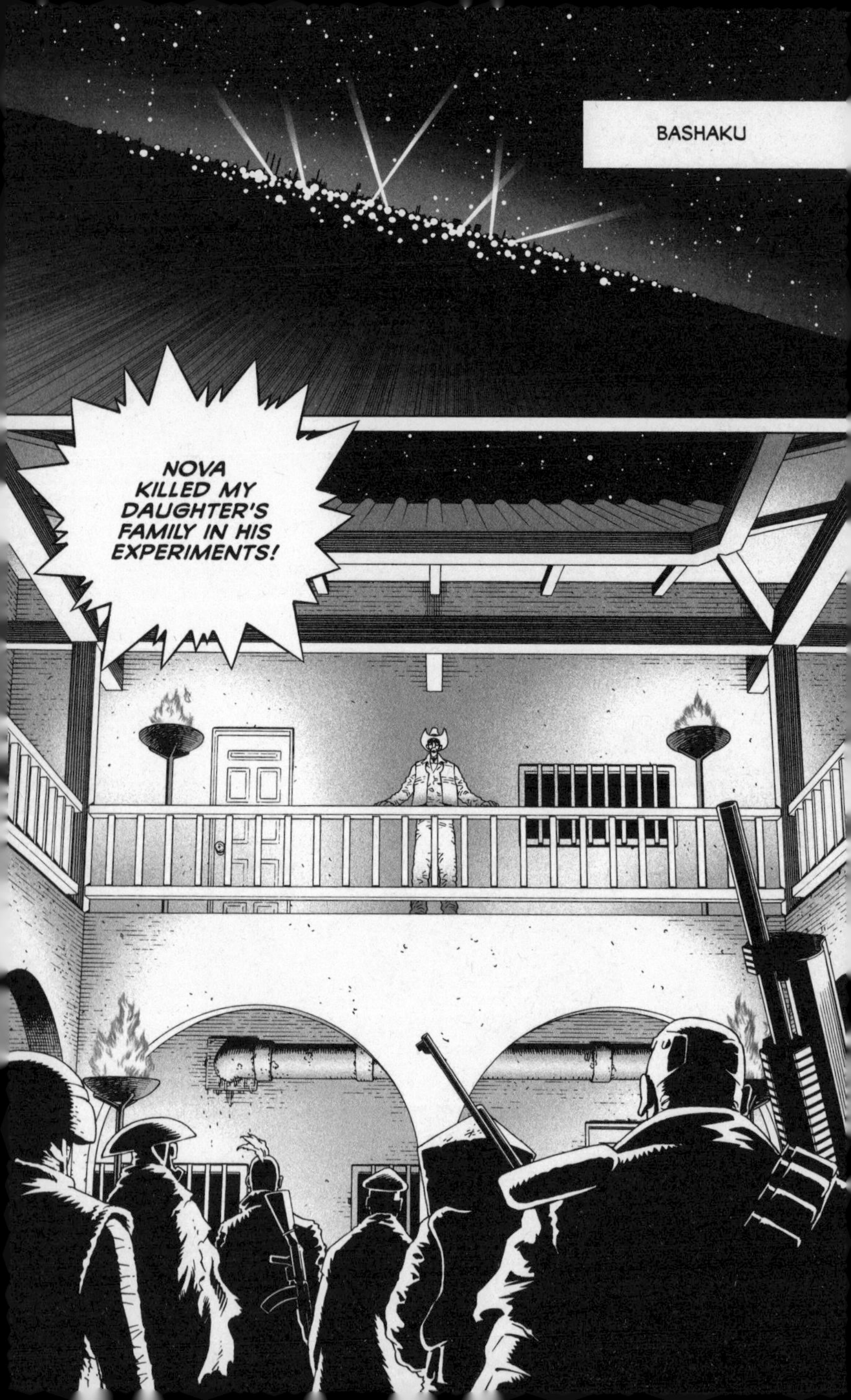
BASHAKU
NOVA KILLED MY DAUGHTER'S FAMILY IN HIS EXPERIMENTS!

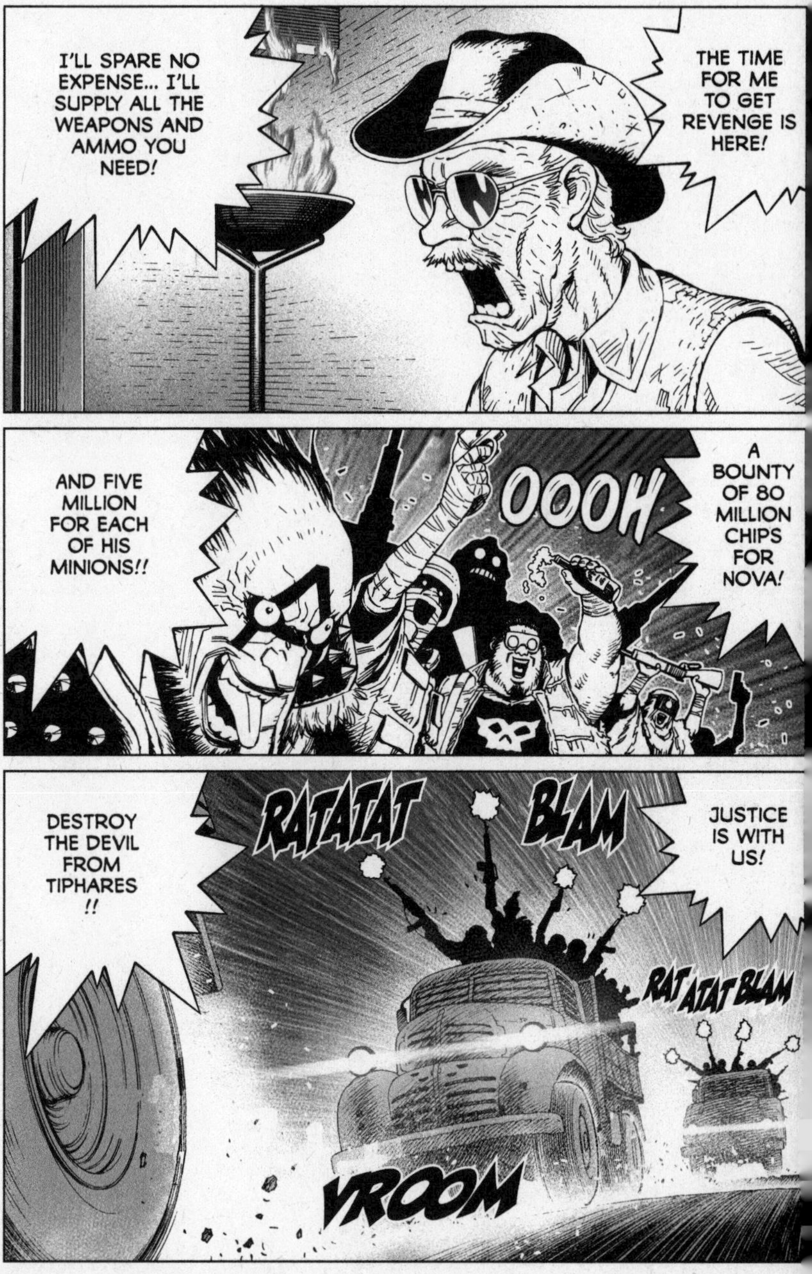
THE TIME FOR ME TO GET REVENGE IS HERE!
I'LL SPARE NO EXPENSE... I'LL SUPPLY ALL THE WEAPONS AND AMMO YOU NEED!
A BOUNTY OF 80 MILLION CHIPS FOR NOVA!
OOOH
AND FIVE MILLION FOR EACH OF HIS MINIONS!!
JUSTICE IS WITH US!
BLAM
RATATAT
DESTROY THE DEVIL FROM TIPHARES !!
RAT ATAT BLAM
VROOM

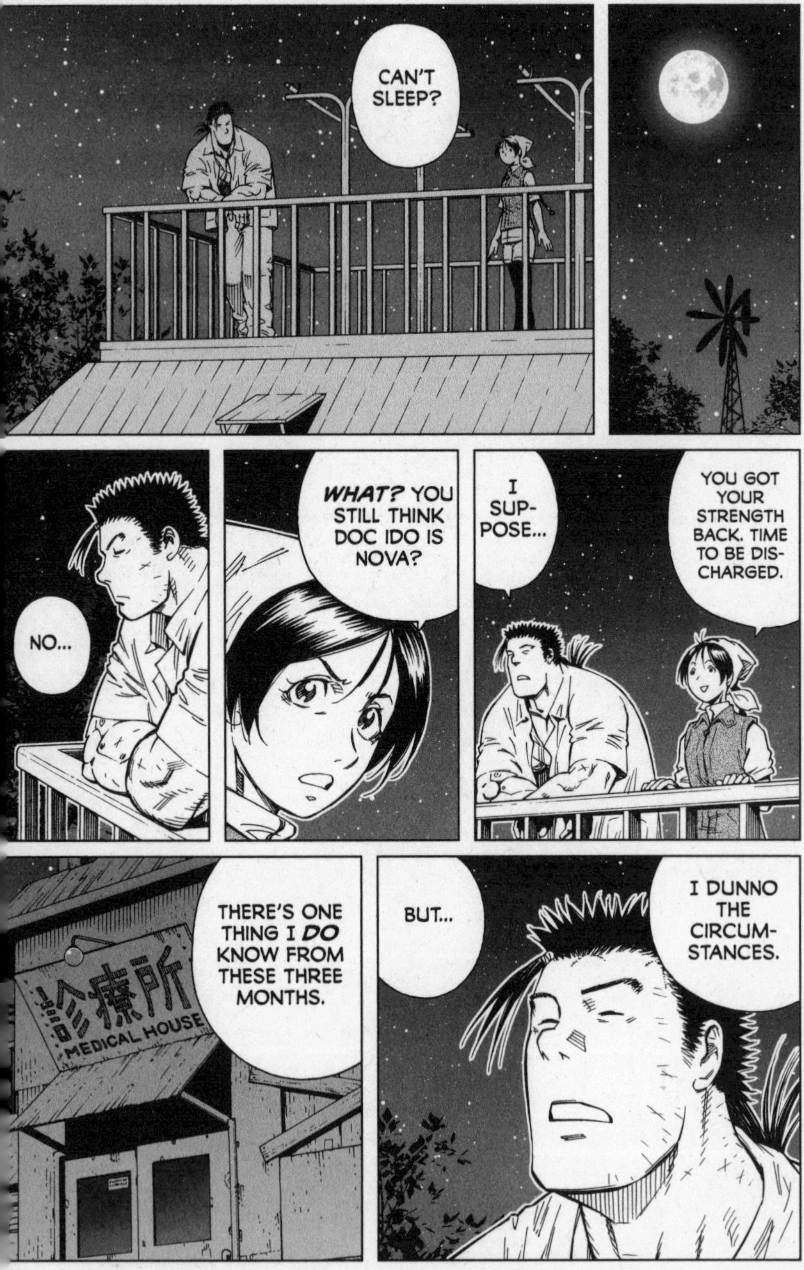
CAN'T SLEEP?
YOU GOT YOUR STRENGTH BACK. TIME TO BE DIS-CHARGED.
I SUP-POSE...
WHAT? YOU STILL THINK DOC IDO IS NOVA?
NO...
I DUNNO THE CIRCUM-STANCES.
BUT...
THERE'S ONE THING I *DO* KNOW FROM THESE THREE MONTHS.
診療所
MEDICAL HOUSE

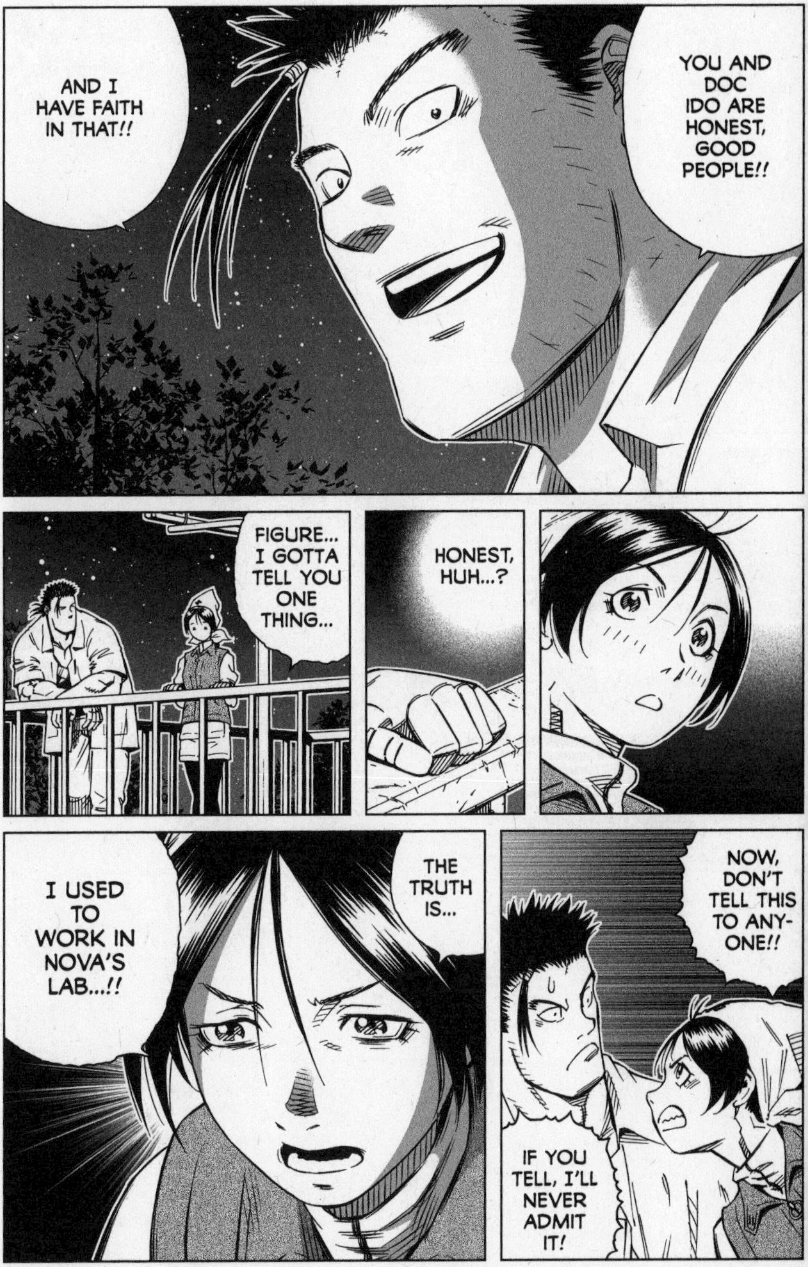
YOU AND DOC IDO ARE HONEST, GOOD PEOPLE!!
AND I HAVE FAITH IN THAT!!
HONEST, HUH...?
FIGURE... I GOTTA TELL YOU ONE THING...
NOW, DON'T TELL THIS TO ANY-ONE!!
IF YOU TELL, I'LL NEVER ADMIT IT!
THE TRUTH IS...
I USED TO WORK IN NOVA'S LAB...!!

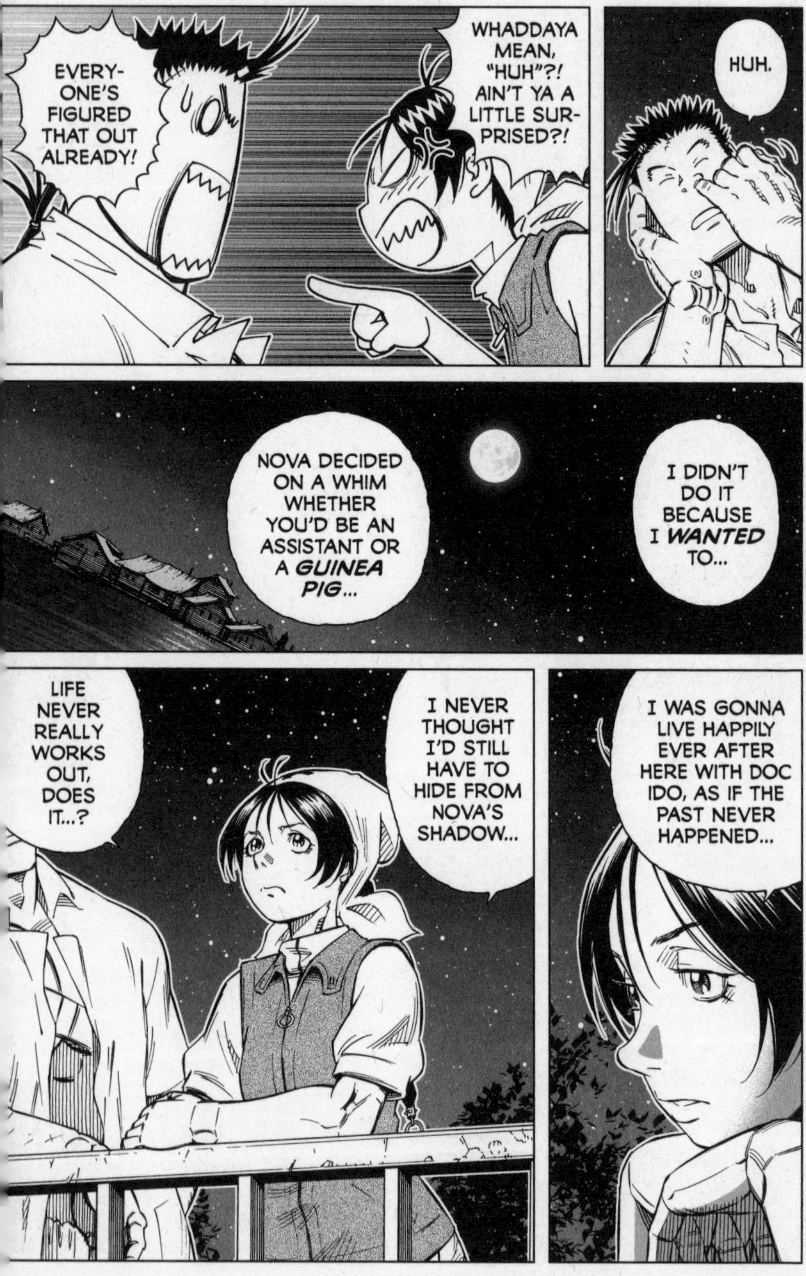
HUH.
WHADDAYA MEAN, "HUH"?! AIN'T YA A LITTLE SUR-PRISED?!
EVERY-ONE'S FIGURED THAT OUT ALREADY!
I DIDN'T DO IT BECAUSE I *WANTED* TO...
NOVA DECIDED ON A WHIM WHETHER YOU'D BE AN ASSISTANT OR A *GUINEA PIG*...
I WAS GONNA LIVE HAPPILY EVER AFTER HERE WITH DOC IDO, AS IF THE PAST NEVER HAPPENED...
I NEVER THOUGHT I'D STILL HAVE TO HIDE FROM NOVA'S SHADOW...
LIFE NEVER REALLY WORKS OUT, DOES IT...?

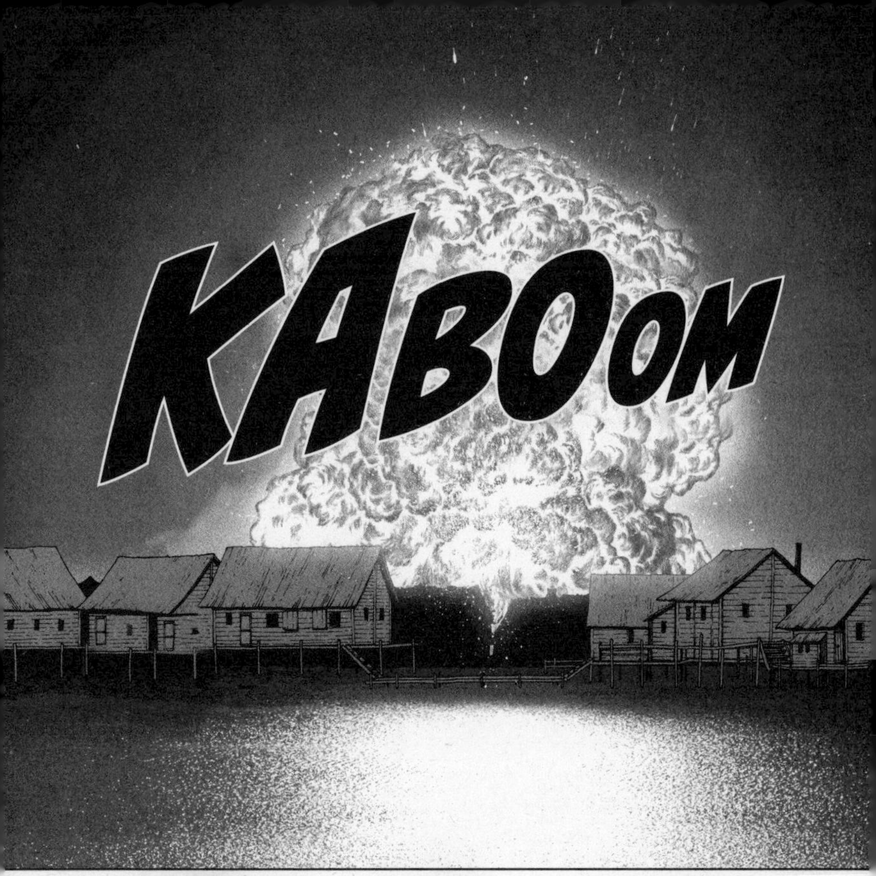
KABOOM

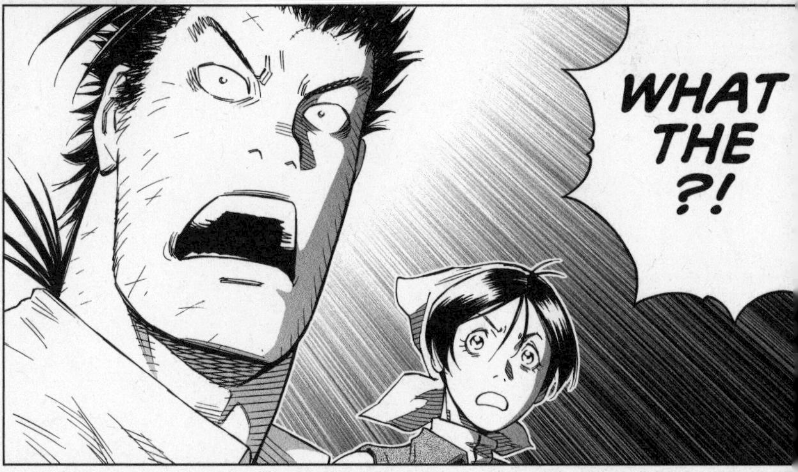
WHAT THE ?!

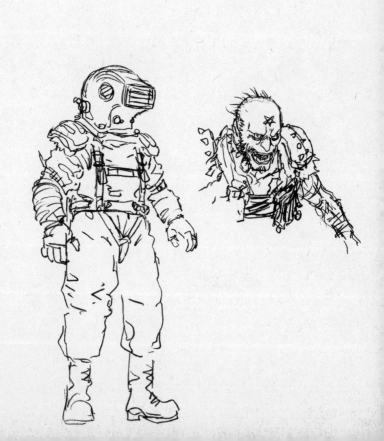

Phase 111: Alita Quest V

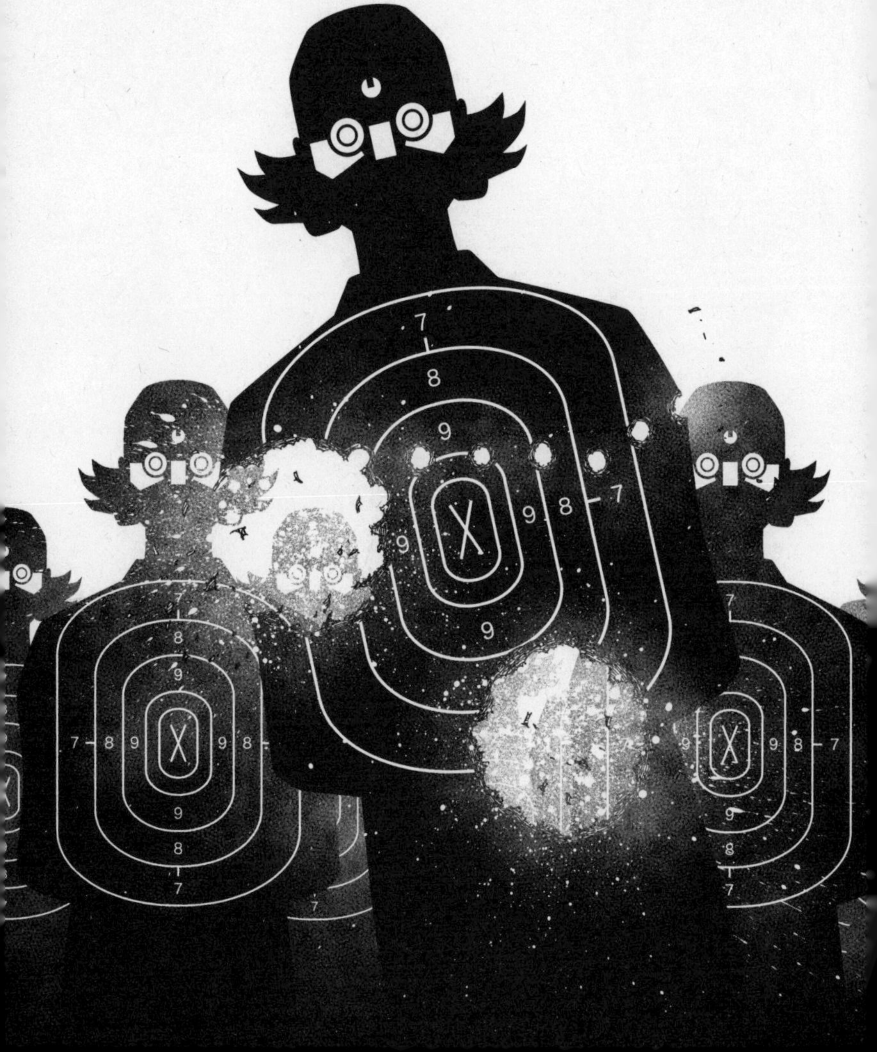
7
8
9
9
9 8 7
9
7
8
9
7 8 9
9 8
9
8
7
7
9
9 8 7
9
8
7

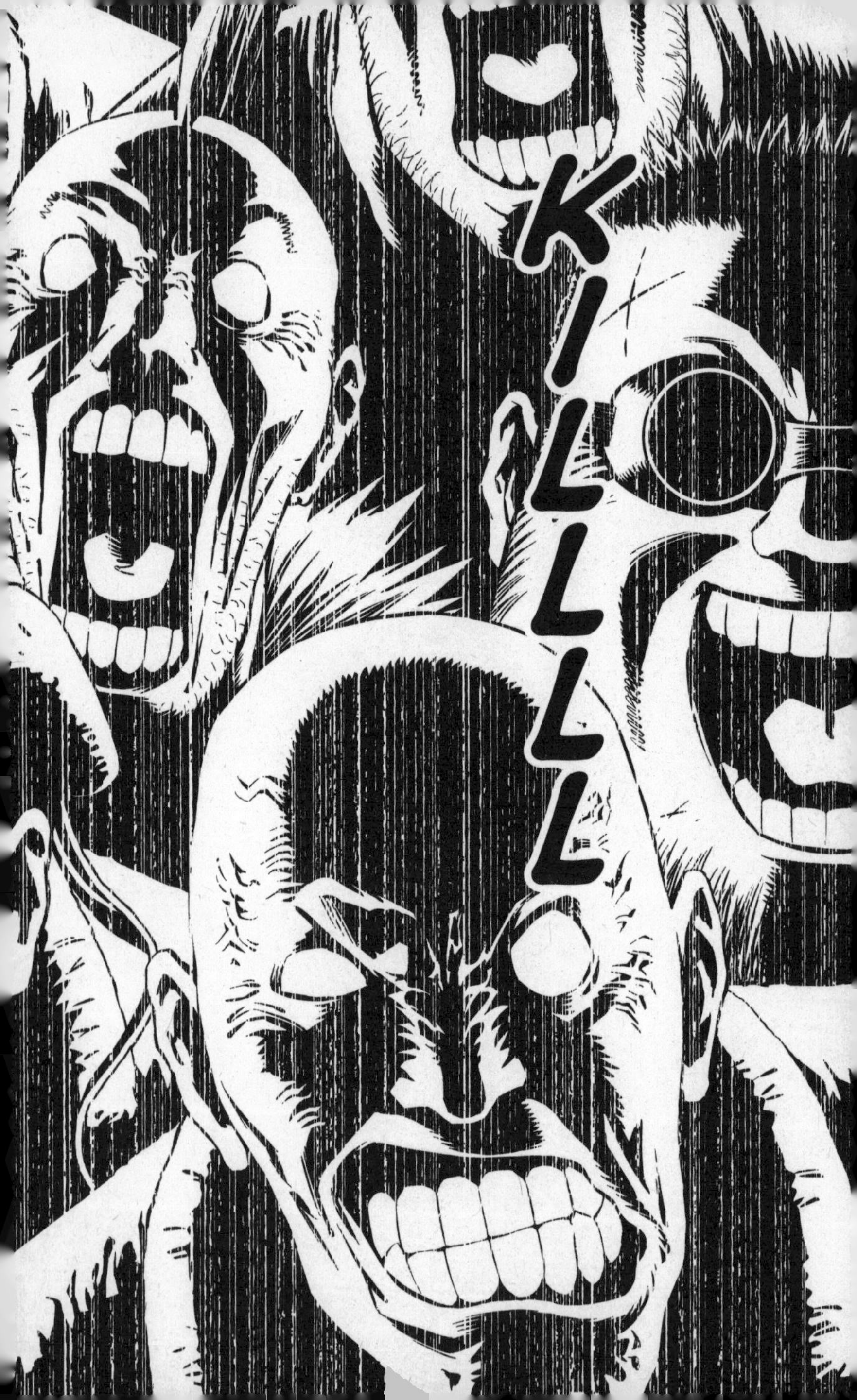
KILLLLL

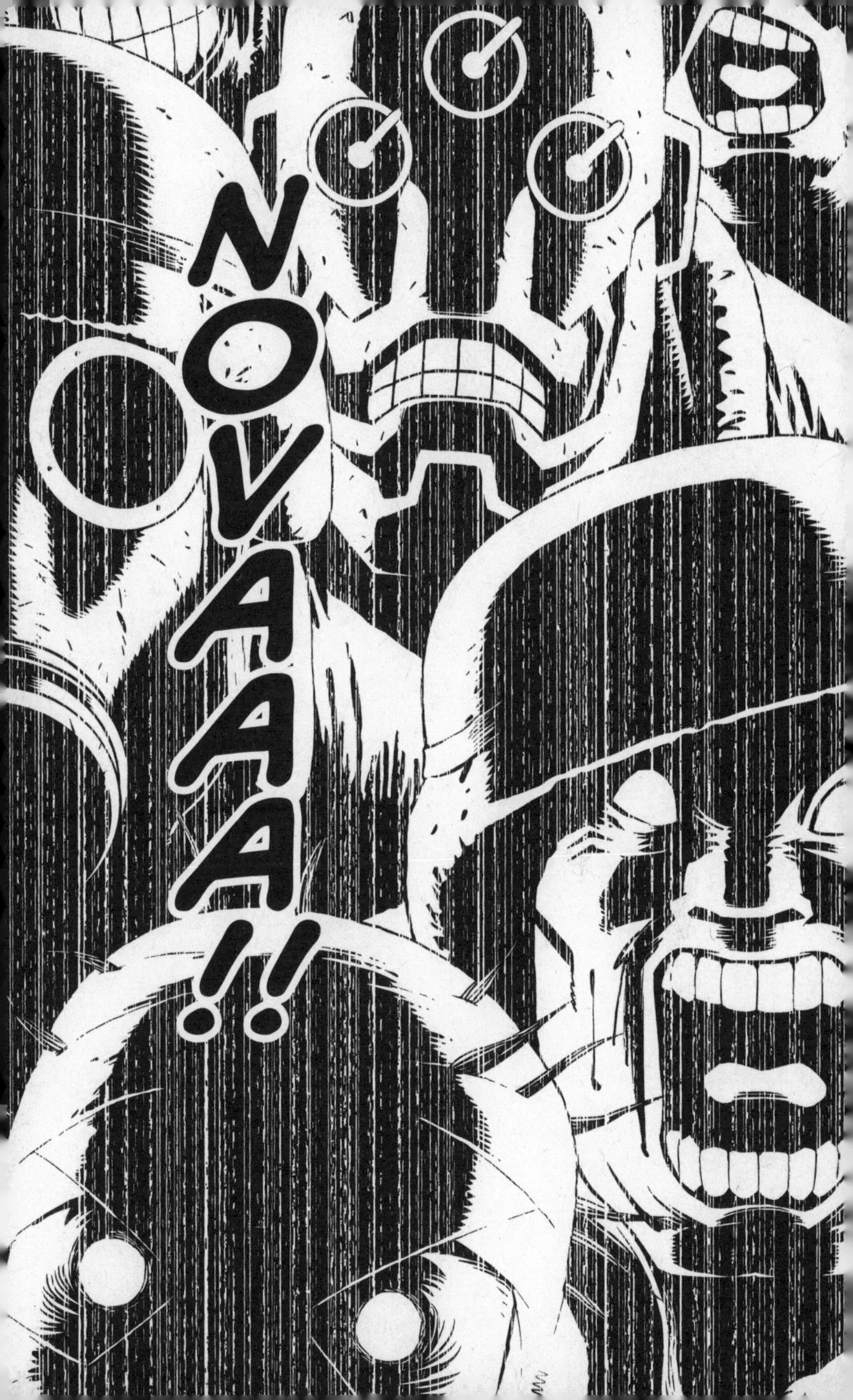
NOVAAA!!

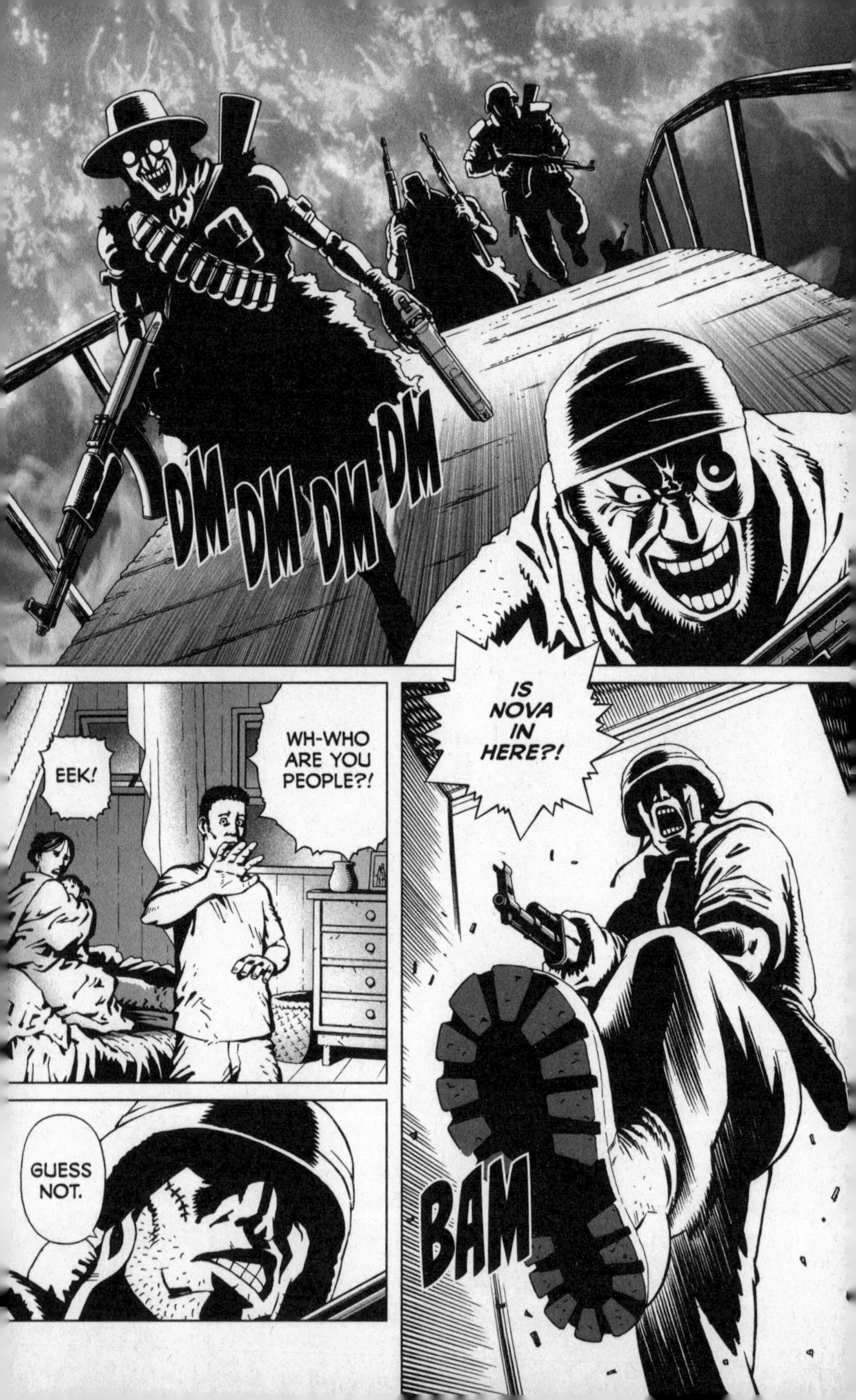
DM DM DM DM
IS NOVA IN HERE?!
BAM
WH-WHO ARE YOU PEOPLE?!
EEK!
GUESS NOT.

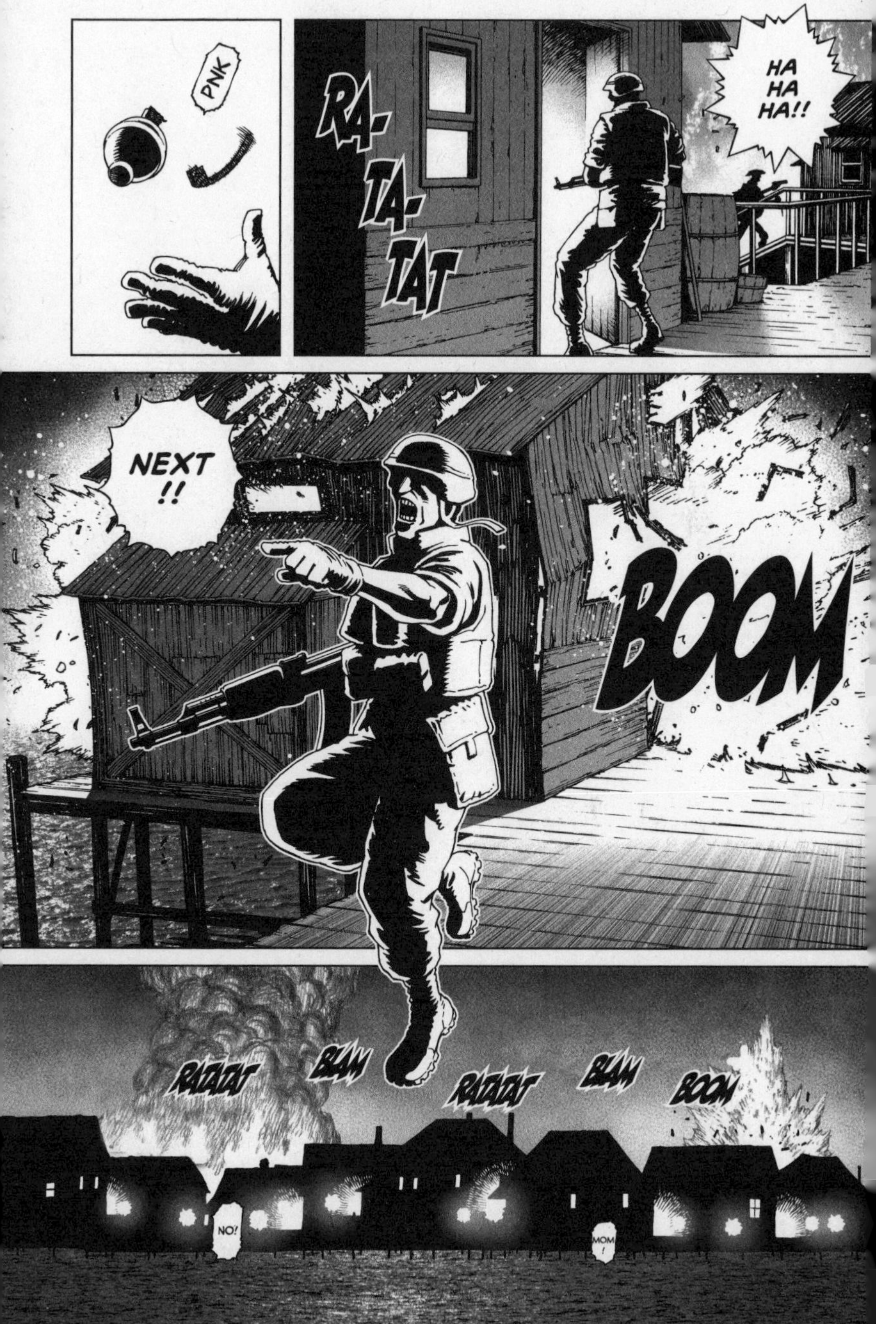
HA HA HA!!
RA-TA-TAT
PNK
NEXT !!
BOOM
BOOM
BLAM
RATATAT
BLAM
RATATAT
MOM!
NO!

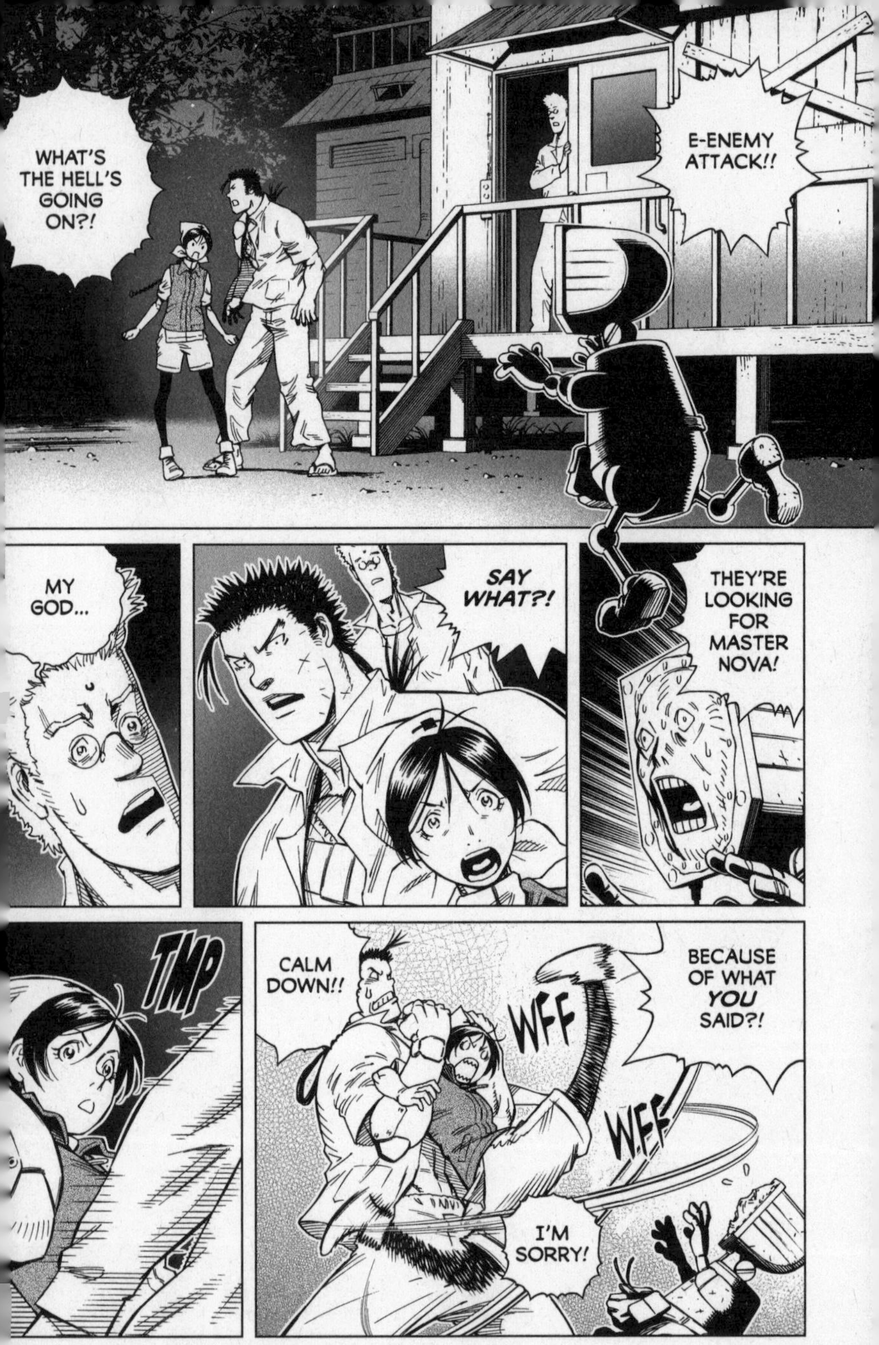
E-ENEMY ATTACK!!
WHAT'S THE HELL'S GOING ON?!
THEY'RE LOOKING FOR MASTER NOVA!
SAY WHAT?!
MY GOD...
BECAUSE OF WHAT YOU SAID?!
CALM DOWN!!
WFF
WFF
I'M SORRY!
TMP

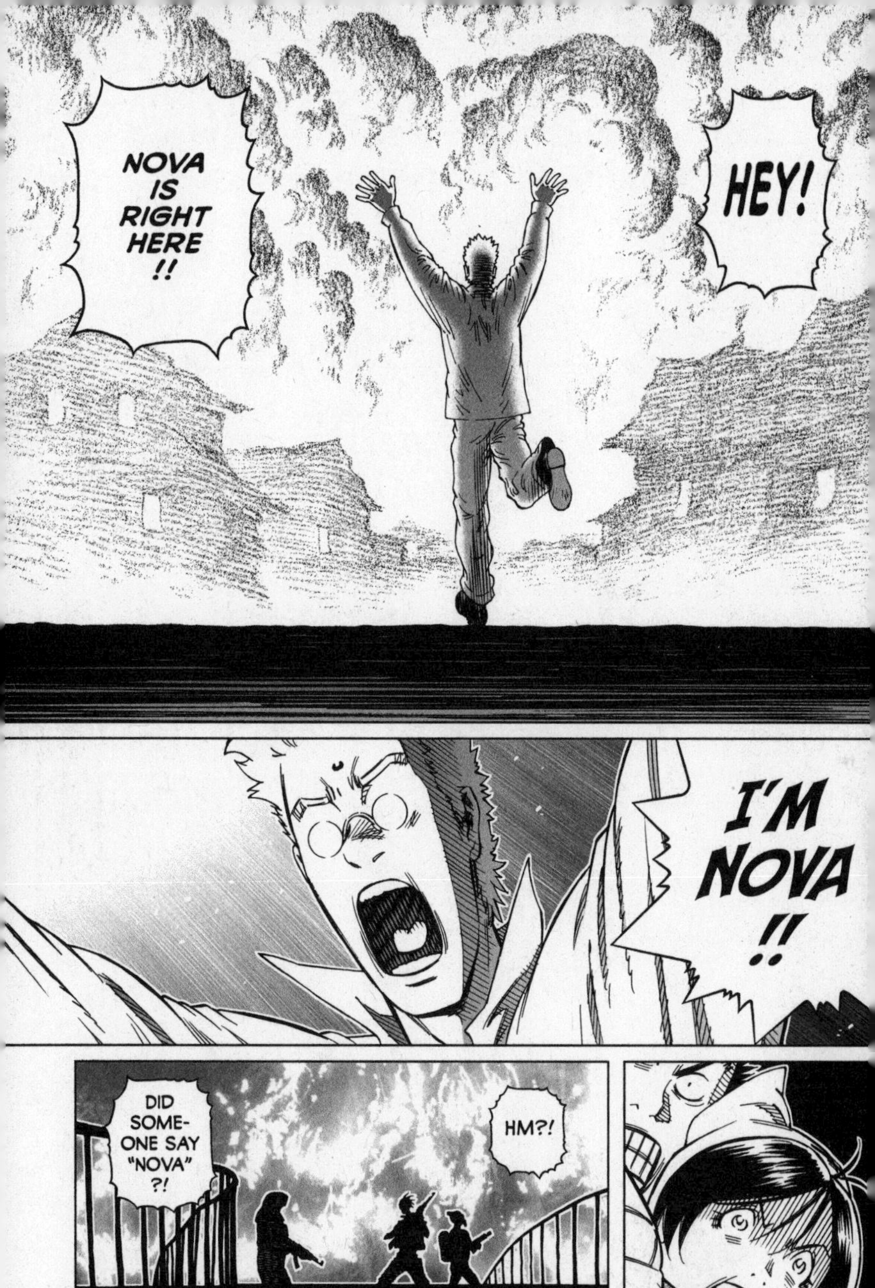
HEY!
NOVA IS RIGHT HERE !!
I'M NOVA !!
HM?!
DID SOME-ONE SAY "NOVA" ?!

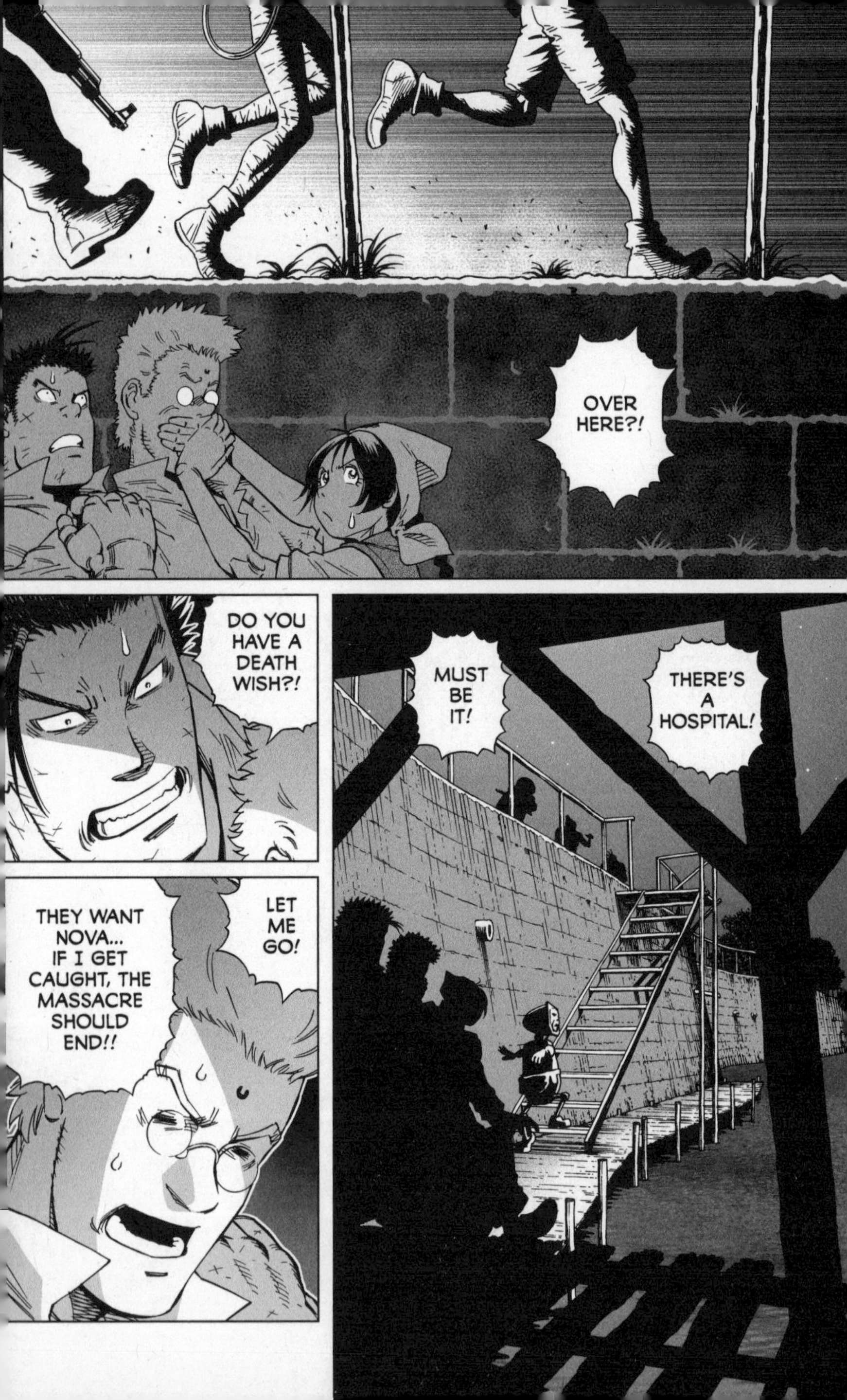
OVER HERE?!
THERE'S A HOSPITAL!
MUST BE IT!
DO YOU HAVE A DEATH WISH?!
LET ME GO!
THEY WANT NOVA... IF I GET CAUGHT, THE MASSACRE SHOULD END!!

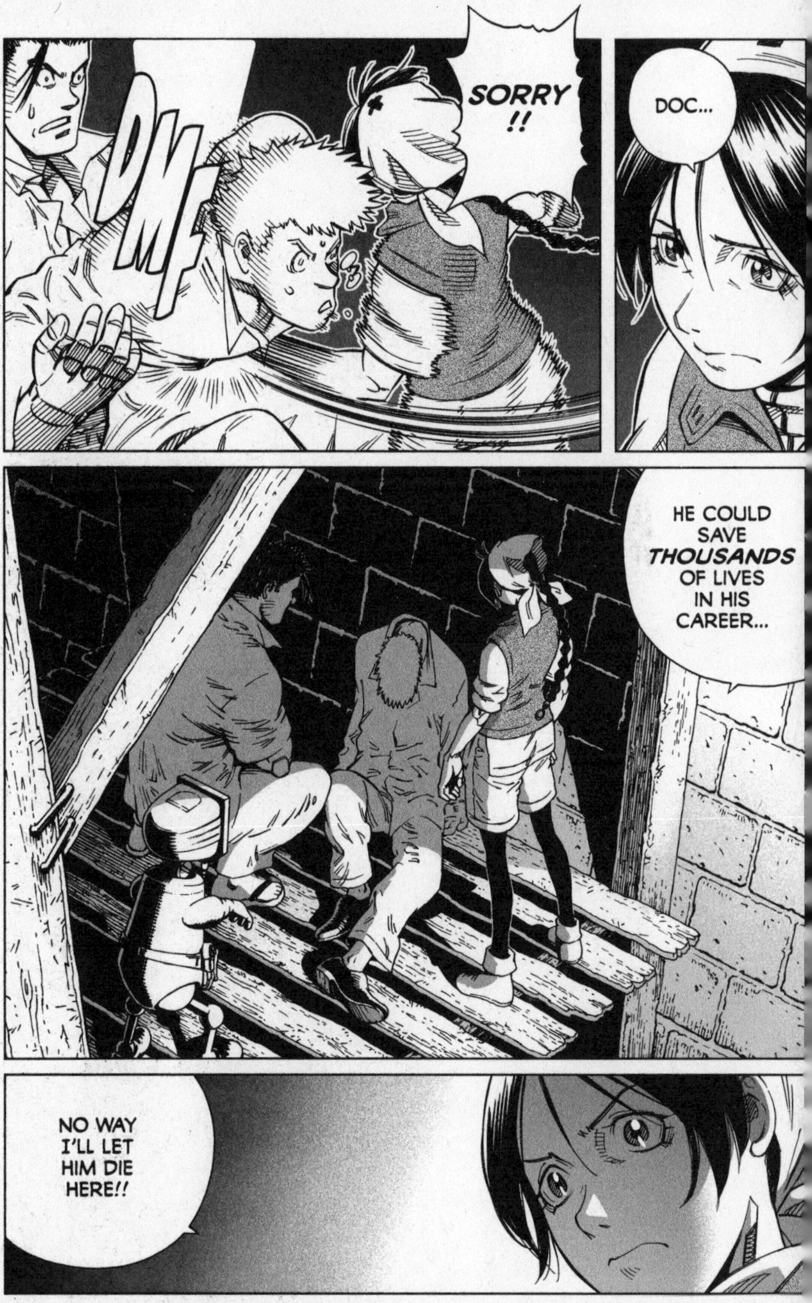
DOC...
SORRY !!
HE COULD SAVE THOUSANDS OF LIVES IN HIS CAREER...
NO WAY I'LL LET HIM DIE HERE!!

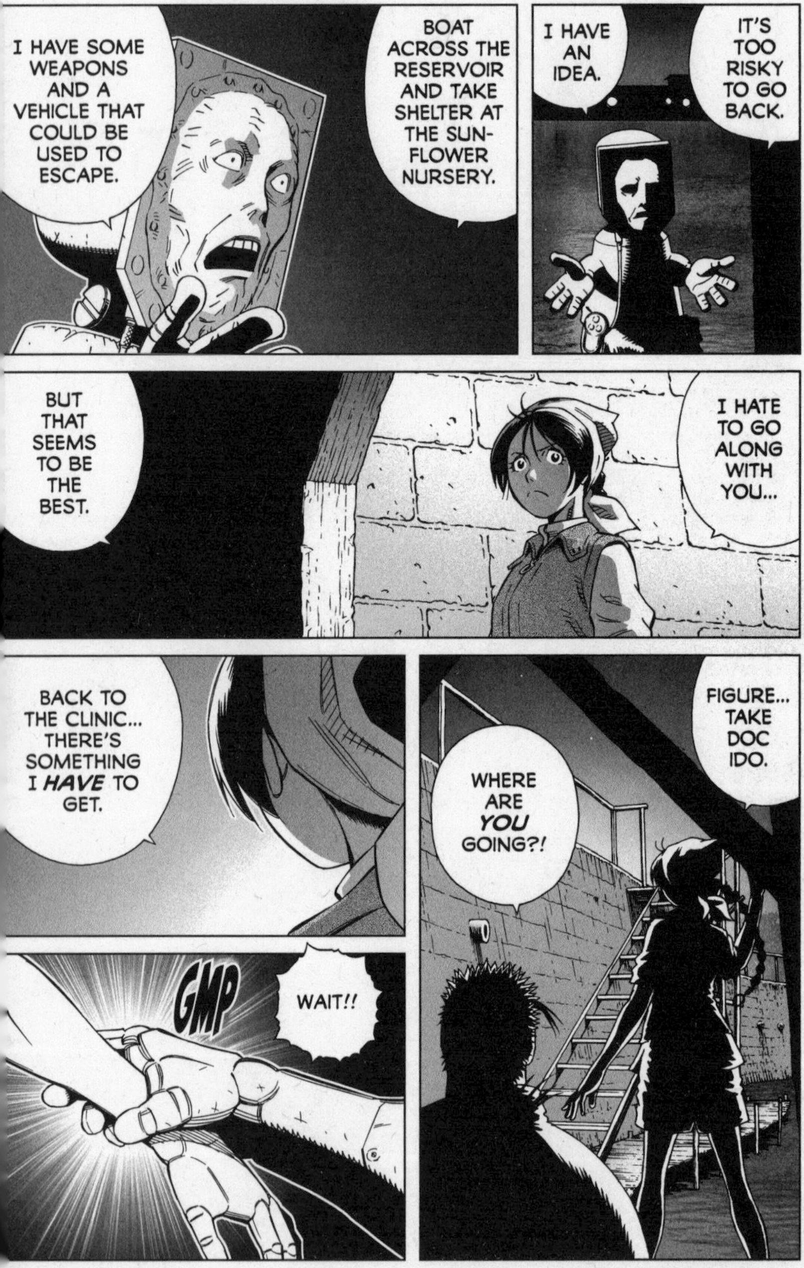
IT'S TOO RISKY TO GO BACK.
I HAVE AN IDEA.
BOAT ACROSS THE RESERVOIR AND TAKE SHELTER AT THE SUN-FLOWER NURSERY.
I HAVE SOME WEAPONS AND A VEHICLE THAT COULD BE USED TO ESCAPE.
I HATE TO GO ALONG WITH YOU...
BUT THAT SEEMS TO BE THE BEST.
FIGURE... TAKE DOC IDO.
WHERE ARE *YOU* GOING?!
BACK TO THE CLINIC... THERE'S SOMETHING I *HAVE* TO GET.
GMP
WAIT!!

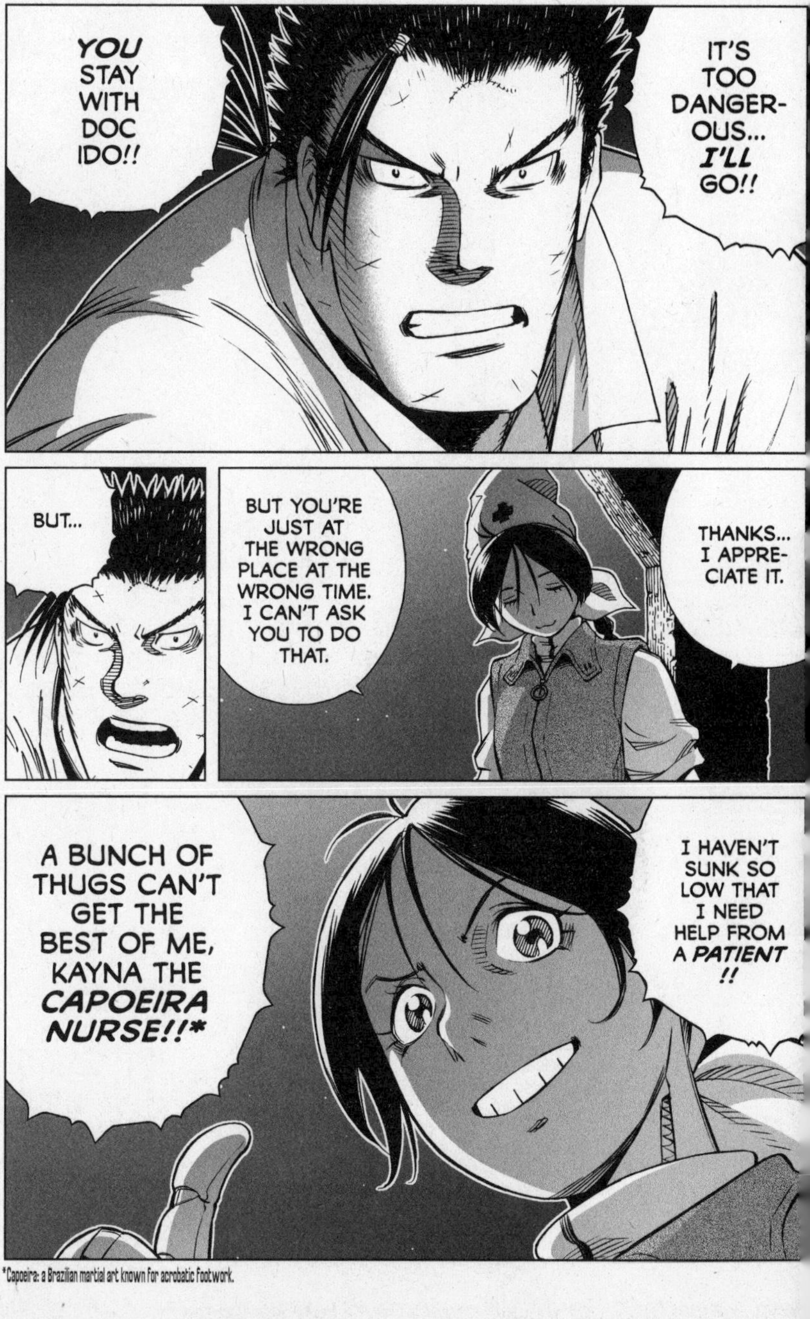
IT'S TOO DANGER-OUS... I'LL GO!!
YOU STAY WITH DOC IDO!!
THANKS... I APPRE-CIATE IT.
BUT YOU'RE JUST AT THE WRONG PLACE AT THE WRONG TIME. I CAN'T ASK YOU TO DO THAT.
BUT...
I HAVEN'T SUNK SO LOW THAT I NEED HELP FROM A PATIENT!!
A BUNCH OF THUGS CAN'T GET THE BEST OF ME, KAYNA THE CAPOEIRA NURSE!!*

*Capoeira: a Brazilian martial art known for acrobatic footwork.

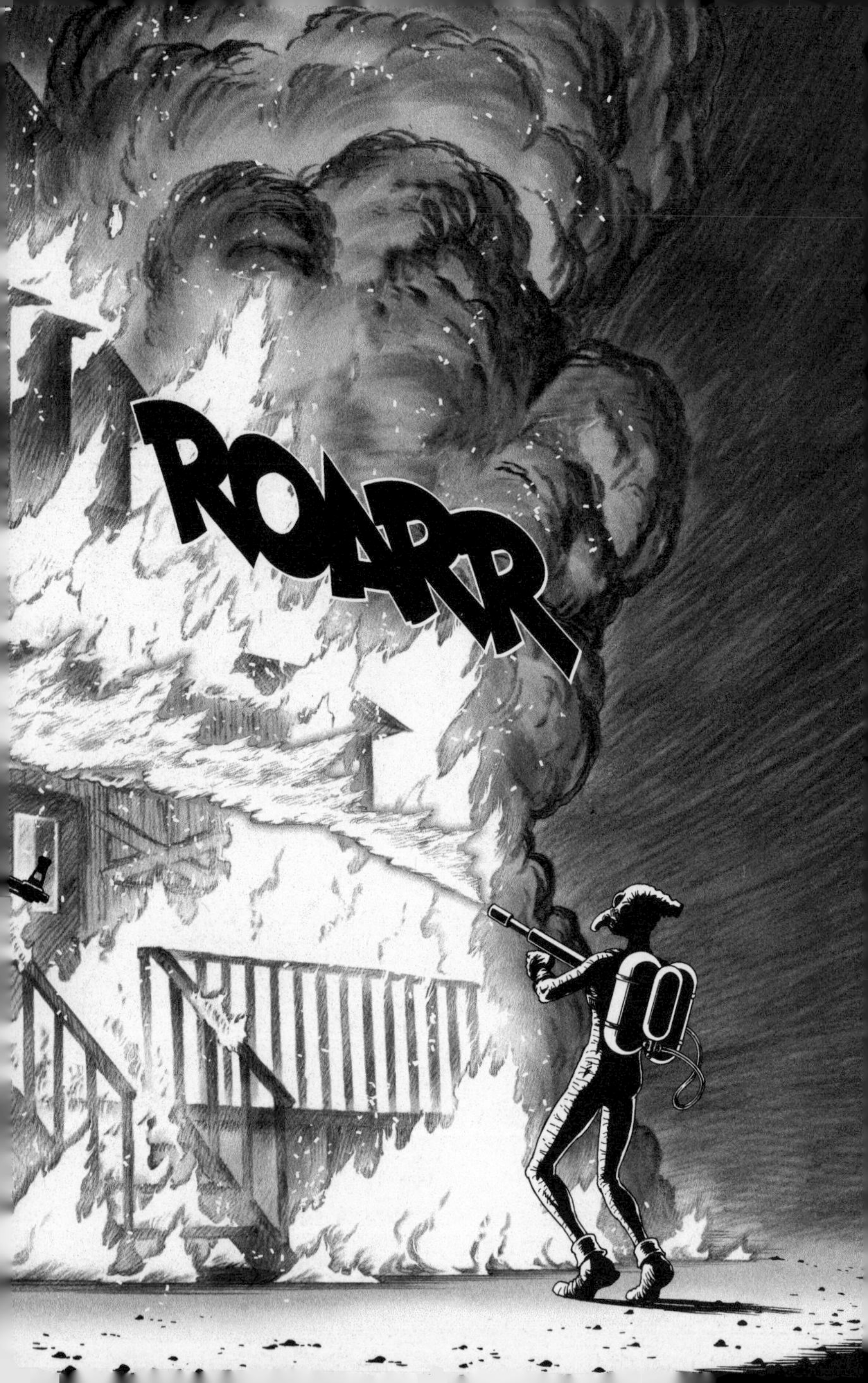
ROARR

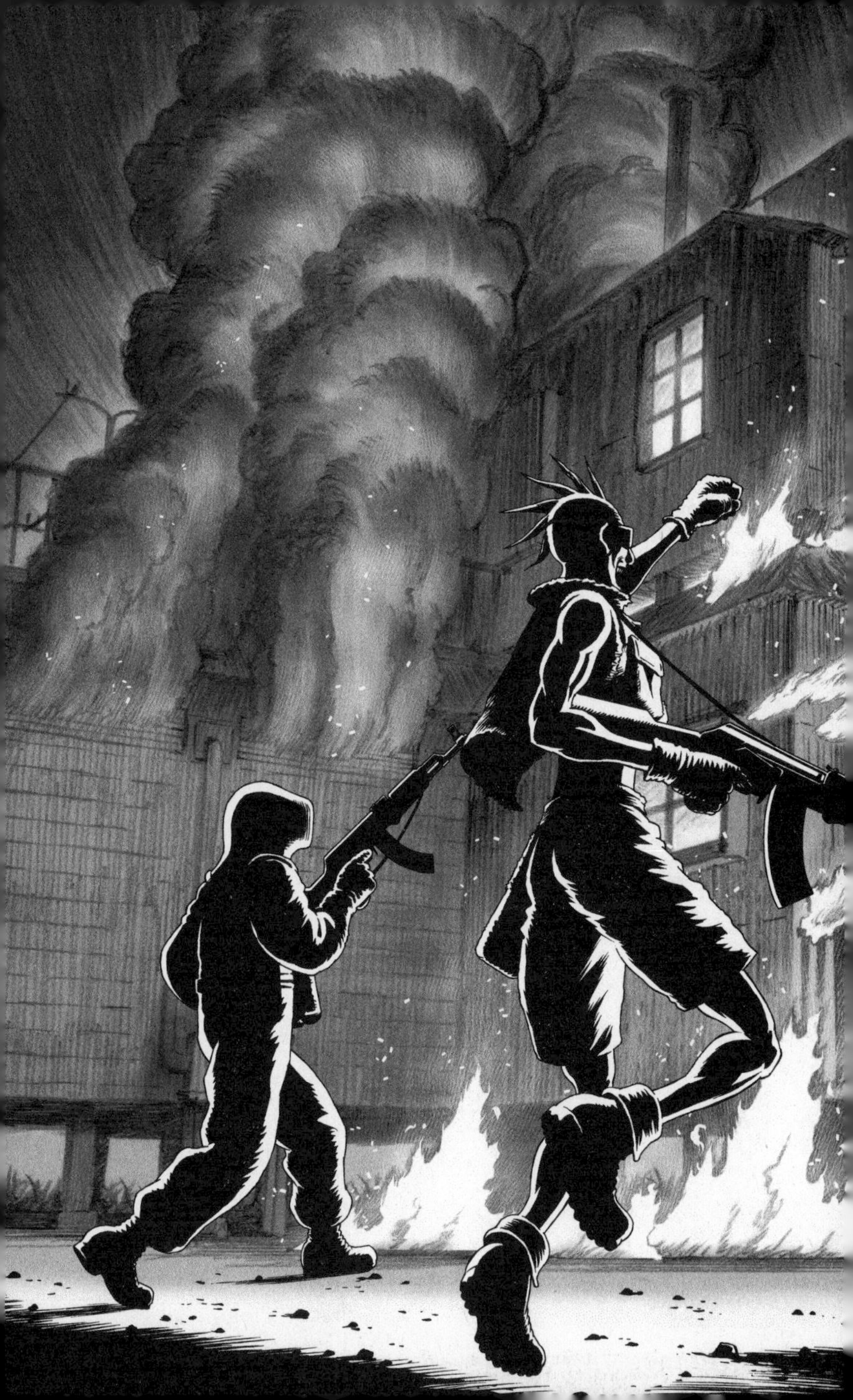

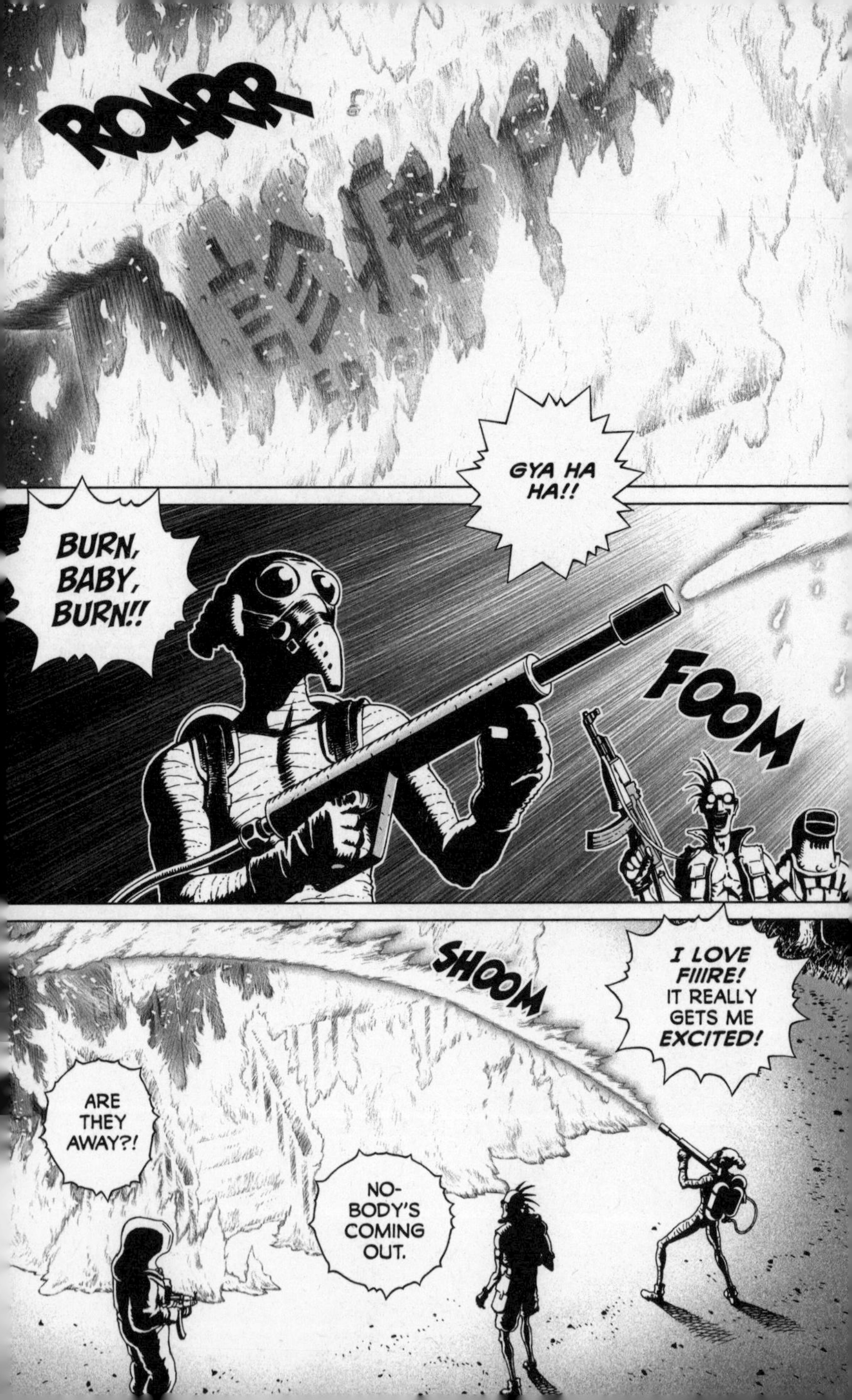
ROARR
GYA HA HA!!
BURN, BABY, BURN!!
FOOM
I LOVE FIIIRE! IT REALLY GETS ME EXCITED!
SHOOM
ARE THEY AWAY?!
NO-BODY'S COMING OUT.

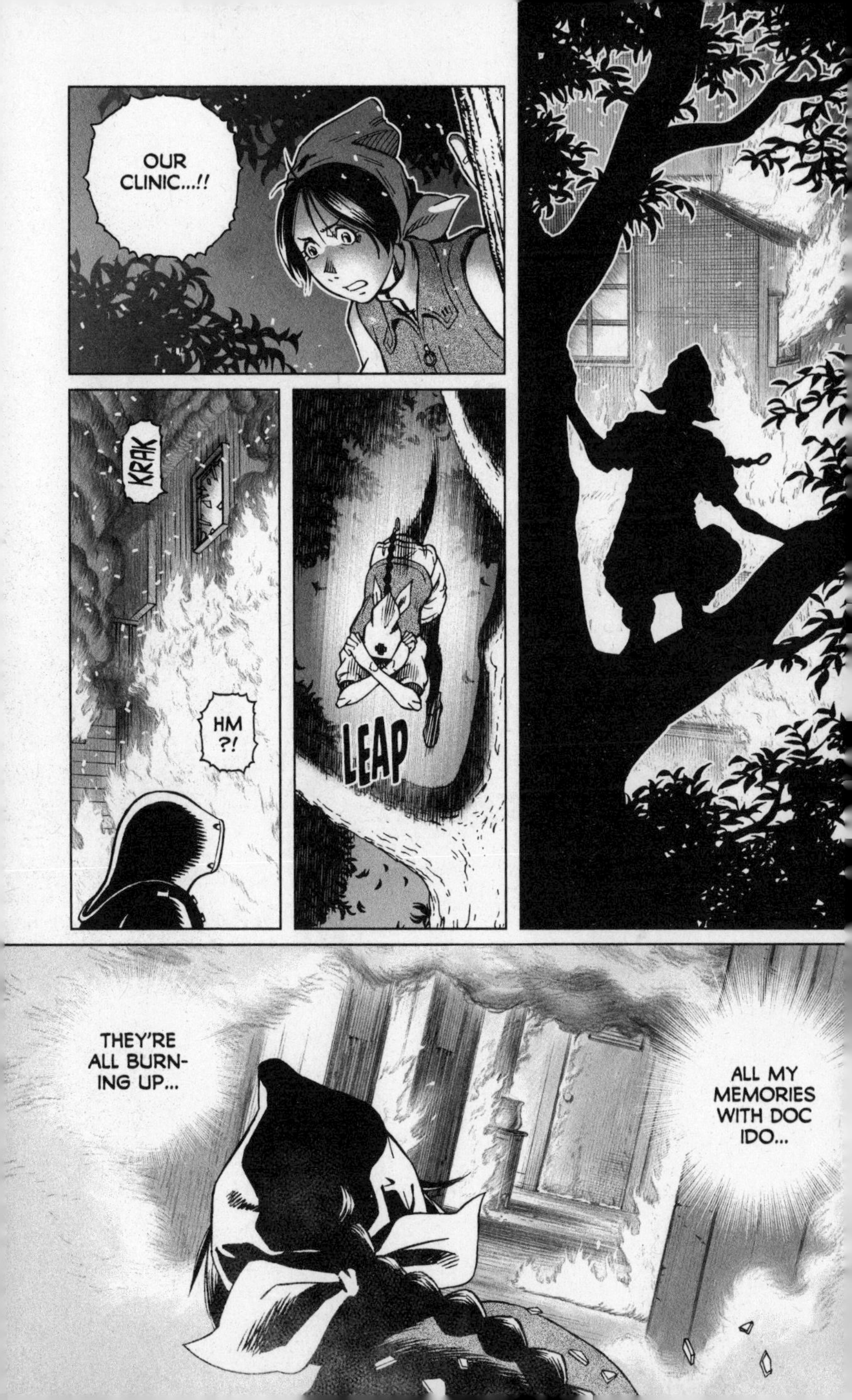
OUR CLINIC...!!
LEAP
KRAK
HM ?!
ALL MY MEMORIES WITH DOC IDO...
THEY'RE ALL BURNING-UP...

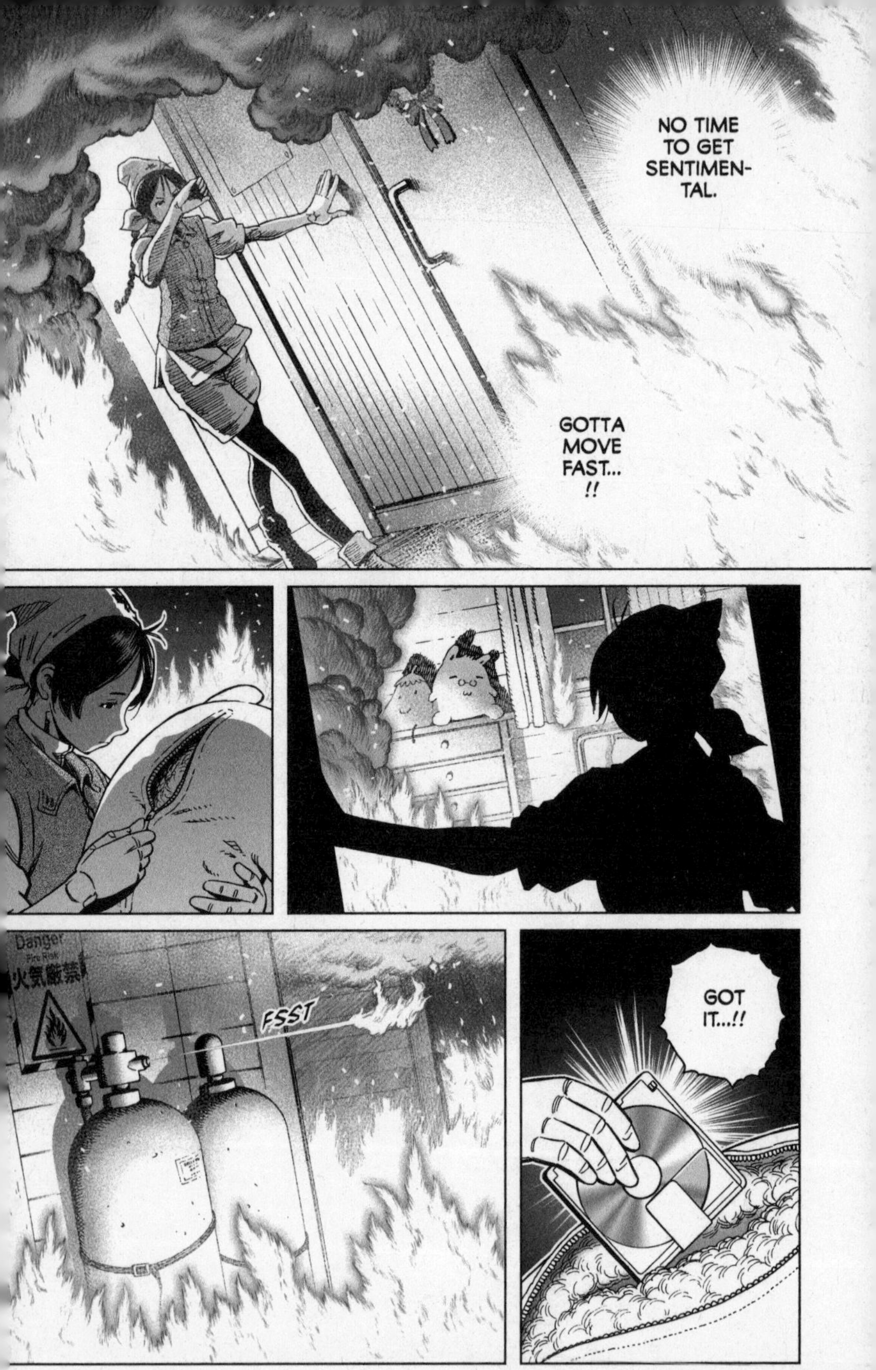
NO TIME TO GET SENTIMEN-TAL.
GOTTA MOVE FAST... !!
GOT IT...!!
Danger
Fire Risk
火気厳禁
FSST

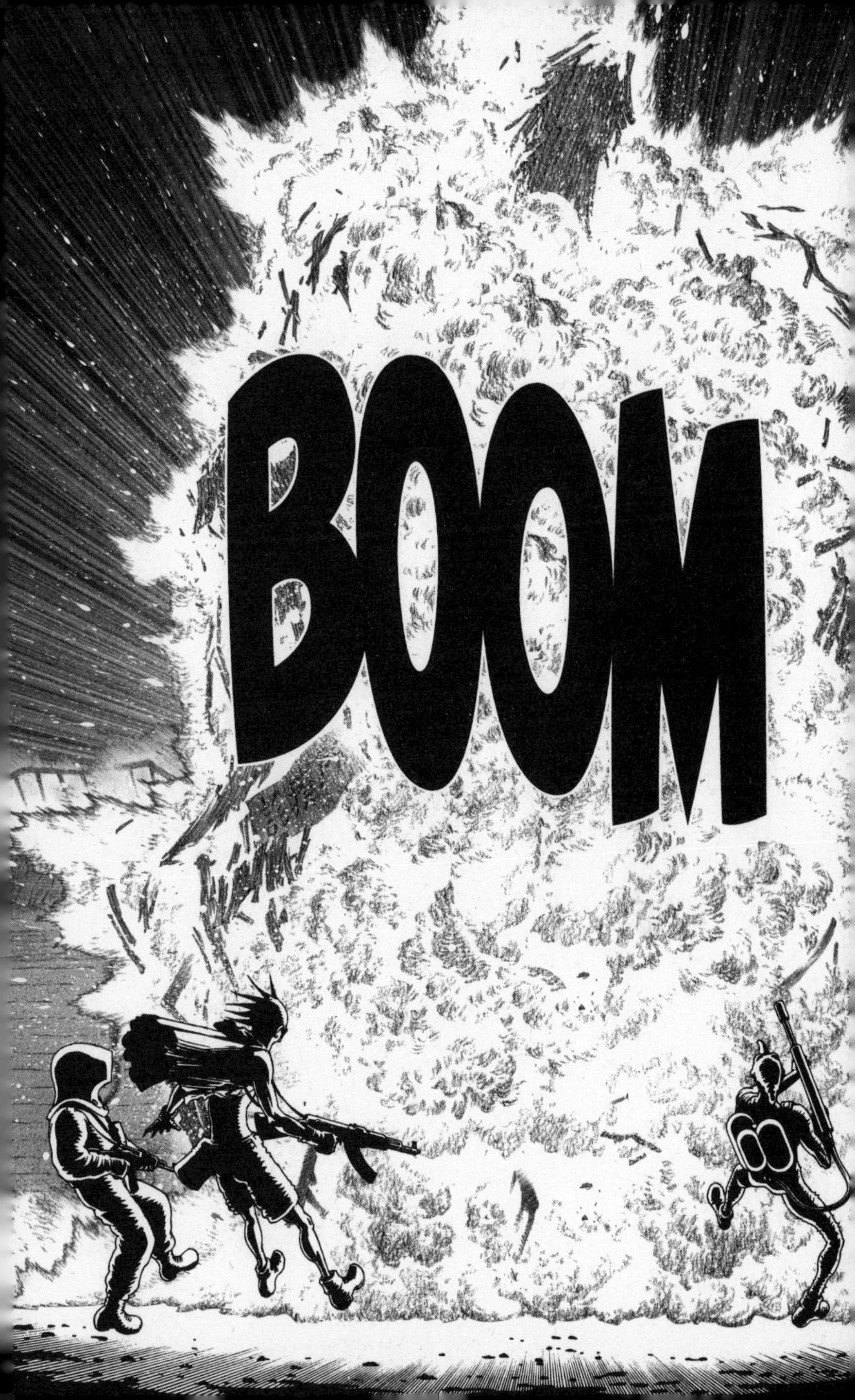
BOOM

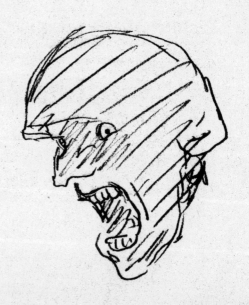

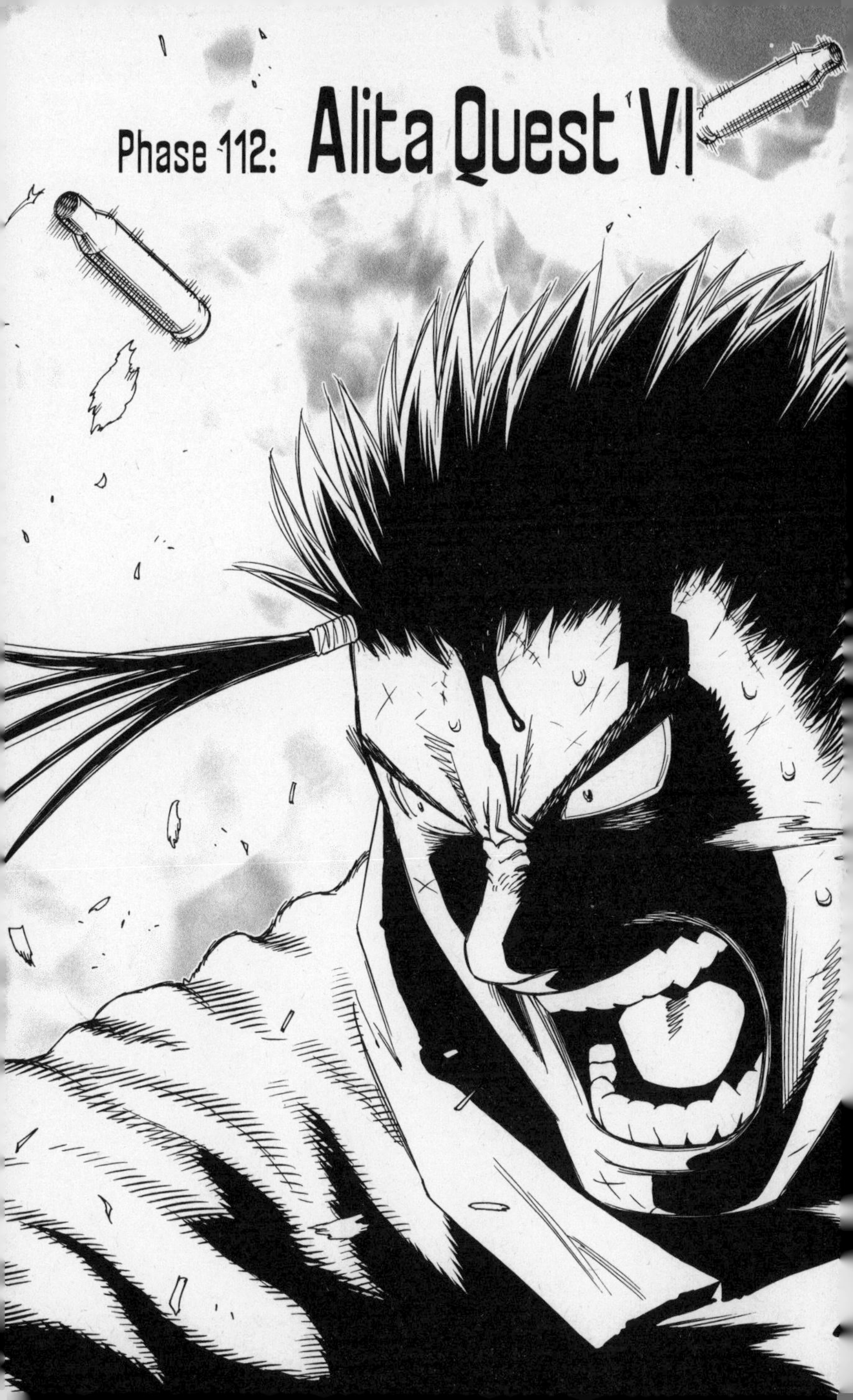
Phase 112: Alita Quest VI

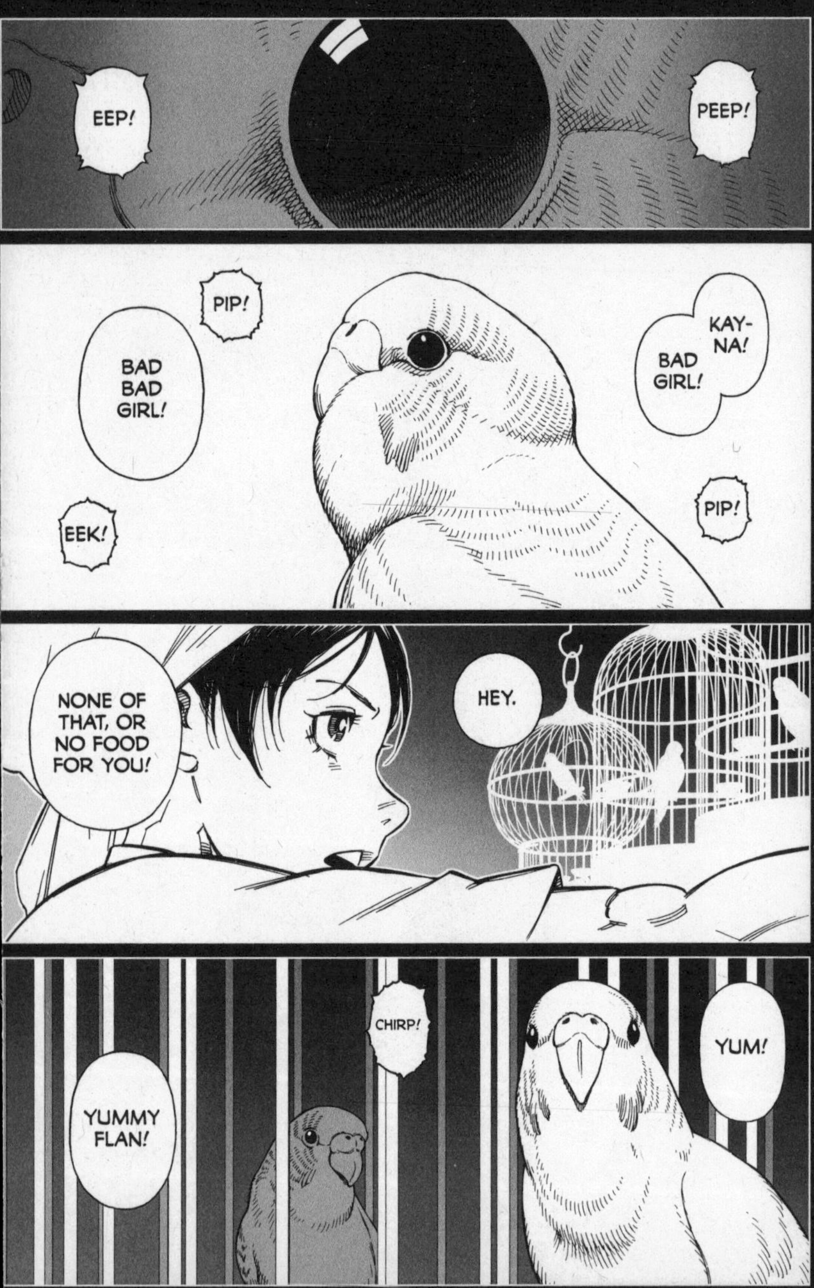

PEEP!
EEP!
KAY-NA! BAD GIRL!
PIP!
BAD BAD GIRL!
PIP!
EEK!
HEY.
NONE OF THAT, OR NO FOOD FOR YOU!
YUM!
CHIRP!
YUMMY FLAN!

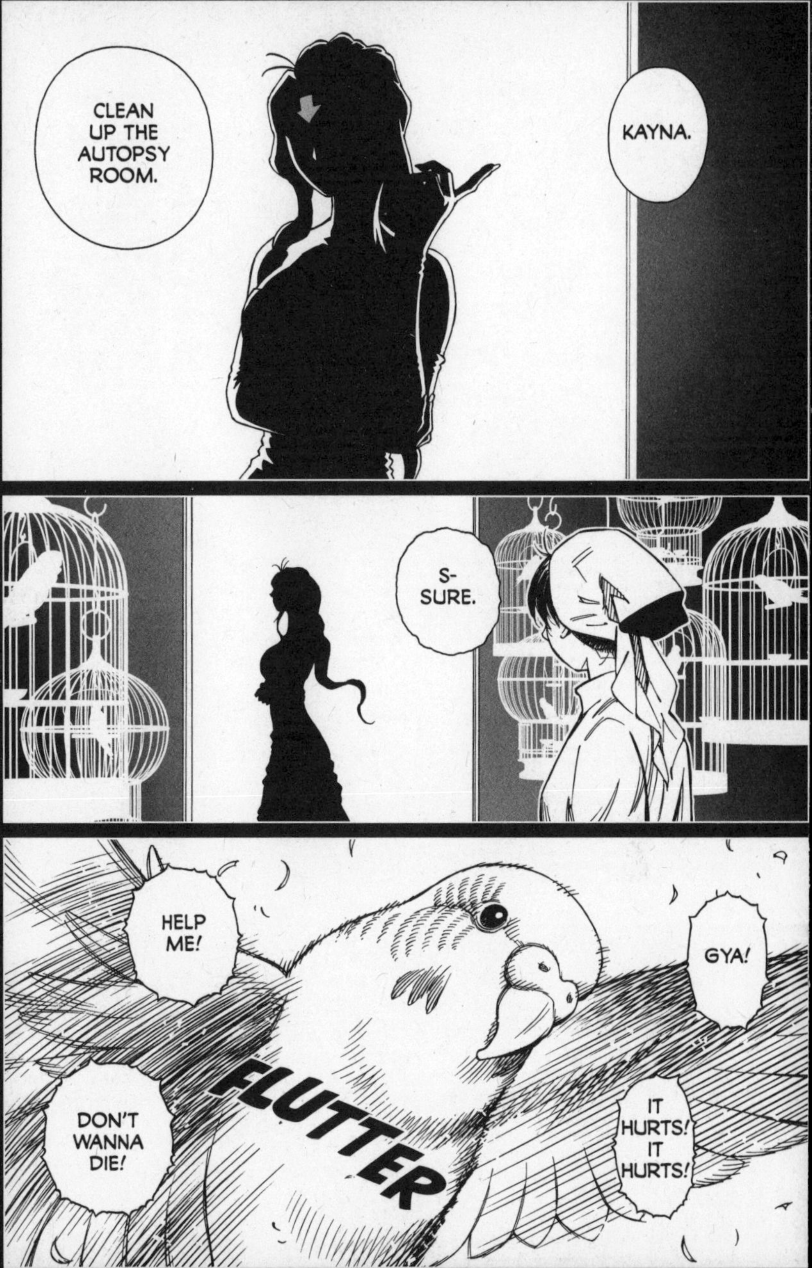
KAYNA.
CLEAN UP THE AUTOPSY ROOM.
S-SURE.
GYA!
HELP ME!
IT HURTS! IT HURTS!
FLUTTER
DON'T WANNA DIE!

UH...

UNH.

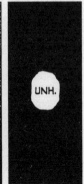

WHAT... HAP- PENED...?

KRAK

THUD

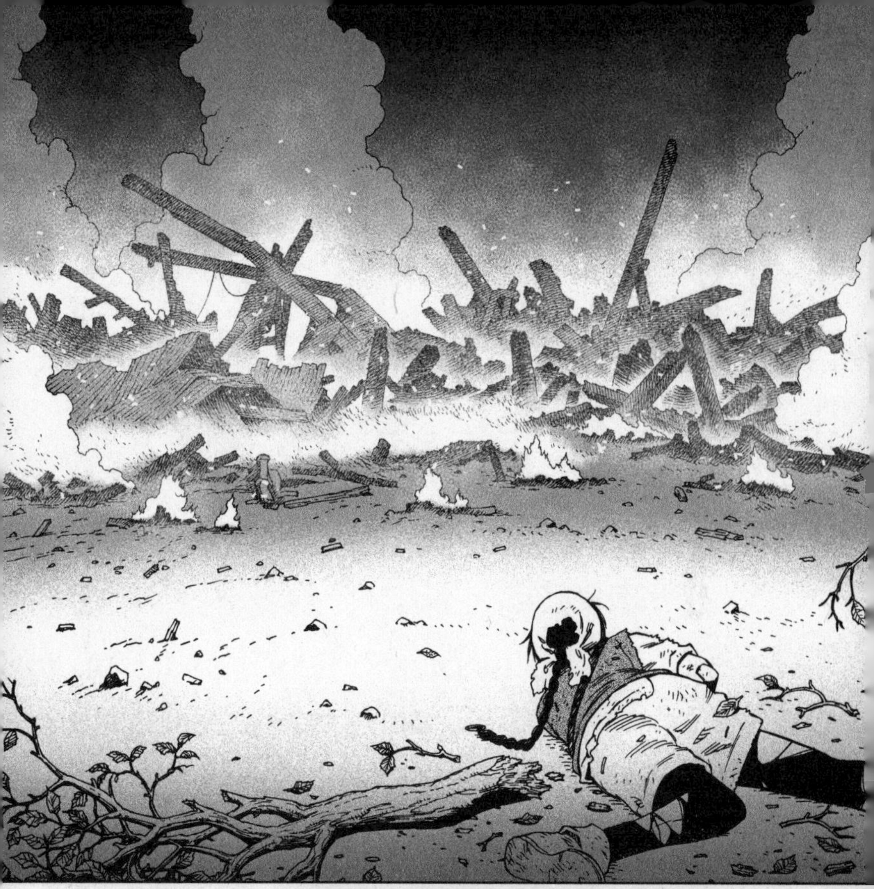
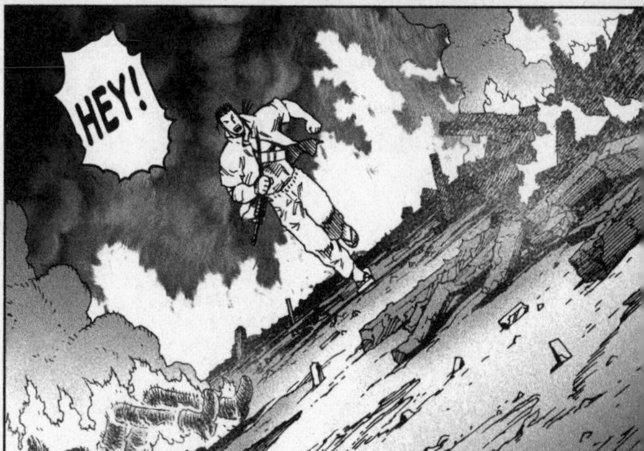
HEY!
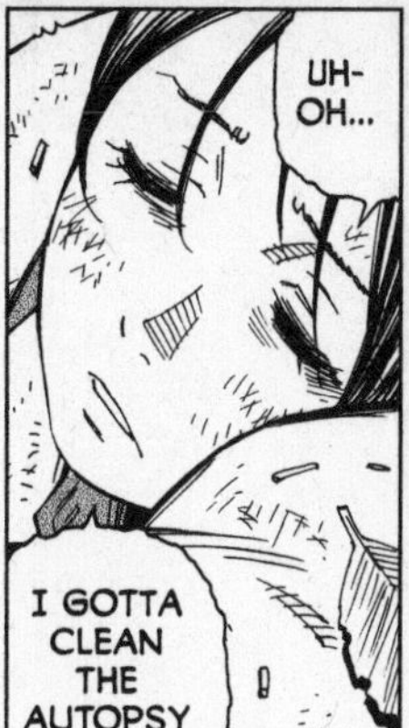
UH-OH...
I GOTTA CLEAN THE AUTOPSY ROOM...

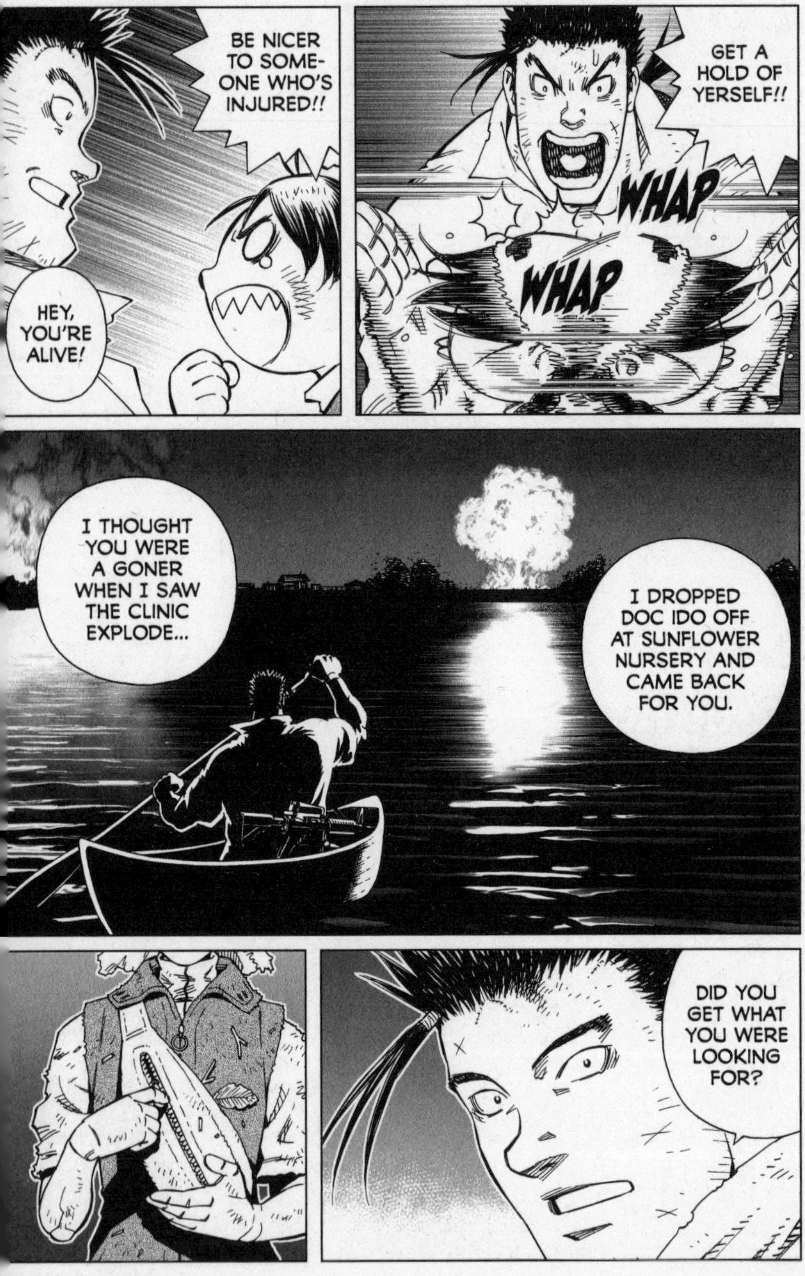
GET A HOLD OF YERSELF!!
WHAP
WHAP
BE NICER TO SOME-ONE WHO'S INJURED!!
HEY, YOU'RE ALIVE!
I THOUGHT YOU WERE A GONER WHEN I SAW THE CLINIC EXPLODE...
I DROPPED DOC IDO OFF AT SUNFLOWER NURSERY AND CAME BACK FOR YOU.
DID YOU GET WHAT YOU WERE LOOKING FOR?

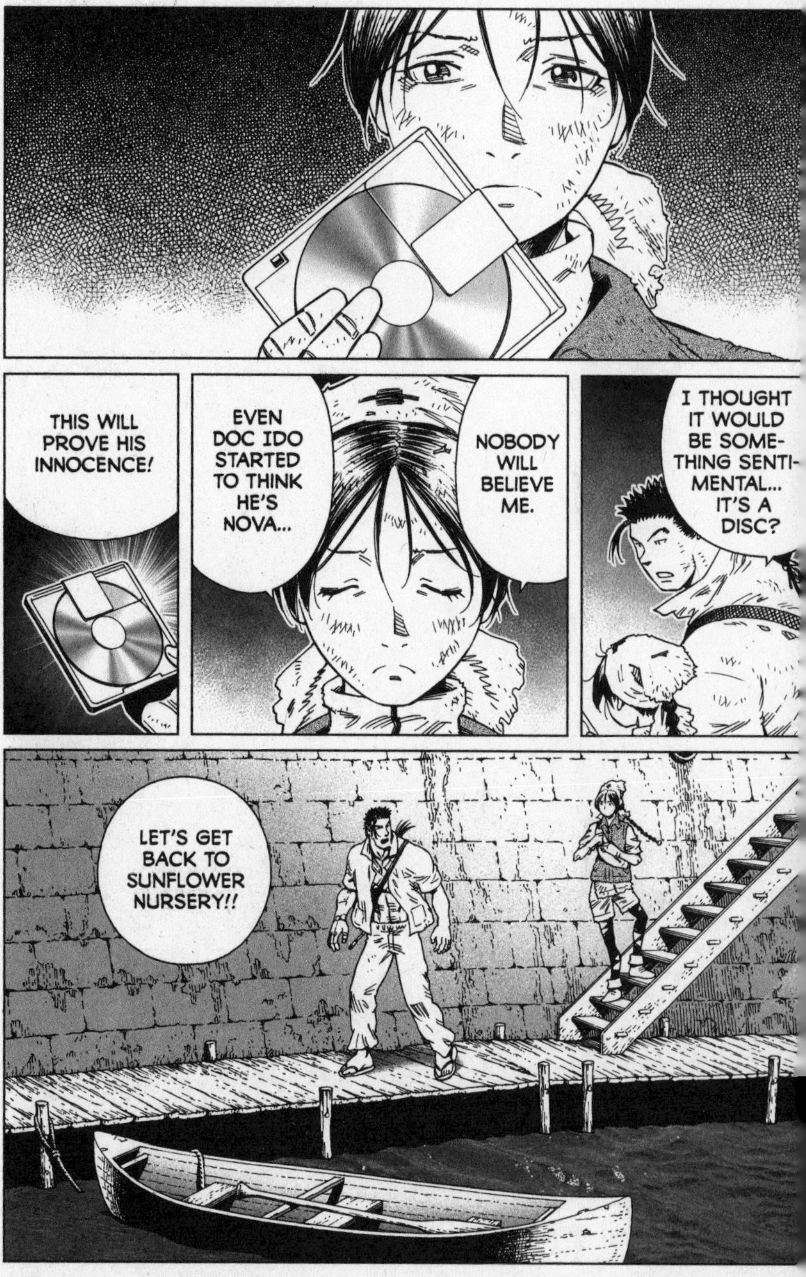
I THOUGHT IT WOULD BE SOME-THING SENTI-MENTAL... IT'S A DISC?
NOBODY WILL BELIEVE ME.
EVEN DOC IDO STARTED TO THINK HE'S NOVA...
THIS WILL PROVE HIS INNOCENCE!
LET'S GET BACK TO SUNFLOWER NURSERY!!

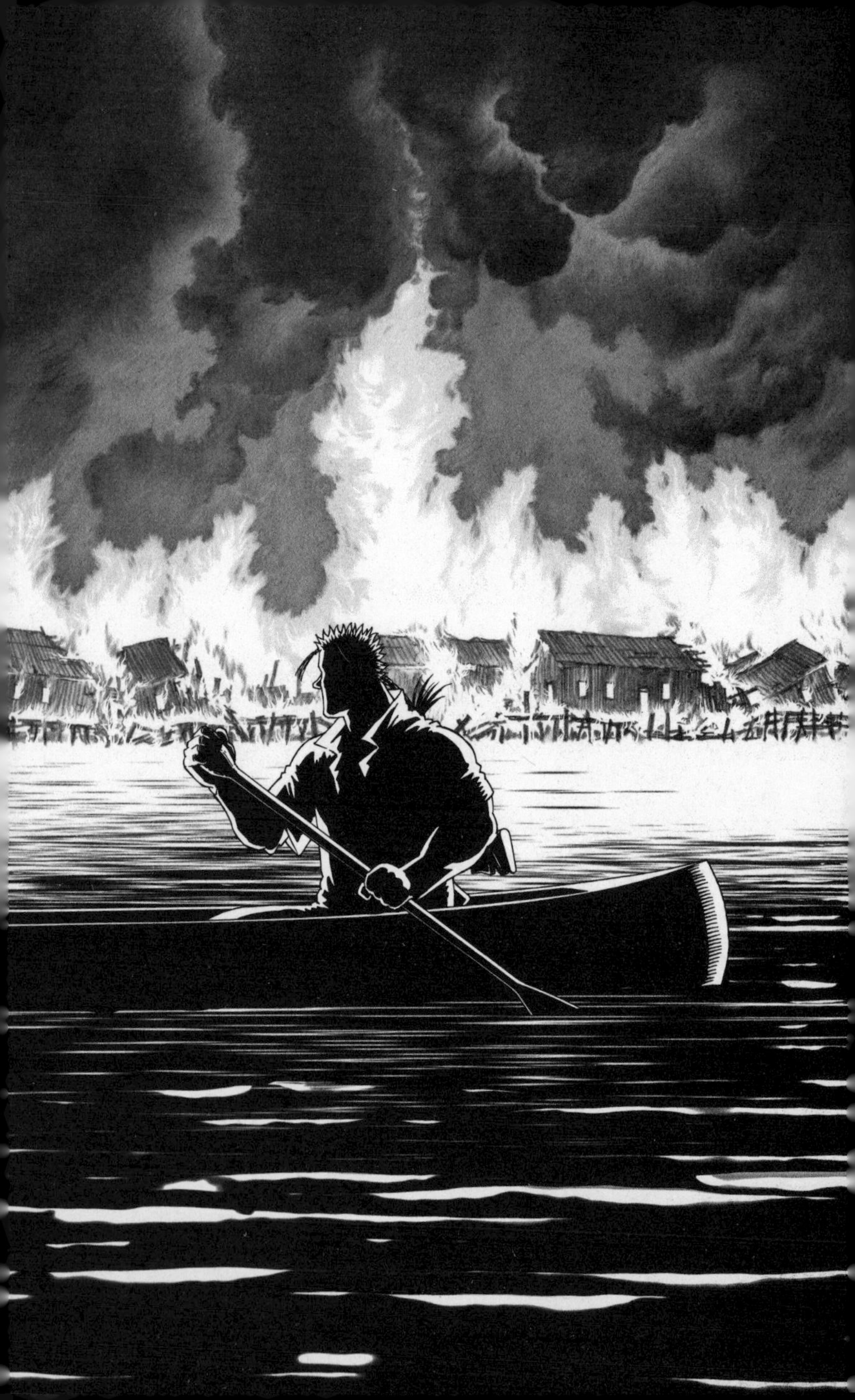

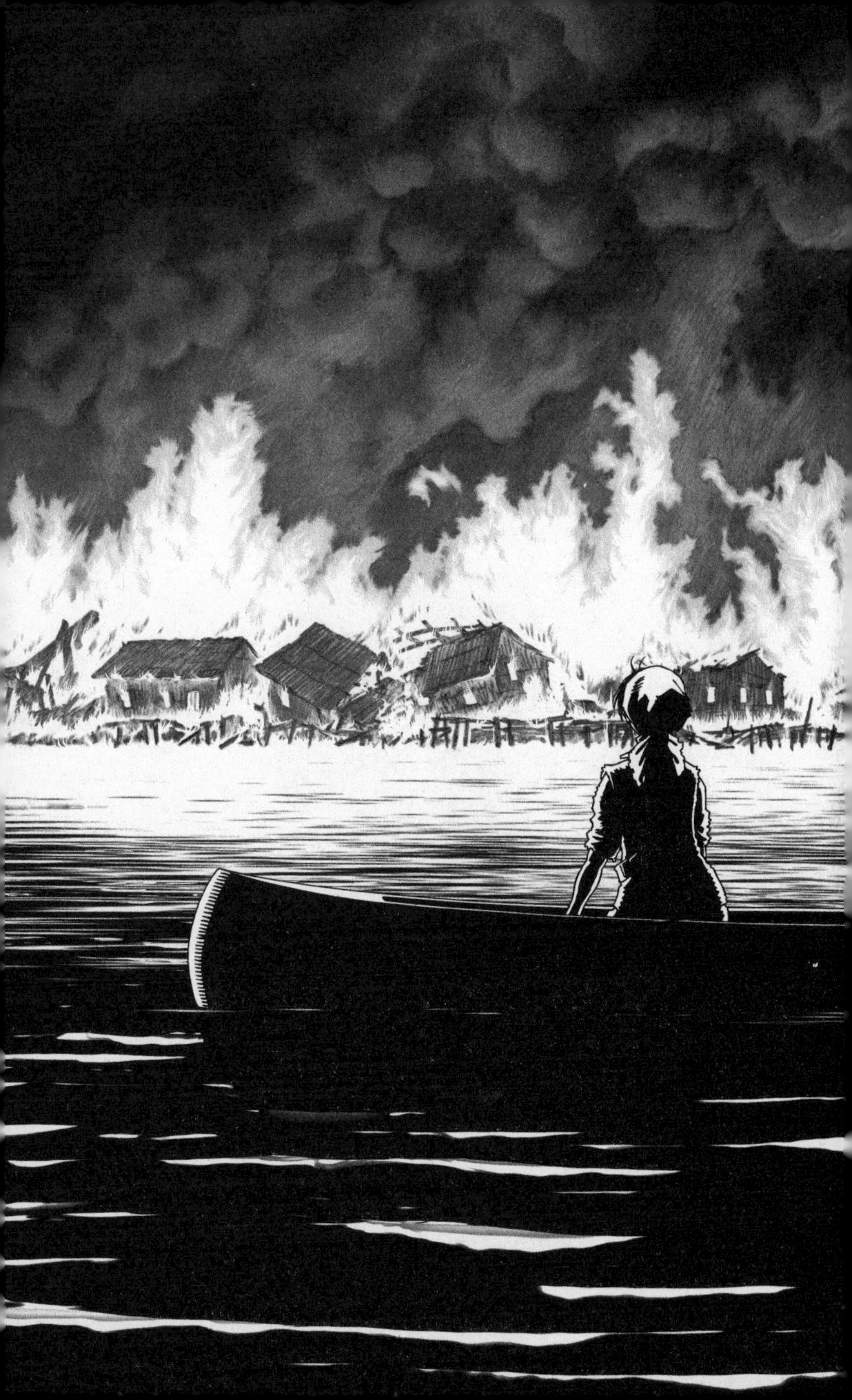

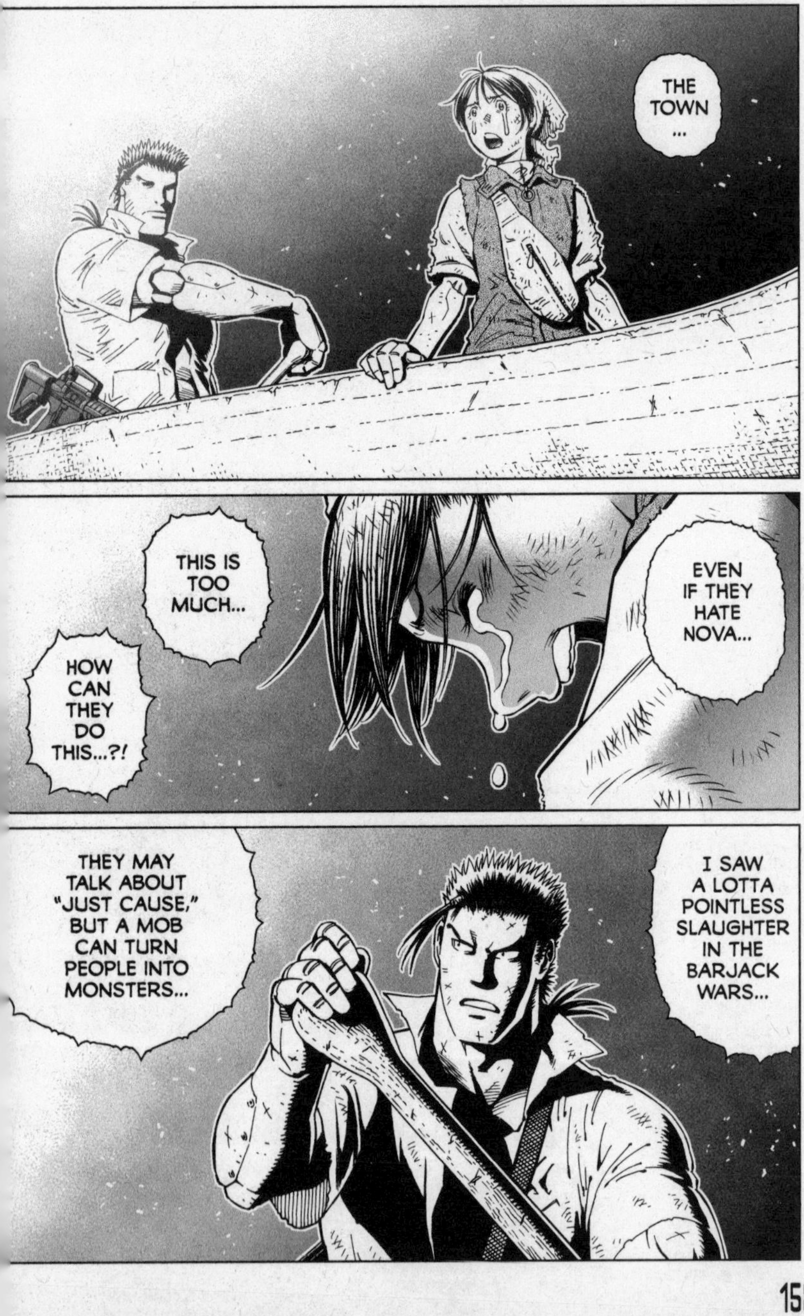
THE TOWN ...
EVEN IF THEY HATE NOVA...
THIS IS TOO MUCH...
HOW CAN THEY DO THIS...?!
I SAW A LOTTA POINTLESS SLAUGHTER IN THE BARJACK WARS...
THEY MAY TALK ABOUT "JUST CAUSE," BUT A MOB CAN TURN PEOPLE INTO MONSTERS...

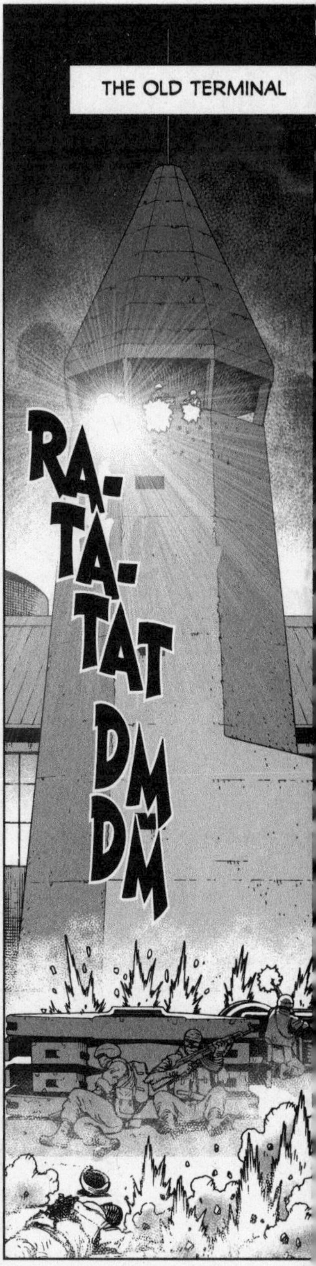
THE OLD TERMINAL
RA-TA-TAT
DMDM DMM

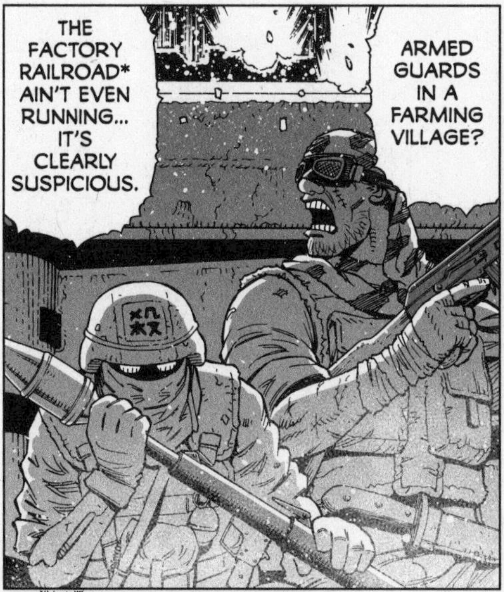
ARMED GUARDS IN A FARMING VILLAGE?
THE FACTORY RAILROAD* AIN'T EVEN RUNNING... IT'S CLEARLY SUSPICIOUS.

*Helmet: Kill

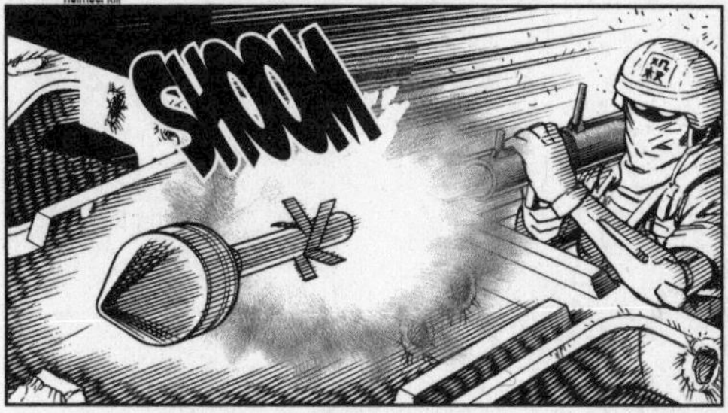
SHOOM

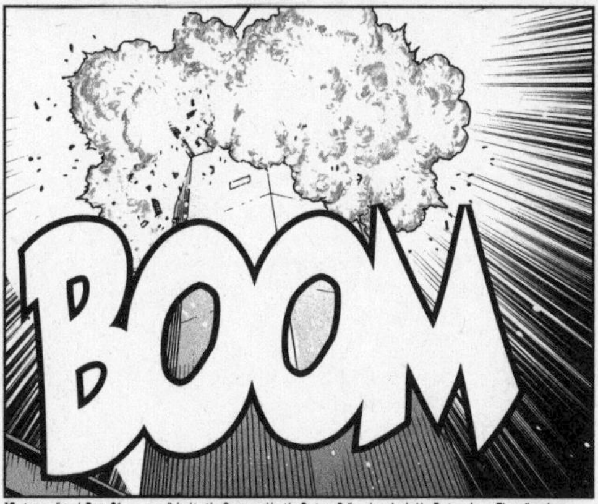
BOOM

*Factory railroad: Farm 21 was once linked to the Scrapyard by the Factory Railroad, and ruled by Factory Law. The railroad was discontinued during the Barjack wars. Now they are autonomous.

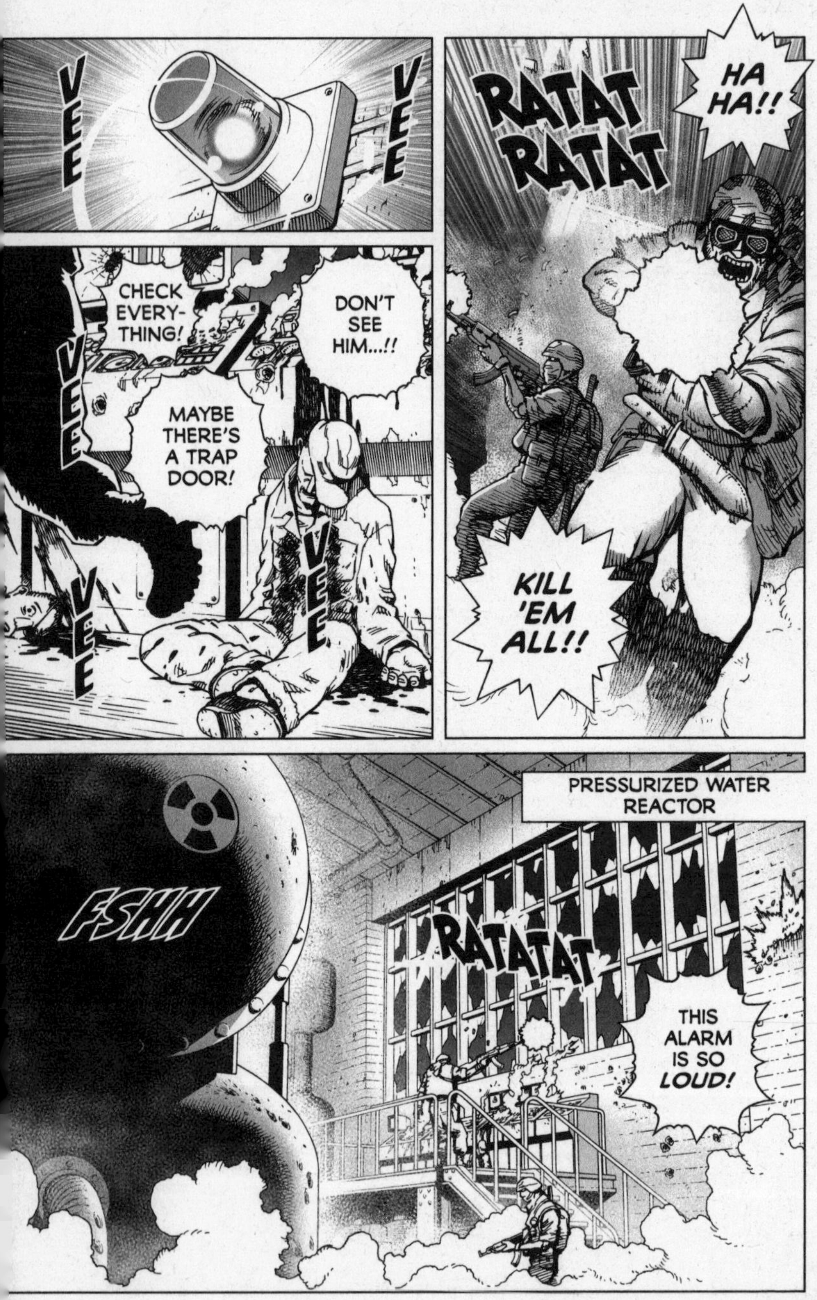
HA HA!!
RATAT RATAT
KILL 'EM ALL!!
VEE VEE
DON'T SEE HIM...!!
CHECK EVERY-THING!
MAYBE THERE'S A TRAP DOOR!
VEE VEE VEE
PRESSURIZED WATER REACTOR
RATATAT
THIS ALARM IS SO *LOUD!*
FSHH

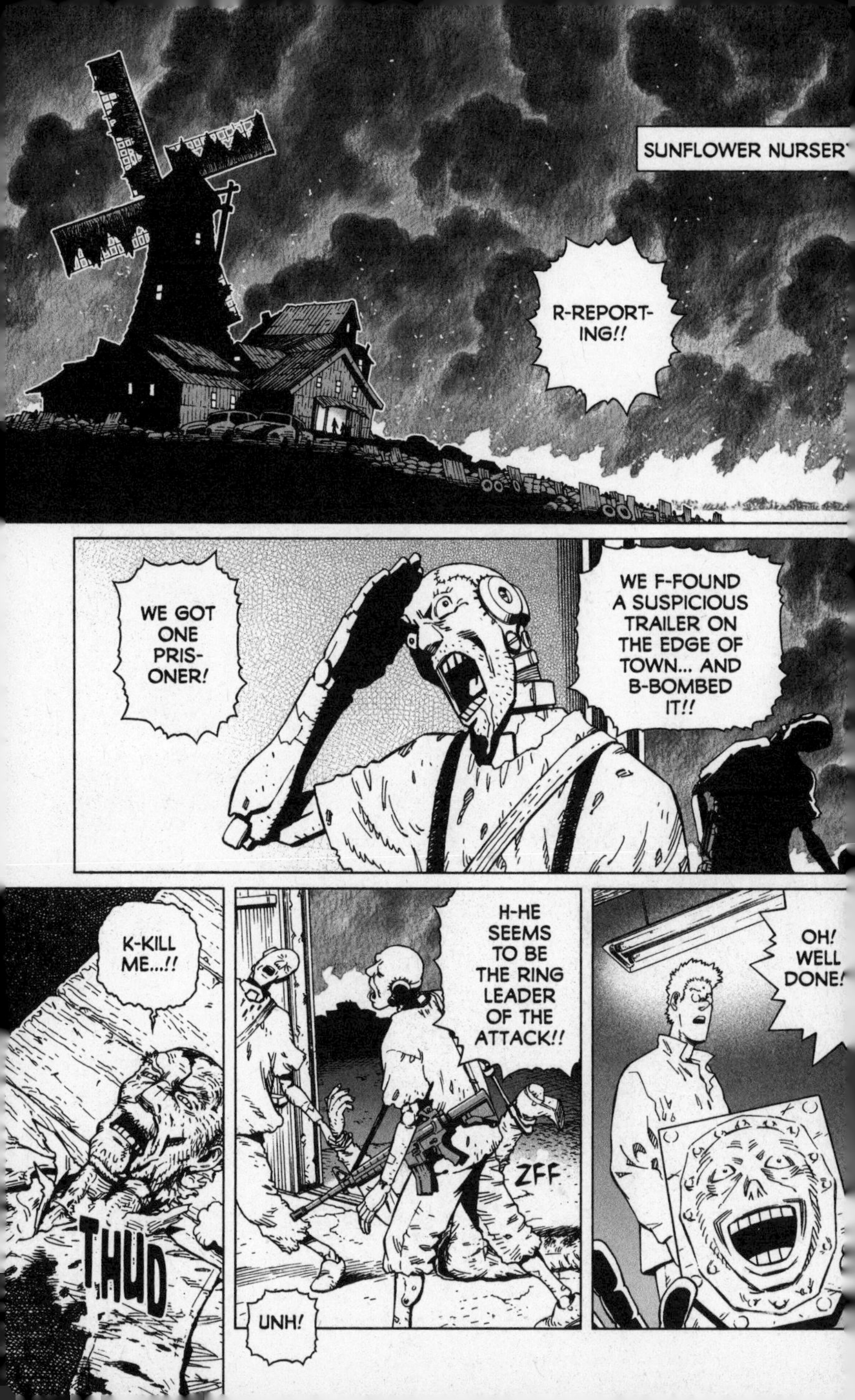
SUNFLOWER NURSER
R-REPORTING!!
WE F-FOUND A SUSPICIOUS TRAILER ON THE EDGE OF TOWN... AND B-BOMBED IT!!
WE GOT ONE PRISONER!
OH! WELL DONE!
H-HE SEEMS TO BE THE RING LEADER OF THE ATTACK!!
ZFF
UNH!
K-KILL ME...!!
THUD

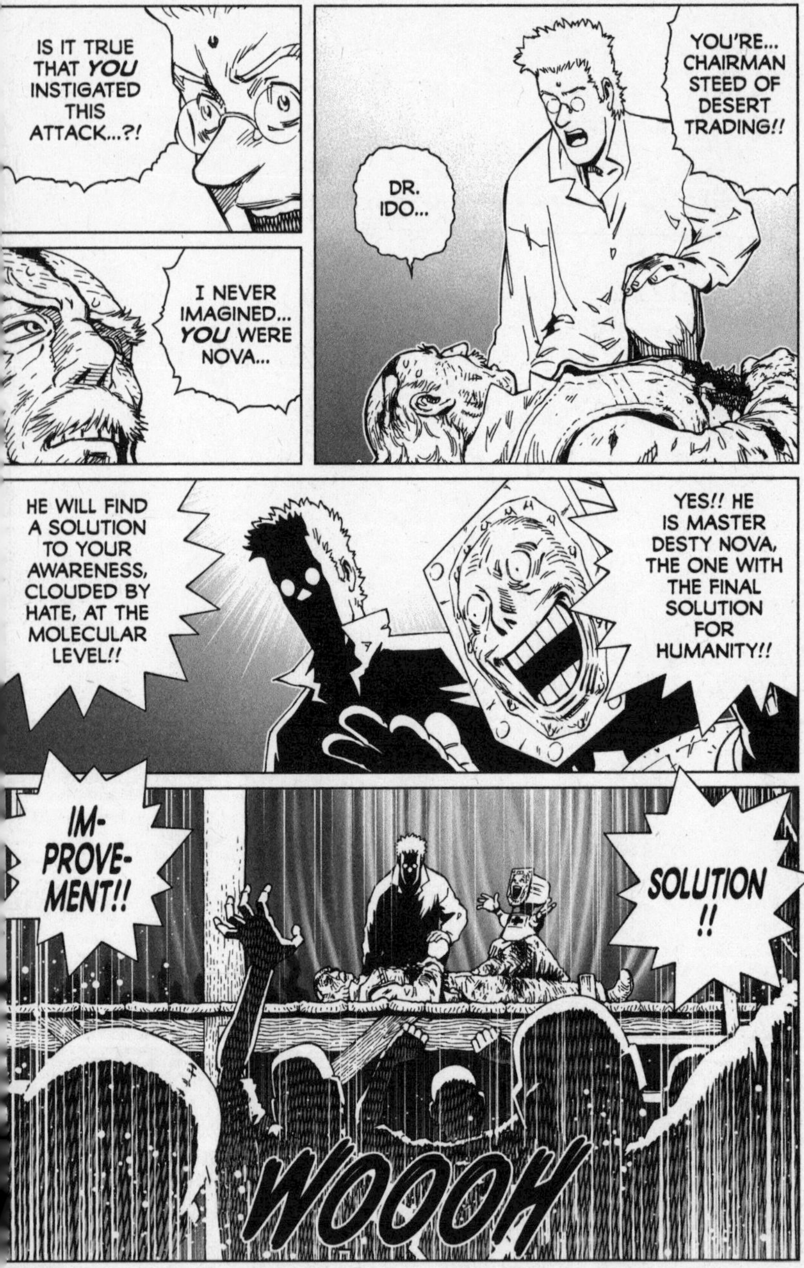
YOU'RE... CHAIRMAN STEED OF DESERT TRADING!!
DR. IDO...
IS IT TRUE THAT *YOU* INSTIGATED THIS ATTACK...?!
I NEVER IMAGINED... *YOU* WERE NOVA...
YES!! HE IS MASTER DESTY NOVA, THE ONE WITH THE FINAL SOLUTION FOR HUMANITY!!
HE WILL FIND A SOLUTION TO YOUR AWARENESS, CLOUDED BY HATE, AT THE MOLECULAR LEVEL!!
SOLUTION !!
IM-PROVE-MENT!!
WOOOH

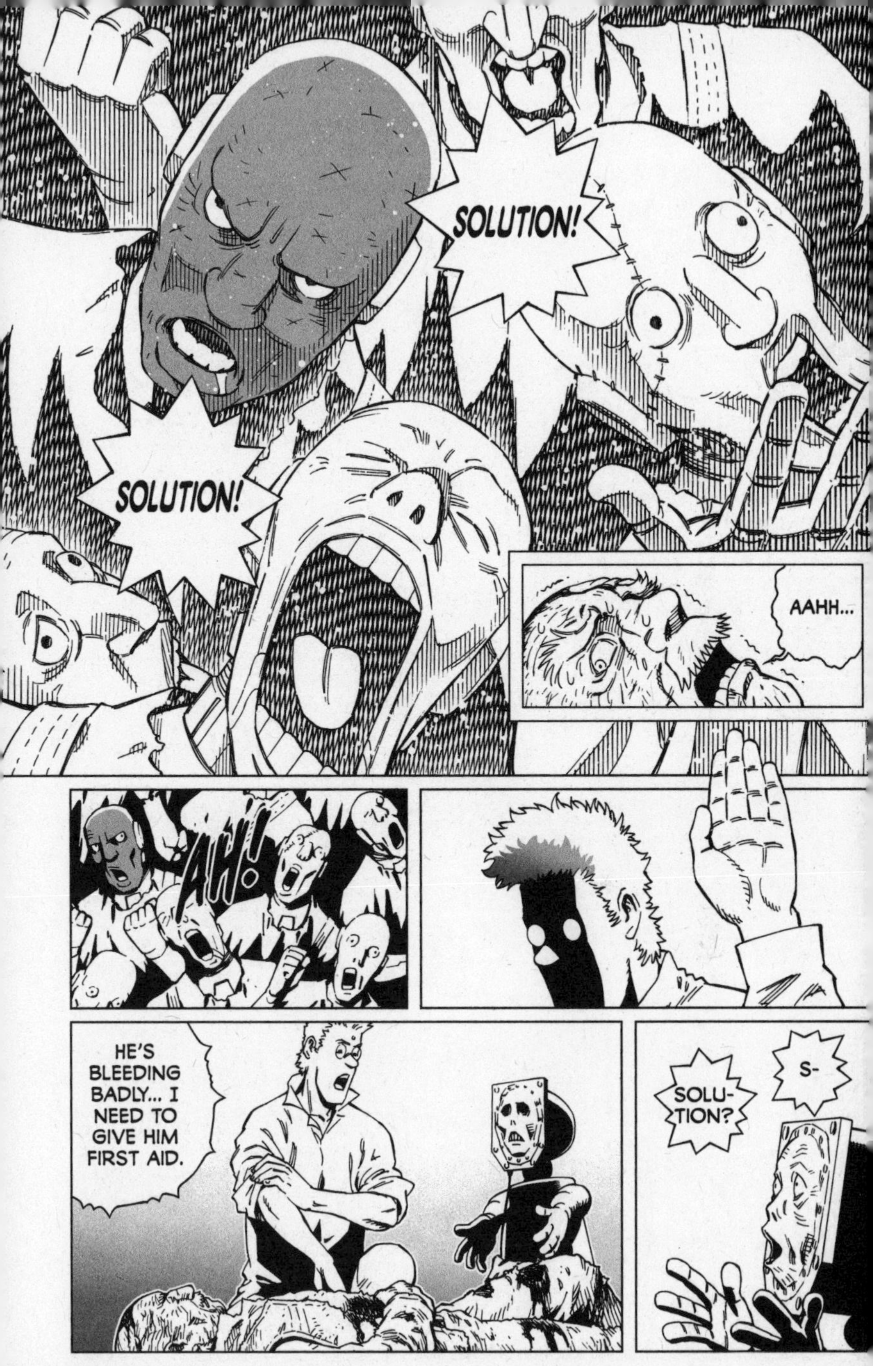
SOLUTION!
SOLUTION!
AAHH...
AW!
S-
SOLU-TION?
HE'S BLEEDING BADLY... I NEED TO GIVE HIM FIRST AID.

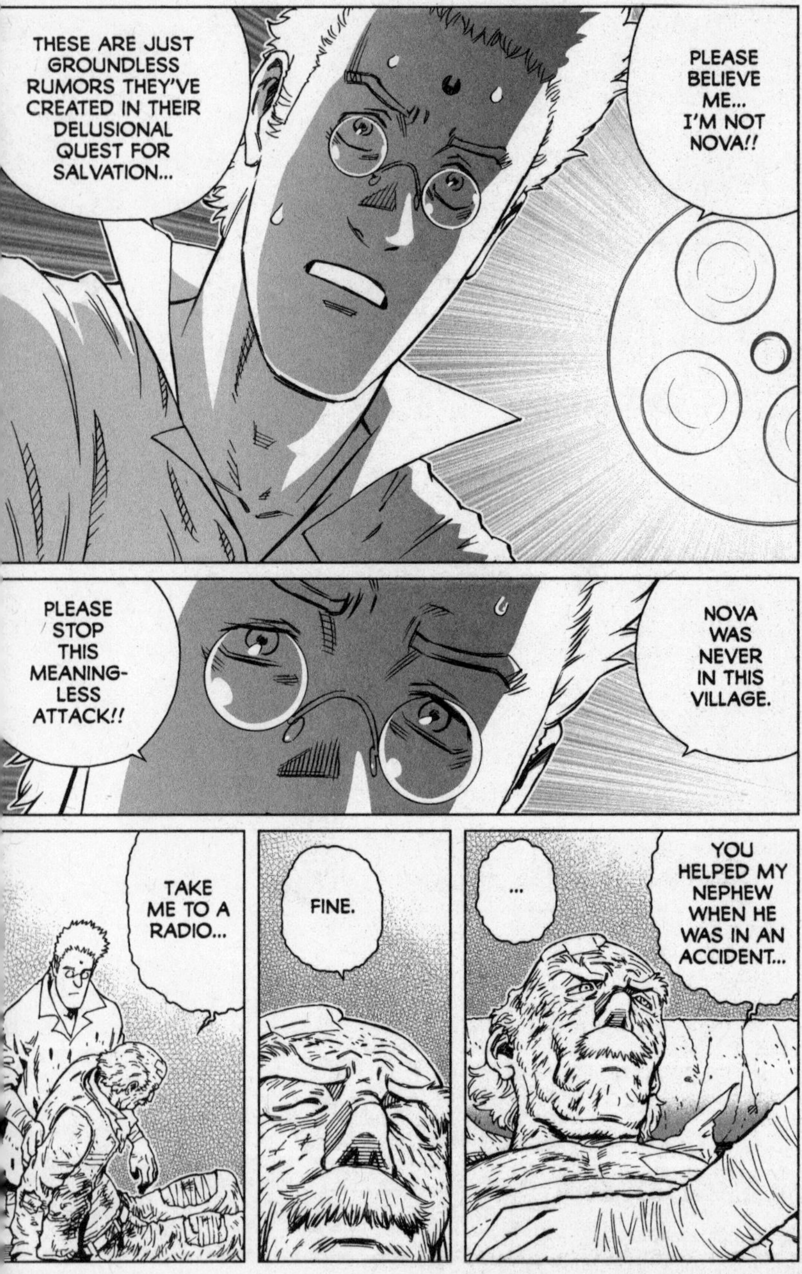
PLEASE BELIEVE ME... I'M NOT NOVA!!
THESE ARE JUST GROUNDLESS RUMORS THEY'VE CREATED IN THEIR DELUSIONAL QUEST FOR SALVATION...
NOVA WAS NEVER IN THIS VILLAGE.
PLEASE STOP THIS MEANINGLESS ATTACK!!
YOU HELPED MY NEPHEW WHEN HE WAS IN AN ACCIDENT...
...
FINE.
TAKE ME TO A RADIO...

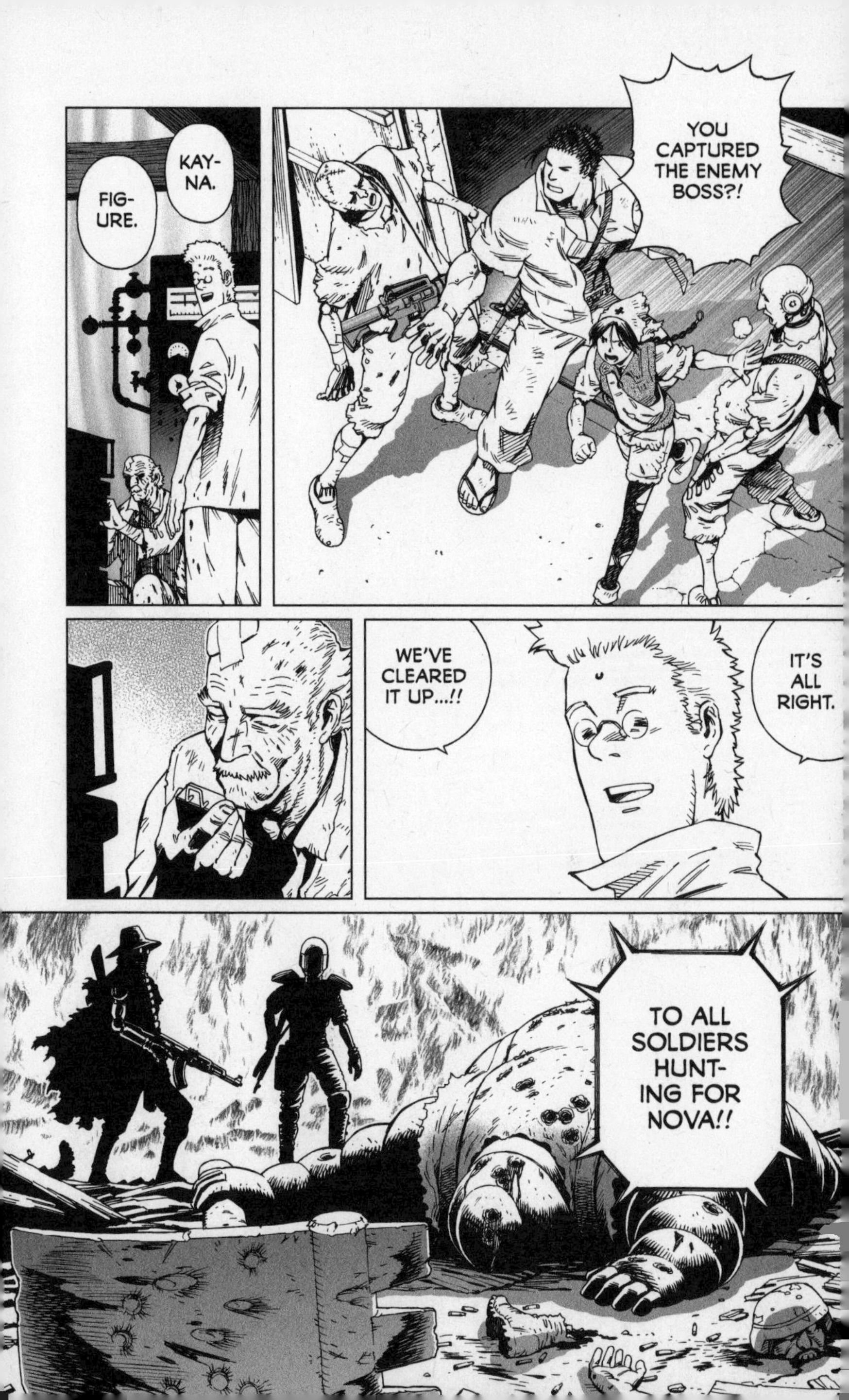
YOU CAPTURED THE ENEMY BOSS?!
KAY-NA.
FIG-URE.
IT'S ALL RIGHT.
WE'VE CLEARED IT UP...!!
TO ALL SOLDIERS HUNT-ING FOR NOVA!!

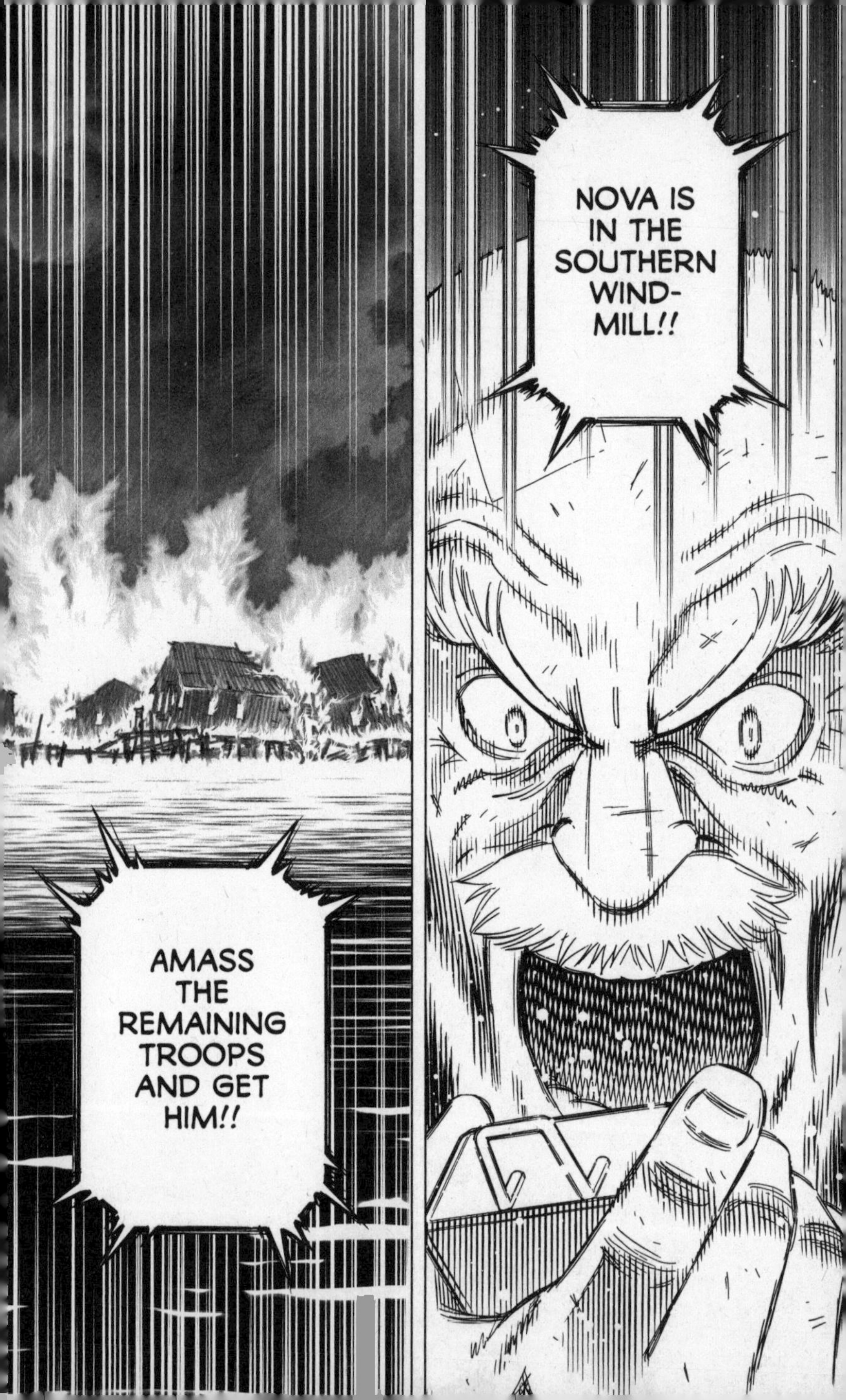
NOVA IS IN THE SOUTHERN WIND-MILL!!
AMASS THE REMAINING TROOPS AND GET HIM!!

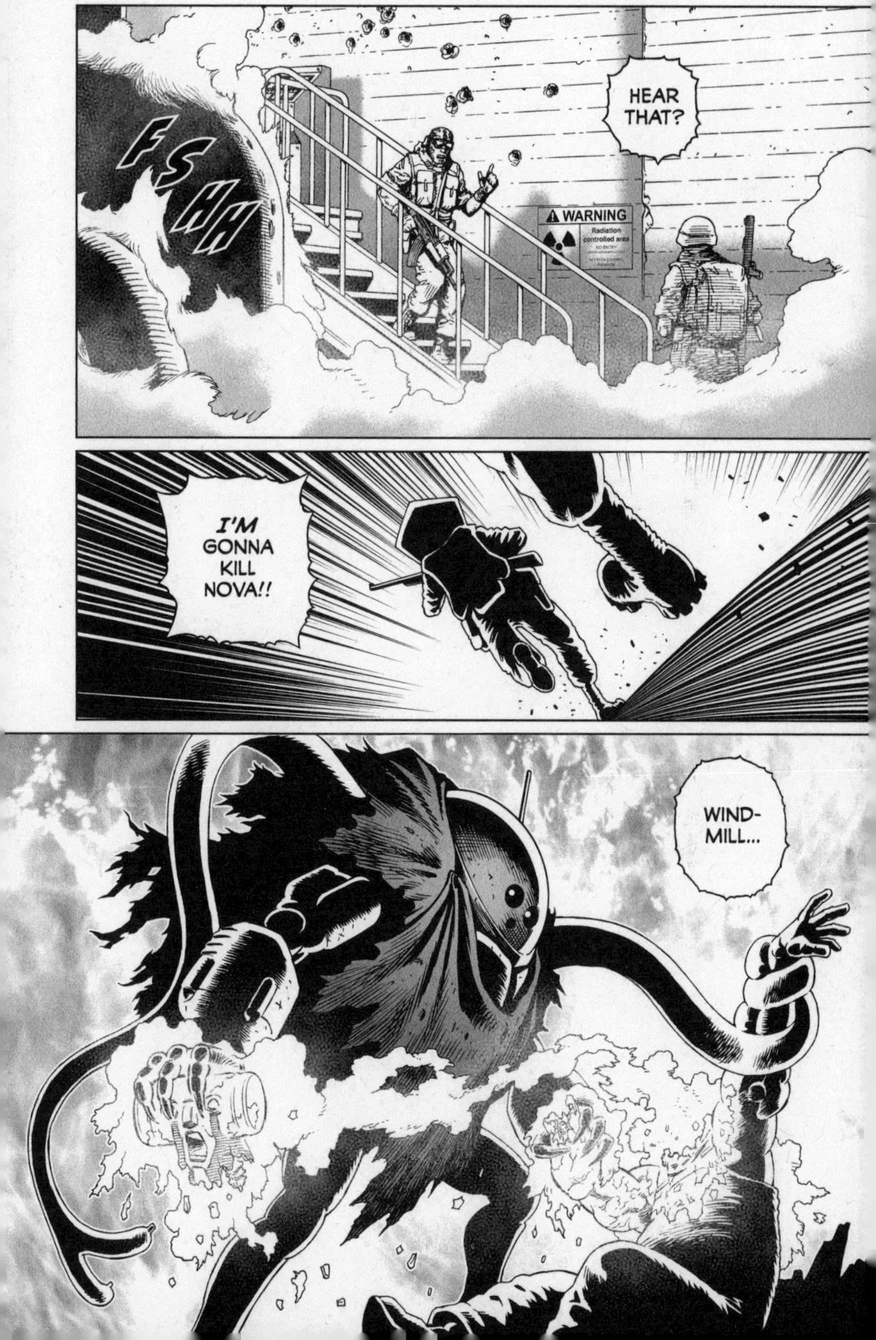
HEAR THAT?
WARNING
Radiation controlled area
NO ENTRY
FSHH
I'M GONNA KILL NOVA!!
WIND-MILL...

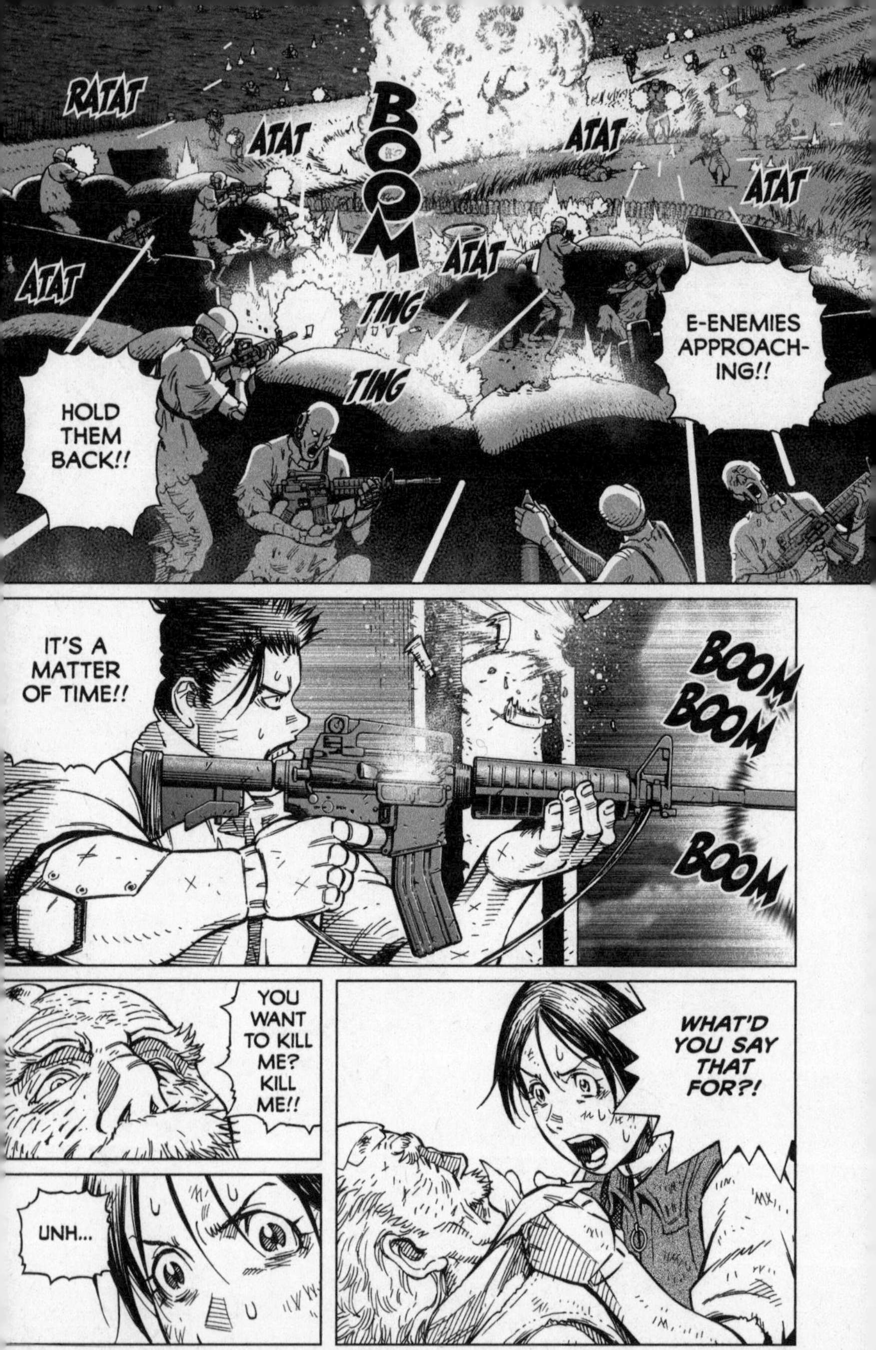
ATAT
ATAT
BOOM
ATAT
RATAT
ATAT
TING
TING
E-ENEMIES APPROACHING!!
ATAT
HOLD THEM BACK!!
BOOM
BOOM
BOOM
IT'S A MATTER OF TIME!!
WHAT'D YOU SAY THAT FOR?!
YOU WANT TO KILL ME? KILL ME!!
UNH...

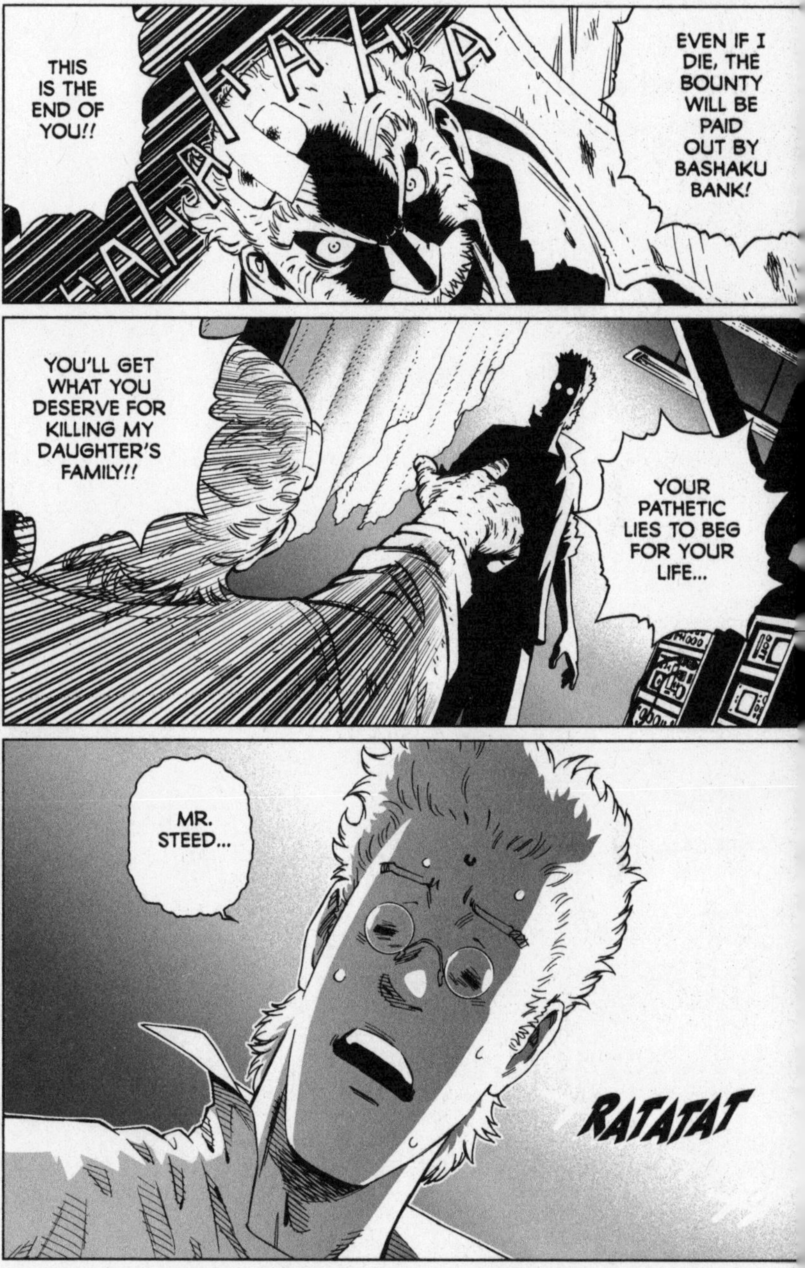

EVEN IF I DIE, THE BOUNTY WILL BE PAID OUT BY BASHAKU BANK!
HAHAHAHA
THIS IS THE END OF YOU!!
YOUR PATHETIC LIES TO BEG FOR YOUR LIFE...
YOU'LL GET WHAT YOU DESERVE FOR KILLING MY DAUGHTER'S FAMILY!!
RATATAT
MR. STEED...

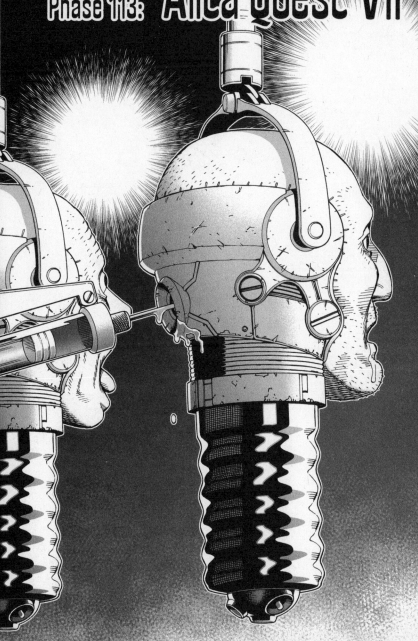

Phase 113: Alita Quest VII

KLANG
WHIR
WHIR
WHIR
WHIR
SHUNK
KOF
WHIRR
KLANG
BING
VEEEMM

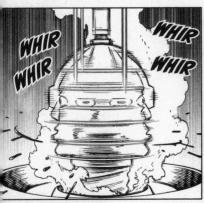

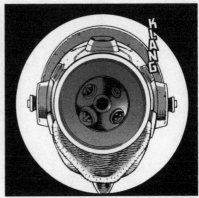

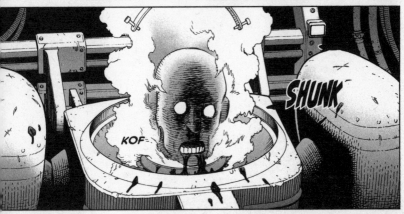

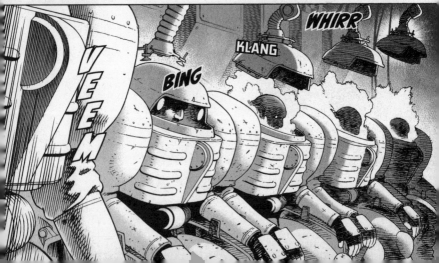

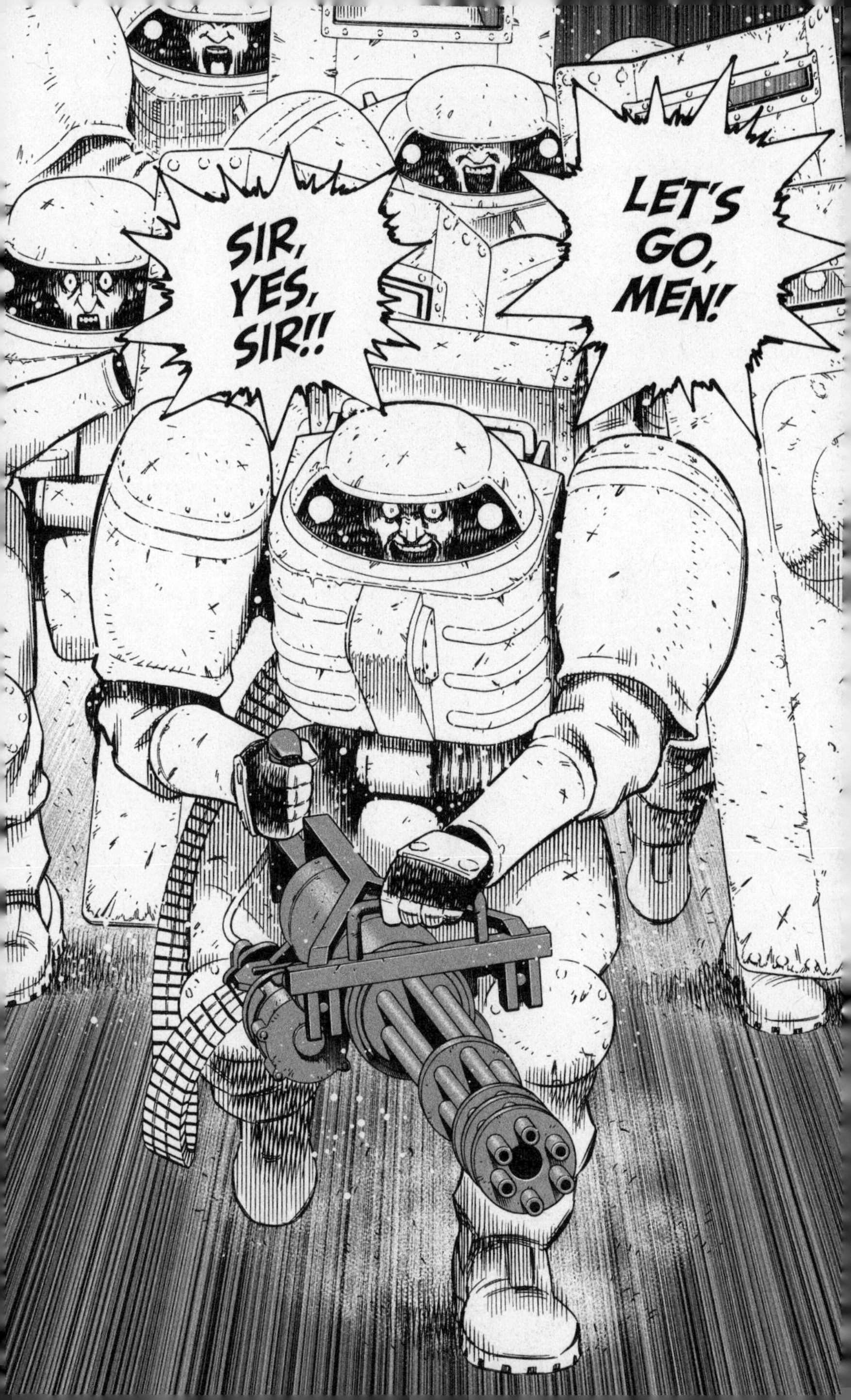
LET'S GO, MEN!
SIR, YES, SIR!!

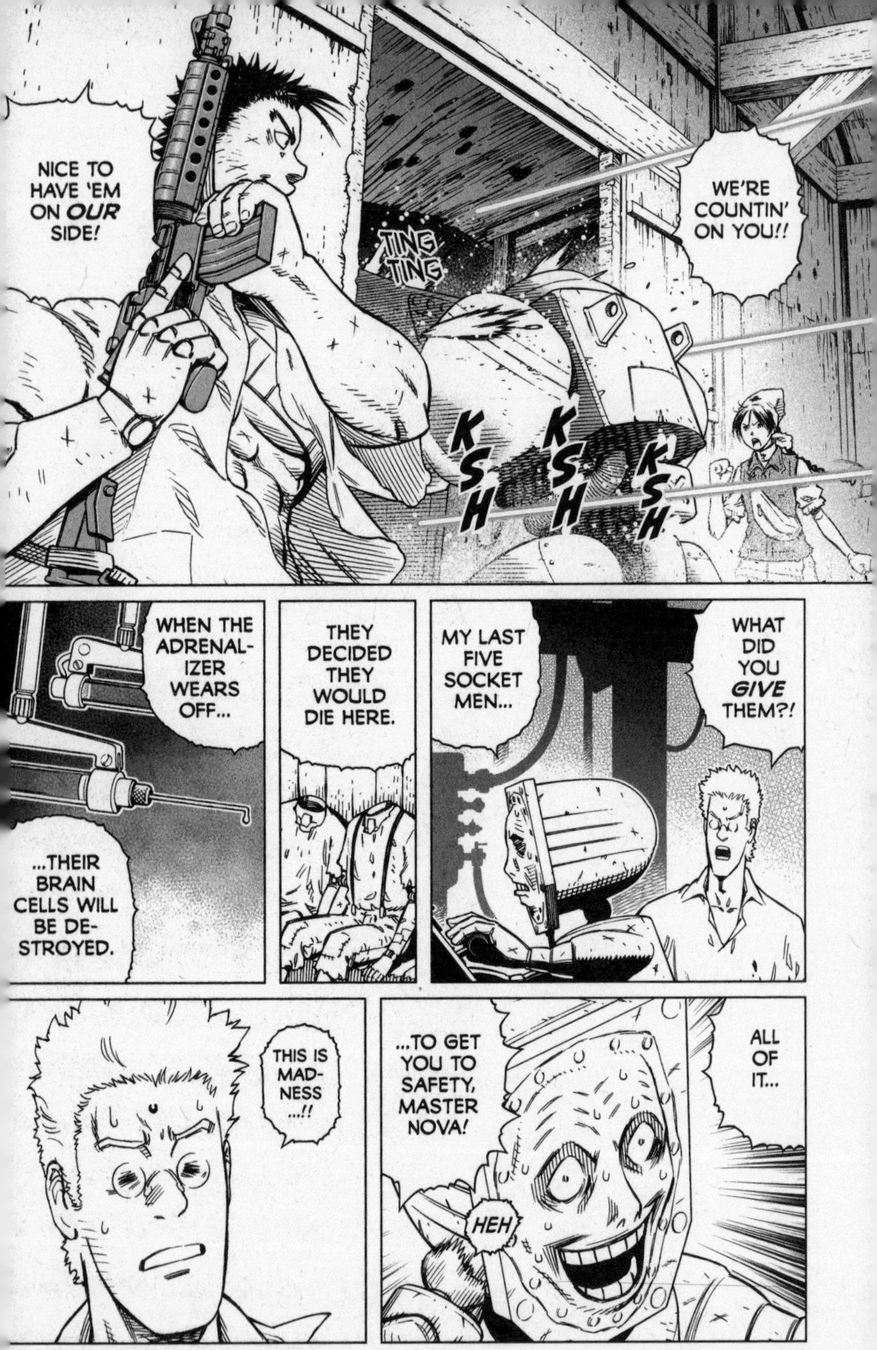
WE'RE COUNTIN' ON YOU!!
TING TING
NICE TO HAVE 'EM ON *OUR* SIDE!
KSH KSH KSH
WHAT DID YOU *GIVE* THEM?!
MY LAST FIVE SOCKET MEN...
THEY DECIDED THEY WOULD DIE HERE.
WHEN THE ADRENALIZER WEARS OFF...
...THEIR BRAIN CELLS WILL BE DESTROYED.
ALL OF IT...
...TO GET YOU TO SAFETY, MASTER NOVA!
HEH
THIS IS MADNESS...!!

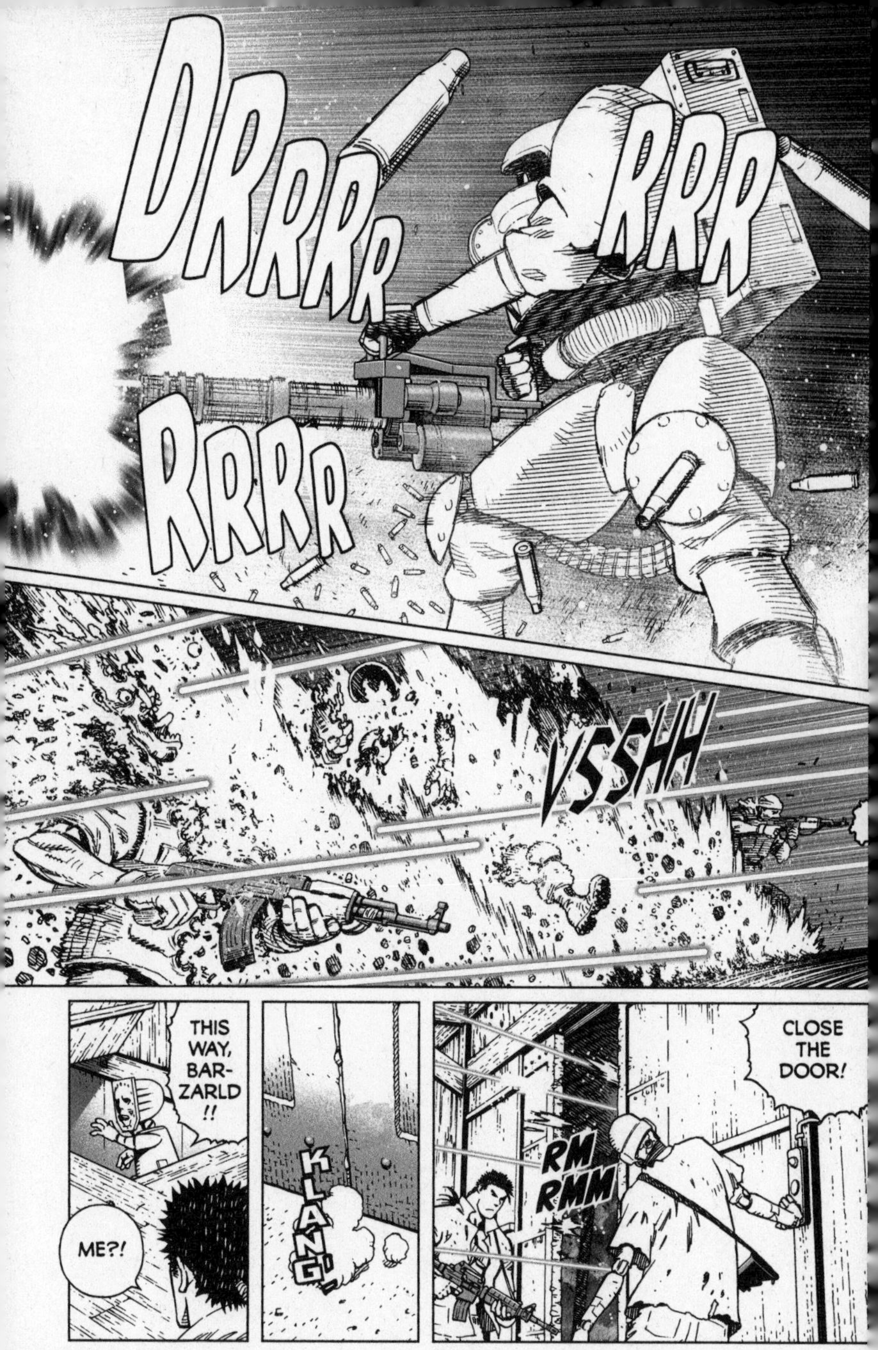
DRRRRR
RRR
RRRR
VSSHH
CLOSE THE DOOR!
RM RMM
KLANG!
THIS WAY, BAR-ZARLD!!
ME?!

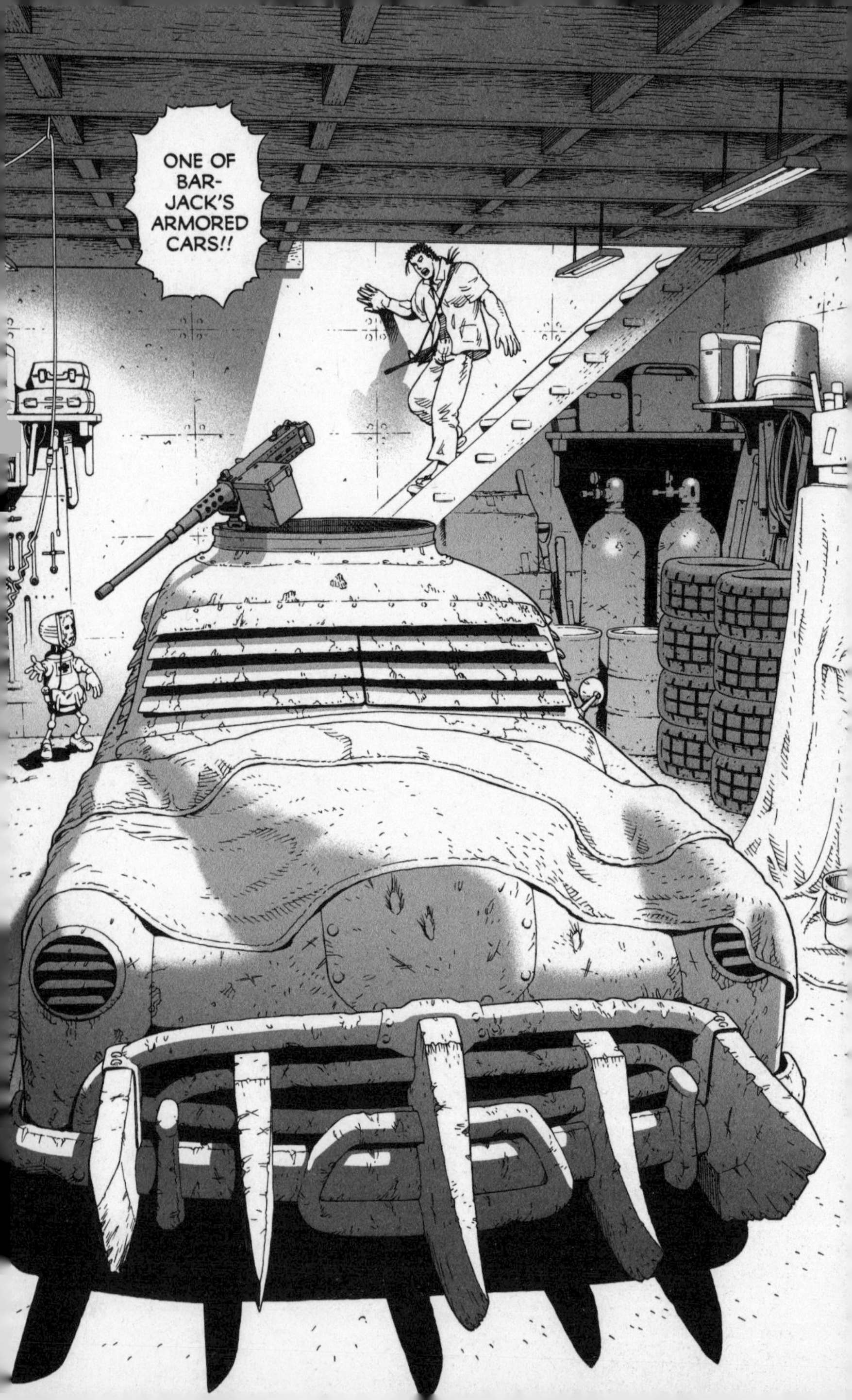
ONE OF BAR-JACK'S ARMORED CARS!!

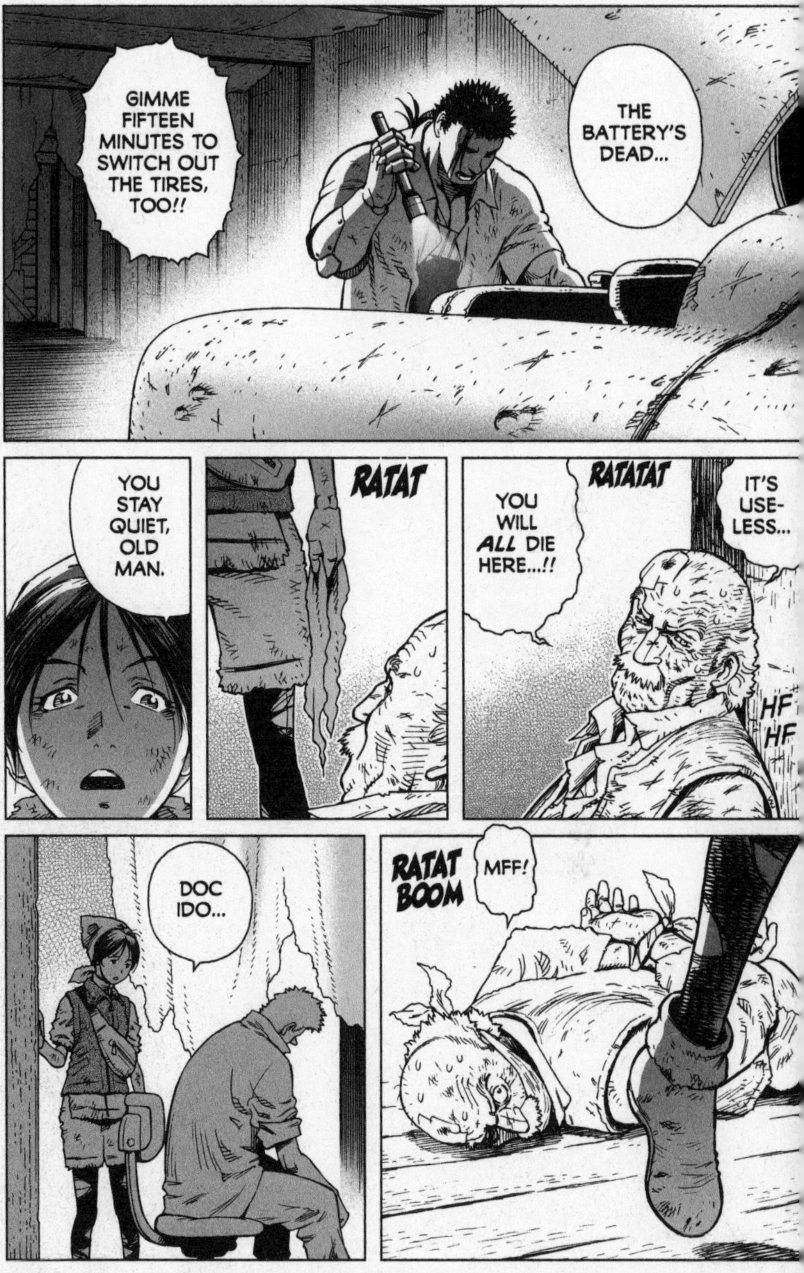
THE BATTERY'S DEAD...
GIMME FIFTEEN MINUTES TO SWITCH OUT THE TIRES, TOO!!
IT'S USELESS...
RATATAT
YOU WILL ALL DIE HERE...!!
HF HF
RATAT
YOU STAY QUIET, OLD MAN.
MFF!
RATAT BOOM
DOC IDO...

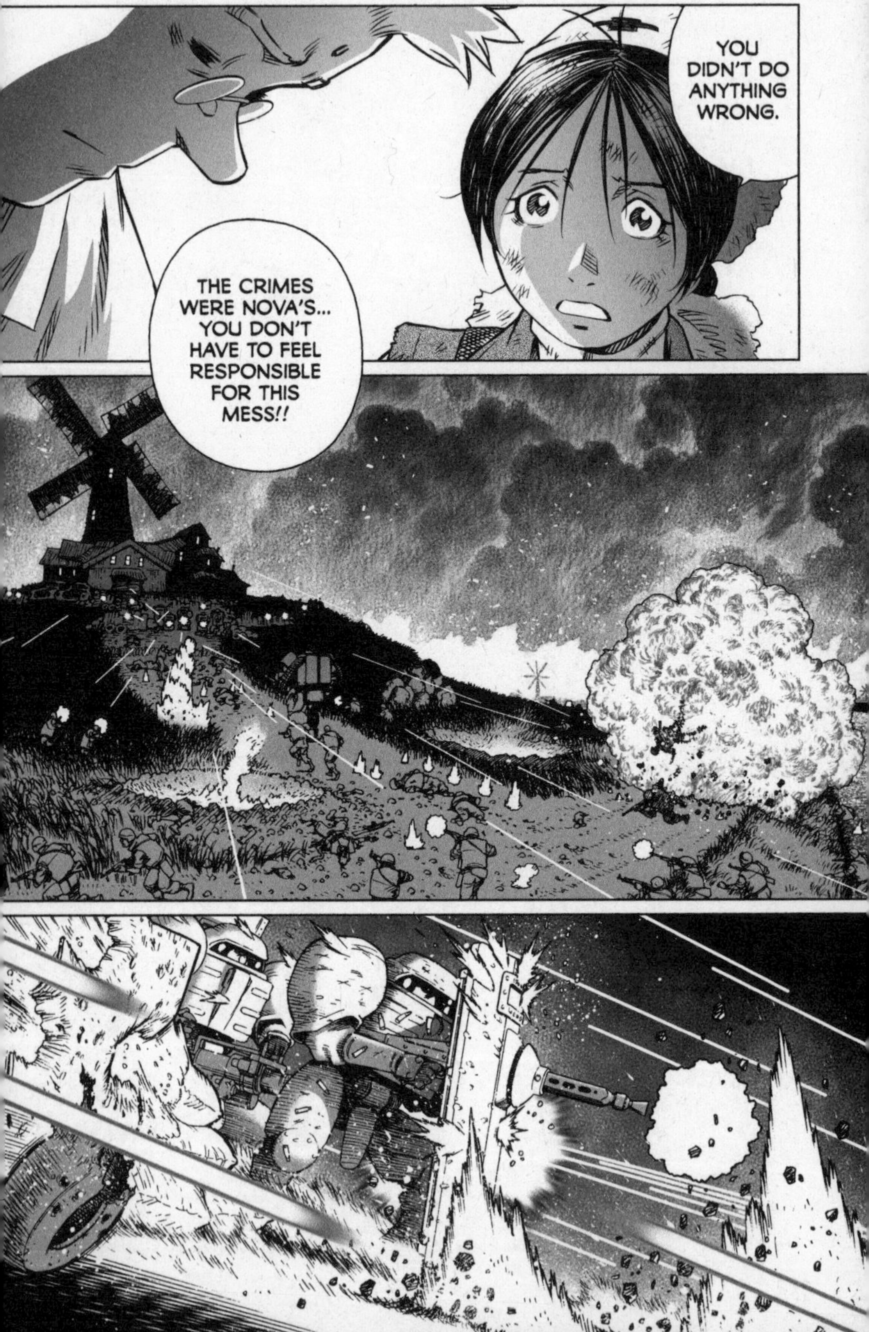
YOU DIDN'T DO ANYTHING WRONG.
THE CRIMES WERE NOVA'S... YOU DON'T HAVE TO FEEL RESPONSIBLE FOR THIS MESS!!

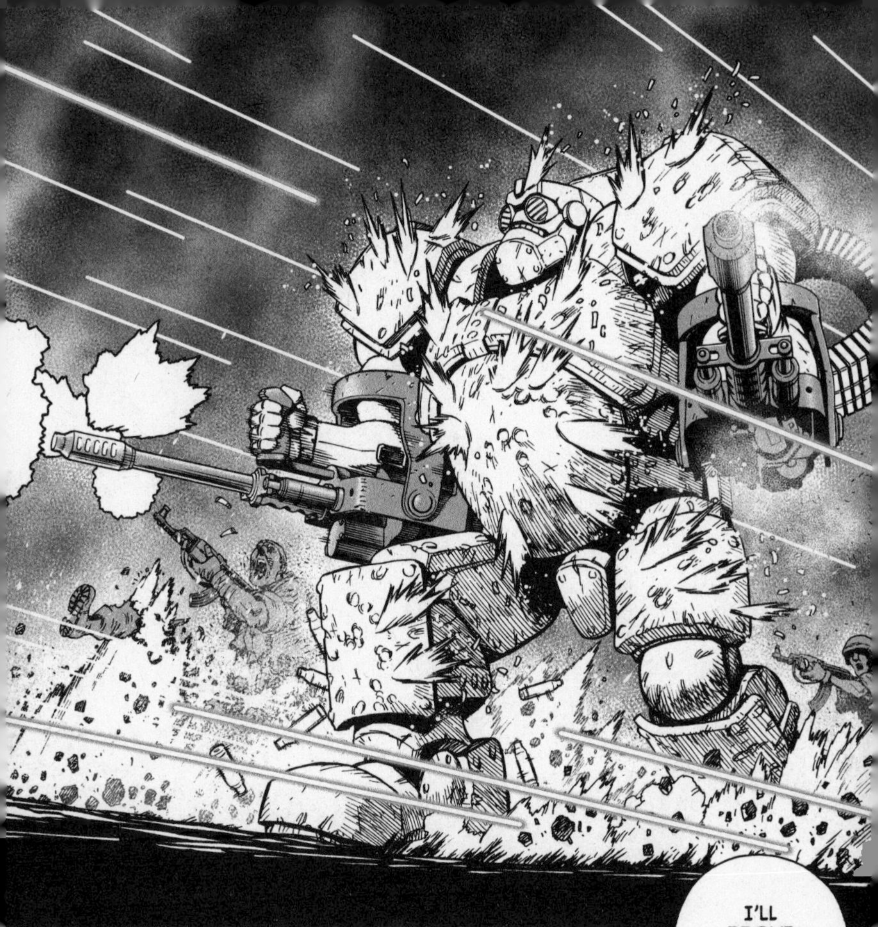

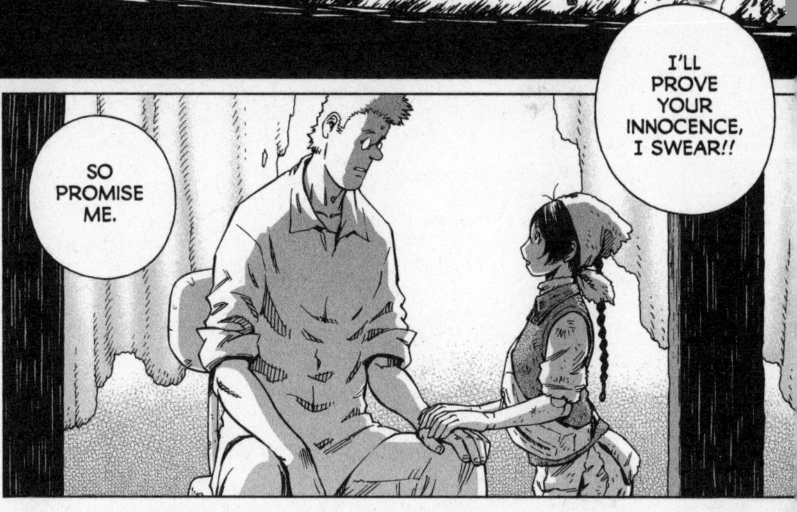
I'LL PROVE YOUR INNOCENCE, I SWEAR!!
SO PROMISE ME.

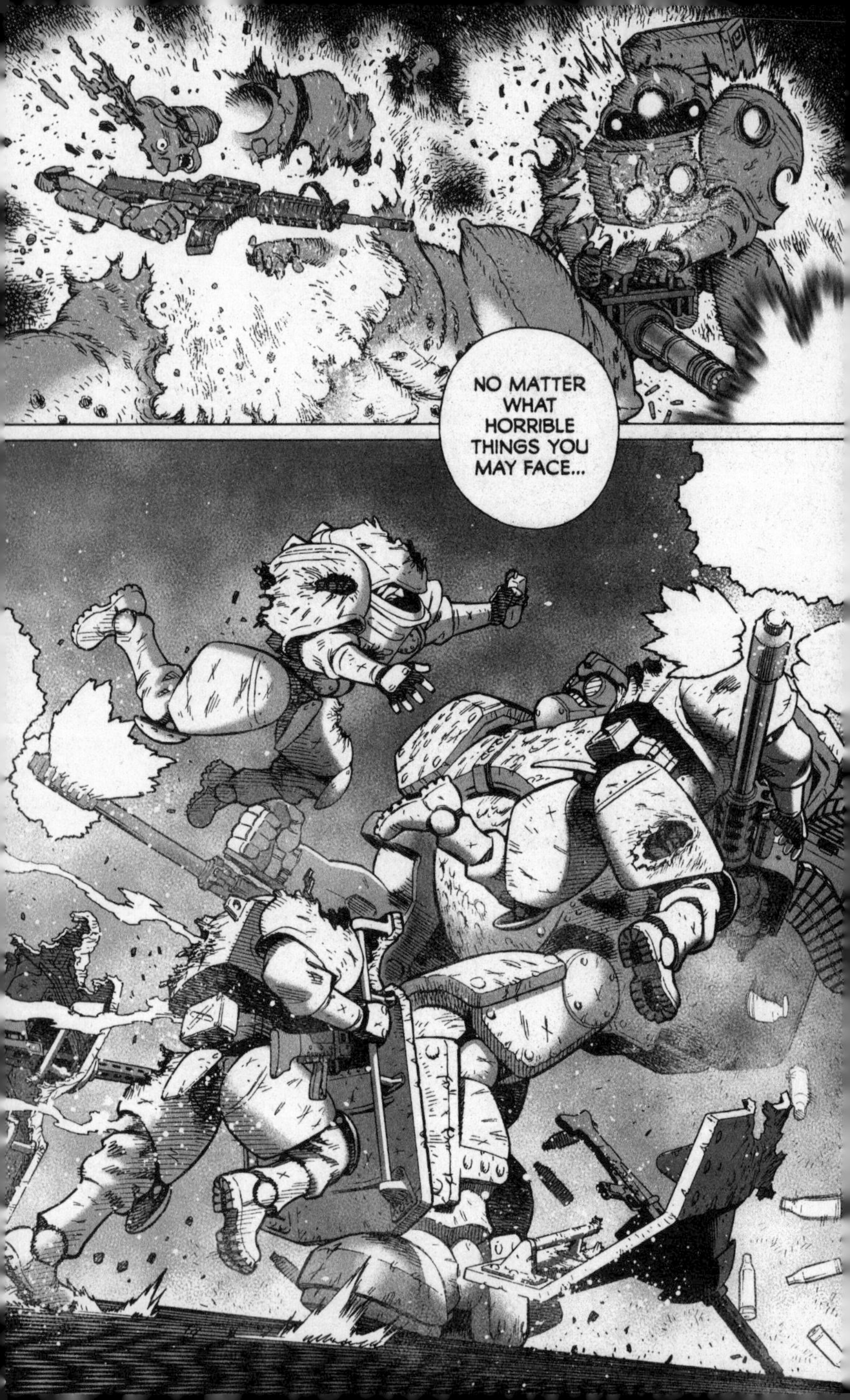
NO MATTER WHAT HORRIBLE THINGS YOU MAY FACE...

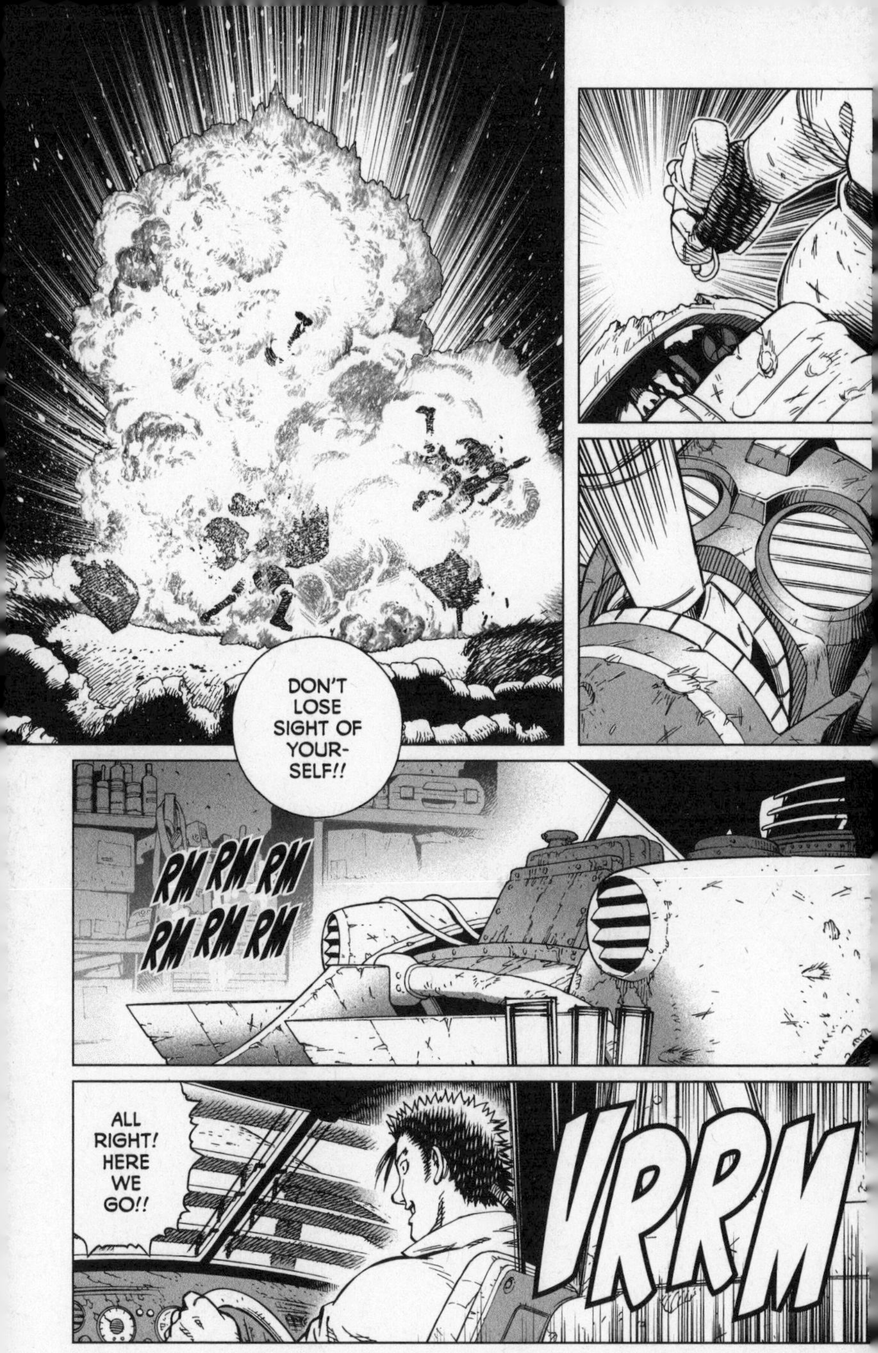
DON'T LOSE SIGHT OF YOUR-SELF!!
RM RM RM RM RM RM
VRRM
ALL RIGHT! HERE WE GO!!

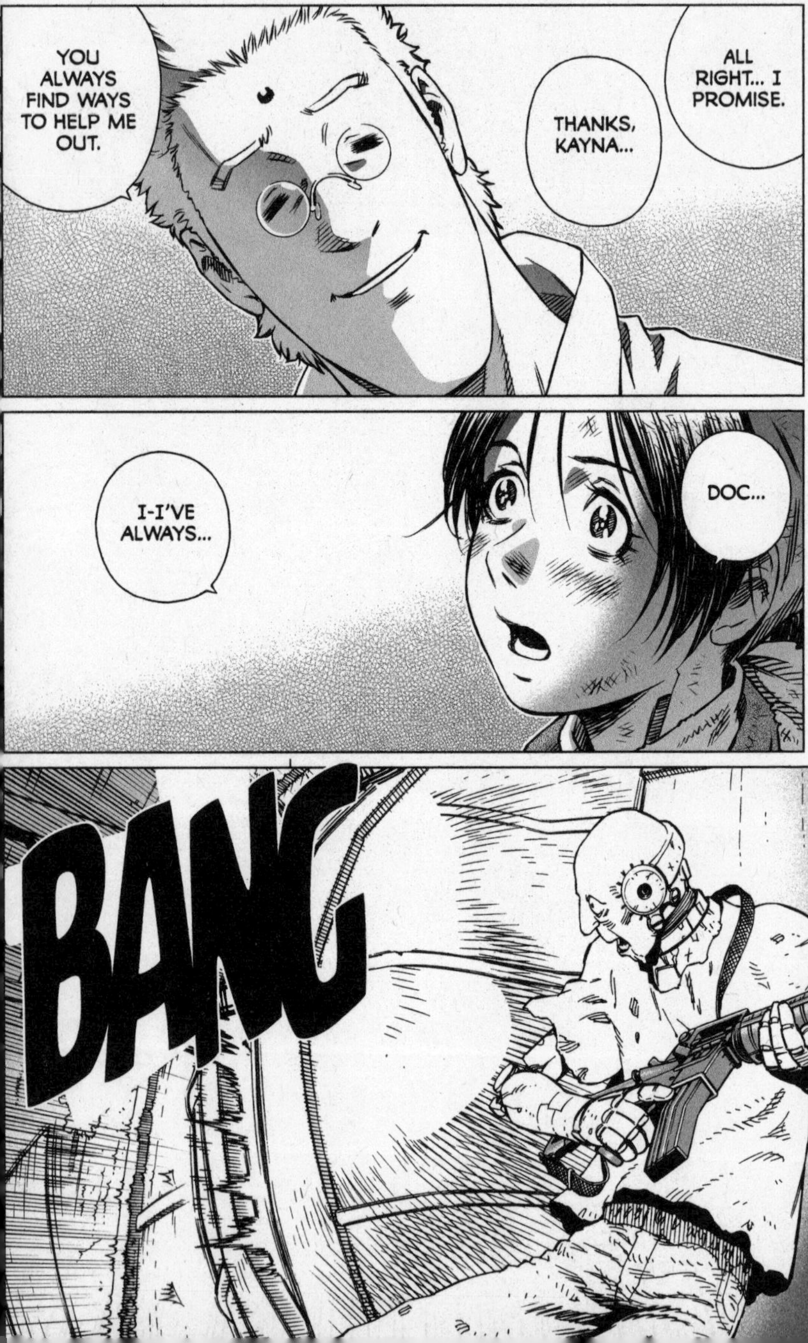
ALL RIGHT... I PROMISE.
THANKS, KAYNA...
YOU ALWAYS FIND WAYS TO HELP ME OUT.
DOC...
I-I'VE ALWAYS...
BANG

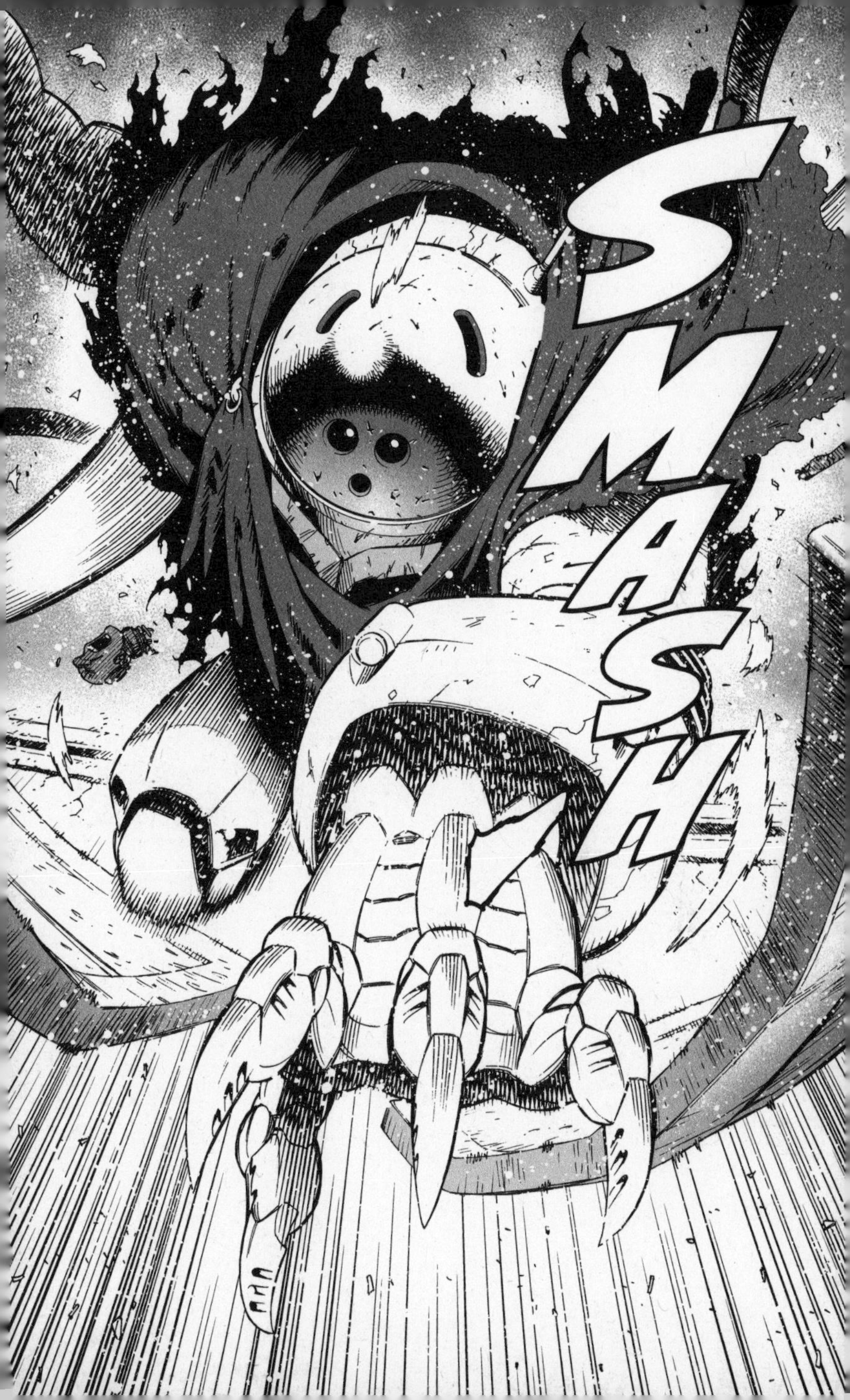
SMASH

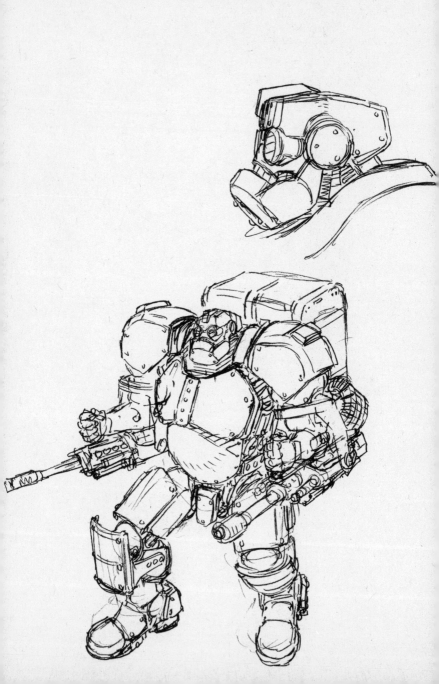

Phase 114: Alita Quest VIII

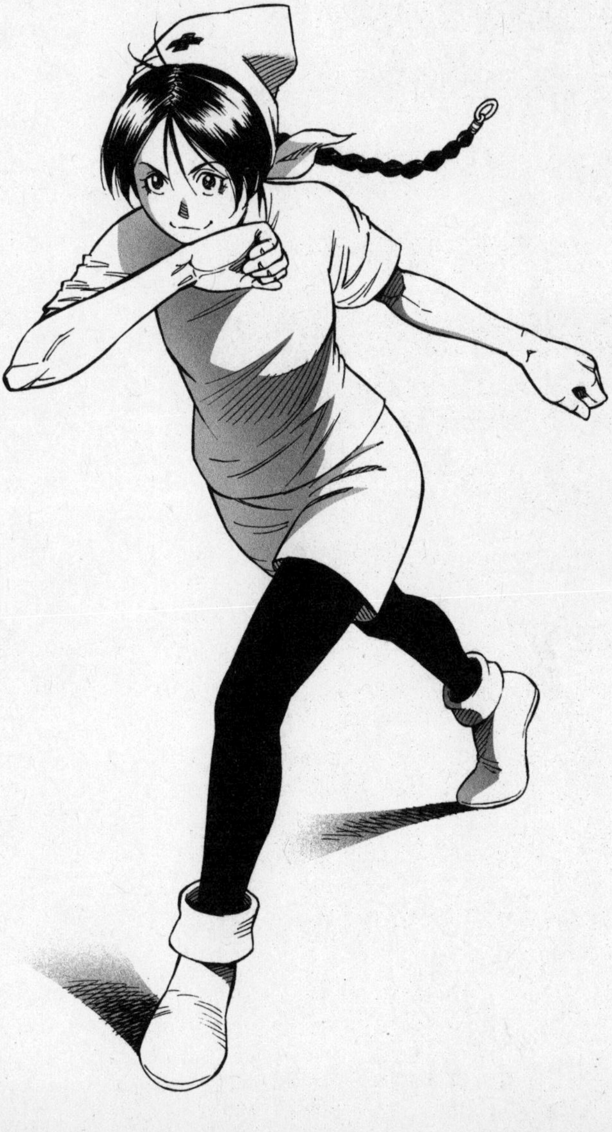

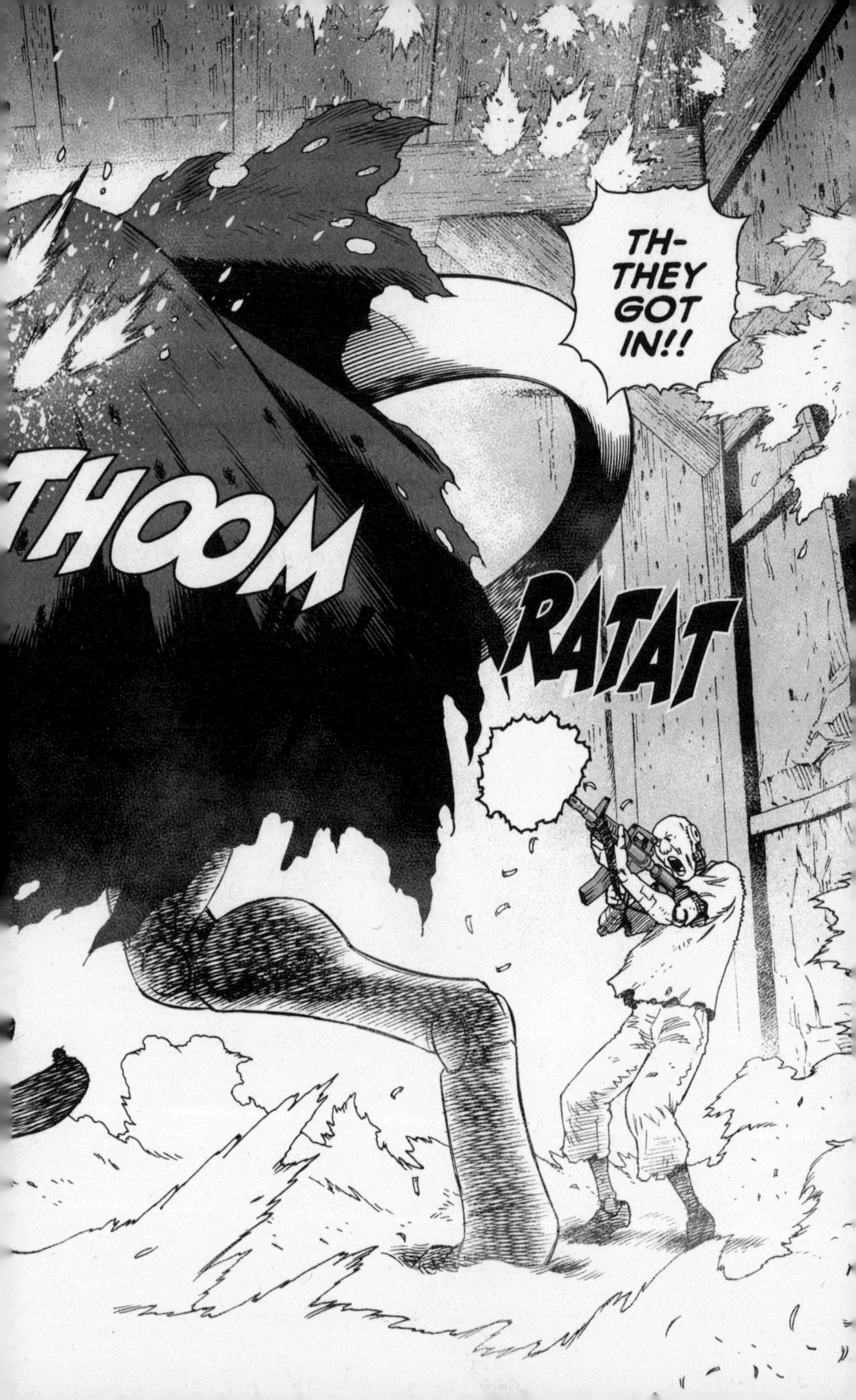
TH- THEY GOT IN!!
THOOM
RATAT

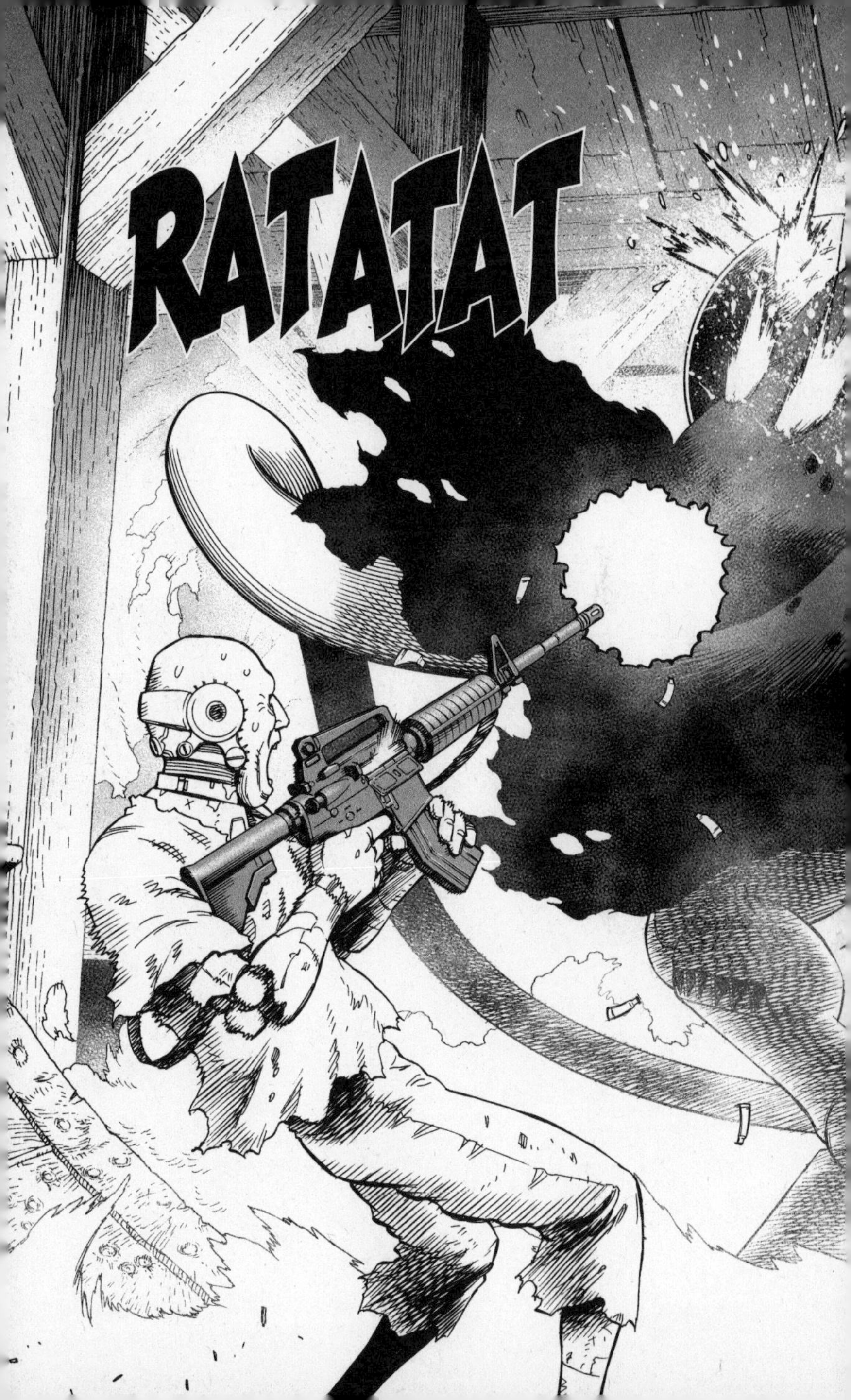
RATATAT

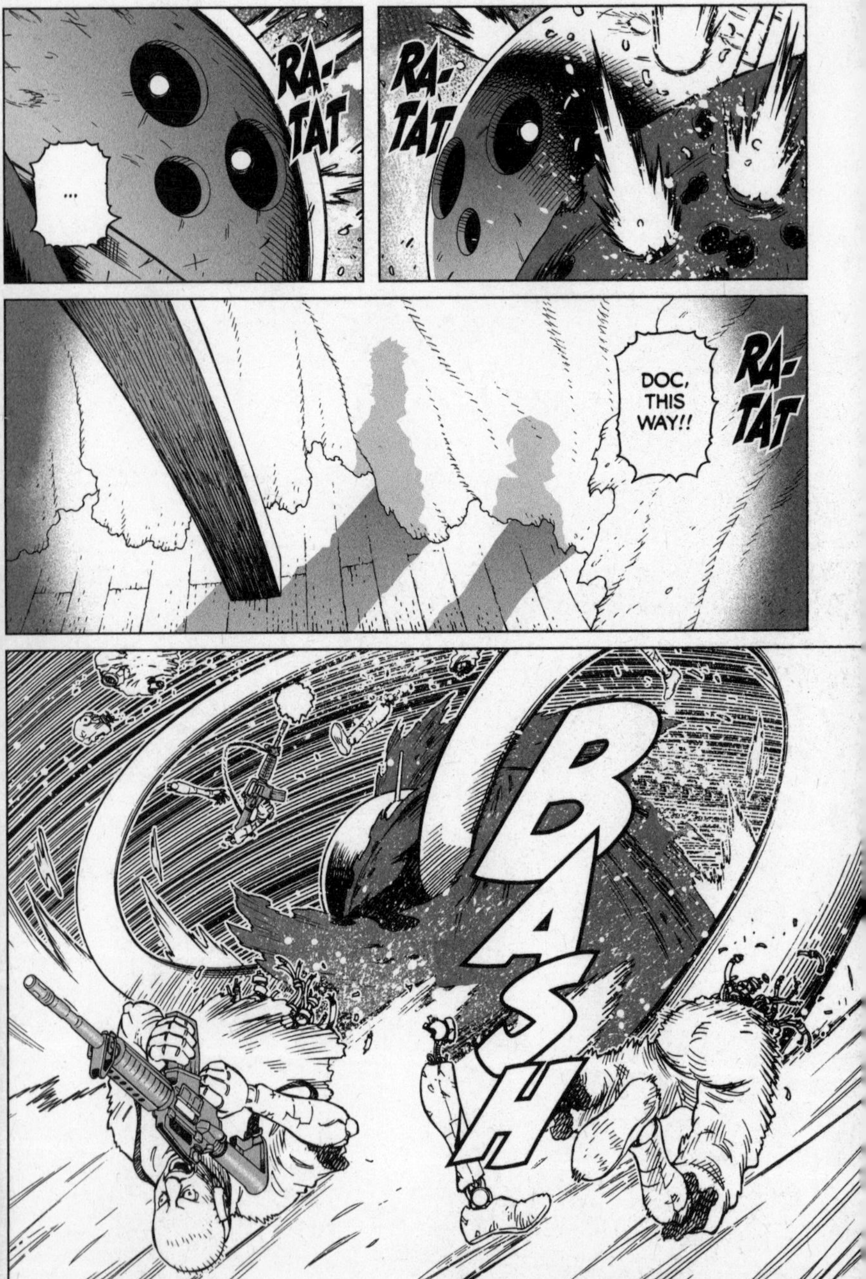
RA-TAT
RA-TAT
...
RA-TAT
DOC, THIS WAY!!
BASH

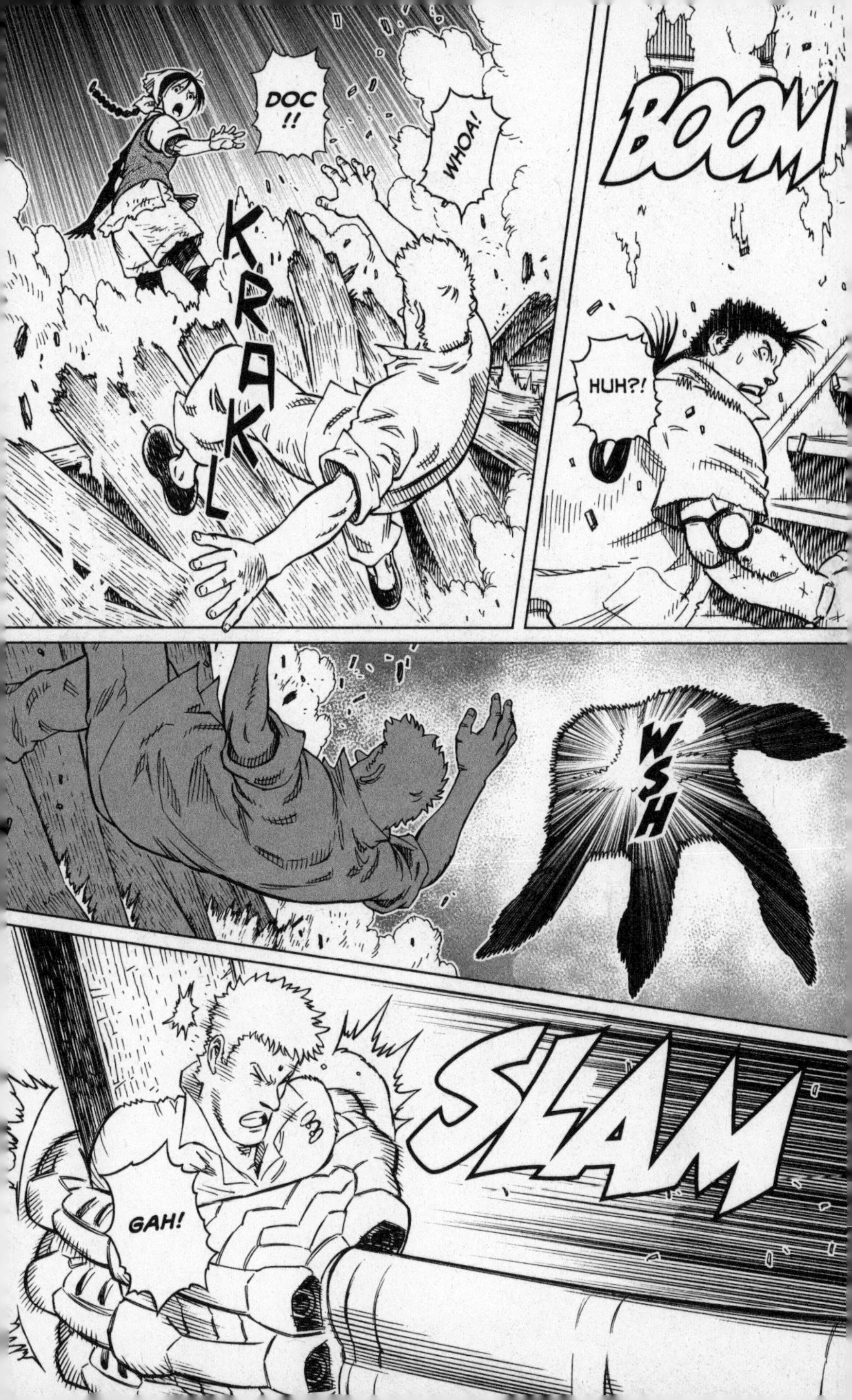
BOOM
HUH?!
WHOA!
DOC !!
KRAKL
WSH
SLAM
GAH!

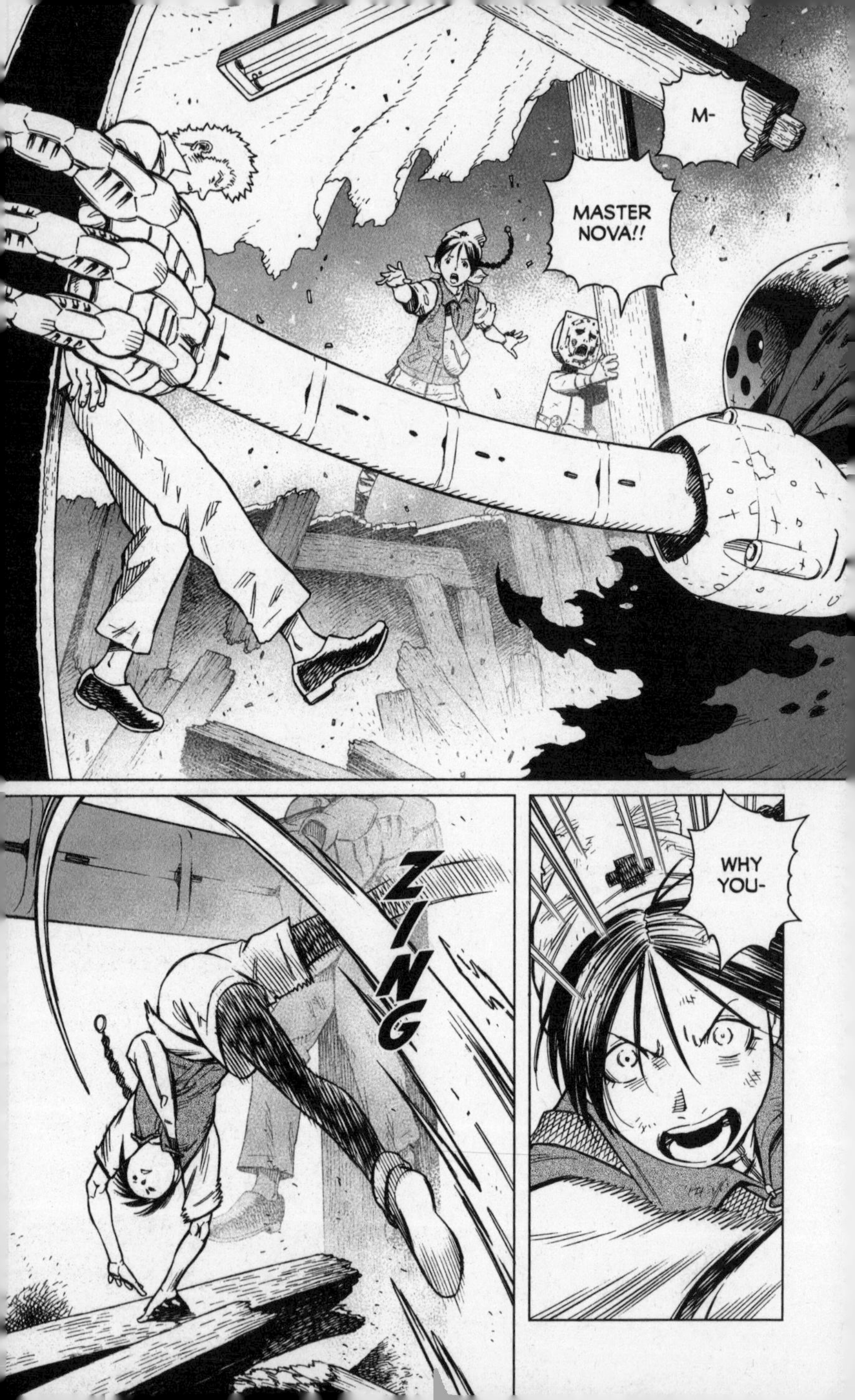
M-
MASTER NOVA!!
WHY YOU-
ZING

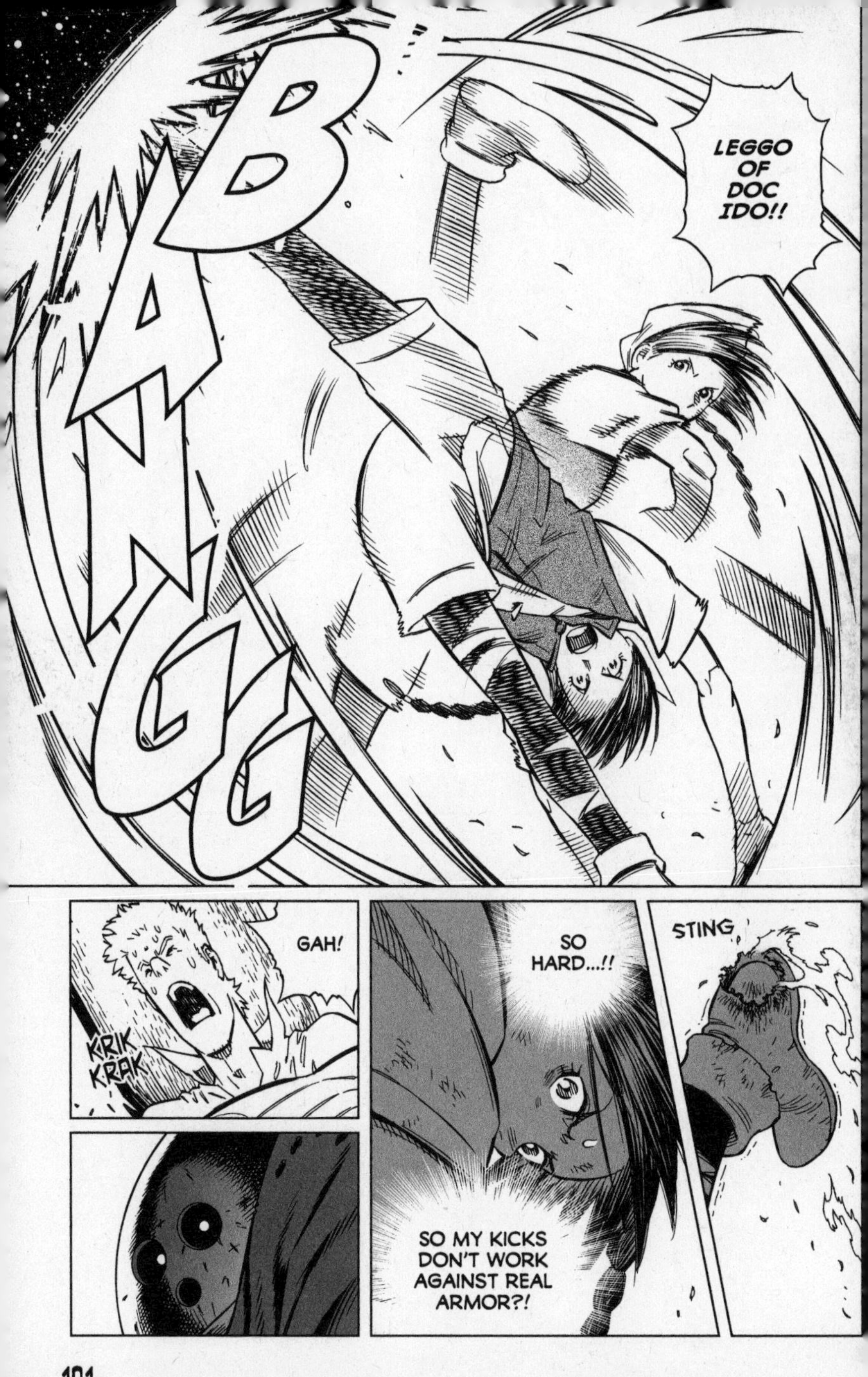
LEGGO OF DOC IDO!!
BANGG
STING
SO HARD...!!
SO MY KICKS DON'T WORK AGAINST REAL ARMOR?!
GAH!
KRIK KRAK

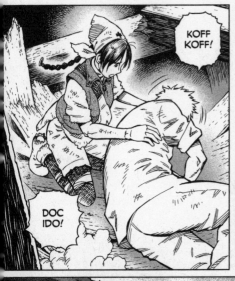

KOFF KOFF!

DOC IDO!

THMP

...ARE NOT NOVA.

YOU...

MFF!!

MM!

WHAT ARE YOU SAY- ING?

WH-

?!

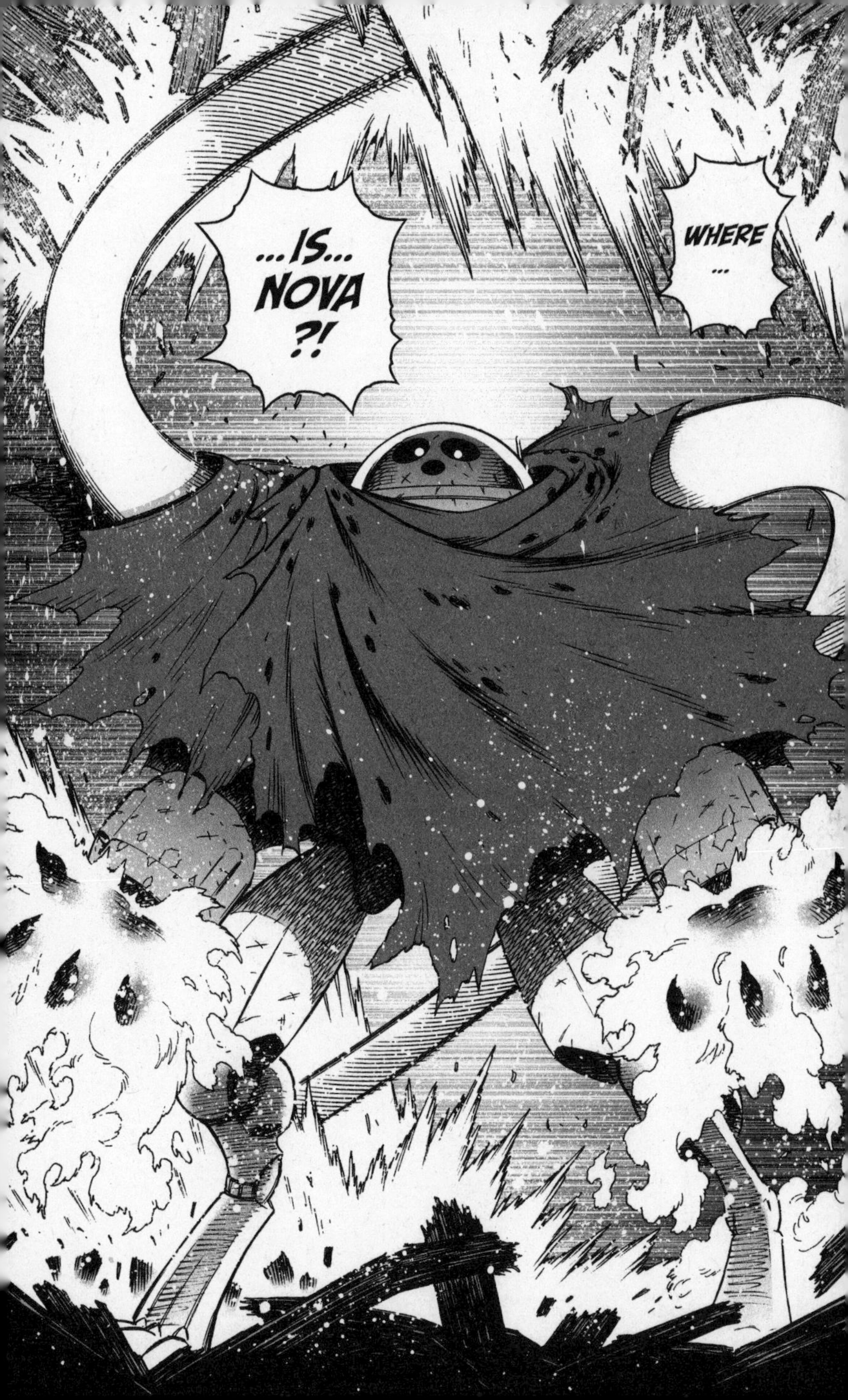
WHERE ...
...IS... NOVA ?!

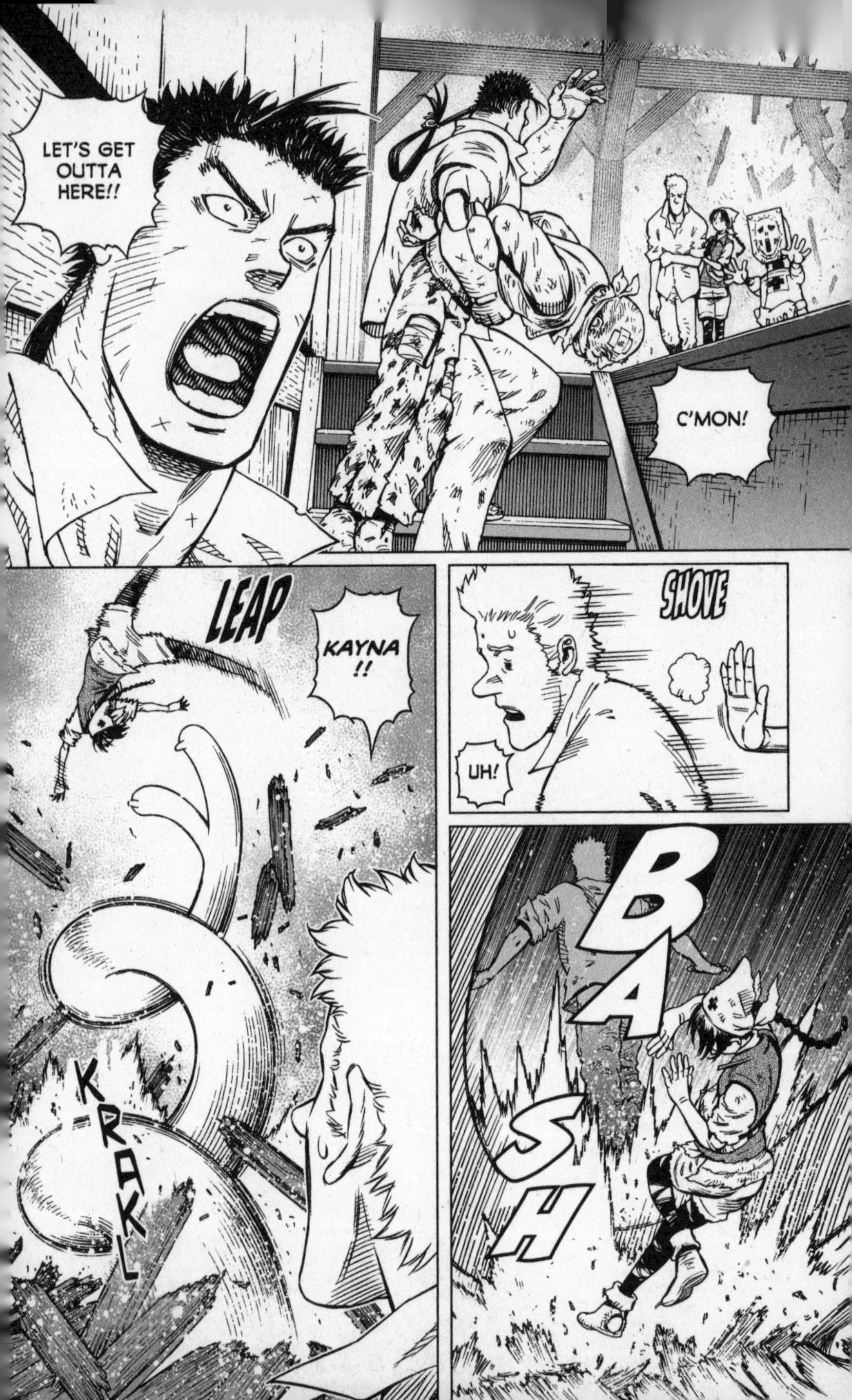
LET'S GET OUTTA HERE!!
C'MON!
SHOVE
UH!
BASH
LEAP
KAYNA!!
KRAKL

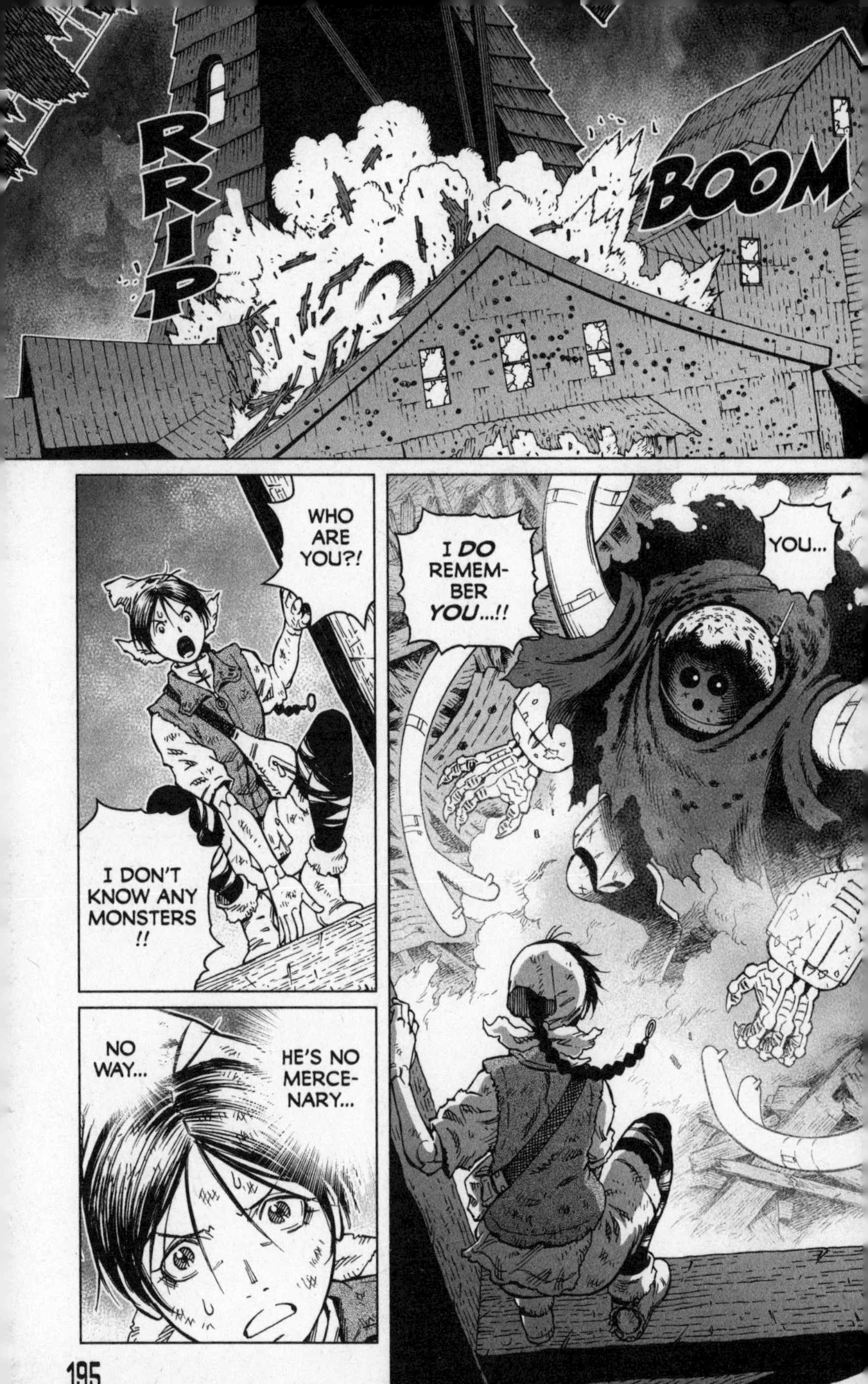
BOOM
RRIP
YOU...
I DO REMEMBER YOU...!!
WHO ARE YOU?!
I DON'T KNOW ANY MONSTERS !!
HE'S NO MERCENARY...
NO WAY...

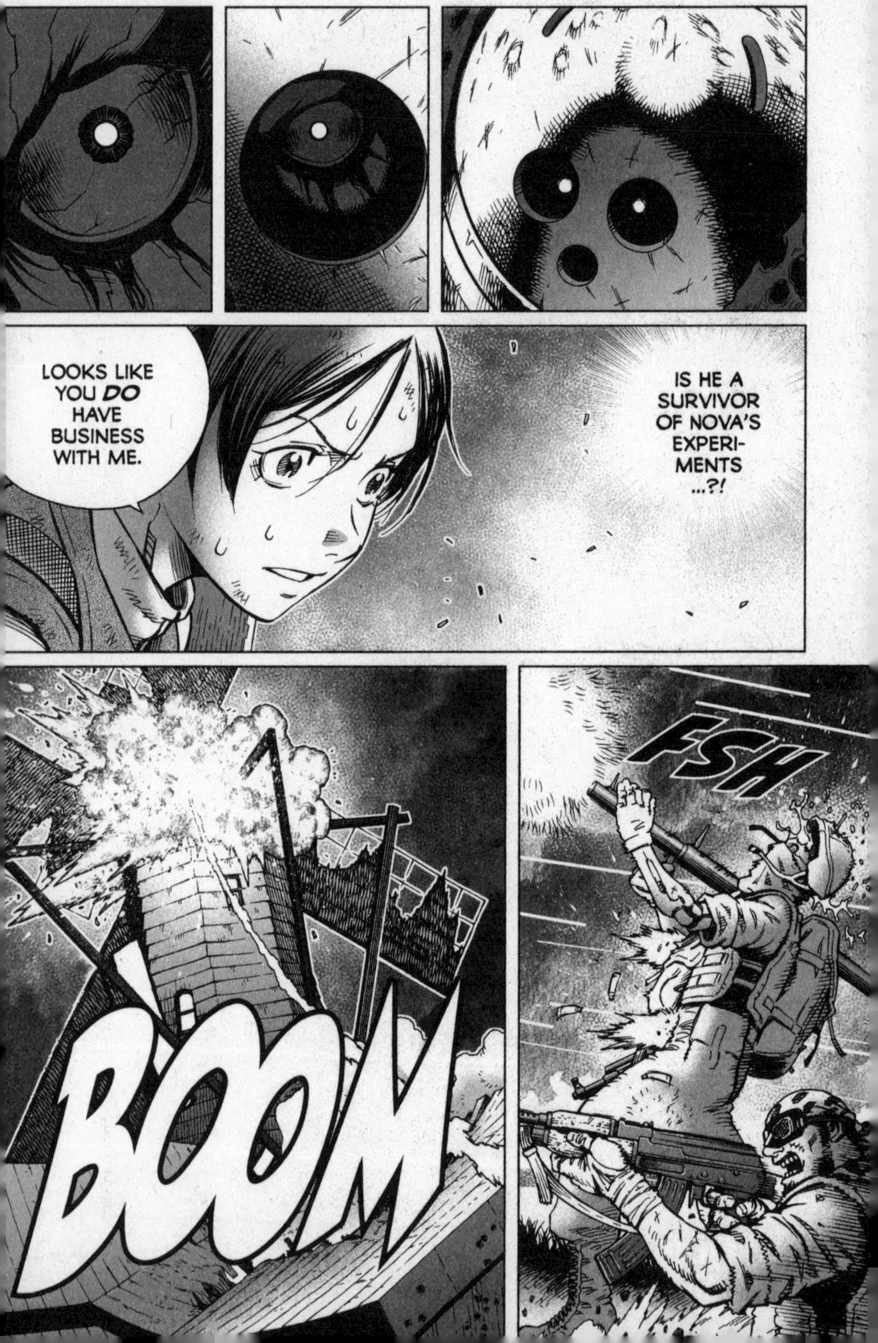
IS HE A SURVIVOR OF NOVA'S EXPERI-MENTS ...?!
LOOKS LIKE YOU *DO* HAVE BUSINESS WITH ME.
FSH
BOOM

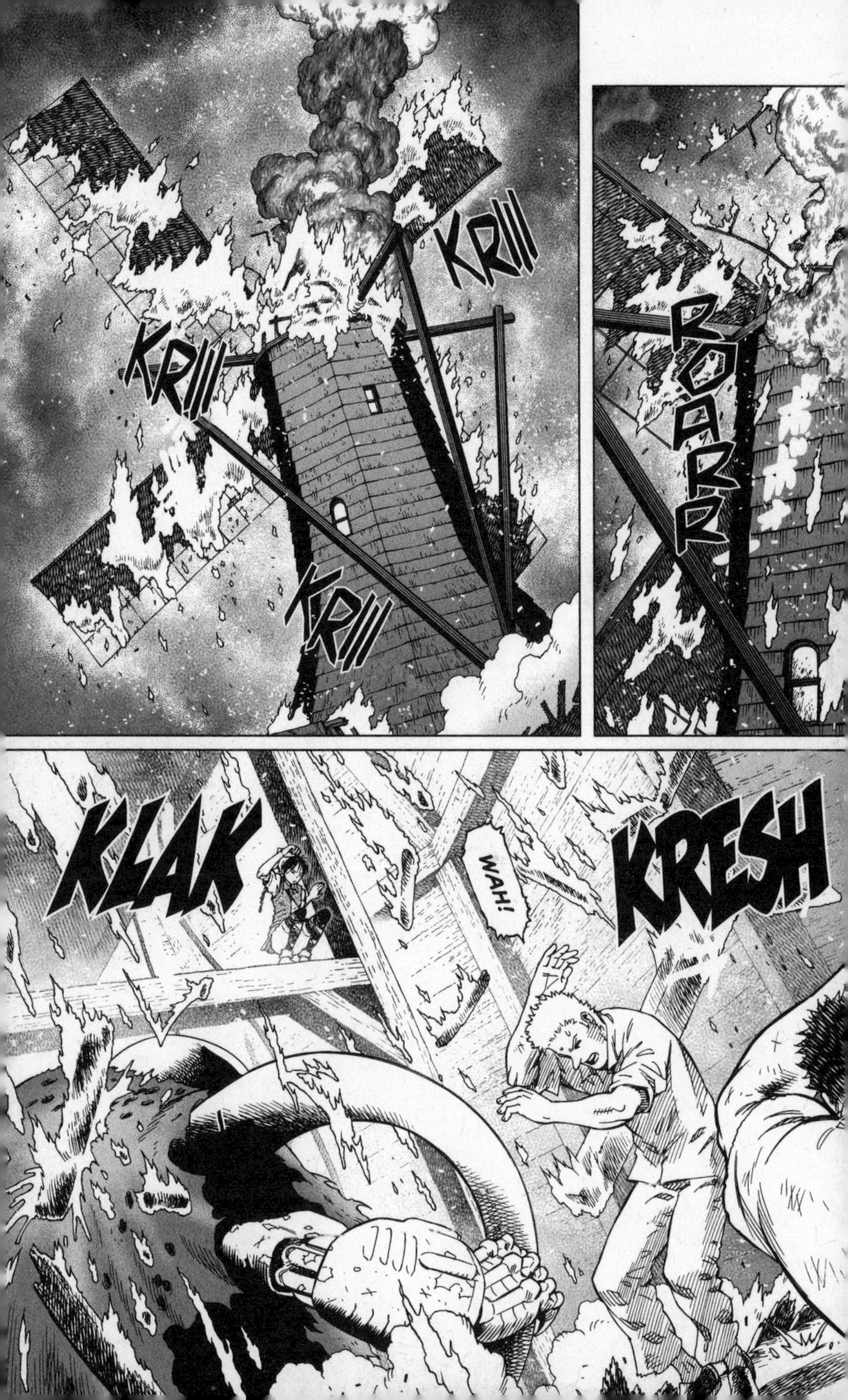
ROARR
KRIII
KRIII
KRIII
KRESH
WAH!
KLAK

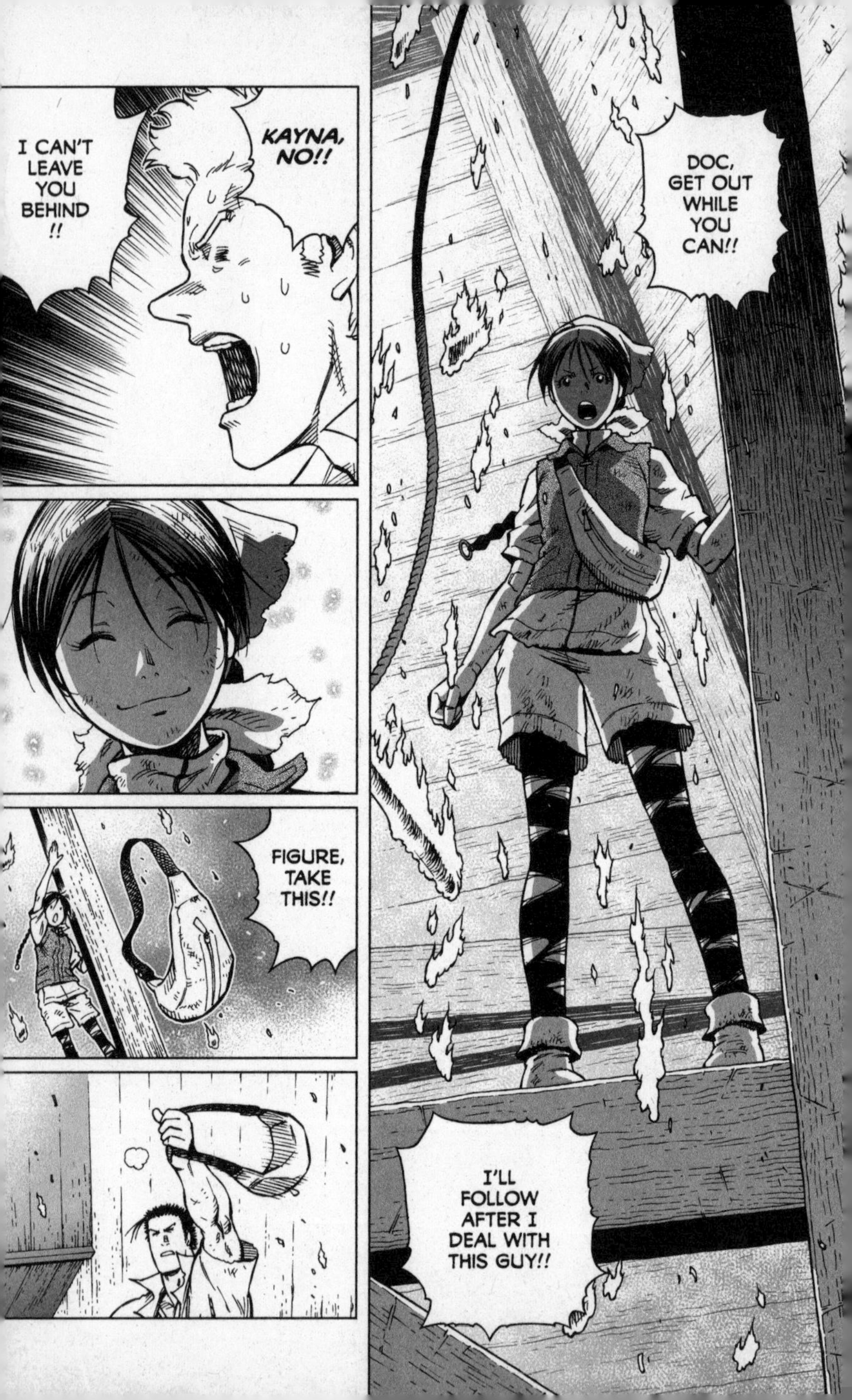
DOC, GET OUT WHILE YOU CAN!!
I'LL FOLLOW AFTER I DEAL WITH THIS GUY!!
KAYNA, NO!!
I CAN'T LEAVE YOU BEHIND!!
FIGURE, TAKE THIS!!

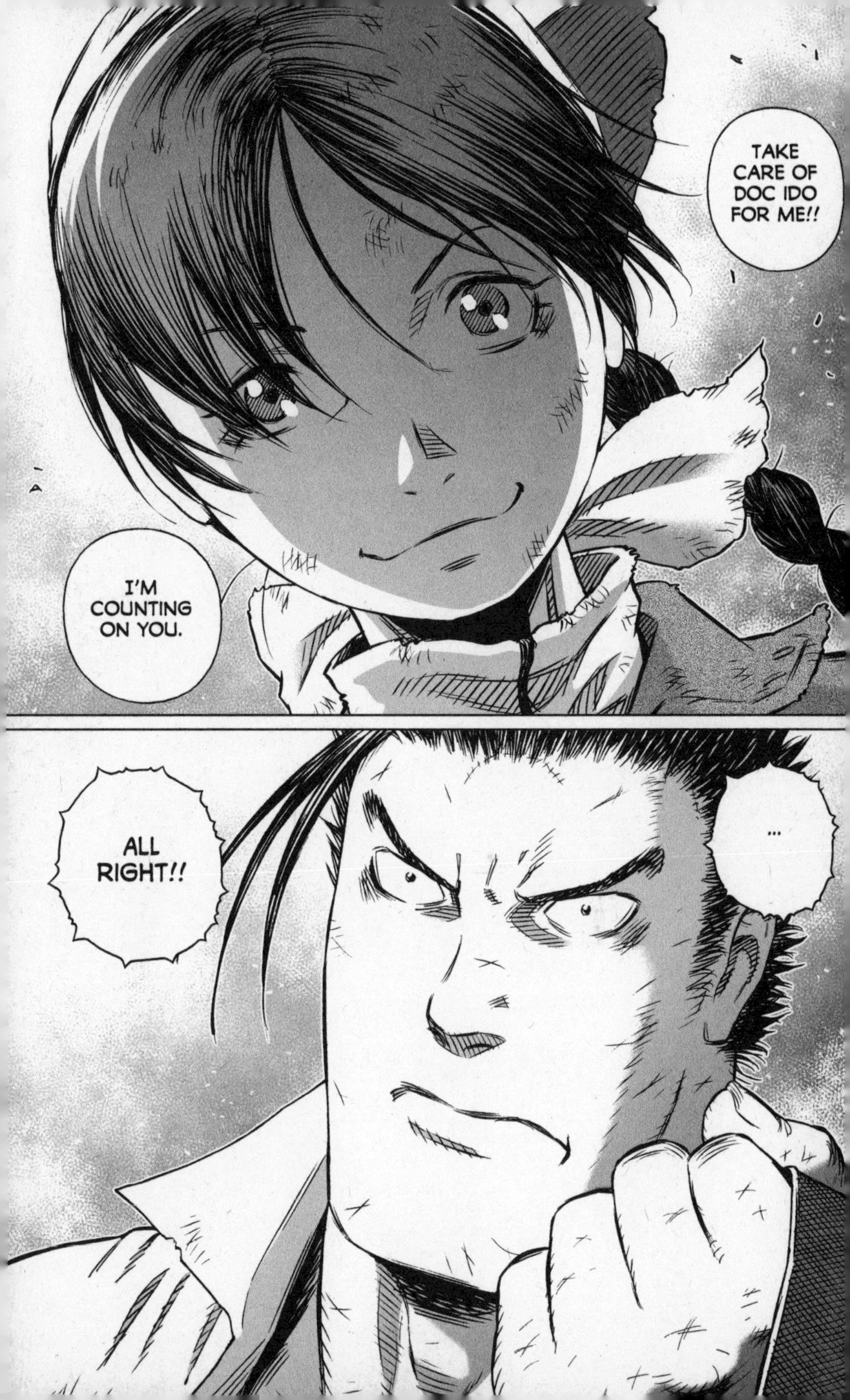
TAKE CARE OF DOC IDO FOR ME!!
I'M COUNTING ON YOU.
...
ALL RIGHT!!

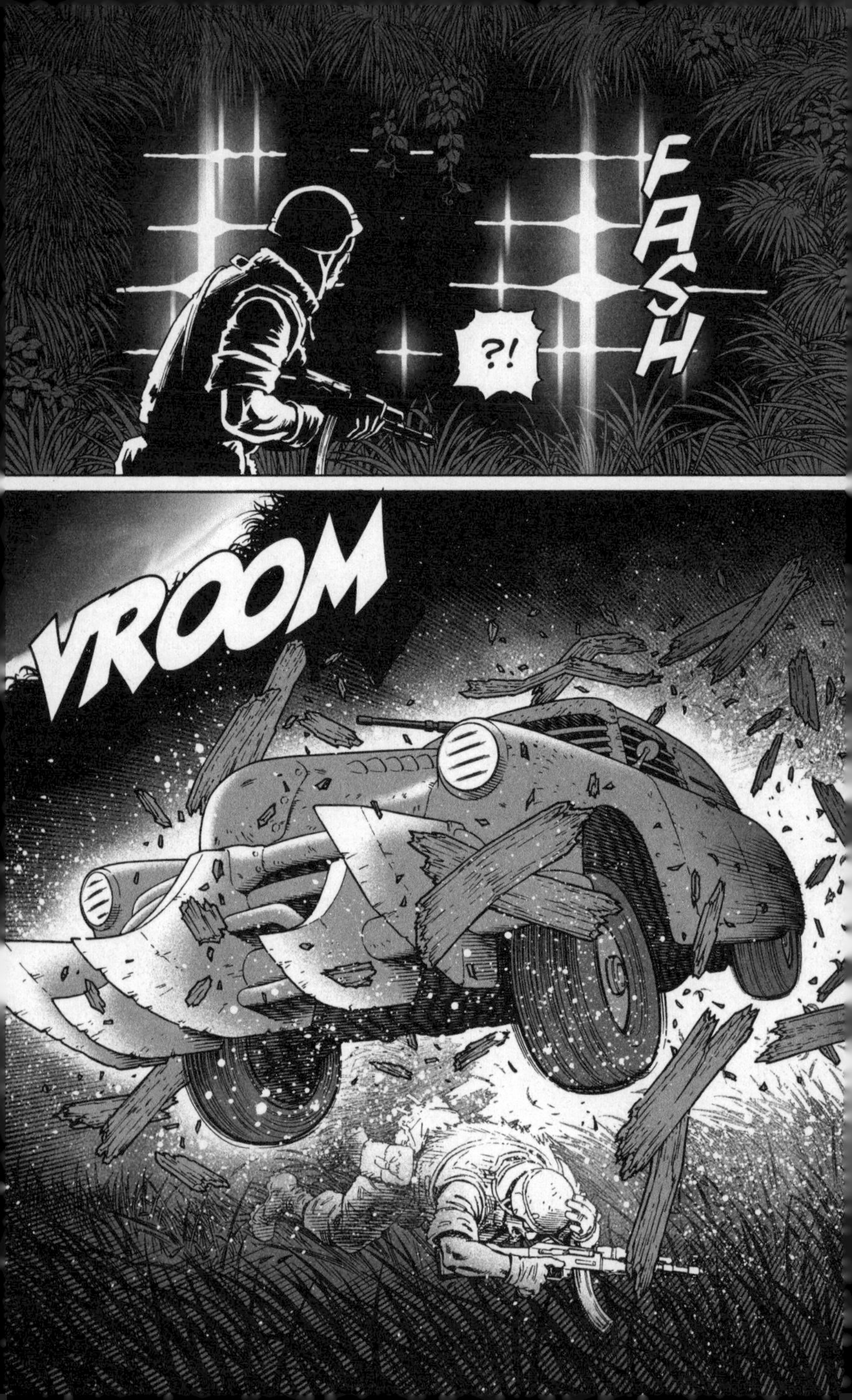
FASH
?!
VROOM

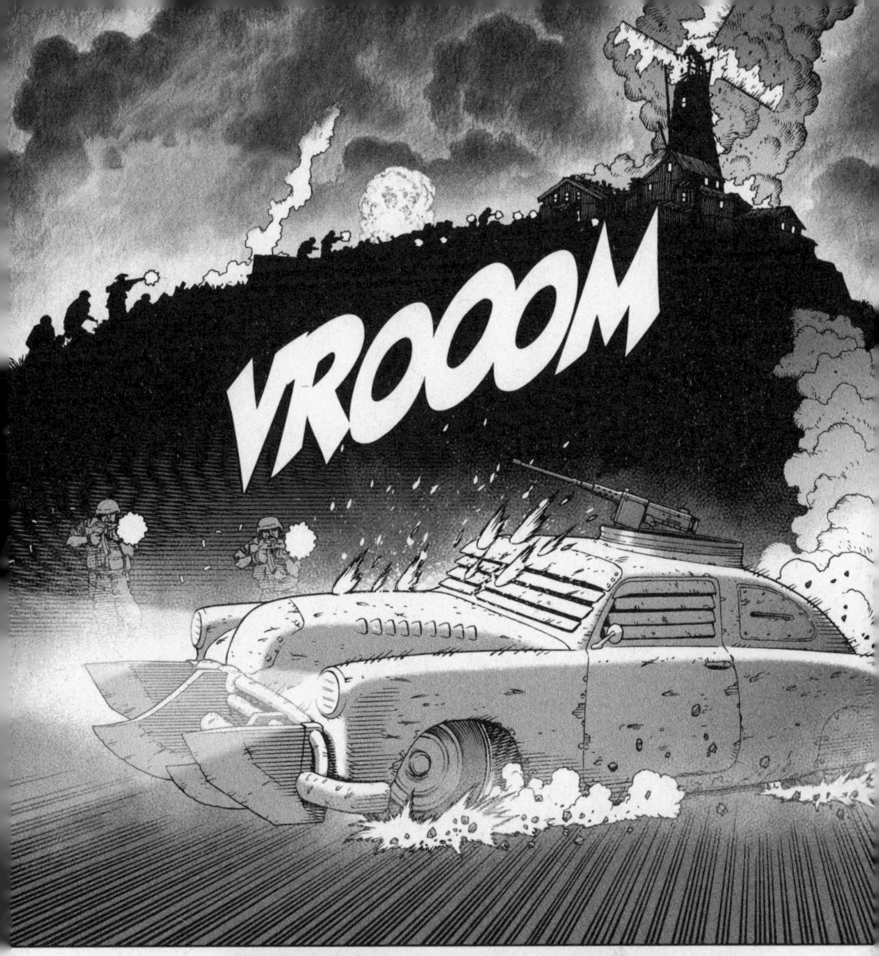
VROOOM

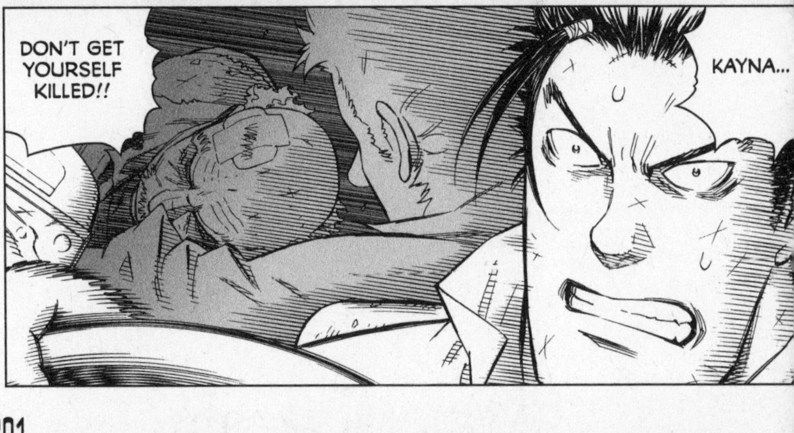
KAYNA...
DON'T GET YOURSELF KILLED!!

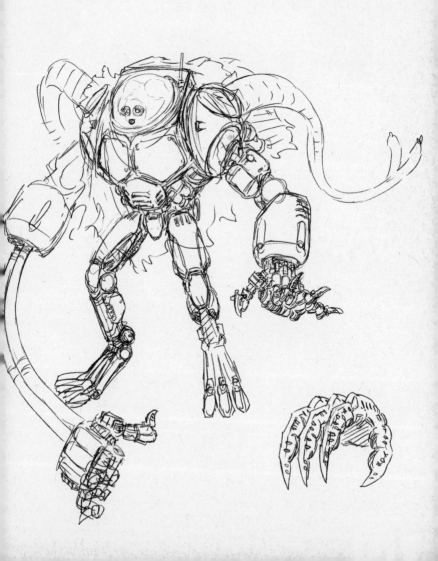

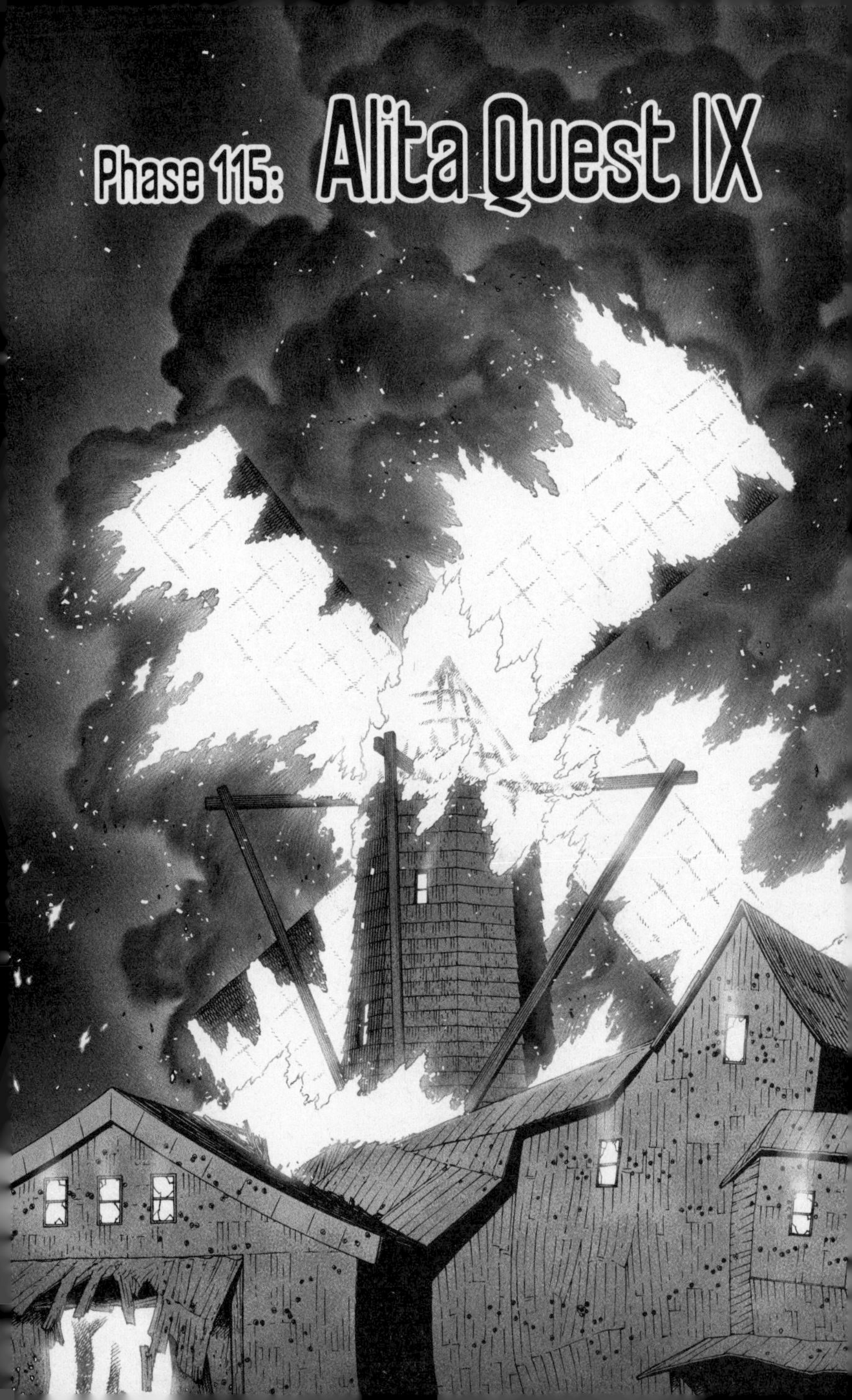
Phase 115: Alita Quest IX

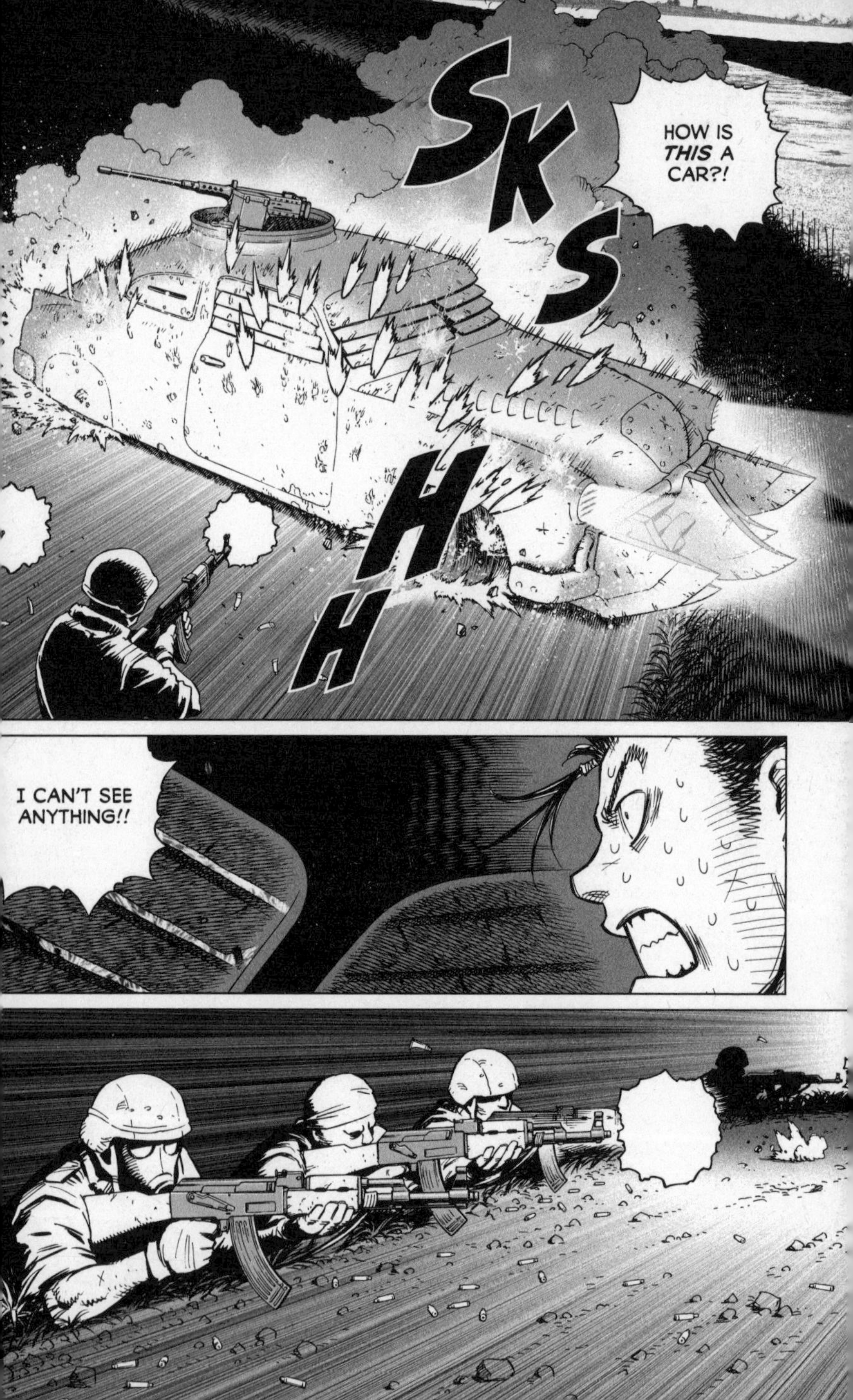
HOW IS *THIS* A CAR?!
SKSHHH
I CAN'T SEE ANYTHING!!

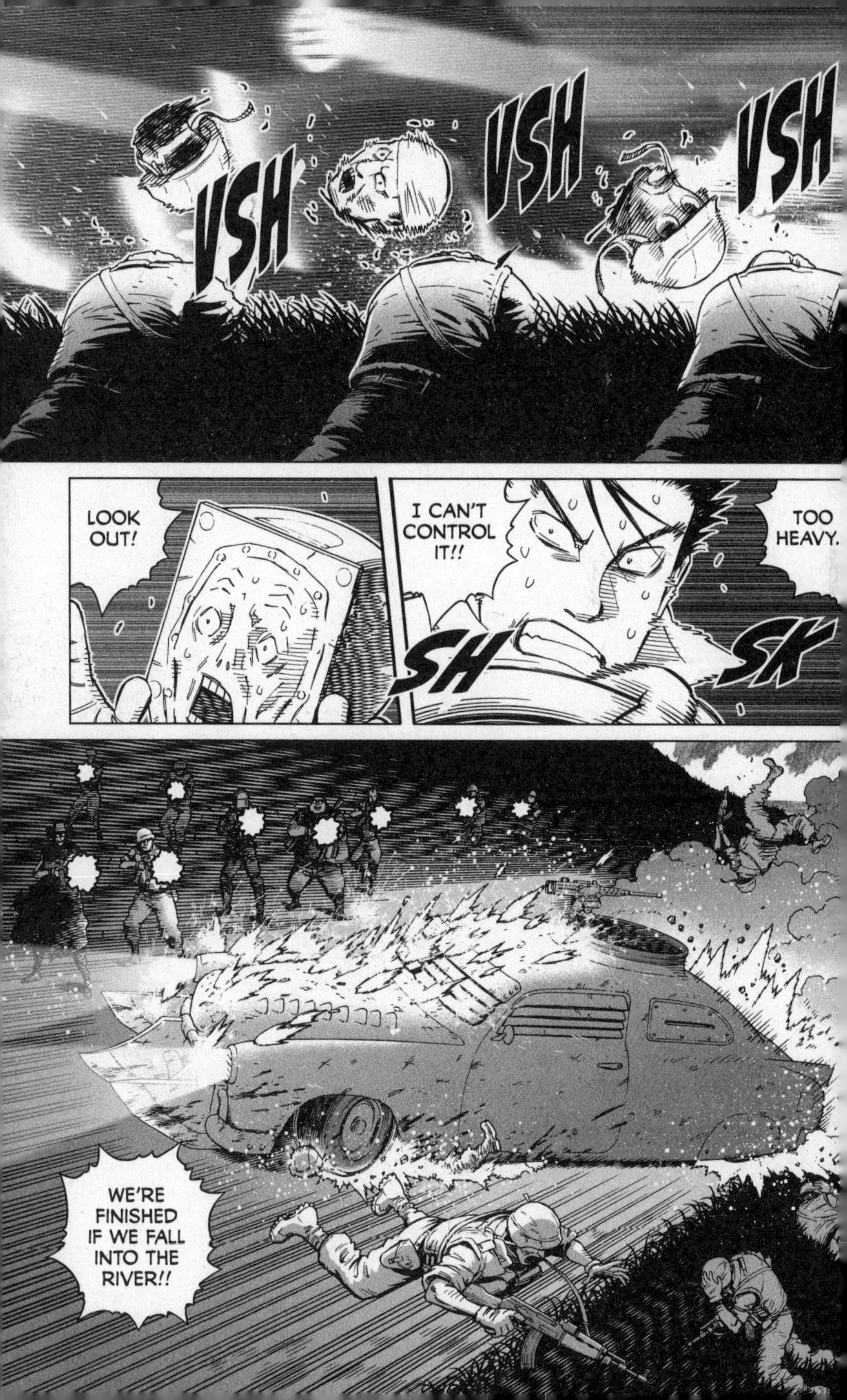
VSH
VSH
VSH
TOO HEAVY.
I CAN'T CONTROL IT!!
SK
SH
LOOK OUT!
WE'RE FINISHED IF WE FALL INTO THE RIVER!!

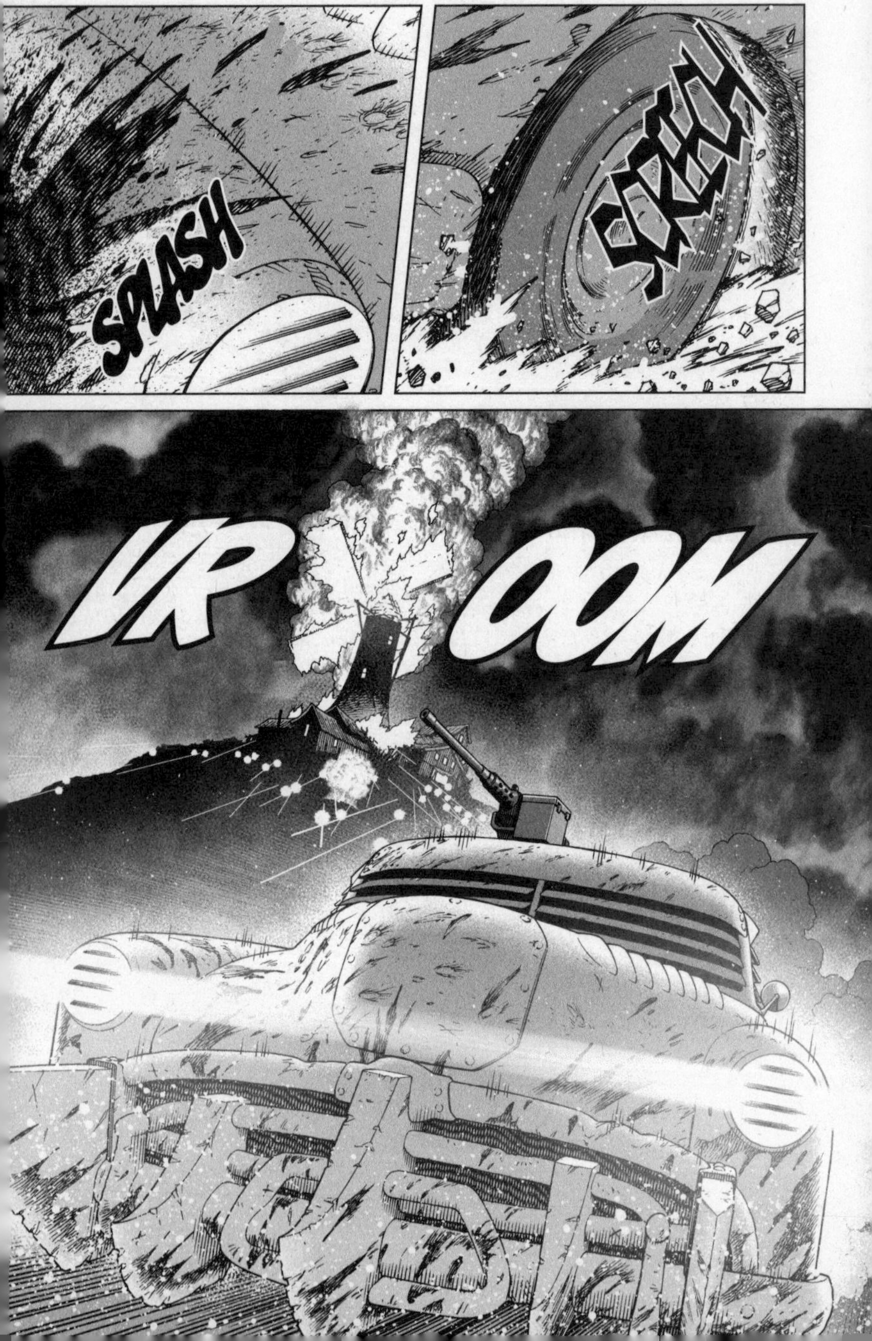
SPLASH
VR OOM

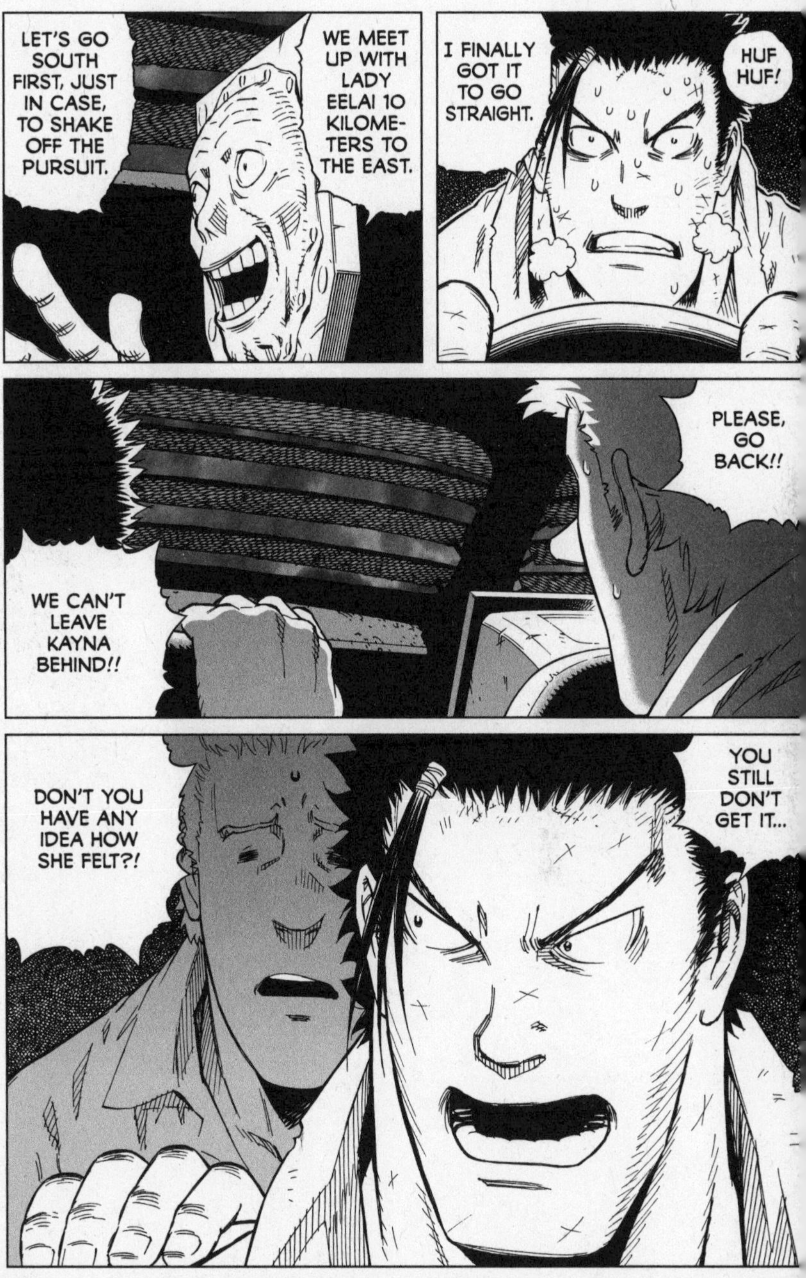
HUF HUF!
I FINALLY GOT IT TO GO STRAIGHT.
WE MEET UP WITH LADY EELAI 10 KILOMETERS TO THE EAST.
LET'S GO SOUTH FIRST, JUST IN CASE, TO SHAKE OFF THE PURSUIT.
PLEASE, GO BACK!!
WE CAN'T LEAVE KAYNA BEHIND!!
YOU STILL DON'T GET IT...
DON'T YOU HAVE ANY IDEA HOW SHE FELT?!

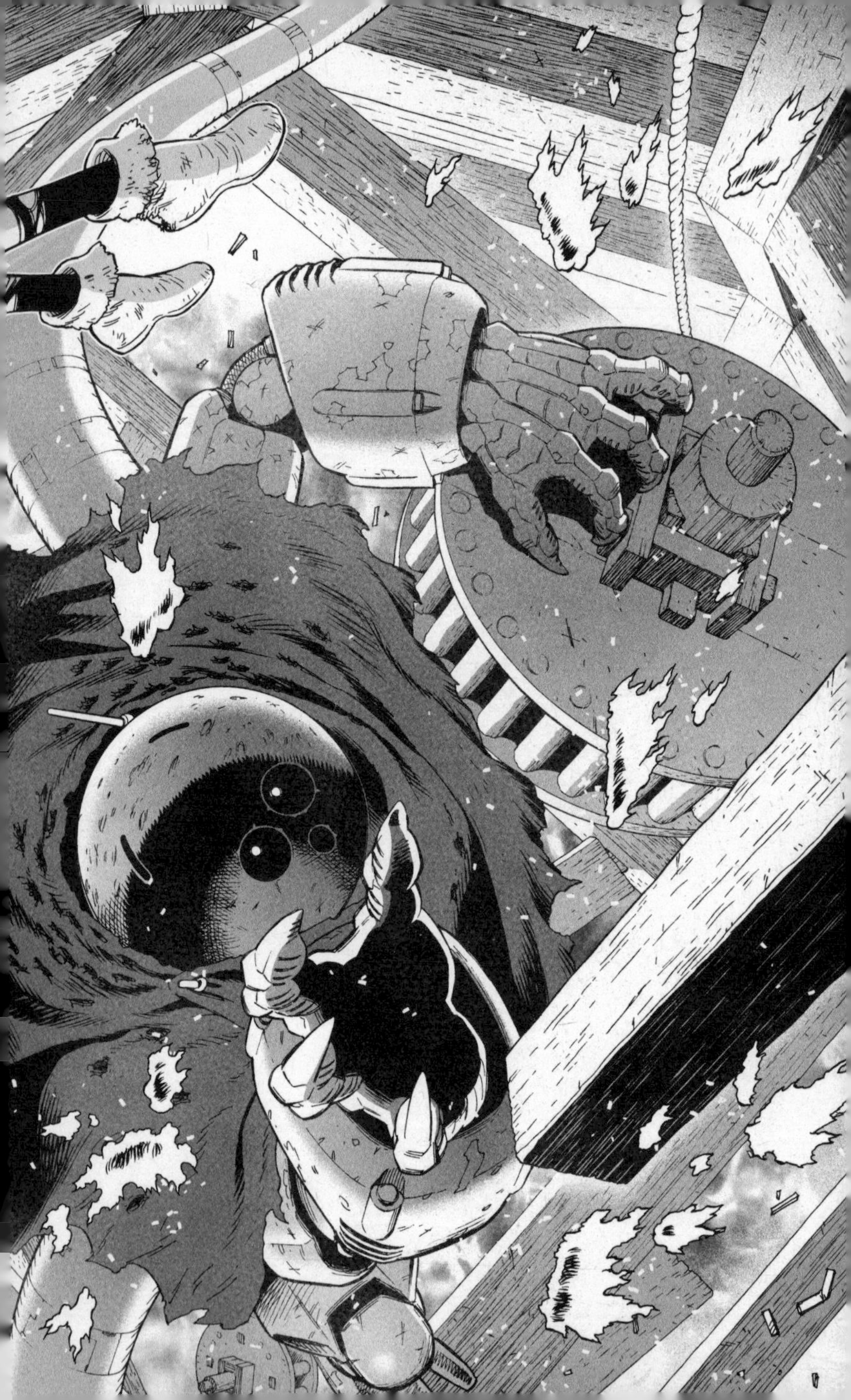

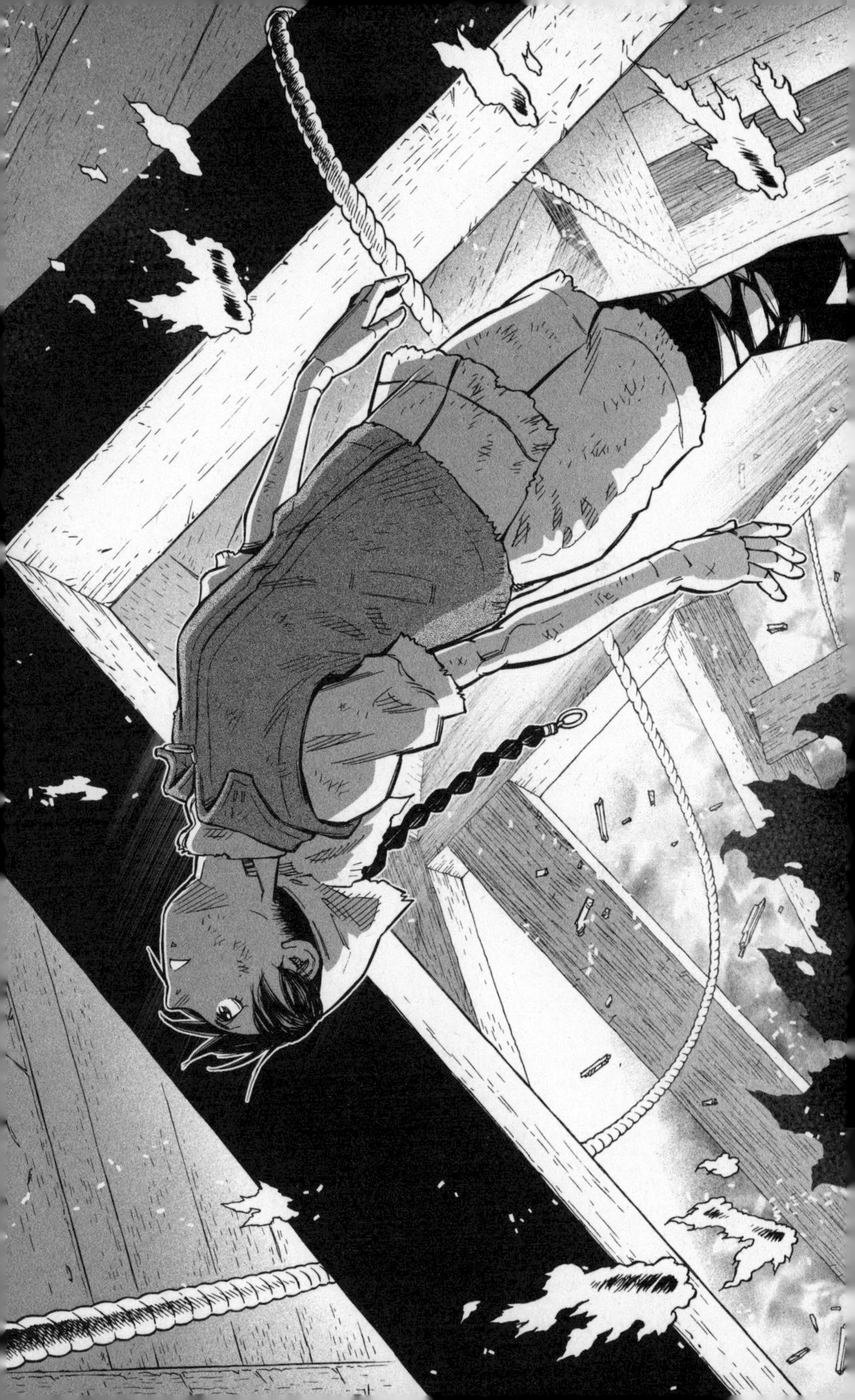

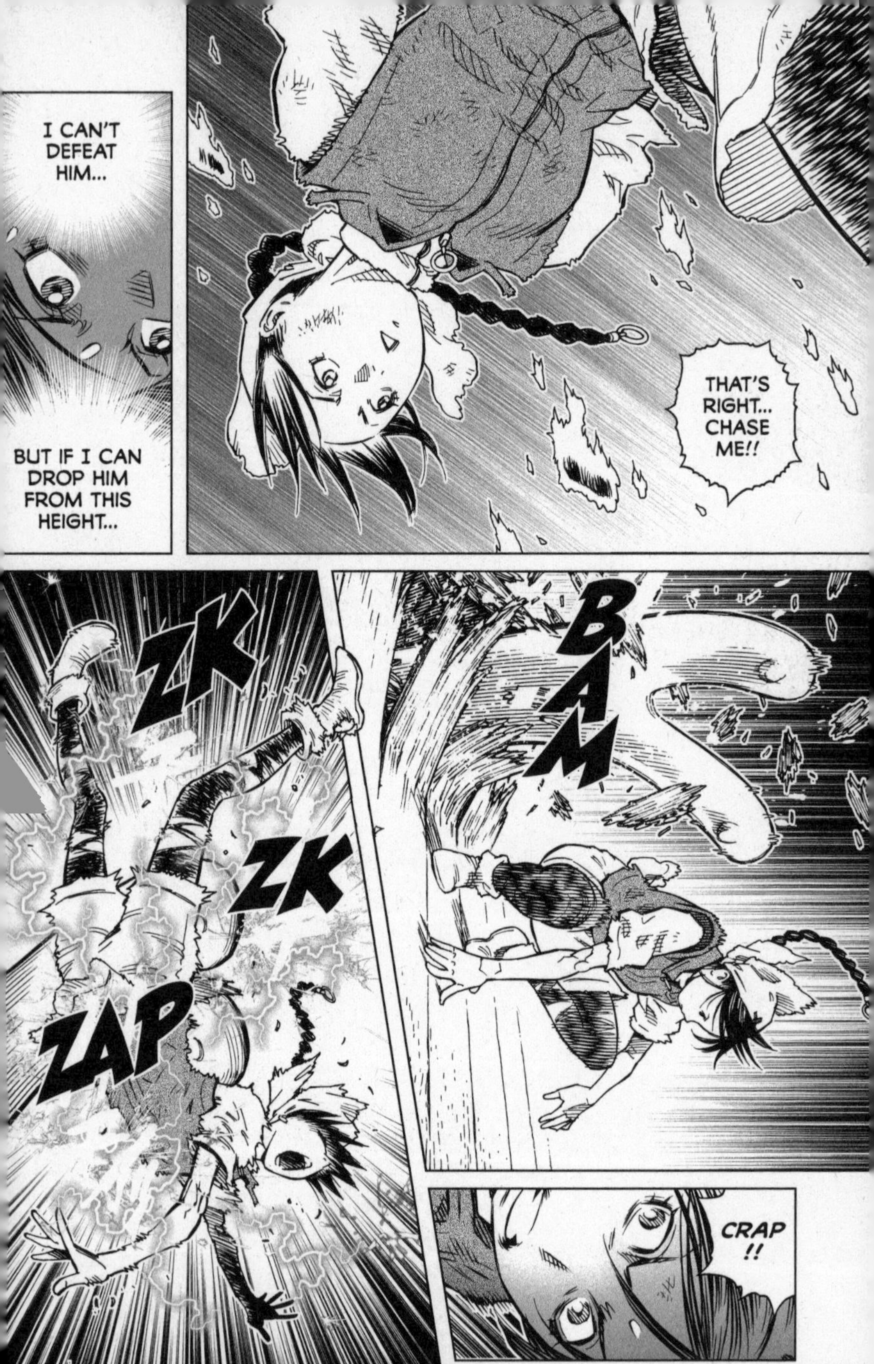
THAT'S RIGHT... CHASE ME!!
I CAN'T DEFEAT HIM...
BUT IF I CAN DROP HIM FROM THIS HEIGHT...
BAM
CRAP!!
ZK
ZK
ZAP

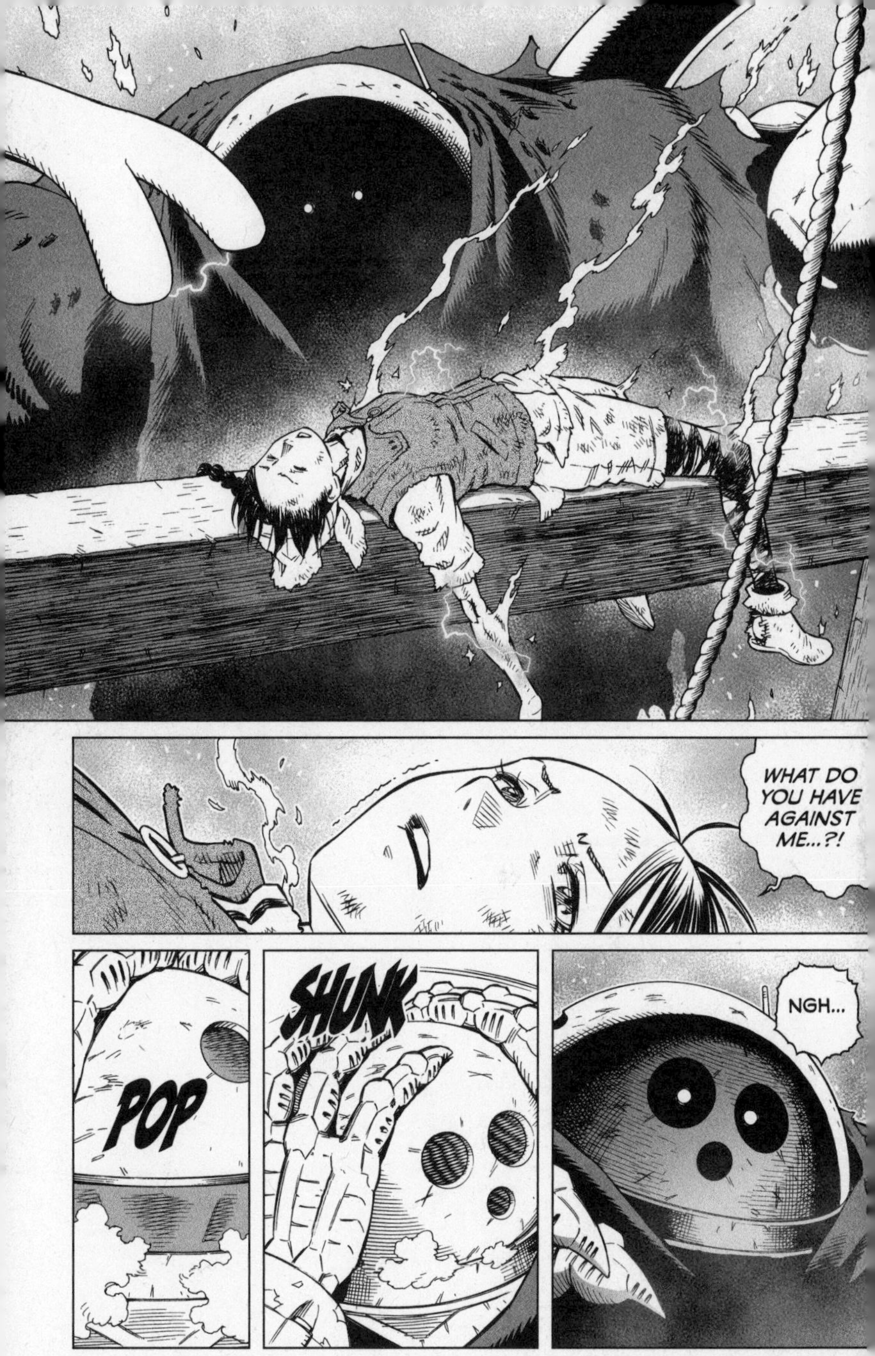
WHAT DO YOU HAVE AGAINST ME...?!
NGH...
SHUNK
POP

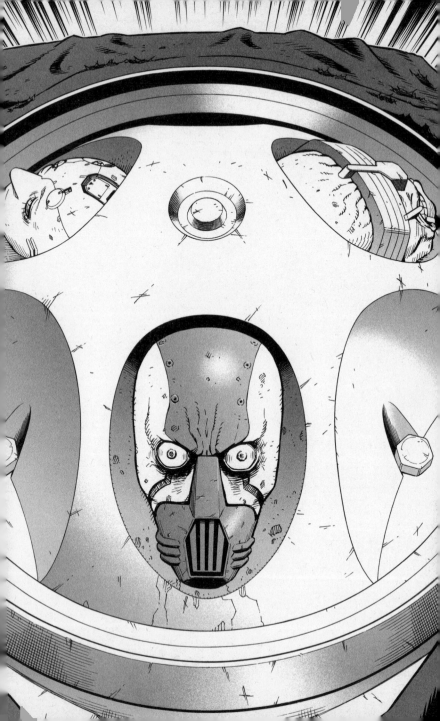

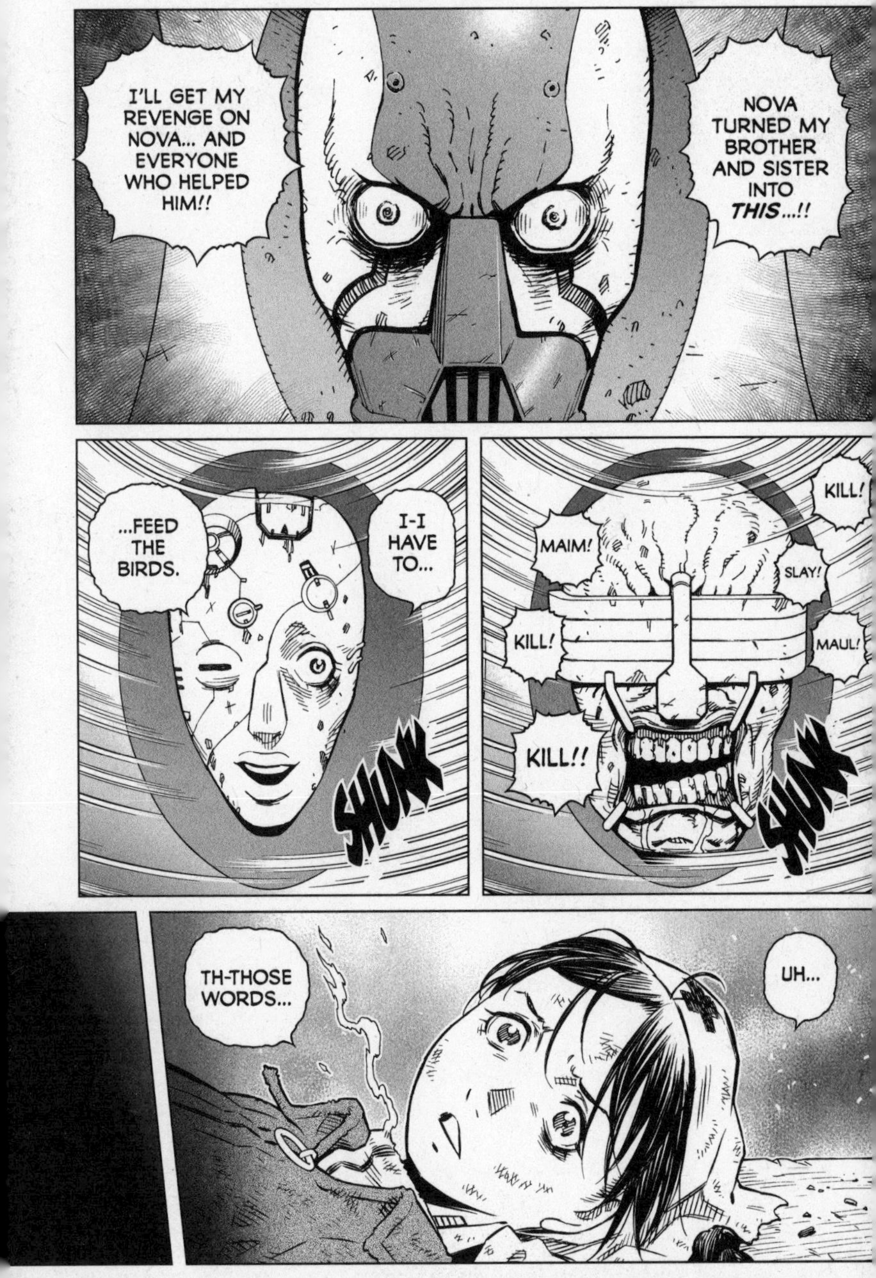
NOVA TURNED MY BROTHER AND SISTER INTO *THIS*...!!
I'LL GET MY REVENGE ON NOVA... AND EVERYONE WHO HELPED HIM!!
KILL!
SLAY!
MAIM!
MAUL!
KILL!
KILL!!
SHUNK
I-I HAVE TO...
...FEED THE BIRDS.
SHUNK
UH...
TH-THOSE WORDS...

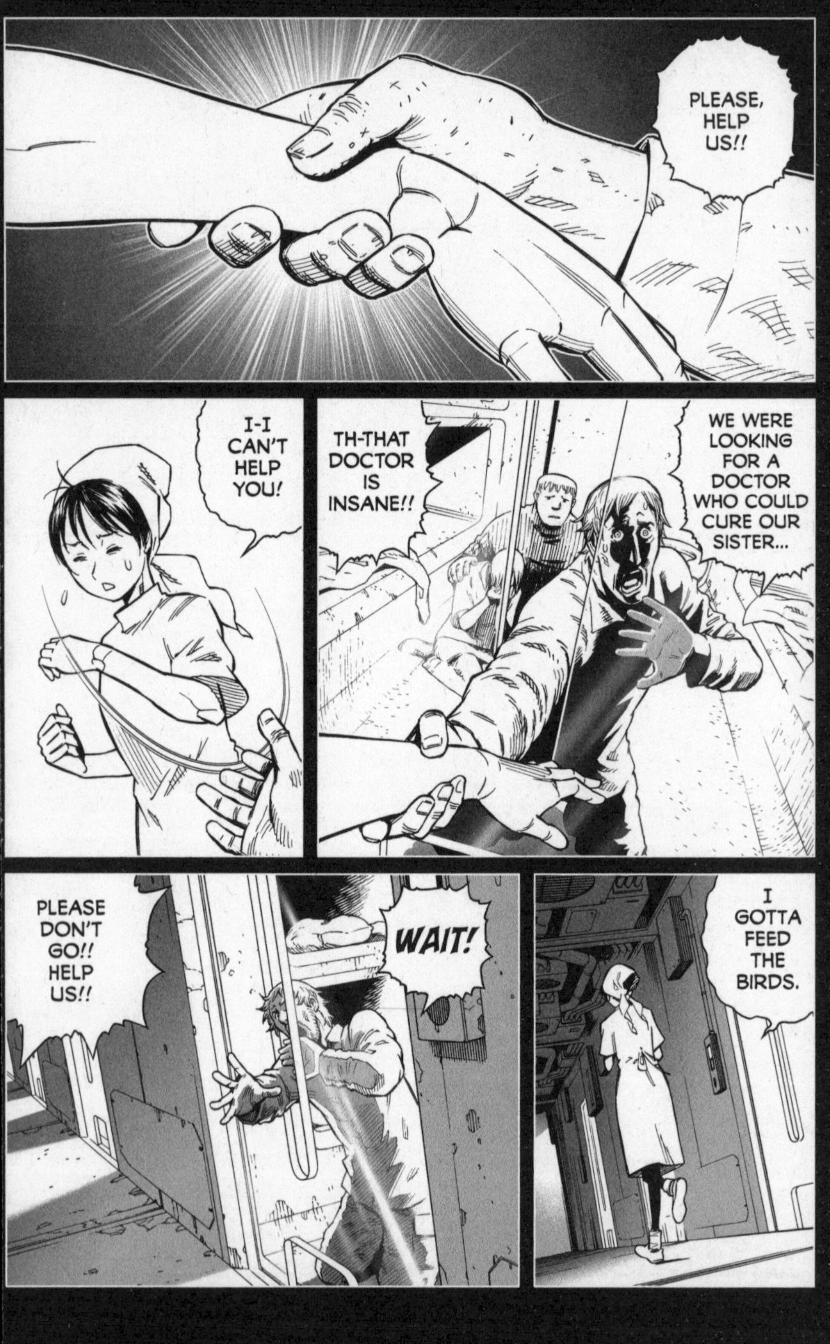
PLEASE, HELP US!!
WE WERE LOOKING FOR A DOCTOR WHO COULD CURE OUR SISTER...
TH-THAT DOCTOR IS INSANE!!
I-I CAN'T HELP YOU!
I GOTTA FEED THE BIRDS.
WAIT!
PLEASE DON'T GO!! HELP US!!

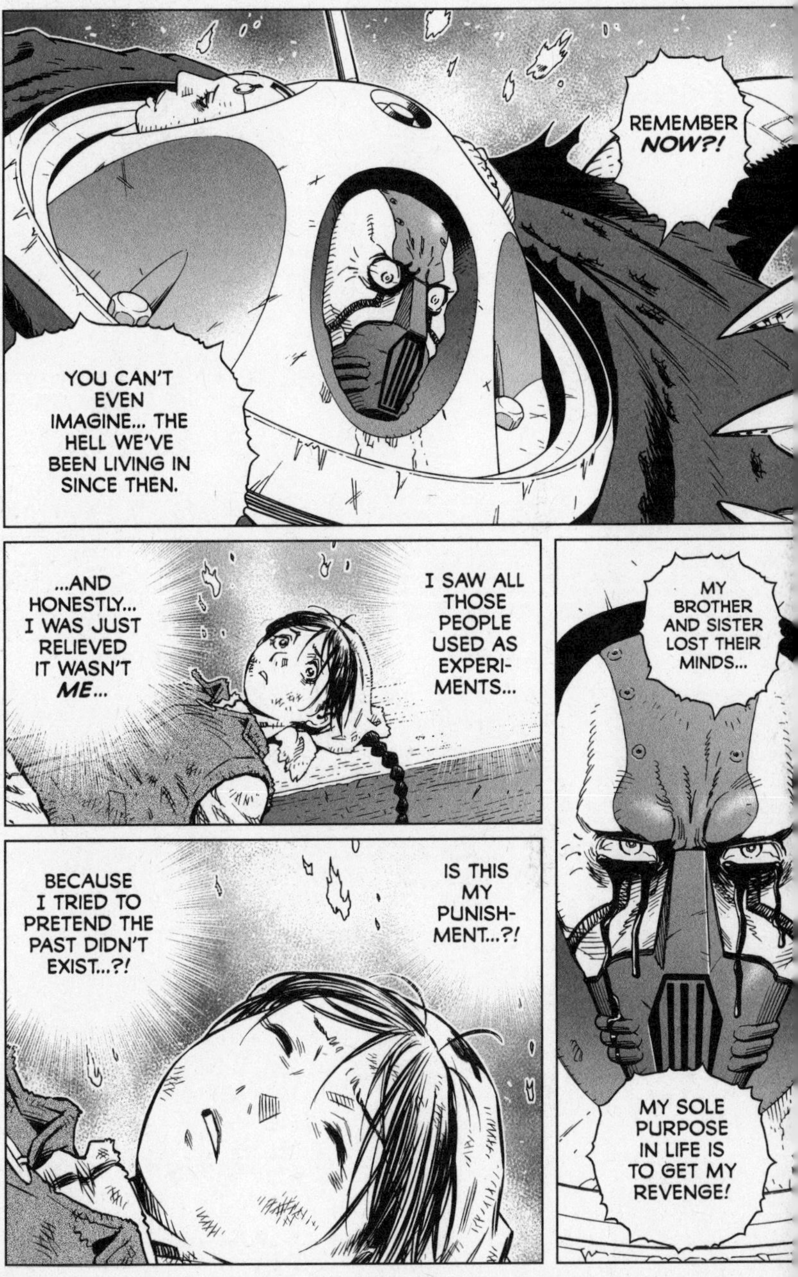
REMEMBER NOW?!
YOU CAN'T EVEN IMAGINE... THE HELL WE'VE BEEN LIVING IN SINCE THEN.
MY BROTHER AND SISTER LOST THEIR MINDS...
MY SOLE PURPOSE IN LIFE IS TO GET MY REVENGE!
I SAW ALL THOSE PEOPLE USED AS EXPERI-MENTS...
...AND HONESTLY... I WAS JUST RELIEVED IT WASN'T ME...
IS THIS MY PUNISH-MENT...?!
BECAUSE I TRIED TO PRETEND THE PAST DIDN'T EXIST...?!

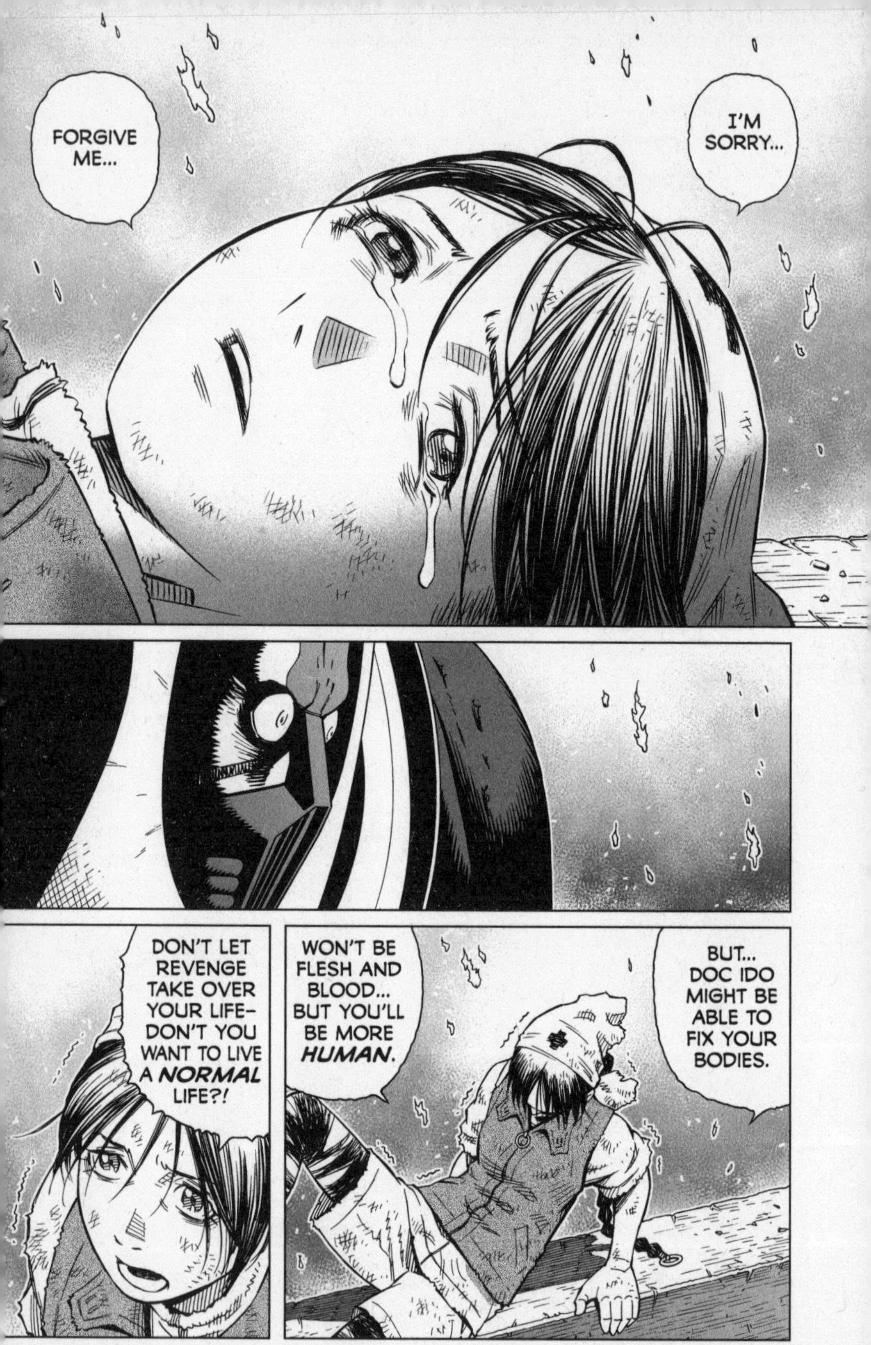
I'M SORRY...
FORGIVE ME...
BUT... DOC IDO MIGHT BE ABLE TO FIX YOUR BODIES.
WON'T BE FLESH AND BLOOD... BUT YOU'LL BE MORE *HUMAN*.
DON'T LET REVENGE TAKE OVER YOUR LIFE– DON'T YOU WANT TO LIVE A *NORMAL* LIFE?!

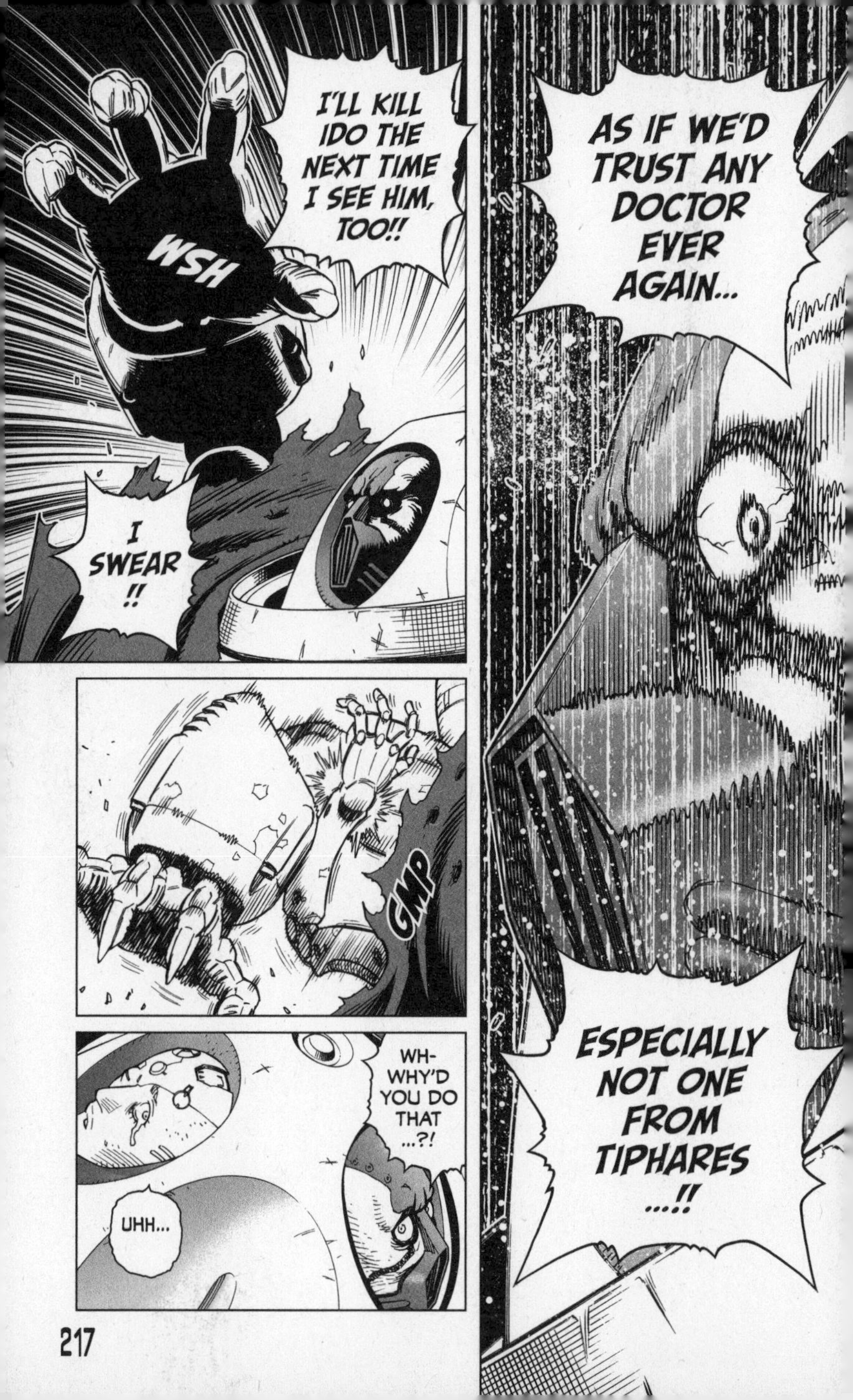
AS IF WE'D TRUST ANY DOCTOR EVER AGAIN...
ESPECIALLY NOT ONE FROM TIPHARES ...!!
I'LL KILL IDO THE NEXT TIME I SEE HIM, TOO!!
WSH
I SWEAR !!
GMP
WH- WHY'D YOU DO THAT ...?!
UHH...

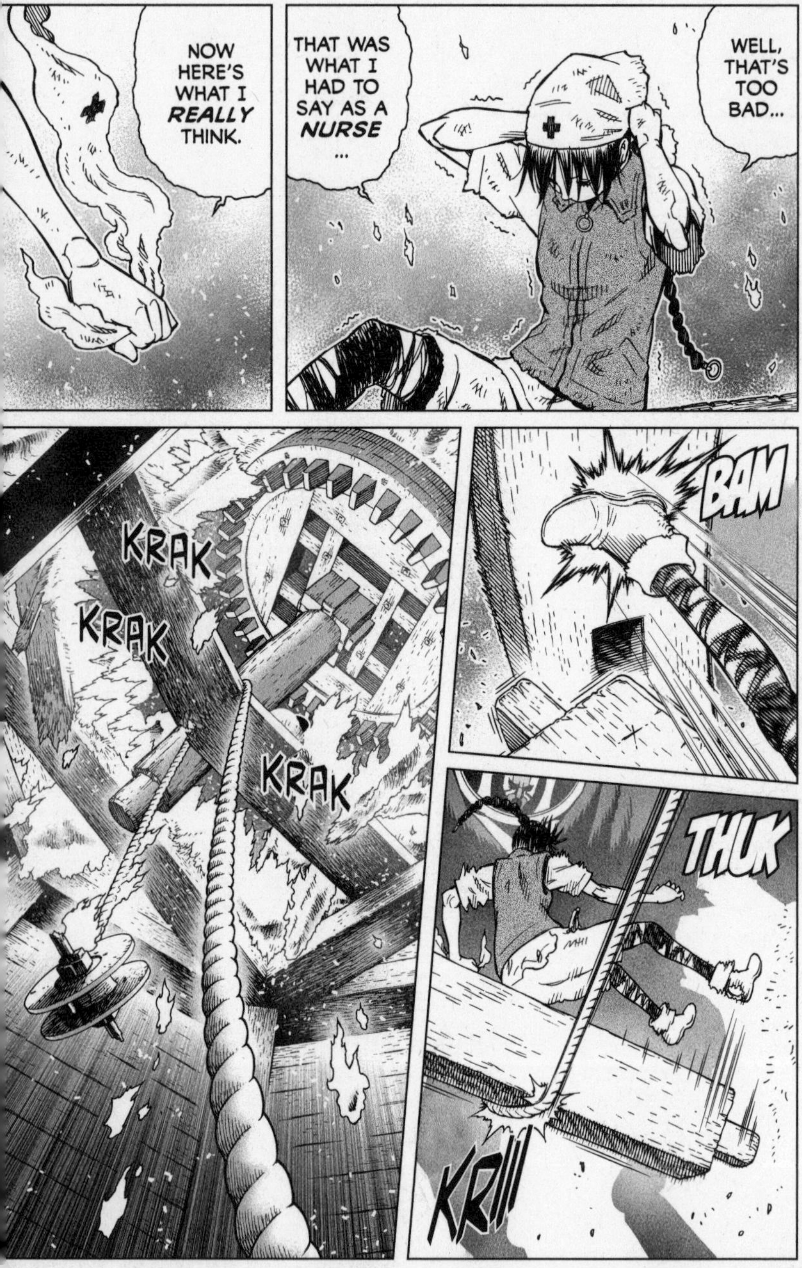
WELL, THAT'S TOO BAD...
THAT WAS WHAT I HAD TO SAY AS A NURSE ...
NOW HERE'S WHAT I REALLY THINK.
BAM
THUK
KRIII
KRAK
KRAK
KRAK

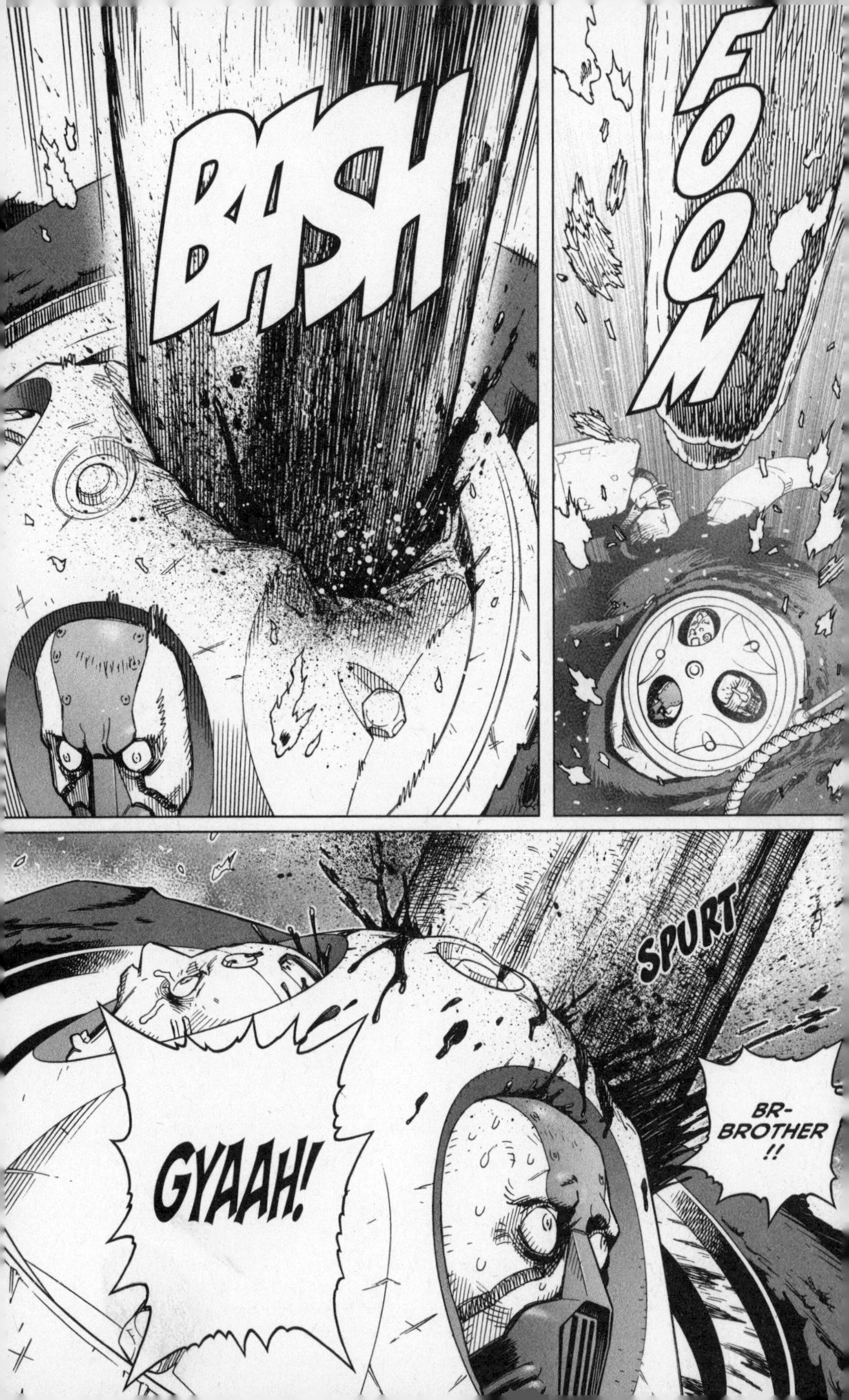
FOOM
BASH
SPURT
BR-BROTHER !!
GYAAH!

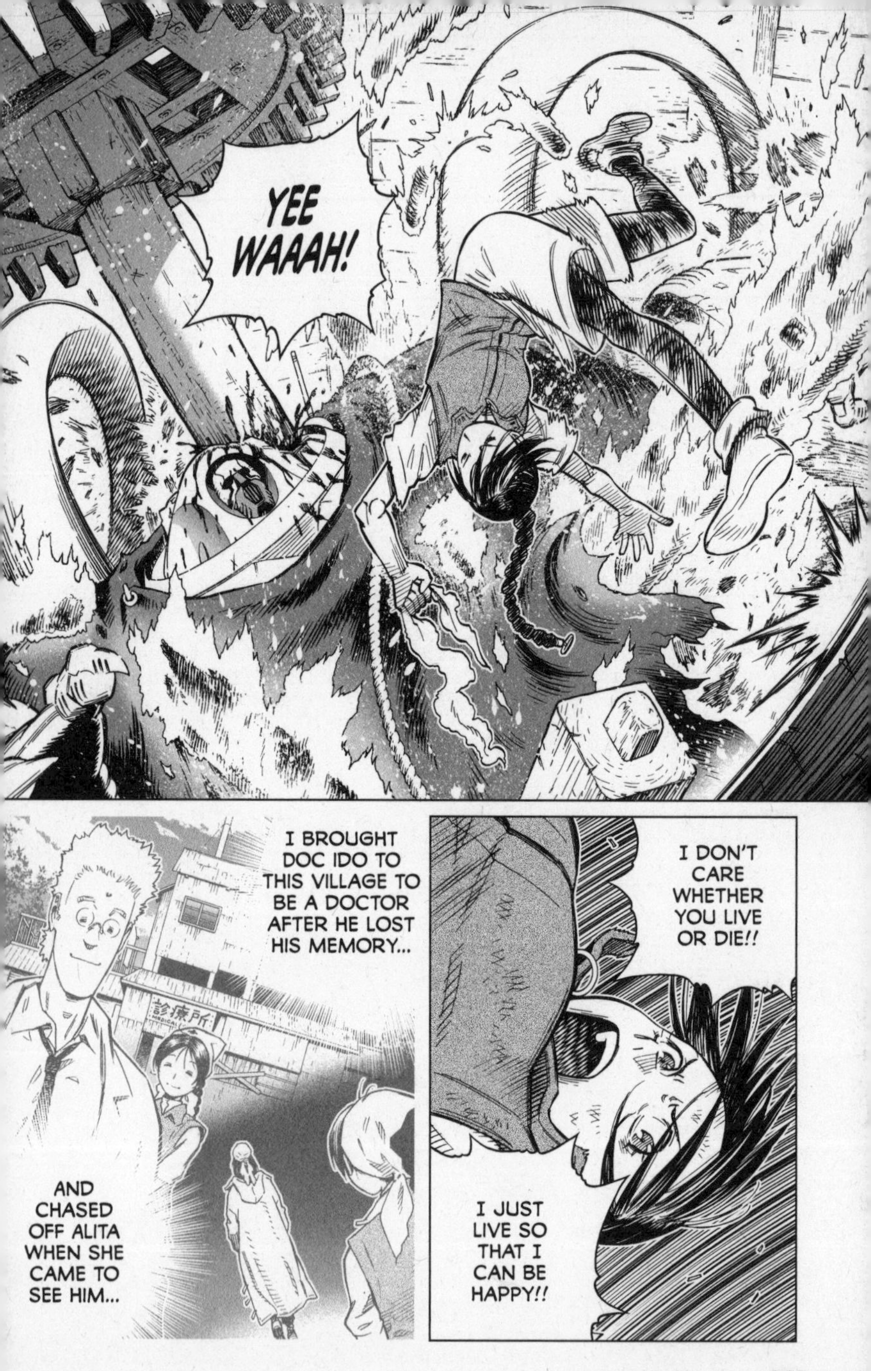
YEE WAAAH!
I DON'T CARE WHETHER YOU LIVE OR DIE!!
I JUST LIVE SO THAT I CAN BE HAPPY!!
I BROUGHT DOC IDO TO THIS VILLAGE TO BE A DOCTOR AFTER HE LOST HIS MEMORY...
診療所
AND CHASED OFF ALITA WHEN SHE CAME TO SEE HIM...

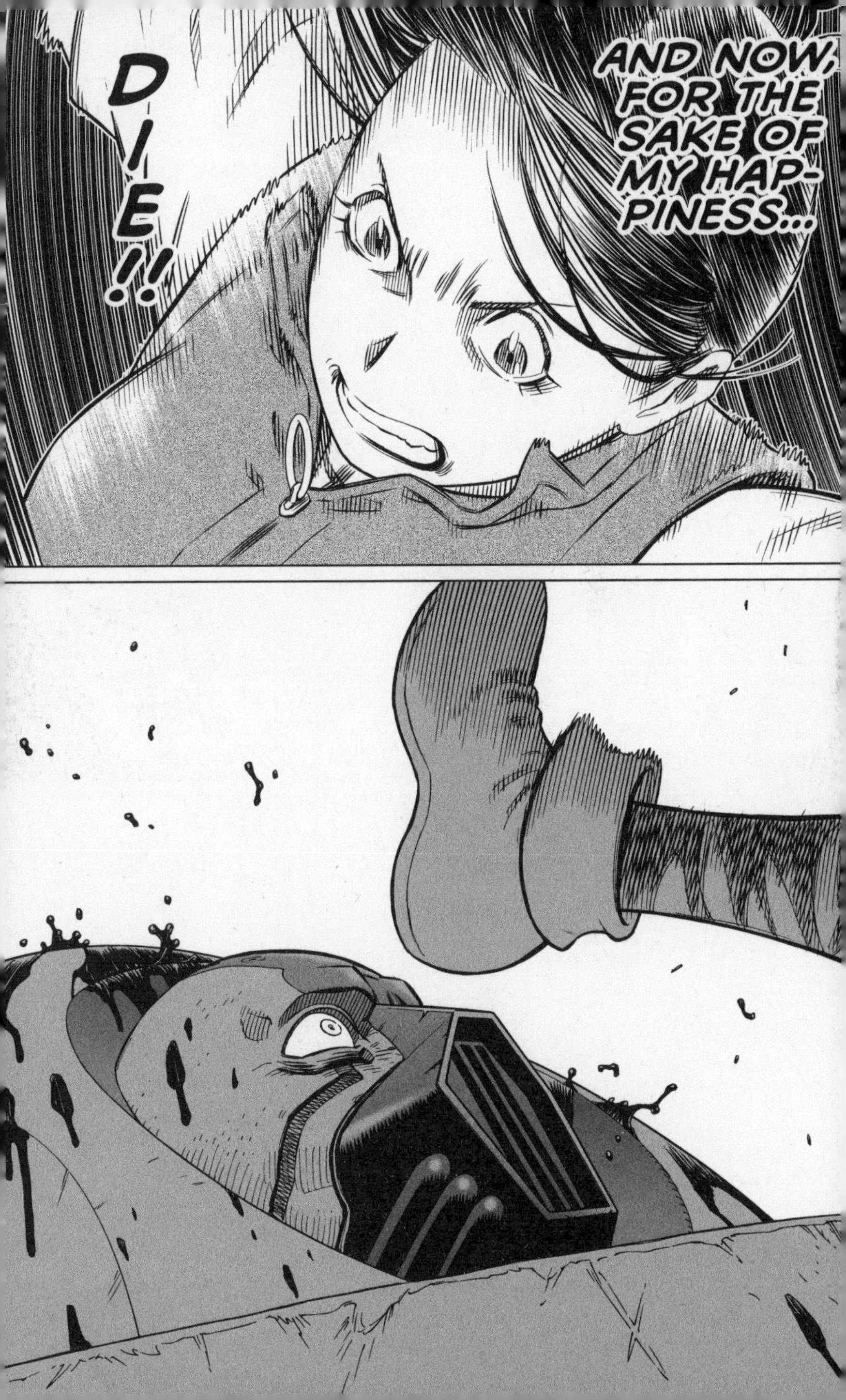
AND NOW, FOR THE SAKE OF MY HAP-PINESS...
DIE!!

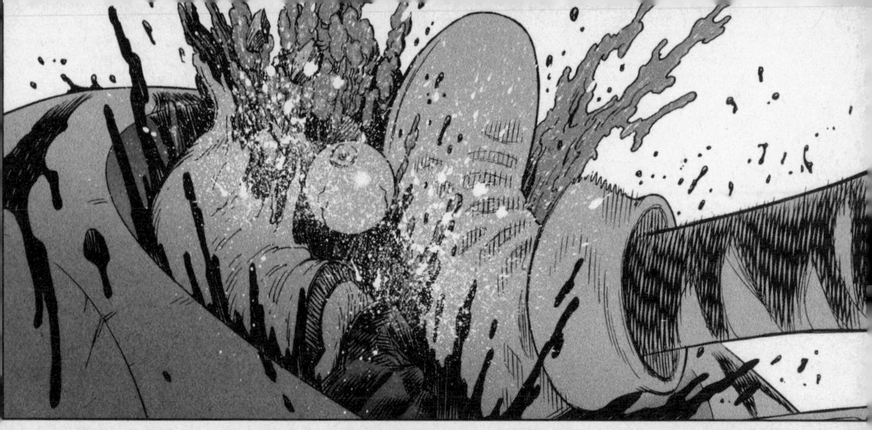

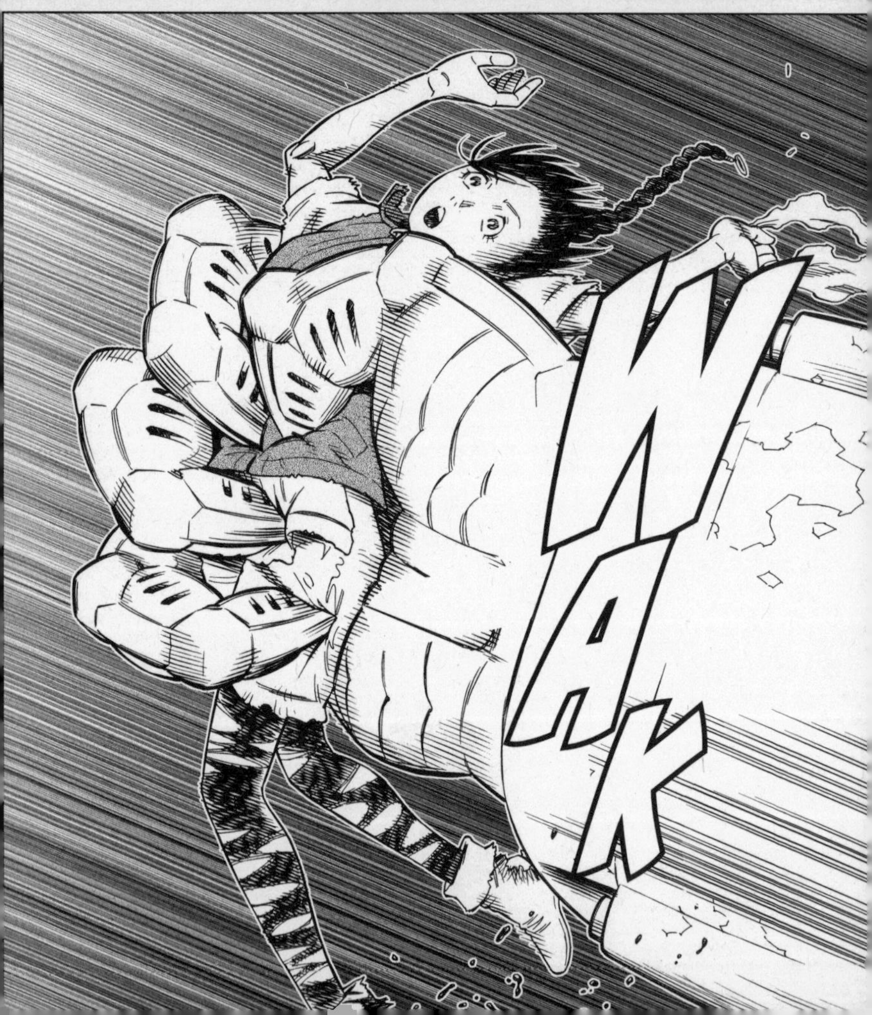
WHAK

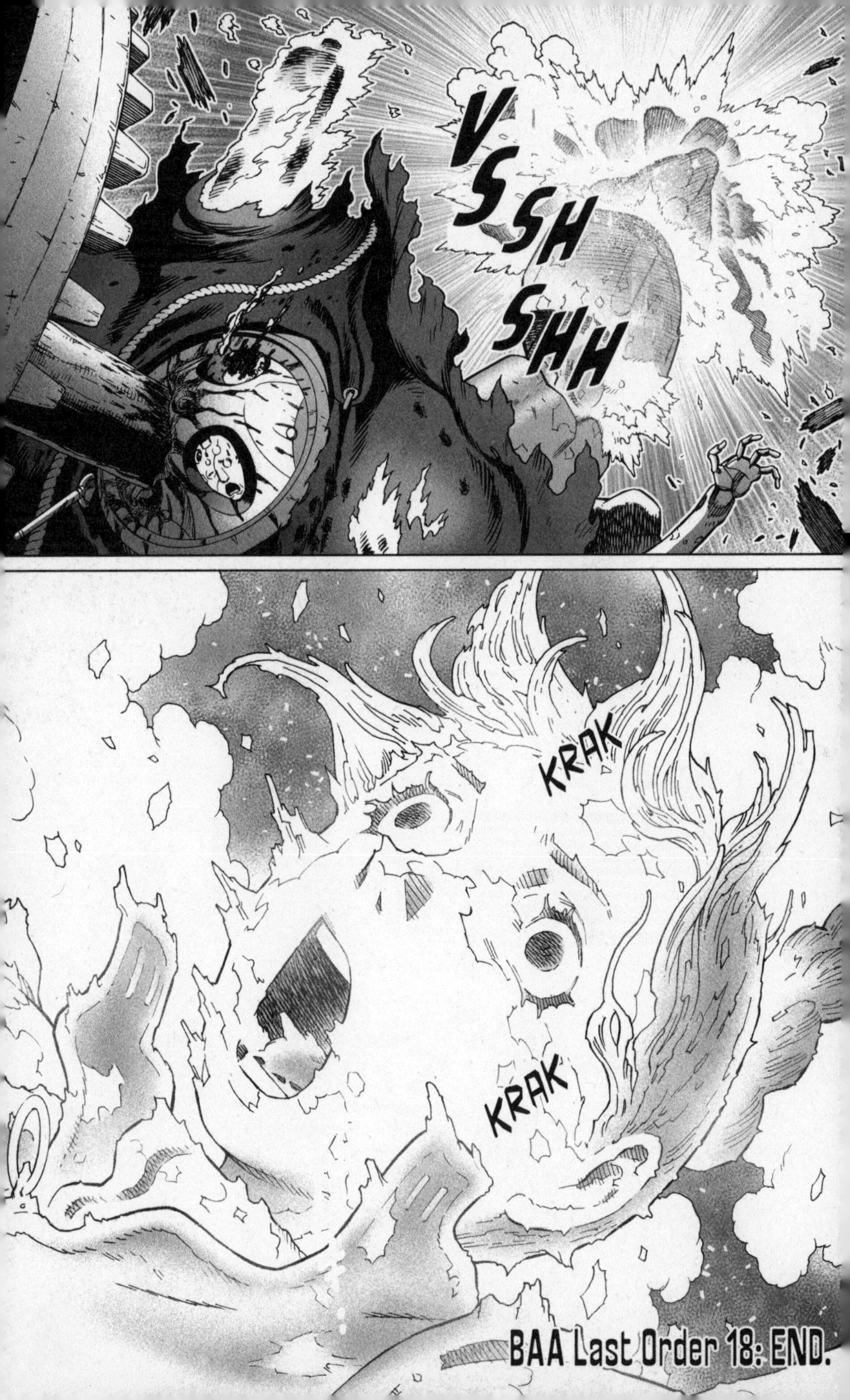
VSSH SHH
KRAK
KRAK
BAA Last Order 18: END.

Figure's Travels: The Surface World

MAP

EARTH IN E.S. 590

The meteor Ix Chel fell in E.S. 55, causing the "Impact Winter" and the end of the world as we know it. Climate change and rising sea levels altered the coastline.

SCRAPYARD

Called Star City under Arthur Farrell's administration. Near the current Kansas City.

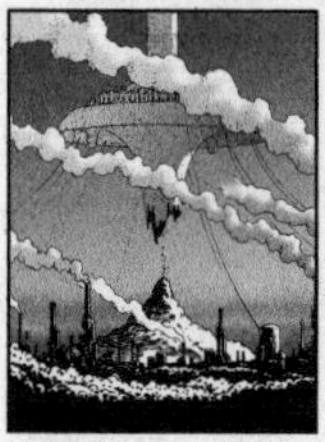

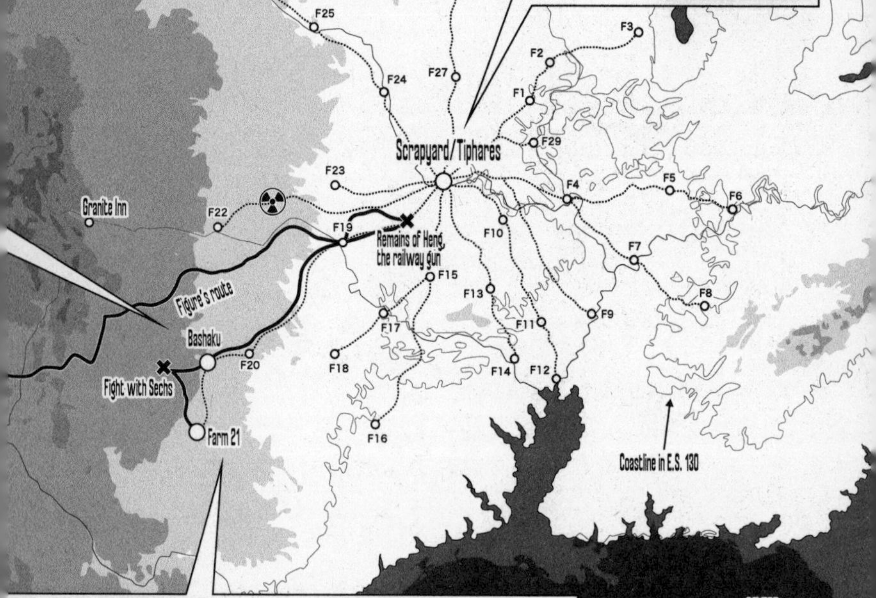

F28
F26
F25
F27
F24
F3
F2
F1
F29
Scrapyard/Tiphares
F23
F4
F5
F6
Granite Inn
F22
F19
Remains of Heng, the railway gun
F10
F7
F15
F8
Figure's route
F13
F9
F17
F11
Bashaku
F20
F18
F14
F12
Fight with Sechs
Farm 21
F16
Coastline in E.S. 130
400Km

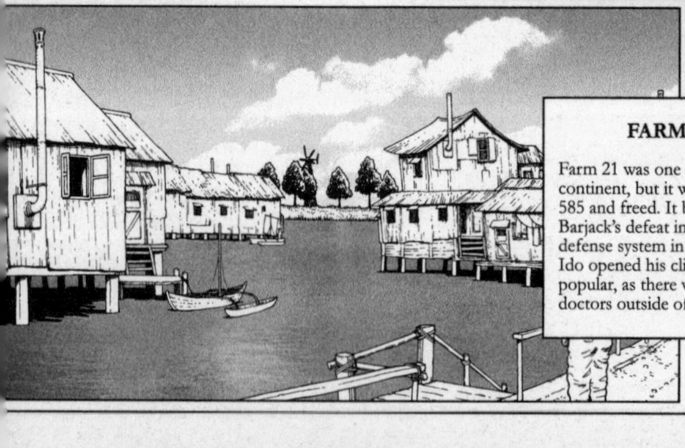

FARM 21/IDO'S CLINIC

Farm 21 was one of 29 Factory-run farms on the continent, but it was taken over by Barjack in E.S. 585 and freed. It became a free-trade farm after Barjack's defeat in E.S. 590, but not having its own defense system in place brought about this tragedy. Ido opened his clinic around E.S. 588. He was quite popular, as there were never enough good cyber doctors outside of the Scrapyard.

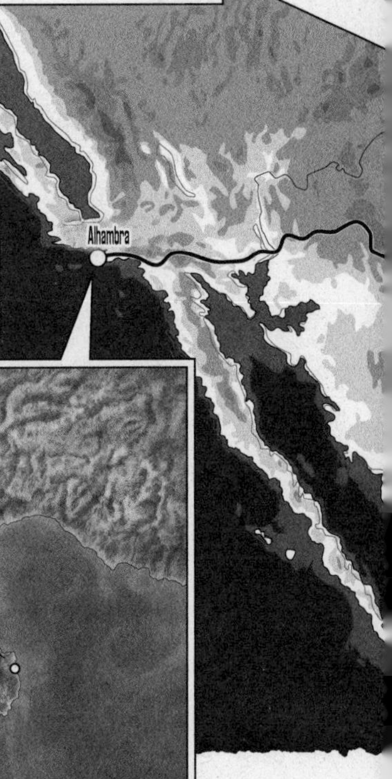

Alhambra

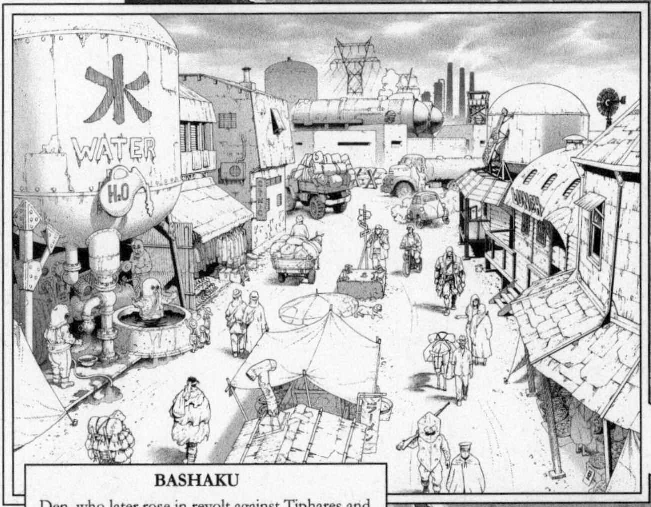

水
WATER
H₂O

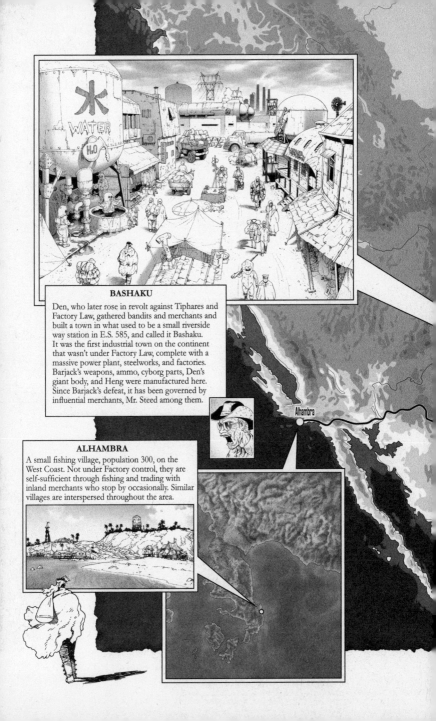

BASHAKU

Den, who later rose in revolt against Tiphares and Factory Law, gathered bandits and merchants and built a town in what used to be a small riverside way station in E.S. 585, and called it Bashaku. It was the first industrial town on the continent that wasn't under Factory Law, complete with a massive power plant, steelworks, and factories. Barjack's weapons, ammo, cyborg parts, Den's giant body, and Heng were manufactured here. Since Barjack's defeat, it has been governed by influential merchants, Mr. Steed among them.

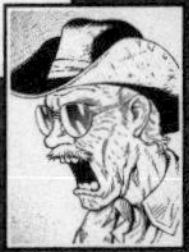

ALHAMBRA

A small fishing village, population 300, on the West Coast. Not under Factory control, they are self-sufficient through fishing and trading with inland merchants who stop by occasionally. Similar villages are interspersed throughout the area.

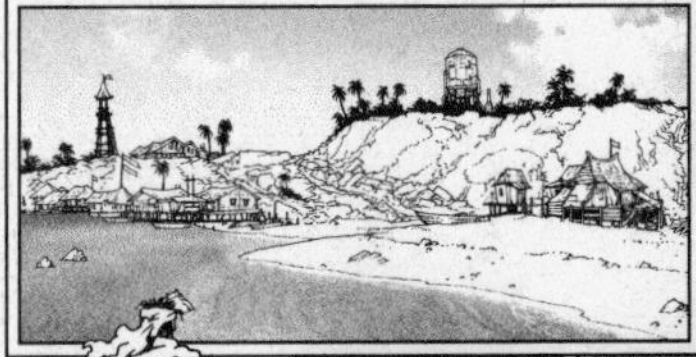

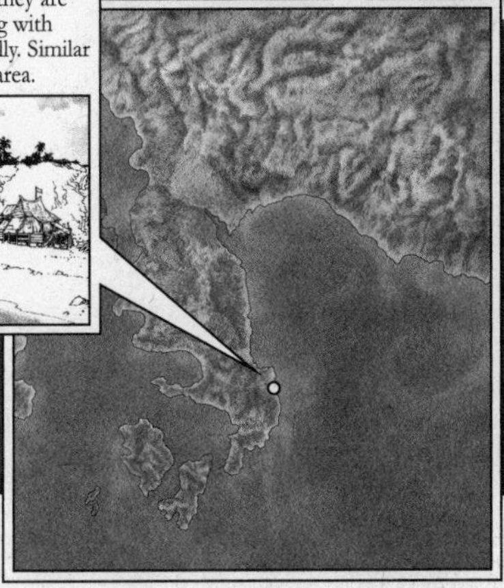

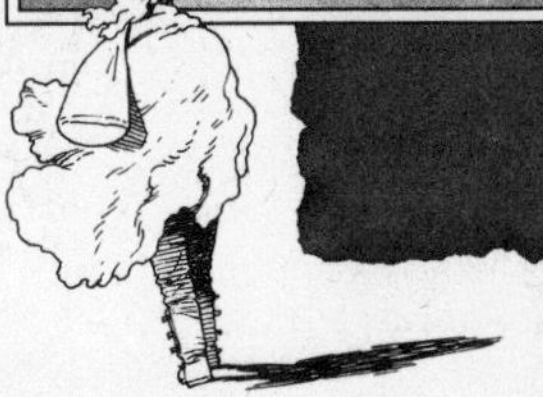

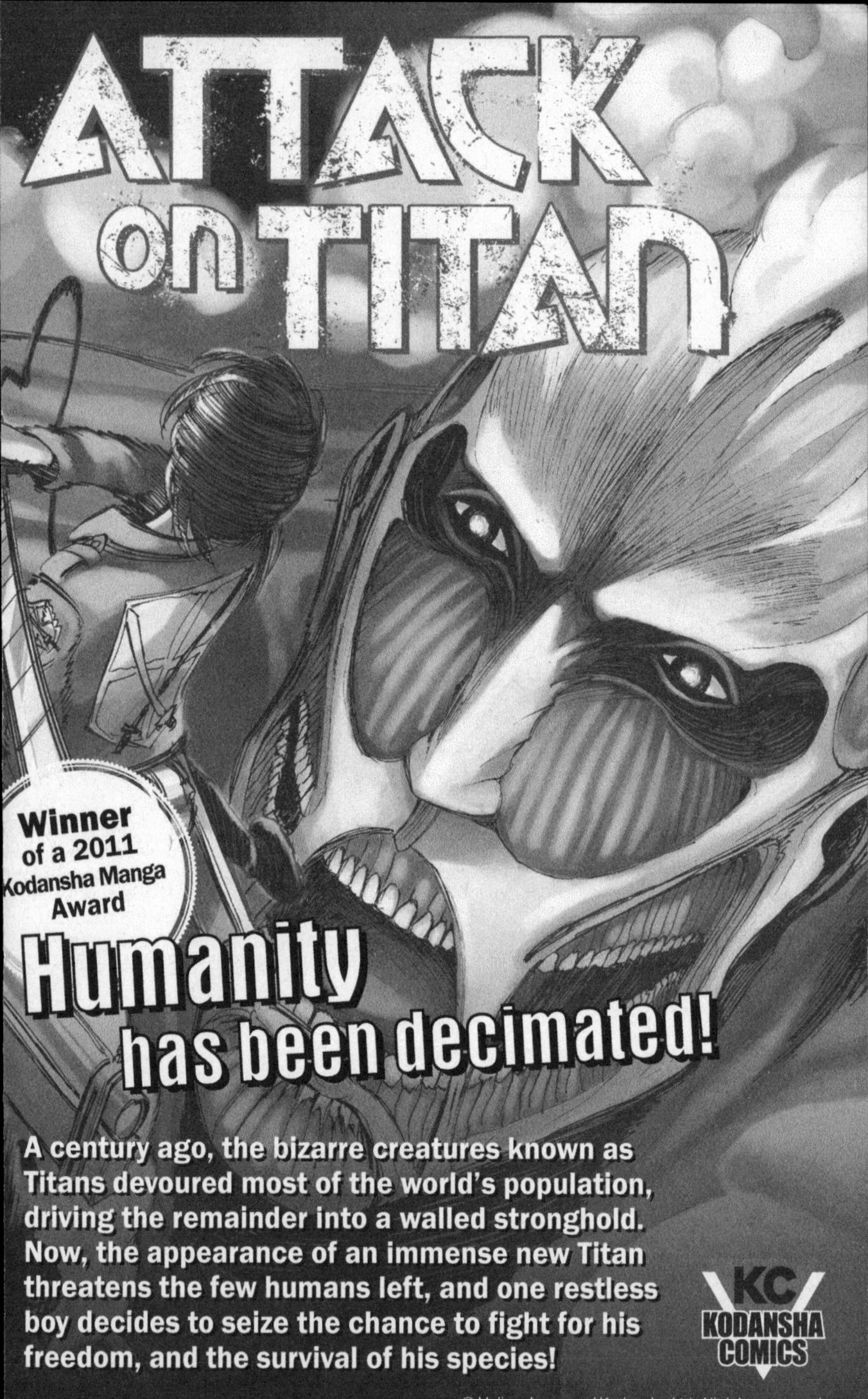

ATTACK ON TITAN

Humanity
has been decimated!

A century ago, the bizarre creatures known as Titans devoured most of the world's population, driving the remainder into a walled stronghold. Now, the appearance of an immense new Titan threatens the few humans left, and one restless boy decides to seize the chance to fight for his freedom, and the survival of his species!

KC
KODANSHA
COMICS

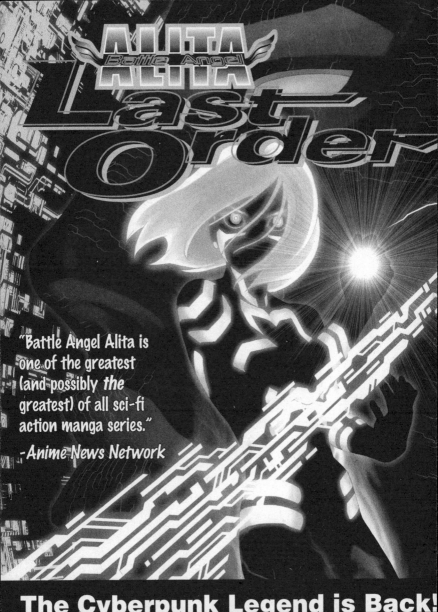

ALITA
Battle Angel
Last Order

"Battle Angel Alita is one of the greatest (and possibly *the* greatest) of all sci-fi action manga series."

-Anime News Network

The Cyberpunk Legend is Back!

In deluxe omnibus editions of 600+ pages, including ALL-NEW original stories by Alita creator Yukito Kishiro!

KODANS
COMIC

MARDOCK
マルドゥック・スクランブル
SCRAMBLE

Created by
Tow Ubukata

×

Manga by
Yoshitoki Oima

I'd rather be dead."

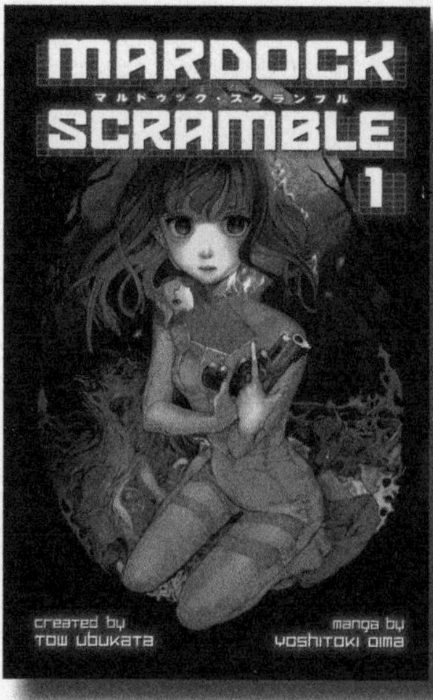
MARDOCK
マルドゥック・スクランブル
SCRAMBLE
1
created by
TOW UBUKATA
manga by
YOSHITOKI OIMA

Ages: 16+

Rune Balot was a lost girl with nothing to live for. A man named Shell took her in and cared for her...until he tried to murder her. Standing at the precipice of death Rune is saved by Dr. Easter, a private investigator, who uses an experimental procedure known as "Mardock Scramble 09." The procedure grants Balot extraordinary abilities. Now, Rune must decide whether to use her new powers to help Dr. Easter bring Shell to justice, or if she even has the will to keep living a life that's been broken so badly.

KC KODANSHA COMICS

VISIT KODANSHACOMICS.COM TO:
- View release date calendars for upcoming volumes
- Find out the latest about upcoming Kodansha Comics series

BLOODY MONDAY

Story by
Ryou Ryumon X **Art by**
Kouji Megumi

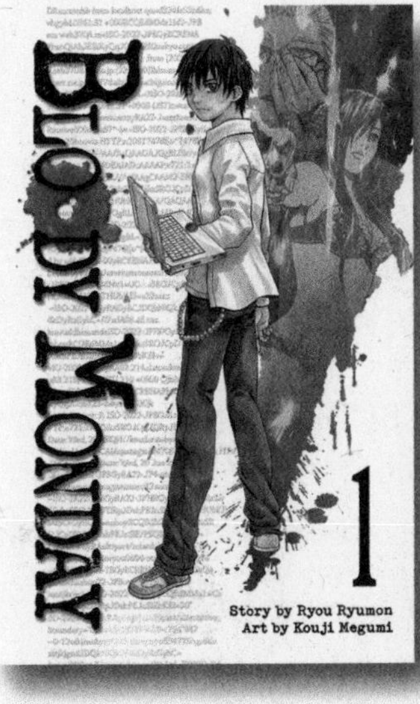
BLOODY MONDAY
1
Story by Ryou Ryumon
Art by Kouji Megumi

Takagi Fujimaru may seem like a regular high school student, but behind the cheery facade lies a genius hacker by the name of Falcon.

When his father is framed for a murder, Falcon uses his brilliant hacking skills to try and protect his sister and clear his father's name.

Special extras in each volume! Read them all!

RATING OT AGES 13+

VISIT WWW.KODANSHACOMICS.COM TO:

- View release date calendars for upcoming volumes
- Find out the latest about new Kodansha Comics series

KC KODANSHA COMICS

ANIMAL LAND

MAKOTO RAIKU

WELCOME TO THE JUNGLE

In a world of animals where the strong eat the weak, Monoko the tanuki stumbles across a strange creature the like of which has never been seen before - **a human baby!**

While the newborn has no claws or teeth to protect itself, it does have the rare ability to speak to and understand all the different animal.

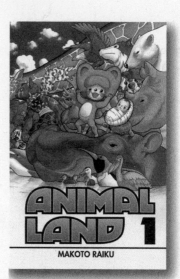

Special extras in each volume! Read them all!

RATING OT AGES 10+

KC
KODANSHA
COMICS

A Kodansha Comics Trade Paperback Original.

Battle Angel Alita: Last Order volume 18 copyright © 2013 Yukito Kishiro
English translation copyright © 2013 Yukito Kishiro

All rights reserved.

Published in the United States by Kodansha Comics, an imprint of Kodansha USA Publishing, LLC, New York.

Publication rights for this English edition arranged through Kodansha Ltd., Tokyo.

First published in Japan in 2013 by Kodansha Ltd., Tokyo, as *Gunnm: Last Order* 18.

ISBN 978-1-61262-297-2

Printed in the United States of America.

www.kodanshacomics.com

9 8 7 6 5 4 3 2 1

Translation: Lillian Olsen
Lettering: Scott O. Brown
Editing: Ben Applegate

TOMARE!

[STOP!]

You're going the wrong way!

Manga is a completely
different
type of reading experience.

To start at the *beginning,*
go to the *end*!

That's right! Authentic manga is read the traditional Japanese way—
from right to left. Exactly the *opposite* of how American books are read.
It's easy to follow: Just go to the other end of the book, and read each
page—and each panel—from the right side to the left side, starting at
the top right. Now you're experiencing manga as it was meant to be!